ISBN 978-1-331-91261-3
PIBN 10253098

English
Français
Deutsche
Italiano
Español
Português

www.forgottenbooks.com

Mythology Photography **Fiction**
Fishing Christianity **Art** Cooking
Essays Buddhism Freemasonry
Medicine **Biology** Music **Ancient
Egypt** Evolution Carpentry Physics
Dance Geology **Mathematics** Fitness
Shakespeare **Folklore** Yoga Marketing
Confidence Immortality Biographies
Poetry **Psychology** Witchcraft
Electronics Chemistry History **Law**
Accounting **Philosophy** Anthropology
Alchemy Drama Quantum Mechanics
Atheism Sexual Health **Ancient History**
Entrepreneurship Languages Sport
Paleontology Needlework Islam
Metaphysics Investment Archaeology
Parenting Statistics Criminology
Motivational

I know no way of judging of the Future bu by he Past."—Patrick Henry.

THE LAST LIVING PASSENGER PIGEON

Now in the Cincinnati Zoological Gardens. Twenty years old in 1912.

REPORT

of a select committee of the Senate of Ohio, in 1857, on a bill proposed to protect the passenger pigeon.

———

"The passenger pigeon needs no protection. Wonderfully prolific, having the vast forests of the North as its breeding grounds, traveling hundreds of miles in search of food, it is here to-day and elsewhere to-morrow, and no ordinary destruction can lessen them, or be missed from the myriads that are yearly produced.

"The snipe (*Scolopax wilsonii*) needs no protection. * * The snipe, too, like the pigeon, will take care of itself, and its yearly numbers can not be materially lessened by the gun."

THE FOLLY OF 1857 AND THE LESSON OF 1912

OUR VANISHING WILD LIFE

ITS
EXTERMINATION AND PRESERVATION

BY

WILLIAM T. HORNADAY, Sc.D.

DIRECTOR OF THE NEW YORK ZOOLOGICAL PARK;
AUTHOR OF "THE AMERICAN NATURAL HISTORY";
EX-PRESIDENT OF THE AMERICAN BISON SOCIETY

WITH MAPS AND ILLUSTRATIONS

"Hew to the line! Let the chips fall where they will."—*Old Exhortation.*
"Nothing extenuate, nor set down aught in malice."—*Othello.*

NEW YORK
CHARLES SCRIBNER'S SONS
1913

Copyright, 1913, by

WILLIAM T. HORNADAY

First Publication, Jan, 1913.

———

SPECIAL NOTICE

For the benefit of the cause that this book represents, the author freely extends to all periodicals and lecturers the privilege of reproducing any of the maps and illustrations in this volume except the bird portraits, the white-tailed deer and antelope, and the maps and pictures specially copyrighted by other persons, and so recorded. This privilege does not cover reproductions in books, without special permission.

———

Clark & Fritts
PRINTERS
209 WEST 38TH STREET
NEW YORK

TO

William Dutcher

FOUNDER AND PRESIDENT OF THE
NATIONAL ASSOCIATION OF AUDUBON SOCIETIES, AND
LIFE-LONG CHAMPION OF AMERICAN BIRDS
THIS VOLUME IS DEDICATED BY
A SINCERE ADMIRER

"I drink to him, he is not here,
Yet I would guard his glory;
A knight without reproach or fear
Should live in song and story."
—*Walsh.*

FOREWORD

The preservation of animal and plant life, and of the general beauty of Nature, is one of the foremost duties of the men and women of to-day It is an imperative duty, because it must be performed at once, for other wise it will be too late. Every possible means of preservation,—senti mental, educational and legislative,—must be employed.

The present warning issues with no uncertain sound, because this great battle for preservation and conservation cannot be won by gentle tones, nor by appeals to the æsthetic instincts of those who have no sense of beauty, or enjoyment of Nature. It is necessary to sound a loud alarm, to present the facts in very strong language, backed up by irrefutable statistics and by photographs which tell no lies, to establish the law and enforce it if needs be with a bludgeon.

This book is such an alarm call. Its forceful pages remind me of the sounding of the great bells in the watch-towers of the cities of the Middle Ages which called the citizens to arms to protect their homes, their liberties and their happiness. It is undeniable that the welfare and happiness of our own and of all future generations of Americans are at stake in this battle for the preservation of Nature against the selfishness, the ignorance, or the cruelty of her destroyers.

We no longer destroy great works of art. They are treasured, and regarded as of priceless value; but we have yet to attain the state of civilization where the destruction of a glorious work of Nature, whether it be a cliff, a forest, or a species of mammal or bird, is regarded with equal abhorrence. The whole earth is a poorer place to live in when a colony of exquisite egrets or birds of paradise is destroyed in order that the plumes may decorate the hat of some lady of fashion, and ultimately find their way into the rubbish heap. The people of all the New England States are poorer when the ignorant whites, foreigners, or negroes of our southern states destroy the robins and other song birds of the North for a mess of pottage.

Travels through Europe, as well as over a large part of the North American continent, have convinced me that nowhere is Nature being destroyed so rapidly as in the United States. Except within our conservation areas, an earthly paradise is being turned into an earthly hades; and it is not savages nor primitive men who are doing this, but men and women who boast of their civilization. Air and water are polluted, rivers and streams serve as sewers and dumping grounds, forests are swept away and fishes are driven from the streams. Many birds are becoming extinct, and certain mammals are on the verge of extermination. Vulgar advertisements hide the landscape, and in all that disfigures the wonderful heritage of the beauty of Nature to-day, we Americans are in the lead.

Fortunately the tide of destruction is ebbing, and the tide of con servation is coming in. Americans are practical. Like all other northern peoples, they love money and will sacrifice much for it, but they are also full of idealism, as well as of moral and spiritual energy. The influence of the splendid body of Americans and Canadians who have turned their best forces of mind and language into literature and into political power for the conservation movement, is becoming stronger every day. Yet we are far from the point where the momentum of conservation is strong enough to arrest and roll back the tide of destruction; and this is especially true with regard to our fast vanishing animal life.

The facts and figures set forth in this volume will astonish all those lovers of Nature and friends of the animal world who are living in a false or imaginary sense of security. The logic of these facts is inexorable. As regards our birds and mammals, the failures of supposed protection in America—under a system of free shooting—are so glaring that we are confident this exposure will lead to sweeping reforms. The author of this work is no amateur in the field of wild-life protection. His ideas concerning methods of reform are drawn from long and successful experience. The states which are still behind in this movement may well give serious heed to his summons, and pass the new laws that are so urgently demanded to save the vanishing remnant.

The New York Zoological Society, which is cooperating with many other organizations in this great movement, sends forth this work in the belief that there is no one who is more ardently devoted to the great cause or rendering more effective service in it than William T. Hornaday. We believe that this is a great book, destined to exert a world-wide influence, to be translated into other languages, and to arouse the de fenders and lovers of our vanishing animal life before it is too late.

HENRY FAIRFIELD OSBORN,

10 December, 1912.   *President of the New York Zoological Society*

PREFACE

The writing of this book has taught me many things. Beyond question, we are exterminating our finest species of mammals, birds and fishes *according to law!*

I am appalled by the mass of evidence proving that throughout the entire United States and Canada, in every state and province, the existing legal system for the preservation of wild life is fatally defective. There is not a single state in our country from which the killable game is not being rapidly and persistently shot to death, legally or illegally, very much more rapidly than it is breeding, with extermination for the most of it close in sight. This statement is not open to argument; for millions of men know that it is literally true. We are living in a fool's paradise.

The rage for wild-life slaughter is far more prevalent to-day throughout the world than it was in 1872, when the buffalo butchers paved the prairies of Texas and Colorado with festering carcasses. From one end of our continent to the other, there is a restless, resistless desire to "kill, *kill!*"

I have been shocked by the accumulation of evidence showing that all over our country and Canada fully nine-tenths of our protective laws have practically been dictated by the killers of the game, and that in all save a very few instances the hunters have been exceedingly careful to provide "open seasons" for slaughter, as long as any game remains to kill!

And yet, the game of North America does not belong wholly and exclusively to the men who kill! The other ninety-seven per cent of the People have vested rights in it, far exceeding those of the three per cent. Posterity has claims upon it that no honest man can ignore.

I am now going to ask both the true sportsman and the people who do not kill wild things to awake, and do their plain duty in protecting and preserving the game and other wild life which belongs partly to us, but chiefly to those who come after us. Can they be aroused, before it is too late?

The time to discuss tiresome academic theories regarding "bag limits" and different "open seasons" as being sufficient to preserve the game, has gone by! We have reached the point where the alternatives are *long closed seasons or a gameless continent;* and we must choose one or the other, speedily. A continent without wild life is like a forest with no leaves on the trees.

The great increase in the slaughter of song birds for food, by the negroes and poor whites of the South, has become an unbearable scourge to our migratory birds,—the very birds on which farmers north and south depend for protection from the insect hordes,—the very birds that are most near and dear to the people of the North. *Song-bird slaughter is growing and spreading,* with the decrease of the game birds! It is a matter that requires instant attention and stern repression. At the present moment it seems that the only remedy lies in federal protection for all migratory birds,—because so many states will not do their duty.

We are weary of witnessing the greed, selfishness and cruelty of "civilized" man toward the wild creatures of the earth. We are sick of tales of slaughter and pictures of carnage. It is time for a sweeping Reformation; and that is precisely what we now demand.

I have been a sportsman myself; but times have changed, and we must change also. When game was plentiful, I believed that it was right for men and boys to kill a limited amount of it for sport and for the table. But the old basis has been swept away by an Army of Destruction that now is almost beyond all control. We must awake, and arouse to the new situation, face it like men, and adjust our minds to the new conditions. The three million gunners of to-day must no longer expect or demand the same generous hunting privileges that were right for hunters fifty years ago, when game was fifty times as plentiful as it is now and there was only one killer for every fifty now in the field.

The fatalistic idea that bag-limit laws can save the game is to-day *the curse of all our game birds, mammals and fishes!* It is a fraud, a delusion and a snare. That miserable fetich has been worshipped much too long. Our game is being exterminated, everywhere, by blind insistence upon "open seasons," and solemn reliance upon "legal bag-limits." If a majority of the people of America feel that so long as there is any game alive there must be an annual two months or four months open season for its slaughter, then assuredly we soon will have a gameless continent.

The only thing that will save the game is by stopping the killing of it! In establishing and promulgating this principle, the cause of wild-life protection greatly needs three things: money, labor, and publicity. With the first, we can secure the second and third. But can we get it,— and *get it in time to save?*

This volume is in every sense a contribution to a Cause; and as such it ever will remain. I wish the public to receive it on that basis. So much important material has drifted straight to it from other hands that this unexpected aid seems to the author like a good omen.

The manuscript has received the benefit of a close and critical reading and correcting by my comrade on the firing-line and esteemed friend, Mr. Madison Grant, through which the text was greatly improved. But for the splendid encouragement and assistance that I have received from him and from Professor Henry Fairfield Osborn the work involved would have borne down rather heavily.

The four chapters embracing the "New Laws Needed; A Roll-Call of the States," were critically inspected, corrected and brought down to date by Dr. T. S. Palmer, our highest authority on the game laws of the Nation and the States. For this valuable service the author is deeply grateful. Of course the author is alone responsible for all the opinions and conclusions herein recorded, and for all errors that appear outside of quotations.

I trust that the Reader will kindly excuse and forget all the typographic and clerical errors that may have escaped me in the rush that had to be made against Time.

UNIVERSITY HEIGHTS, NEW YORK,   W. T. H.
    December 1, 1912.

CONTENTS

ILLUSTRATIONS

MAPS

OUR VANISHING WILD LIFE

PART I. EXTERMINATION

CHAPTER I

THE FORMER ABUNDANCE OF WILD LIFE

"By my labors my vineyard flourished. But Ahab came. Alas! for Naboth."

In order that the American people may correctly understand and judge the question of the extinction or preservation of our wild life, it is necessary to recall the near past. It is not necessary, however, to go far into the details of history; for a few quick glances at a few high points will be quite sufficient for the purpose in view.

Any man who reads the books which best tell the story of the development of the American colonies of 1712 into the American nation of 1912, and takes due note of the wild-life features of the tale, will say without hesitation that when the American people received this land from the bountiful hand of Nature, it was endowed with a magnificent and all-pervading supply of valuable wild creatures. The pioneers and the early settlers were too busy even to take due note of that fact, or to comment upon it, save in very fragmentary ways.

Nevertheless, the wild-life abundance of early American days survived down to so late a period that it touched the lives of millions of people now living. Any man 55 years of age who when a boy had a taste for "hunting,"—for at that time there were no "sportsmen" in America, —will remember the flocks and herds of wild creatures that he saw. and which made upon his mind many indelible impressions.

"Abundance" is the word with which to describe the original animal life that stocked our country, and all North America, only a short half-century ago. Throughout every state, on every shore-line, in all the millions of fresh water lakes, ponds and rivers, on every mountain range, in every forest, *and even on every desert*, the wild flocks and herds held sway. It was impossible to go beyond the settled haunts of civilized man and escape them.

It was a full century after the complete settlement of New England and the Virginia colonies that the wonderful big-game fauna of the great plains and Rocky Mountains was really discovered; but the bison millions, the antelope millions, the mule deer, the mountain sheep and mountain goat were there, all the time. In the early days, the millions of pinnated grouse and quail of the central states attracted no serious attention from the American people-at-large; but they lived and flourished just the same, far down in the seventies, when the greedy market gunners systematically slaughtered them, and barreled them up for "the market," while the foolish farmers calmly permitted them to do it.

We obtain the best of our history of the former abundance of North American wild life first from the pages of Audubon and Wilson; next, from the records left by such pioneers as Lewis and Clark, and last from the testimony of living men. To all this we can, many of us, add observations of our own.

To me the most striking fact that stands forth in the story of American wild life one hundred years ago is the wide extent and thoroughness of its distribution. Wide as our country is, and marvelous as it is in the diversity of its climates, its soils, its topography, its flora, its riches and its poverty, Nature gave to each square mile and to each acre a generous quota of wild creatures, according to its ability to maintain living things. No pioneer ever pushed so far, or into regions so difficult or so remote, that he did not find awaiting him a host of birds and beasts. Sometimes the pioneer was not a good hunter; usually he was a stupid fisherman; but the "game" was there, nevertheless. The time was when every farm had its quota.

The part that the wild life of America played in the settlement and development of this continent was so far-reaching in extent, and so enormous in potential value, that it fairly staggers the imagination. From the landing of the Pilgrims down to the present hour the wild game has been the mainstay and the resource against starvation of the pathfinder, the settler, the prospector, and at times even the railroad-builder. In view of what the bison millions did for the Dakotas, Montana, Wyoming, Kansas and Texas, it is only right and square that those states should now do something for the perpetual preservation of the bison species and all other big game that needs help.

For years and years, the antelope millions of the Montana and Wyoming grass-lands fed the scout and Indian-fighter, freighter, cowboy and surveyor, ranchman *and sheep-herder;* but thus far I have yet to hear of one Western state that has ever spent one penny directly for the preservation of the antelope! And to-day we are in a hand-to-hand fight in Congress, and in Montana, with the Wool-Growers Association, which maintains in Washington a keen lobbyist to keep aloft the tariff on wool, and prevent Congress from taking 15 square miles of grass lands on Snow Creek, Montana, for a National Antelope Preserve. All that the wool-growers want is the entire earth, all to themselves. Mr. McClure, the Secretary of the Association says:

"The proper place in which to preserve the big game of the West is in city parks, where it can be protected."

To the colonist of the East and pioneer of the West, the white-tailed deer was an ever present help in time of trouble. Without this omnipresent animal, and the supply of good meat that each white flag represented, the commissariat difficulties of the settlers who won the country as far westward as Indiana would have been many times greater than they were. The backwoods Pilgrim's progress was like this:

Trail, deer; cabin, deer; clearing; bear, corn, deer; hogs, deer; cattle, wheat, independence.

And yet, how many men are there to-day, out of our ninety millions of Americans and pseudo-Americans, who remember with any feeling of gratitude the part played in American history by the white-tailed deer? Very few! How many Americans are there in our land who now preserve that deer for sentimental reasons, and because his forbears were nation-builders? As a matter of fact, are there any?

On every eastern pioneer's monument, the white-tailed deer should figure; and on those of the Great West, the bison and the antelope should be cast in enduring bronze, *"lest we forget!"*

The game birds of America played a different part from that of the deer, antelope and bison. In the early days, shotguns were few, and shot was scarce and dear. The wild turkey and goose were the smallest birds on which a rifleman could afford to expend a bullet and a whole charge of powder. It was for this reason that the deer, bear, bison, and elk disappeared from the eastern United States while the game birds yet remained abundant. With the disappearance of the big game came the fat steer, hog and hominy, the wheat-field, fruit orchard and poultry galore.

The game birds of America, as a class and a mass, have not been swept away to ward off starvation or to rescue the perishing. Even back in the sixties and seventies, very, very few men of the North thought of killing prairie chickens, ducks and quail, snipe and woodcock, in order to keep the hunger wolf from the door. The process was too slow and uncertain; and besides, the really-poor man rarely had the gun and ammunition. Instead of attempting to live on birds, he hustled for the staple food products that the soil of his own farm could produce.

First, last and nearly all the time, the game birds of the United States as a whole, have been sacrificed on the altar of Rank Luxury, to tempt appetites that were tired of fried chicken and other farm delicacies. To-day, even the average poor man hunts birds for the joy of the outing, and the pampered epicures of the hotels and restaurants buy game birds, and eat small portions of them, solely to tempt jaded appetites. If there is such a thing as "class" legislation, it is that which permits a few sordid market-shooters to slaughter the birds of the whole people in order to sell them to a few epicures.

The game of a state belongs to the whole people of the state. The Supreme Court of the United States has so decided. (Geer vs. Connecticut). If it is abundant, it is a valuable asset. The great value of the game birds of America lies not in their meat pounds as they lie upon the table, but in the temptation they annually put before millions of field-weary farmers and desk-weary clerks and merchants to get into their beloved hunting togs, stalk out into the lap of Nature, and say "Begone, dull Care!"

And the man who has had a fine day in the painted woods, on the bright waters of a duck-haunted bay, or in the golden stubble of September, can fill his day and his soul with six good birds just as well as with sixty. The idea that in order to enjoy a fine day in the open a man must kill a wheel-barrow load of birds, is a mistaken idea; and if obstinately adhered to, it becomes vicious! The Outing in the Open is the thing,—not the blood-stained feathers, nasty viscera and Death in the game-bag. One quail on a fence is worth more to the world than ten in a bag.

The farmers of America have, by their own supineness and lack of foresight, permitted the slaughter of a stock of game birds which, had it been properly and wisely conserved, would have furnished a good annual shoot to every farming man and boy of sporting instincts through the past, right down to the present, and far beyond. They have allowed millions of dollars worth of *their* birds to be coolly snatched away from them by the greedy market-shooters.

There is one state in America, and so far as I know *only one*, in which there is at this moment an old-time abundance of game-bird life. That is the state of Louisiana. The reason is not so very far to seek. For the birds that do not migrate,—quail, wild turkeys and doves,—the cover is yet abundant. For the migratory game birds of the Mississippi Valley, Louisiana is a grand central depot, with terminal facilities that are unsurpassed. Her reedy shores, her vast marshes, her long coast line and abundance of food furnish what should be not only a haven but a heaven for ducks and geese. After running the gauntlet of guns all the way from Manitoba and Ontario to the Sunk Lands of Arkansas, the shores of the Gulf must seem like heaven itself.

The great forests of Louisiana shelter deer, turkeys, and fur-bearing animals galore; and rabbits and squirrels abound.

Naturally, this abundance of game has given rise to an extensive industry in shooting for the market. The "big interests" outside the state send their agents into the best game districts, often bringing in their own force of shooters. They comb out the game in enormous quantities, without leaving to the people of Louisiana any decent and fair quid-pro-quo for having despoiled them of their game and shipped a vast annual product outside, to create wealth elsewhere.

At present, however, we are but incidentally interested in the short-sightedness of the people of the Pelican State. As a state of oldtime abundance in killable game, the killing records that were kept in the year 1909–10 possess for us very great interest. They throw a startling search-light on the subject of this chapter,—the former abundance of wild life.

From the records that with great pains and labor were gathered by the State Game Commission, and which were furnished me for use here by President Frank M. Miller, we set forth this remarkable exhibit of old-fashioned abundance in game, A.D. 1909.

OFFICAL RECORD OF GAME KILLED IN LOUISIANA DURING THE SEASON (12 MONTHS) OF 1909–10

BIRDS

Wild Ducks, sea and river	3,176,000
Coots	280,740
Geese and Brant	202,210
Snipe, Sandpiper and Plover	606,635
Quail (Bob-White)	1,140,750
Doves	310,660
Wild Turkeys	2,219
Total number of game birds killed	5,719,214

MAMMALS

Deer	5,470
Squirrels and Rabbits	690,270
Total of game mammals	695,740
Fur-bearing mammals	1,971,922
Total of mammals	2,667,662
Grand total of birds and mammals	8,386,876

Of the thousands of slaughtered robins, it would seem that no records exist. It is to be understood that the annual slaughter of wild life in Louisiana never before reached such a pitch as now. Without drastic measures, what will be the inevitable result? Does any man suppose that even the wild millions of Louisiana can long withstand such slaughter as that shown by the official figures given above? It is wildly impossible

But the darkest hour is just before the dawn. At the session of the Louisiana legislature that was held in the spring of 1912, great improvements were made in the game laws of that state. The most important feature was the suppression of wholesale market hunting, by persons who are not residents of the state. A very limited amount of game may be sold and served as food in public places, but the restrictions placed upon this traffic are so effective that they will vastly reduce the annual slaughter. In other respects, also, the cause of wild life protection gained much; for which great credit is due to Mr. Edward A. McIlhenny.

It is the way of Americans to feel that because game is abundant in a given place at a given time, it always will be abundant, and may therefore be slaughtered without limit. That was the case last winter in California during the awful slaughter of band-tailed pigeons, as will be noted elsewhere.

It is time for all men to be told in the plainest terms that there never has existed, anywhere in historic times, a volume of wild life so great that civilized man could not quickly exterminate it by his methods of de-

SHALL WE LEAVE ANY ONE OF THEM OPEN?

struction. Lift the veil and look at the stories of the bison, the passenger pigeon, the wild ducks and shore birds of the Atlantic coast, and the fur-seal.

As reasoning beings, it is our duty to heed the lessons of history, and not rush blindly on until we perpetrate a continent destitute of wild life.

CHAPTER II

EXTINCT SPECIES OF NORTH AMERICAN BIRDS

For educated, civilized Man to exterminate a valuable wild species of living things is a crime. It is a crime against his own children, and posterity.

No man has a right, either moral or legal, to destroy or squander an inheritance of his children that he holds for them in trust. And man, the wasteful and greedy spendthrift that he is, has not created even the humblest of the species of birds, mammals and fishes that adorn and enrich this earth. "The earth is THE LORD'S, and the fulness thereof!" With all his wisdom, man has not evolved and placed here so much as a ground-squirrel, a sparrow or a clam. It is true that he has juggled with the wild horse and sheep, the goats and the swine, and produced some hardy breeds that can withstand his abuse without going down before it; but as for species, he has not yet created and placed here even so much as a protozoan.

The wild things of this earth are *not* ours, to do with as we please. They have been given to us *in trust*, and we must account for them to the generations which will come after us and audit our accounts.

But man, the shameless destroyer of Nature's gifts, blithely and persistently exterminates one species after another. Fully ten per cent of the human race consists of people who will lie, steal, throw rubbish in parks, and destroy forests and wild life whenever and wherever they can do so without being stopped by a policemen and a club. These are hard words, but they are absolutely true. From ten per cent (or more) of the human race, the high moral instinct which is honest without compulsion *is absent*. The things that seemingly decent citizens,—men posing as gentlemen,—will do to wild game when they secure great chances to slaughter, are appalling. I could fill a book of this size with cases in point.

To-day the women of England, Europe and elsewhere are directly promoting the extermination of scores of beautiful species of wild birds by the devilish persistence with which they buy and wear feather ornaments made of their plumage. They are just as mean and cruel as the truck-driver who drives a horse with a sore shoulder and beats him on the street. But they do it! And appeals to them to do otherwise they laugh to scorn, saying, "I will wear what is fashionable, when I please and where I please!" As a famous bird protector of England has just written me, "The women of the smart set are beyond the reach of appeal or protest."

To-day, the thing that stares me in the face every waking hour, like a grisly spectre with bloody fang and claw, is *the extermination of species.* To me, that is a horrible thing. It is wholesale murder, no less. It is capital crime, and a black disgrace to the races of civilized mankind. I say "civilized mankind," because savages don't do it!

There are three kinds of extermination:

The practical extermination of a species means the destruction of its members to an extent so thorough and widespread that the species disappears from view, and living specimens of it can not be found by seeking for them. In North America this is to-day the status of the whooping crane, upland plover, and several other species. If any individuals are living, they will be met with only by accident.

The absolute extermination of a species means that not one individual of it remains alive. Judgment to this effect is based upon the lapse of time since the last living specimen was observed or killed. When five years have passed without a living "record" of a wild specimen, it is time to place a species in the class of the totally extinct.

Extermination in a wild state means that the only living representatives are in captivity or otherwise under protection. This is the case of the heath hen and David's deer, of China. The American bison is saved from being wholly extinct as a wild animal by the remnant of about 300 head in northern Athabasca, and 49 head in the Yellow-stone Park.

It is a serious thing to exterminate a species of any of the vertebrate animals. There are probably millions of people who do not realize that civilized (!) man is the most persistently and wickedly wasteful of all the predatory animals. The lions, the tigers, the bears, the eagles and hawks, serpents, and the fish-eating fishes, all live by destroying life; but they kill only what they think they can consume. If something is by chance left over, it goes to satisfy the hunger of the humbler creatures of prey. *In a state of nature, where wild creatures prey upon wild creatures, such a thing as wanton, wholesale and utterly wasteful slaughter is almost unknown!*

When the wild mink, weasel and skunk suddenly finds himself in the midst of scores of man's confined and helpless domestic fowls, or his caged gulls in a zoological park, an unusual criminal passion to murder for the joy of killing sometimes seizes the wild animal, and great slaughter is the result.

From the earliest historic times, it has been the way of savage man, red, black, brown and yellow, to kill as the wild animals do,—only what he can use, or *thinks* he can use. The Cree Indian impounded small herds of bison, and sometimes killed from 100 to 200 at one time; but it was to make sure of having enough meat and hides, and because he expected to use the product. I think that even the worst enemies of the plains Indians hardly will accuse them of killing large numbers of bison, elk or deer merely for the pleasure of seeing them fall, or taking only their teeth.

It has remained for the wolf, the sheep-killing dog and civilized man to make records of wanton slaughter which puts them in a class together,

SIX RECENTLY EXTERMINATED NORTH AMERICAN BIRDS

Great Auk   Labrador Duck
Eskimo Curlew   Pallas Cormorant
Passenger Pigeon   Carolina Parrakeet

and quite apart from other predatory animals. When a man can kill bison for their tongues alone, bull elk for their "tusks" alone, and shoot a whole colony of hippopotami,—actually damming a river with their bloated and putrid carcasses, all untouched by the knife,—the men who do such things must be classed with the cruel wolf and the criminal dog.

It is now desirable that we should pause in our career of destruction long enough to look back upon what we have recently accomplished in the total extinction of species, and also note what we have blocked out for the immediate future. Here let us erect a monument to the dead species of our own times.

It is to be doubted whether, up to this hour, any man has made a list of the species of North American birds that have become extinct during the past sixty years. The specialists have no time to spare from their compound differential microscopes, and the bird-killers are too busy with shooting, netting and clubbing to waste any time on such trifles as exterminated species. What does a market-shooter care about birds that can not be killed a second time? As for the farmers, they are so busy raising hogs and prices that their best friends, the birds, get scant attention from them,—until a hen-hawk takes a chicken!

Down South, the negroes and poor whites may slaughter robins for food by the ten thousand; but does the northern farmer bother his head about a trifle of that kind? No, indeed. Will he contribute any real money to help put a stop to it? Ask him yourself.

Let us pause long enough to reckon up some of our expenditures in species, and in millions of individuals. Let us set down here, in cold blood, a list of the species of our own North American birds that have been totally exterminated in our own times. After that we will have something to say about other species that soon will be exterminated; and the second task is much greater than the first.

Roll Call of the Dead Species of American Birds

The Great Auk, — *Plautus impennis*, (Linn.), was a sea-going diving bird about the size of a domestic goose, related to the guillemots, murres and puffins. For a bird endowed only with flipper-like wings, and therefore absolutely unable to fly, this species had an astonishing geographic range. It embraced the shores of northern Europe to North Cape, southern Greenland, southern Labrador, and the Atlantic coast of North America as far south as Massachusetts. Some say, "as far south as Massachusetts, the Carolinas and Florida," but that is a large order, and I leave the A.O.U. to prove that if it can. In the life history of this bird, a great tragedy was enacted in 1800 by sailors, on Funk Island, north of Newfoundland, where men were landed by a ship, and spent several months slaughtering great auks and trying out their fat for oil. In this process, the bodies of thousands of auks were burned as fuel, in working up the remains of tens of thousands of others.

On Funk Island, a favorite breeding-place, the great auk was exterminated in 1840, and in Iceland in 1844. Many natives ate this bird with relish, and being easily captured, either on land or sea, the commercialism of its day soon obliterated the species. The last living specimen was seen in 1852, and the last dead one was picked up in Trinity Bay, Ireland, in 1853. There are about 80 mounted and unmounted skins in existence, four skeletons, and quite a number of eggs. An egg is worth about $1200 and a good mounted skin at least double that sum.

THE LABRADOR DUCK, — *Camptorhynchus labradoricus*, (Gmel.).— This handsome sea-duck, of a species related to the eider ducks of arctic waters, became totally extinct about 1875, before the scientific world even knew that its existence was threatened. With this species, the exact and final cause of its extinction is to this day unknown. It is not at all probable, however, that its unfortunate,blotting out from our bird fauna was due to natural causes, and when the truth becomes known, it is very probable that the hand of man will be revealed.

The Labrador duck bred in Labrador, and once frequented our Atlantic coast as far south as Chesapeake Bay; but it is said that it never was very numerous, at least during the twenty-five years preceding its disappearance. About thirty-five skins and mounted museum specimens are all that remain to prove its former existence, and I think there is not even one skeleton.

THE PALLAS CORMORANT,— *Carbo perspicillatus*, (Pallas).—In 1741, when the Russian explorer, Commander Bering, discovered the Bering or Commander Islands, in the far-north Pacific, and landed upon them, he also discovered this striking bird species. Its plumage both above and below was a dark metallic green, with blue iridescence on the neck and purple on the shoulders. A pale ring of naked skin around each eye suggested the Latin specific name of this bird. The Pallas cormorant became totally extinct, through causes not positively known, about 1852.

THE PASSENGER PIGEON, — *Ectopistes migratoria*, (Linn.).—We place this bird in the totally-extinct class, not only because it is extinct in a wild state, but only one solitary individual, a twenty-year-old female in the Cincinnati Zoological Gardens, now remains alive. One living specimen and a few skins, skeletons and stuffed specimens are all that remain to show for the uncountable millions of pigeons that swarmed over the United States, only yesterday as it were!

There is no doubt about where those millions have gone. They went down and out by systematic, wholesale slaughter for the market and the pot, before the shotguns, *clubs* and *nets* of the earliest American pot-hunters. Wherever they nested they were slaughtered.

It is a long and shameful story, but the grisly skeleton of its Michigan chapter can be set forth in a few words. In 1869, from the town of Hartford, Mich., *three car loads* of dead pigeons were shipped to market each day for *forty days*, making a total of 11,880,000 birds. It is recorded that another Michigan town marketed 15,840,000 in two years. (See Mr. W. B. Mershon's book, "The Passenger Pigeon.")

Alexander Wilson, the pioneer American ornithologist, was the man who seriously endeavored to estimate by computations the total number of passenger pigeons in one flock that was seen by him. Here is what he has said in his "American Ornithology":

"To form a rough estimate of the daily consumption of one of these immense flocks, let us first attempt to calculate the numbers of that above mentioned, as seen in passing between Frankfort and the Indiana territory. If we suppose this column to have been one mile in breadth (and I believe it to have been much more) and that it moved at the rate of one mile in a minute, four hours, the time it continued passing, would make its whole length two hundred and forty miles. Again, supposing that each square yard of this moving body comprehended three pigeons; the square yards in the whole space multiplied by three would give 2,230,272,000 pigeons! An almost inconceivable multitude, and yet probably far below the actual amount."

*   *

"Happening to go ashore one charming afternoon, to purchase some milk at a house that stood near the river, and while talking with the people within doors, I was suddenly struck with astonishment at a loud rushing roar, succeeded by instant darkness, which, on the first moment, I took for a tornado about to overwhelm the house and every thing around in destruction. The people observing my surprise, coolly said, 'It is only the pigeons!' On running out I beheld a flock, thirty or forty yards in width, sweeping along very low, between the house and the mountain or height that formed the second bank of the river. These continued passing for more than a quarter of an hour, and at length varied their bearing so as to pass over the mountains, behind which they disappeared before the rear came up.

"In the Atlantic States, though they never appear in such unparalleled multitudes, they are sometimes very numerous; and great havoc is then made amongst them with the gun, the clap-net, and various other implements of destruction. As soon as it is ascertained in a town that the pigeons are flying numerously in the neighborhood, the gunners rise *en masse;* the clap-nets are spread out on suitable situations, commonly on an open height in an old buckwheat field, four or five live pigeons, *with their eyelids sewed up,** are fastened on a movable stick, a small hut of branches is fitted up for the fowler at the distance of forty or fifty yards. By the pulling of a string, the stick on which the pigeons rest is alternately elevated and depressed, which produces a fluttering of their wings, similar to that of birds alighting. This being perceived by the passing flocks, they descend with great rapidity, and finding corn, buckwheat, etc, strewed about, begin to feed, and are instantly, by the pulling of a cord, covered by the net. In this manner ten, twenty, and even thirty dozen have been caught at one sweep. Meantime the air is

---

*To-day, we think that the fowlers of the rocollos of northern Italy are very cruel in their methods of catching song-birds wholesale for the market (chapter xi); but our own countrymen of Wilson's day were just as cruel in the method described above.

darkened with large bodies of them moving in various directions; the woods also swarm with them in search of acorns, and the thundering of musquetry is perpetual on all sides from morning to night. Wagon loads of them are poured into market, where they sell from fifty to twenty-five and even twelve cents per dozen; and pigeons become the order of the day at dinner, breakfast and supper, until the very name becomes sickening."

*   *   *   *   *

The range of the passenger pigeon covered nearly the whole United States from the Atlantic coast westward to the Rocky Mountains. A few bold pigeons crossed the Rocky Mountains into Oregon, northern California and Washington, but only as "stragglers," few and far between. The wide range of this bird was worthy of a species that existed in millions, and it was persecuted literally all along the line. The greatest slaughter was in Michigan, Ohio and Pennsylvania. In 1848 Massachusetts gravely passed a law protecting the *netters* of wild pigeons from foreign interference! There was a fine of $10 for damaging nets, or frightening pigeons away from them. This was on the theory that the pigeons were so abundant they could not by any possibility ever become scarce, and that pigeon-slaughter was a legitimate industry.

In 1867, the State of New York found that the wild pigeon needed protection, and enacted a law to that effect. The year 1868 was the last year in which great numbers of passenger pigeons nested in that State. Eaton, in "The Birds of New York," said that "millions of birds occupied the timber along Bell's Run, near Ceres, Alleghany County, on the Pennsylvania line."

In 1870, Massachusetts gave pigeons protection except during an "open season," and in 1878 Pennsylvania elected to protect pigeons on their nesting grounds.

The passenger pigeon millions were destroyed so quickly, and so thoroughly *en masse*, that the American people utterly failed to comprehend it, and for thirty years obstinately refused to believe that the species had been suddenly wiped off the map of North America. There was years of talk about the great flocks having "taken refuge in South America," or in Mexico, and being still in existence. There were surmises about their having all "gone out to sea," and perished on the briny deep.

A thousand times, at least, wild pigeons have been "reported" as having been "seen." These rumors have covered nearly every northern state, the whole of the southwest, and California. For years and years we have been patiently writing letters to explain over and over that the band-tailed pigeon of the Pacific coast, and the red-billed pigeon of Arizona and the southwest are neither of them the passenger pigeon, and never can be.

There was a long period wherein we believed many of the pigeon reports that came from the states where the birds once were most numerous; but that period has absolutely passed. During the past five years large cash rewards, aggregating about $5000, have been offered for the discovery of one nesting pair of genuine passenger pigeons. Many persons have claimed this reward (of Professor C. F. Hodge, of Clark University, Worcester, Mass.), and many claims have been investigated. The results have disclosed many *mourning doves*, but not one pigeon. Now we understand that the quest is closed, and hope has been abandoned.

The passenger pigeon is a dead species. The last wild specimen (so we believe) that ever will reach the hands of man, was taken near Detroit, Michigan, on Sept. 14, 1908, and mounted by C. Campion. That is the one definite, positive record of the past ten years.

The fate of this species should be a lasting lesson to the world at large. Any wild bird or mammal species can be exterminated by commercial interests in twenty years time, or less.

THE ESKIMO CURLEW,—*Numenius borealis*, (Forst.). This valuable game bird once ranged all along the Atlantic coast of North America, and wherever found it was prized for the table. It preferred the fields and meadows to the shore lines, and was the companion of the plovers of the uplands, expecially the golden plover. "About 1872," says Mr. Forbush, "there was a great flight of these birds on Cape Cod and Nantucket. They were everywhere; and enormous numbers were killed. They could be bought of boys at six cents apiece. Two men killed $300 worth of these birds at that time."

Apparently, that was the beginning of the end of the "dough bird," which was another name for this curlew. In 1908 Mr. G. H. Mackay stated that this bird and the golden plover had decreased 90 per cent in fifty years, and in the last ten years of that period 90 per cent of the remainder had gone. "Now (1908)," says Mr. Forbush, "ornithologists believe that the Eskimo curlew is practically extinct, as only a few specimens have been recorded since the beginning of the twentieth century." The very last record is of two specimens collected at Waco, York County, Nebraska, in March, 1911, and recorded by Mr. August Eiche. Of course, it is possible that other individuals may still survive; but so far as our knowledge extends, the species is absolutely dead.

*   *   *   *   *

In the West Indies and the Guadeloupe Islands, five species of macaws and parrakeets have passed out without any serious note of their disappearance on the part of the people of the United States. It is at least time to write brief obituary notices of them.

We are indebted to the Hon. Walter Rothschild, of Tring, England, for essential facts regarding these species as set forth in his sumptuous work "Extinct Birds".

THE CUBAN TRICOLORED MACAW,—*Ara tricolor*, (Gm.). In 1875, when the author visited Cuba and the Isle of Pines, he was informed by Professor Poey that he was "about ten years too late" to find this fine species alive. It was exterminated for food purposes, about 1864, and only four specimens are known to be in existence.

GOSSE'S MACAW,—*Ara gossei*, (Roth.).—This species once inhabited the Island of Jamaica. It was exterminated about 1800; and so far as known not one specimen of it is in existence.

GUADELOUPE MACAW,—*Ara guadeloupensis*, (Clark).—All that is known of the life history of this large bird is that once it inhabited the Guadeloupe Islands. The date and history of its disappearance are both unknown, and there is not one specimen of it in existence.

YELLOW-WINGED GREEN PARROT,—*Amazona olivacea*, (Gm.).—Of the history of this Guadeloupe species, also, nothing is known, and there appear to be no specimens of it in existence.

PURPLE GUADELOUPE PARRAKEET,—*Anodorhynchus purpurescens*, (Rothschild).—This is another dead species, that once lived in the Guadeloupe Islands, and passed away silently and unnoticed at the time, leaving no records of its existence, and no specimens.

THE CAROLINA PARRAKEET,—*Conuropsis carolinensis*, (Linn.), brings us down to the present moment. To this charming little green-and-yellow bird, we are in the very act of bidding everlasting farewell. Ten specimens remain alive in captivity, six of which are in the Cincinnati Zoological Garden, three are in the Washington Zoological Park and one is in the New York Zoological Park.

Regarding wild specimens, it is possible that some yet remain, in some obscure and *neglected* corner of Florida; but it is extremely doubtful whether the world ever will find any of them alive. Mrs. Minnie Moore Willson, of Kissimee, Fla., reports the species as totally extinct in Florida. Unless we would strain at a gnat, we may just as well enter this species in the dead class; for there is no reason to hope that any more wild specimens ever will be found.

The former range of this species embraced the whole southeastern and central United States. From the Gulf it extended to Albany, N. Y., northern Ohio and Indiana, northern Iowa, Nebraska, central Colorado and eastern Texas, from which it will be seen that once it was widely distributed. It was shot because it was destructive to fruit and for its plumage, and many were trapped alive, to be kept in captivity. I know that one colony, near the mouth of the Sebastian River, east coast of Florida, was exterminated in 1898 by a local hunter, and I regret to say that it was done in the hope of selling the living birds to a New York bird-dealer. By holding bags over the holes in which the birds were nesting, the entire colony, of about 16 birds, was caught.

Everywhere else than in Florida, the Carolina parrakeet has long been extinct. In 1904 a flock of 13 birds was seen near Lake Okechobee; but in Florida many calamities can overtake a flock of birds in eight years. The birds in captivity are not breeding, and so far as perpetuation by them is concerned, they are only one remove from mounted museum specimens. This parrakeet is the only member of its order that ranged into the United States during our own times, and with its disappearance the Order Psittaciformes totally disappears from our country.

CHAPTER III

THE NEXT CANDIDATES FOR OBLIVION

In the world of human beings, murder is the most serious of all crimes. To take from a man that which no one ever can restore to him, his life, is murder; and its penalty is the most severe of all penalties.

There are circumstances under which the killing of a wild animal may be so wanton, so revolting and so utterly reprehensible that the act may justly be classed as murder. The man who kills a walrus from the deck of a steamer that he knows will not stop; the man who wantonly killed the whole colony of hippopotami that Mr. Dugmore photographed in life; the man who last winter shot bull elk in Wyoming for their two ugly and shapeless teeth, and the man who wantonly shot down a half-tame deer "for fun" near Carmel, Putnam County, New York, in the summer of 1912,—all were guilty of *murdering* wild animals.

The murder of a wild animal species consists in taking from it that which man with all his cunning and all his preserves and breeding can not give back to it,—its God-given place in the ranks of Living Things. Where is man's boasted intelligence, or his sense of proportion, that every man does not see the monstrous moral obliquity involved in the destruction of a species!

If the beautiful Taj Mehal at Agra should be destroyed by vandals, the intelligent portion of humanity would be profoundly shocked, even though the hand of man could at will restore the shrine of sorrowing love. To-day the great Indian rhinoceros, certainly one of the most wonderful four-footed animals still surviving, is actually being exterminated; and even the people of India and England are viewing it with an indifference that is appalling. Of course there are among Englishmen a great many sportsmen and several zoologists who really care; but they do not constitute one-tenth of one per-cent of the men who ought to care!

In the museums, we stand in awe and wonder before the fossil skeleton of the Megatherium, and the savants struggle to unveil its past, while the equally great and marvelous *Rhinoceros indicus* is being rushed into oblivion. We marvel at the fossil shell of the gigantic turtle called *Collosochelys atlas*, while the last living representatives of the gigantic land tortoises are being exterminated in the Galapagos Islands and the Sychelles, for their paltry oil and meat; and only one man (Hon. Walter Rothschild) is doing aught to save any of them in their haunts, where they can breed. The dodo of Mauritius was exterminated by swine, whose bipedal descendents have exterminated many other species since that time.

A failure to appreciate either the beauty or the value of our living birds, quadrupeds and fishes is the hall-mark of arrested mental development and ignorance. The victim is *not always to blame;* but in this practical world the cornerstone of legal jurisprudence is the inexorable principle that "ignorance of the law excuses no man."

These pages are addressed to my countrymen, and the world at large, not as a reproach upon the dead Past which is gone beyond recall, but in the faint hope of somewhere and somehow arousing forces that will reform the Present and save the Future. The extermination of wild species that now is proceeding throughout the world, is a dreadful thing. It is not only injurious to the economy of the world, but it is a shame and a disgrace to the civilized portion of the human race.

It is of little avail that I should here enter into a detailed description of each species that now is being railroaded into oblivion. The bookshelves of intelligent men and women are filled with beautiful and adequate books on birds and quadrupeds, wherein the status of each species may be determined, almost without effort. There is time and space only in which to notice the most prominent of the doomed species, and perhaps discuss a few examples by way of illustration. Here is a

PARTIAL LIST OF NORTH AMERICAN BIRDS THREATENED WITH

EARLY EXTERMINATION

WHOOPING CRANE	PECTORAL SANDPIPER
TRUMPETER SWAN	BLACK-CAPPED PETREL
AMERICAN FLAMINGO	AMERICAN EGRET
ROSEATE SPOONBILL	SNOWY EGRET
SCARLET IBIS	WOOD DUCK
LONG-BILLED CURLEW	BAND-TAILED PIGEON
HUDSONIAN GODWIT	HEATH HEN
UPLAND PLOVER	SAGE GROUSE
RED-BREASTED SANDPIPER	PRAIRIE SHARP-TAIL
GOLDEN PLOVER	PINNATED GROUSE
DOWITCHER	WHITE-TAILED KITE
WILLET	

THE WHOOPING CRANE.—This splendid bird will almost certainly be the next North American species to be totally exterminated. It is the only new world rival of the numerous large and showy cranes of the old world; for the sandhill crane is not in the same class as the white, black and blue giants of Asia. We will part from our stately *Grus americanus* with profound sorrow, for on this continent we ne'er shall see his like again.

The well-nigh total disappearance of this species has been brought close home to us by the fact that there are less than half a dozen individuals alive in captivity, while in a wild state the bird is so rare as to be quite unobtainable. For example, for nearly five years an English gen-

WHOOPING CRANES IN THE ZOOLOGICAL PARK
Very Soon this Species will Become Totallv Extinct.

tlemen has been offering $1,000 for a pair, and the most enterprising bird collector in America has been quite unable to fill the order. So far as our information extends, the last living specimen captured was taken six or seven years ago. The last wild birds seen and reported were observed by Ernest Thompson Seton, who saw five below Fort Mc-Murray, Saskatchewan, October 16th, 1907, and by John F. Ferry, who saw one at Big Quill Lake, Saskatchewan, in June, 1909.

The range of this species once covered the eastern two-thirds of the continent of North America. It extended from the Atlantic coast to the Rocky Mountains, and from Great Bear Lake to Florida and Texas. Eastward of the Mississippi it has for twenty years been totally extinct, and the last specimens taken alive were found in Kansas and Nebraska.

THE TRUMPETER SWAN.—Six years ago this species was regarded as so nearly extinct that a doubting ornithological club of Boston refused to believe on hearsay evidence that the New York Zoological Park contained a pair of living birds, and a committee was appointed, to investigate in person, and report. Even at that time, skins were worth all the way from $100 to $150 each; and when swan skins sell at either of those figures it is because there are people who believe that the species either is on the verge of extinction, or has passed it. The pair referred to above was acquired in 1900. Since that time, Dr. Leonard C. Sanford procured in 1910 two living birds from a bird dealer who obtained them on the coast of Virginia. We have done our utmost to induce our pair to breed, but without any further results than nest-building.

The loss of the trumpeter swan (*Olor americanus*) will not be so great, nor felt so keenly, as the blotting out of the whooping crane. It so closely resembles the whistling swan that only an ornithologist can recognize the difference, a yellow spot on the side of the upper mandible, near its base. The whistling swan yet remains in fair numbers, but it is to be feared that soon it will go as the trumpeter has gone.

THE AMERICAN FLAMINGO, SCARLET IBIS AND ROSEATE SPOONBILL are three of the most beautiful and curious water-haunting birds of the tropics. Once all three species inhabited portions of the southern United States; but now all three are gone from our star-spangled bird fauna. The brilliant scarlet plumage of the flamingo and ibis, and the exquisite pink rose-color and white of the spoonbill naturally attracted the evil eyes of the "milliner's taxidermists" and other bird-butchers. From Florida these birds quickly vanished. The six great breeding colonies of Flamingoes on Andros Island, Bahamas, have been reduced to two, and from Prof. E. A. Goeldi, of the State Museum Goeldi, Para, Brazil, have come bitter complaints of the slaughter of scarlet ibises in South America by plume-hunters in European pay.

I know not how other naturalists regard the future of the three species named above, but my opinion is that unless the European feather trade is quickly stopped as to wild plumage, they are absolutely certain to be shot into total oblivion, within a very few years. The plumage of these birds has so much commercial value, for fishermen's flies as well as for women's hats, that the birds will be killed as long as their feathers can be sold and any birds remain alive.

Zoologically, the flamingo is the most odd and interesting bird on the American continent except the emperor penguin. Its beak baffles description, its long legs and webbed feet are a joke, its nesting habits are amazing, and its food habits the despair of most zoological-garden keepers. Millions of flamingos inhabit the shores of a number of small lakes in the interior of equatorial East Africa, but that species is not brilliant scarlet all over the neck and head, as is the case with our species.

If the American flamingo, scarlet ibis and roseate spoonbill, one or all of them, are to be saved from total extinction, efforts must be made in each of the countries in which they breed and live. Their preservation is distinctly a burden upon the countries of South America that lie eastward of the Andes, and on Yucatan, Cuba and the Bahamas. The time has come when the Government of the Bahama Islands should sternly forbid the killing of any more flamingos, on any pretext whatever; and if the capture of living specimens for exhibition purposes militates against the welfare of the colonies, *they should forbid that also.*

THE UPLAND PLOVER, OR "BARTRAMIAN SANDPIPER."—Apparently this is the next shore-bird species that will follow the Eskimo curlew into oblivion. Four years ago,—a long period for a species that is on the edge of extermination,—Mr. E. H. Forbush* wrote of it as follows:

"The Bartramian Sandpiper, commonly known as the Upland Plover, a bird which formerly bred on grassy hills all over the State and migrated southward along our coasts in great flocks, is in imminent danger of extirpation. A few still breed in Worcester and Berkshire Counties, or Nantucket, so there is still a nucleus which, if protected, may save the species. Five reports from localities where this bird formerly bred give it as nearing extinction, and four as ex.inct. This is one of the most useful of all birds in grass land, feeding largely on grasshoppers and cutworms. It is one of the finest of all birds for the table. An effort should be made at once to save this useful species."

THE BLACK-CAPPED PETREL, (*Aestrelata hasitata*).—This species is already recorded in the A. O. U. "Check list" as extinct; but it appears that this may not as yet be absolutely true. On January 1, 1912, a strange thing happened. A much battered and exhausted black-capped petrel was picked up alive in Central Park, New York, taken to the menagerie, and kept there during the few days that it survived. When it died it was sent to the American Museum; and this may easily prove to be the last living record for that species. In reality, this species might as well be listed with those totally extinct. Formerly it ranged from the Antilles to Ohio and Ontario, and the causes of its blotting out are not yet definitely known.

This ocean-going bird once had a wide range overseas in the temperate areas of the North Atlantic. It is recorded from Ulster County, New York, New Hampshire, Kentucky, Ohio, Virginia and Florida. It was about of the size of the common tern.

THE CALIFORNIA CONDOR, (*Gymnogyps californianus*).—I feel that the existence of this species hangs on a very slender thread. This is due to its alarmingly small range, the insignificant number of individuals now living, the openness of the species to attack, and the danger of its extinction by poison. Originally this remarkable bird,—the largest North American bird of prey,—ranged as far northward as the Columbia River, and southward for an unknown distance. Now its range is reduced to seven counties in southern California, although it is said to extend from Monterey Bay to Lower California, and eastward to Arizona.

Regarding the present status and the future of this bird, I have been greatly disturbed in mind. When a unique and zoologically important species becomes reduced in its geographic range to a small section of a single state, it seems to me quite time for alarm. For some time I have counted this bird as one of those threatened with early extermination, and as I think with good reason. In view of the swift calamities that now seem able to fall on species like thunderbolts out of clear skies, and wipe them off the earth even before we know that such a fate is impend-

*"Special Report on the Decrease of Certain Birds, and its Causes."—Mass. State Board of Agriculture, 1908.

CALIFORNIA CONDOR
Now Living in the New York Zoological Park.

ing, no species of seven-county distribution is safe. Any species that is limited to a few counties of a single state is liable to be wiped out in five years, by poison, or traps, or lack of food.

On order to obtain the best and also the most conservative information regarding this species, I appealed to the Curator of the Museum of Verbetrate Zoology, of the University of California. Although written in the mountain wilds, I promptly received the valuable contribution that appears below. As a clear, precise and conservative survey of an important species, it is really a model document.

THE STATUS OF THE CALIFORNIA CONDOR IN 1912

By Joseph Grinnell

"To my knowledge, the California Condor has been definitely observed within the past five years in the following California counties: Los Angeles, Ventura, Santa Barbara, San Luis Obispo, Monterey, Kern, and Tulare. In parts of Ventura, Santa Barbara, San Luis Obispo and Kern counties the species is still fairly common, for a large bird, probably equal in numbers to the golden eagle in those regions that are suited to it. By suitable country I mean cattle-raising, mountainous territory, of which there are still vast areas, and which are not likely to be put to any other use for a very long time, if ever, on account of the lack of water.

"While in Kern County last April, I was informed by a reliable man who lives near the Tejon Rancho that he had counted twenty-five condors in a single day, since January 1 of the present year. These were on the Tejon Rancho, which is an enormous cattle range covering parts of the Tehachapi and San Emigdio Mountains.

"Our present state law provides complete protection for the condor and its eggs; and the State Fish and Game Commission, in granting permits for collectors, always adds the phrase— 'except the California condor and its eggs.' I know of two special permits having been issued, but neither of these were used; that is, no 'specimens' have been taken since 1908, as far as I am aware.

"In my travels about the state, I have found that practically everyone knows that the condor is protected. Still, there is always the hunting element who do not hesitate to shoot anything alive and out of the ordinary, and a certain percentage of the condors are doubtless picked off each year by such criminals. It is possible, also, that the mercenary egg-collector continues to take his annual rents, though if this is done it is kept very quiet. It is my impression that the present fatalities from all sources are fully balanced by the natural rate of increase.

"There is one factor that has militated against the condor more than any other one thing; namely, the restriction in its food source. Its forage range formerly included most of the great valleys adjacent to its mountain retreats. But now the valleys are almost entirely devoted to agriculture, and of course far more thickly settled than formerly.

"The mountainous areas where the condor is making its last stand seem to me likely to remain adapted to the bird's existence for many years,—fifty years, if not longer. Of course, this is conditional upon the maintenance and enforcement of the present laws. There is also the enlightenment of public sentiment in regard to the preservation of wild life, which I believe can be depended upon. This is a matter of general education, which is, fortunately, and with no doubt whatever, progressing at a quite perceptible rate.

"Yes; I should say that the condor has a fair chance to survive, in limited numbers.

"Another bird which in my opinion is far nearer extinction than the condor, so far as California is concerned, is the white-tailed kite. This is a perfectly harmless bird, but one which harries over the marshes, where it has been an easy target for the idle duck-hunter. Then, too, its range was limited to the valley bottoms, where human settlement is increasingly close. I know of only *two* live pairs within the state last year!

"Finally, let me remark that the rate of increase of the California condor is not one whit less than that of the band-tailed pigeon! Yet, there is no protection at all for the latter in this state, even in the nesting season; and thousands were shot last spring, in the unprecedented concentration of the species in the southern coast counties. (See Chambers' in *The Condor* for May, 1912, p. 108.)"

The California Condor is one of the only two species of condor now living, and it is the only one found in North America. As a matter of national pride, and a duty to posterity, the people of the United States can far better afford to lose a million dollars from their national treasury than to allow that bird to become extinct. Its preservation for all coming time is distinctly a white man's burden upon the state of California. The laws now in force for the condor's protection are not half adequate! I think there is no law by which the accidental poisoning of those birds, by baits put out for coyotes and foxes, can be stopped. A law to prevent the use of poisoned meat baits anywhere in southern California, should be enacted at the next session of California's legislature. The fine for molesting a condor should be raised to $500, with a long prison-term as an alternative. A competent, interested game warden should be appointed *solely for the protection of the condors*. It is time to count those birds, keep them under observation, and have an annual report upon their condition.

THE HEATH HEN.—But for the protection that has been provided for it by the ornithologists of Massachusetts, and particularly Dr. George W. Field, William Brewster and John E. Thayer, the heath hen or eastern pinnated grouse would years ago have become totally extinct. New York, New Jersey and Massachusetts began to protect that species entirely too late. It was given five-year close seasons, without avail. Then it was given ten-year close seasons, but it was *too late!*

To-day, the species exists only in one locality, the island of Martha's Vineyard, and concerning its present status, Mr. Forbush has recently furnished us the following clear statement:

"The heath hens increased for two years after the Massachusetts Fish and Game Commission established a reservation for them, but in 1911 they had not increased. There are probably about two hundred birds extant.

"I found a great many marsh hawks on the Island and the Commission did not kill them, believing them to be beneficial. In watching them, I concluded that they were catching the young heath hens. A large number of these hawks have been shot and their stomachs sent to Washington for examination, as I was too busy at the time to examine them. So far as I know, no report of the examination has been made, but Dr. Field himself examined a few of the stomachs and found the remains of the heath hen in some.

"The warden now says that during the past two years, the heath hen has not increased, but I can give you no definite evidence of this. I am quite sure they are being killed by natives of the island and that at least one collector supplies birds for museums. We are trying to get evidence of this.

I believe if the heath hen is to be increased in numbers and brought back to this country, we shall have to have more than one warden on the reservation and, eventually, we shall have to establish the bird on the mainland also. "

From the "American Natural History"

PINNATED GROUSE, OR "PRAIRIE CHICKEN"

The Pinnated Grouse, Sage Grouse and Prairie Sharp-Tail.—
In view of the fate of the grouse of the United States, as it has been
wrought out thus far in all the more thickly settled areas, and particularly in view of the history of the heath hen, we have no choice but to
regard all three of the species named above as absolutely certain to
become totally extinct, within a short period of years, unless the conditions surrounding them are immediately and radically changed for the
better. Personally, I do not believe that the gunners and game-hogs of
Minnesota, Montana, Nebraska, Idaho, Washington, Oregon and California will permit any one of those species to be saved.

If the present open seasons prevail in the states that I have mentioned above, no power on earth can save those three species of grouse
from the fate of the heath hen. To-day their representatives exist only
in small shreds and patches, and from fully nineteen-twentieths of their
original ranges they are forever gone.

The sage grouse will be the first species to go. It is the largest, the
most conspicuous, the one most easily found, and the biggest mark for
the gunner. Those who have seen this bird in its native sage-brush well
understand how fatally it is exposed to slaughter.

Many appeals have been made in behalf of the pinnated grouse; but
the open seasons continue. The gunners of the states in which a few
remnants still exist are determined to have them, all; and the state
legislatures seem disposed to allow the killers to have their way. It

SAGE GROUSE
The First of the Upland Game Birds that
will Become Extinct

may be however, that like New York with the heath hen, they will arouse and virtuously lock the stable door—after the horse has been stolen!

THE SNOWY EGRET AND AMERICAN EGRET, (*Egretta candidissima and Herodias egretta*).—These unfortunate birds, cursed for all time by the commercially valuable "aigrette" plumes that they bear, have had a very narrow escape from total extinction in the United States, despite all the efforts made to save them. The "plume-hunters" of the millinery trade have been, *and still are*, determined to have the last feather and the last drop of egret blood. In an effort to stop the slaughter in at least one locality in Florida, Warden Guy Bradley was killed by a plume-hunter, who of course escaped all punishment through the heaven-born "sympathy" of a local jury.

Of the bloody egret slaughter in Florida, not one-tenth of the whole story ever has been told. Millions of adult birds,—all there were,—were killed *in the breeding season*, when the plumes were ripe for the market; and millions of young birds starved in their nests. It was a common thing for a rookery of several hundred birds to be attacked by the plume-hunters, and in two or three days utterly destroyed. The same bloody work is going on to-day in Venezuela and Brazil; and the stories and "affidavits" stating that the millions of egret plumes being shipped annually from those countries are "shed feathers," "picked up off the ground," are absolute lies. The men who have sworn to those lies are perjurers, and should be punished for their crimes. (See Chapter XIII).

By 1908, the plume-hunters had so far won the fight for the egrets that Florida had been swept almost as bare of these birds as the Colorado desert.

Until Mr. E. A. McIlhenny's egret preserve, at Avery Island, Louisiana, became a pronounced success, we had believed that our two egrets soon would become totally extinct in the United States. But Mr. McIlhenny has certainly saved those birds to our fauna. In 1892 he started an egret and heron preserve, close beside his house on Avery Is-

Photo by E. A. McIlhenny

SNOWY EGRETS IN THE McILHENNY EGRET PRESERVE

t is at This Period That the Parent Birds are Killed for Their Plumes, and the Young Starve in the Nest

land. By 1900 it was an established success. To-day 20,000 pairs of egrets and herons are living and breeding in that bird refuge, and the two egret species are safe in at least one spot in our own country.

Three years ago, I think there were not many bird-lovers in the United States, who believed it possible to prevent the total extinction of both egrets from our fauna. All the known rookeries accessible to plume-hunters had been totally destroyed. Two years ago, the secret discovery of several small, hidden colonies prompted William Dutcher, President of the National Association of Audubon Societies, and Mr. T. Gilbert Pearson, Secretary, to attempt the protection of those colonies. With a fund contributed for the purpose, wardens were hired and duly commissioned. As previously stated, one of those wardens was shot dead in cold blood by a plume hunter. The task of guarding swamp rookeries from the attacks of money-hungry desperadoes to whom the accursed plumes were worth their weight in gold, is a very chancy proceeding. There is now one warden in Florida who says that "before they get my rookery they will first have to get me."

Thus far the protective work of the Audubon Association has been successful. Now there are twenty colonies, which contain all told, about 5,000 egrets and about 120,000 herons and ibises which are guarded by the Audubon wardens. One of the most important is on Bird Island, a mile out in Orange Lake, central Florida, and it is ably defended by Oscar E. Baynard. To-day, the plume hunters who do not dare to raid the guarded rookeries are trying to study out the lines of flight of the birds, to and from their feeding-grounds, and shoot them in transit. Their motto is—"Anything to beat the law, and get the plumes." It is there that the state of Florida should take part in the war.

The success of this campaign is attested by the fact that last year a number of egrets were seen in eastern Massachusetts,—for the first time in many years. And so to-day the question is, can the wardens continue to hold the plume-hunters at bay?

THE WOOD-DUCK (*Aix sponsa*), by many bird-lovers regarded as the most beautiful of all American birds, is threatened with extinction in all the states that it still inhabits with the exception of eight. Long ago (1901) the U. S. Biological Survey sounded a general alarm for this species by the issue of a special bulletin regarding its disappearance, and advising its protection by long close seasons. To their everlasting honor, eight states responded, by the enactment of long close-season laws. This is the

ROLL OF HONOR

CONNECTICUT	NEW JERSEY
MAINE	NEW YORK
MASSACHUSETTS	VERMONT
NEW HAMPSHIRE	WEST VIRGINIA

WOOD DUCK
Regularly Killed as "Food" in 15 States

And how is it with the other states that number the wood-duck in their avian faunas? I am ashamed to tell; but it is necessary that the truth should be known.

Surely we will find that if the other states have not the grace to protect this bird on account of its exquisite beauty they will not penalize it by extra long open seasons.

A number of them have taken pains to provide extra long OPEN *seasons on this species, usually of five or six months!!* And this for a bird so exquisitely beautiful that shooting it for the table is like dining on birds of paradise. Here is a partial list of the

Wood-Duck-Eating States (1912)

Georgia kills and eats the Wood-duck from		Sept.	1,	to Feb.	1.
Indiana, Iowa and Kansas do so "		Sept.	1,	to Apr.	15.
Kentucky, (extra long!) does so "		Aug.	15,	to Apr.	1.
Louisiana (extra long!) " " "		Sept.	1,	to Mar.	1.
Maryland " " "		Nov.	1,	to Apr.	1.
Michigan " " "		Oct.	15	to Jan.	1.
Nebraska (extra long!) " " "		Sept.	1,	to Apr.	1.
Ohio " " "		Sept.	1,	to Jan.	1.
Pennsylvania, (extra long!) " " '		Sept.	1,	to Apr.	11
Rhode Island, " " " " "		Aug.	15,	to Apr.	1.
South Carolina " " " " "		Sept.	1,	to Mar.	1.
South Dakota " " " " "		Sept.	10,	to Apr.	10.
Tennessee " " " " "		Aug.	1,	to Apr.	15.
Virginia " " "		Aug.	1,	to Jan.	1.
Wisconsin " " "		Sept.	1,	to Jan.	1.

The above are the states that really possess the wood-duck and that should give it, one and all, a series of five-year close seasons. Now, is not the record something to blush for?

Is there in those fifteen states *nothing* too beautiful or too good to go into the pot?

THE WOODCOCK (*Philohela minor*), is a bird regarding which my bird-hunting friends and I do not agree. I say that as a species it is steadily disappearing, and presently will become extinct, unless it is accorded better protection. They reply: "Well, I can show you where there are woodcock yet!"

A few months ago a Nova Scotian writer in *Forest and Stream* came out with the bold prediction that three more years of the usual annual slaughter of woodcock will bring the species to the verge of extinction in that Province.

It is such occurrences as this that bring the end of a species:

"Last fall [1911, at Norwalk, Conn.] we had a good flight of wood-cock, and it is a shame the way they were slaughtered. I know of a number of cases where twenty were killed by one gun in the day, and heard of one case of fifty. This is all wrong, and means the end of the woodcock, if continued. There is no doubt we need a bag limit on wood-cock, as much as on quail or partridge." ("Woodcock" in *Forest and Stream*, Mar. 2, 1912.)

As far back as 1901, Dr. A. K. Fisher of the Biological Survey pre-dicted that the woodcock and wood-duck would both become extinct unless better protected. As yet, the better protection demanded has not materialized to any great extent.

Says Mr. Forbush, State Ornithologist of Massachusetts, in his admirable "Special Report," p. 45:

"The woodcock is decreasing all over its range in the East, and needs the strongest protection. Of thirty-eight Massachusetts reports, thirty-six state that "woodcock are decreasing," "rare" or "extinct," while one states that they are holding their own, and one that they are increas-ing slightly since the law was passed prohibiting their sale."

Let not any honest American or Canadian sportsman lullaby him-self into the belief that the woodcock is safe from extermination. As sure as the world, it is *going!* The fact that a little pocket here or there contains a few birds does not in the slightest degree disprove the main fact. If the sportsmen of this country desire to save the seed stock of woodcock, they must give it *everywhere* five or ten-year close seasons, and *do it immediately!*

OUR SHORE BIRDS IN GENERAL.—This group of game birds will be the first to be exterminated in North America *as a group*. Of all our birds, these are the most illy fitted to survive. They are very con-spicuous, very unwary, easy to find if alive, and easy to shoot. Never in my life have any shore birds except woodcock and snipe appealed to me as real game. They are too easy to kill, too trivial when killed, and some of them are too rank and fishy on the plate. As game for men I place them on a level with barnyard ducks or orchard turkeys. I would as soon be caught stealing a sheep as to be seen trying to shoot fishy yellow legs or little joke sandpipers for the purpose of feeding upon them. And yet, thousands of full-grown men, some of them six feet high, grow indignant and turn red in the face at the mention of a law to give all the shore birds of New York a five-year close season.

But for all that, gentlemen of the gun, there are exactly two alterna tives between which you shall choose:

(1) Either give the woodcock of the eastern United States just *ten times* the protection that it now has, or (2) bid the species a long farewell. If you elect to slaughter old *Philohela minor* on the altar of Selfishness, then it will be in order for the millions of people who do not kill birds to say whether that proposal shall be consummated or not.

Read if you please Mr. W. A. McAtee's convincing pamphlet (Biological Survey, No. 79), on "Our Vanishing Shore Birds," reproduced in full in Chapter XXIII. He says: "Throughout the eastern United States, shore birds are fast vanishing. Many of them have been so reduced that *extermination seems imminent.* So averse to shore birds are present conditions [of slaughter] that the wonder is that any escape. All the shore birds of the United States are in great need of better protection. . . Shore birds have been hunted until only a remnant of their once vast numbers are left. Their limited powers of reproduction, coupled with the natural vicissitudes of the breeding period, make their increase slow, and peculiarly expose them to danger of extermination. So great is their economic value that their retention in the game list and their destruction by sportsmen is a serious loss to agriculture."

And yet, here in New York state there are many men who think they "know," who indignantly scoff at the idea that our shore birds need a five-year close season to help save them from annihilation. The writer's appeal for this at a recent convention of the New York State Fish, Game and Forest League fell upon deaf ears, and was not even seriously discussed.

The shore-birds must be saved; and just at present it seems that the only persons who will do it are those who are *not* sportsmen, and who never kill game! If the sportsmen persist in refusing to act, to them we must appeal.

Besides the woodcock and snipe, the species that are most seriously threatened with extinction at an early date are the following

Species in Great Danger

Willet	*Catoptrophorus semipalmatus*
Dowitcher	*Macrorhamphus griseus*
Knot: Red-Breasted Sandpiper	*Tryngites subruficollis*
Upland Plover	*Bartramia longicauda*
Golden Plover	*Charadrius dominicus*
Pectoral Sandpiper	*Pisobia maculata*

Of these fine species, Mr. Forbush, whose excellent knowledge of the shore birds of the Atlantic coast is well worth the most serious consideration, says that the upland plover, or Bartramian sandpiper, "is in immi-

THE GRAY SQUIRREL, A FAMILIAR FRIEND WHEN PROTECTED

nent danger of extinction. Five reports from localities where this bird formerly bred give it as nearing extinction, and four as extinct. This is one of the most useful of all birds in grass land, feeding largely on grass-hoppers and cutworms. . . . There is no difference of opinion in regard to the diminution of the shore birds; the reports from all quarters are the same. It is noteworthy that practically all observers agree that, considering all species, these birds have fallen off about 75 per cent within twenty-five to forty years, and that several species are nearly extirpated.''

In 1897 when the Zoological Society published my report on the ''Extermination of Our Birds and Mammals,'' we put down the decrease in the volume of bird life in Massachusetts during the previous fifteen years at twenty-seven per cent. The later and more elaborate investigations of Mr. Forbush have satisfactorily vindicated the accuracy of that estimate.

There are other North American birds that easily might be added to the list of those now on the road to oblivion; but surely the foregoing citations are sufficient to reveal the present desperate conditions of our bird life in general. Now the question is: What are the great American people going to do about it?

THE GRAY SQUIRREL.—The gray squirrel is in danger of extermination. Although it is our most beautiful and companionable small wild animal, and really unfit for food, Americans have strangely elected to class it as "game," and shoot it to death, *to eat!* And this in stall-fed America, in the twentieth century! Americans are the only white people in the world who eat squirrels. It would be just as reasonable, and no more barbarous, to kill domestic cats and eat them. Their flesh would taste quite as good as squirrel flesh and some of them would afford quite as good "sport."

Every intelligent person knows that in the United States the deadly shot-gun is rapidly exterminating every bird and every small mammal that is classed as "game," and which legally may be killed, even during two months of the twelve. The market gunners slaughter ducks, grouse, shore birds and rabbits as if we were all starving.

The beautiful gray squirrel has clung to life in a few of our forests and wood-lots, long after most other wild mammals have disappeared; but throughout at least ninety-five per cent. of its original area, it is now extinct. During the past thirty years I have roamed the woods of my state in several widely separated localities,—the Adirondacks, Catskills, Berkshires, western New York and elsewhere, and in all that time I have seen only *three* wild gray squirrels outside of city parks.

Except over a very small total area, the gray squirrel is already gone from the wild fauna of New York State!

Do the well-fed people of America wish to have this beautiful animal entirely exterminated? Do they wish the woods to become wholly lifeless? Or, do they desire to bring back some of the wild creatures, and keep them for their children to enjoy?

There is no wild mammal that responds to protection more quickly than the gray squirrel. In two years' time, wild specimens that are set free in city parks learn that they are safe from harm and become almost fearless. They take food from the hands of visitors, and climb into their arms. One of the most pleasing sights of the Zoological Park is the enjoyment of visitors, young and old, in "petting" our wild gray squirrels.

We ask the Boy Scouts of America to bring back this animal to each state where it belongs, by securing for it from legislatures and governors the perpetual closed seasons that it imperatively needs. It is not much to ask. This can be done by writing to members of the legislatures and requesting a suitable law. Such a request will be both right and reasonable; and three states have already granted it.

The gray squirrel is naturally the children's closest wild-animal friend. Surely every farmer boy would like to have colonies of gray squirrels around him, to keep him company, and furnish him with entertainment. A wood-lot without squirrels and chipmunks is indeed a lifeless place. For $20 anyone can restock any bit of woods with the most companionable and most beautiful tree-dweller that nature has given us.

The question now is, which will you choose—a gray squirrel colony to every farm, or lifeless desolation?

We ask every American to lend a hand to save Silver-Tail.

CHAPTER IV

EXTINCT AND NEARLY EXTINCT SPECIES OF MAMMALS

When we pause and consider the years, the generations and the ages that Nature spends in the production of a high vertebrate species, the preservation of such species from extermination should seriously concern us. As a matter of fact, in modern man's wild chase after wealth and pleasure, it is only one person out of every ten thousand who pauses to regard such causes, unless cornered by some protectionist fanatic, held fast and coerced to listen.

We are not discussing the animals of the Pleistocene, or the Eocene, or any period of the far-distant Past. We are dealing with species that have been ruthlessly, needlessly and wickedly destroyed by man during our own times; species that, had they been given a fair chance, would be alive and well to-day.

In reckless waste of blood and treasure, the nineteenth century has much for which to answer. Wars and pillage, fires, earthquakes and volcanoes are unhappily unavoidable. Like the poor of holy writ, we have them with us always. But the destruction of animal life is in a totally different category from the accidental calamities of life. It is deliberate, cold-blooded, persistent, and in its final stage, *criminal!* Worst of all, there is no limit to the devilish persistence of the confirmed destroyer, this side of the total extinction of species. No polar night is too cold, no desert inferno is too hot for the man who pursues wild life for commercial purposes. The rhytina has been exterminated in the far north, the elephant seals on Kerguelen are being exterminated in the far south, and midway, in the desert mountains of Lower California a fine species of mountain sheep is rapidly being shot into oblivion.

Large Mammals Completely Exterminated

The Arizona Elk, (*Cervus merriami*). — Right at our very door, under our very noses and as it were only yesterday, a well-defined species of American elk has been totally exterminated. Until recently the mountains of Arizona and New Mexico were inhabited by a light-colored elk of smaller size than the Wyoming species, whose antlers possessed on each side only one brow tine instead of two. The exact history of the blotting out of that species has not yet been written, but it seems that its final extinction occurred about 1901. Its extermination was only a routine incident of the devilish general slaughter of American big game that by 1900 had wiped out nearly everything killable over a large portion of the Rocky Mountain region and the Great Plains.

The Arizona elk was exterminated before the separate standing of the species had been discovered by naturalists, and before even *one* skin had been preserved in a museum! In 1902 Mr. E. W. Nelson described the species from two male skulls,—all the material of which he knew. Since that time, a third male skull, bearing an excellent pair of antlers, has been discovered by Mr. Ferdinand Kaegebehn, a member of the New York Zoological Society, and presented to our National Collection of Heads and Horns. It came from the Santa Catalina Mountains, Arizona, in 1884. The species was first exterminated in the central and northern mountains of Arizona, probably twenty years ago, and made its last stand in northwestern New Mexico. Precisely when it became extinct there, its last abiding place, we do not know, but in time the facts may appear.

THE QUAGGA, (*Equus quagga*).—Before the days of Livingstone, Gordon-Cumming and Anderson, the grassy plains and half-forested hills of South Africa were inhabited by great herds of a wild equine species that in its markings was a sort of connecting link between the striped zebras and the stripeless wild asses. The quagga resembled a wild ass with a few zebra stripes around its neck, and no stripes elsewhere.

There is no good reason why a mammal that is not in any one of the families regularly eaten by man should be classed as a game animal. White men, outside of the western border of the continent of Europe, do not eat horses; and by this token there is no reason why a zebra should be shot as a "game" animal, any more than a baboon. A big male baboon is dangerous; a male zebra is not.

Nevertheless, white men have elected to shoot zebras as game; and under this curse the unfortunate quagga fell to rise no more. The species was shot to a speedy death by sportsmen, and by the British and Dutch farmers of South Africa. It became extinct about 1875, and to-day there are only 18 specimens in all the museums of the world.

THE BLAUBOK, (*Hippotragus leucophaeus*).—The first of the African antelopes to become extinct in modern times was a species of large size, closely related to the roan antelope of to-day, and named by the early Dutch settlers of Cape Colony the blaubok, which means "blue-buck." It was snuffed out of existence in the year 1800, so quickly and so thoroughly that, like the Arizona elk, it very nearly escaped the annals of natural history. According to the careful investigations of Mr. Graham Renshaw, there are only eight specimens in existence in all the museums of Europe. In general terms it may be stated that this species has been extinct for about a century.

DAVID'S DEER, (*Elaphurus davidianus*).—We enter this species with those that are totally extinct, because this is true of it so far as its wild state is concerned. It is a deer nearly as large as the red deer of Europe, with 3-tined antlers about equal in total length to those of the red deer. Its most striking differential character is its *long tail*, a feature that among the deer of the world is quite unique.

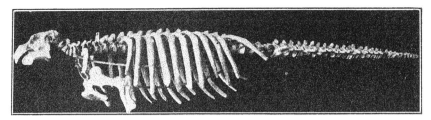

SKELETON OF A RHYTINA, OR ARCTIC SEA-COW
In the United States National Museum

Originally this species inhabited "northern Mongolia" (China), but in a wild state it became extinct before its zoological standing became known to the scientific world. The species was called to the attention of zoologists by a Roman Catholic missionary, called Father David, and when finally described it was named in his honor.

· At the outbreak of the Boxer Rebellion, in 1900, there were about 200 specimens living in the imperial park of China, a short distance south of Pekin; but during the rebellion, all of them were killed and eaten, thus totally exterminating the species from Asia.

Fortunately, previous to that calamity (in 1894), the Duke of Bedford had by considerable effort and expenditure procured and established in his matchless park surrounding Woburn Abbey, England, a herd of eighteen specimens of this rarest of all deer. That nucleus has thriven and increased, until in 1910 it contained thirty-four head. Owing to the fact that all the living female specimens of this remarkable species are concentrated in one spot, and perfectly liable to be wiped out in one year by riot, war or disease, there is some cause for anxiety. The writer has gone so far as to suggest the desirability of starting a new herd of David's deer, at some point far distant from England, as an insurance measure against the possibility of calamity at Woburn. Excepting two or three specimens in European zoological gardens that have been favored by the Duke of Bedford, there are no living specimens outside of Woburn Park.

THE RHYTINA, *(Rhytina gigas)*.—The most northerly Sirenian that (so far as we know) ever inhabited the earth, lived on the Commander Islands in the northern end of Behring Sea, and was exterminated by man, for its oil and its flesh, about 1768. It was first made known to the world by Steller, in 1741, and must have become extinct near the beginning of the nineteenth century.

The rhytina belonged to the same mammalian Order as the manatee of Florida and South America, and the dugong of Australia. The largest manatee that Florida has produced, so far as we know, was thirteen feet long. The rhytina attained a length of between thirty and thirty-five feet, and a weight of 6,000 pounds or over. The flesh of this animal, like that of the manatee and dugong, must have been edible, and surely was prized by the hungry sailors and natives of its time. It is not strange

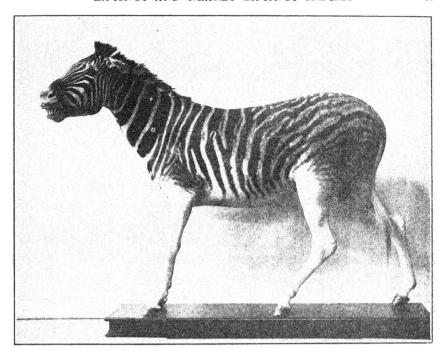

BURCHELL'S ZEBRA, IN THE U. S. NATIONAL MUSEUM
Now Believed to be Totally Extinct

that such a species was quickly exterminated by man, in the arctic regions. The wonder is that it ever existed at a latitude so outrageous for a Sirenian, an animal which by all precedents should prefer life in temperate or warm waters.

BURCHELL'S ZEBRA (*Equus burchelli typicus*).—The foundation type of what now is the Burchell group of zebras, consisting of four or five sub-species of the original species of *burchelli*, is an animal abundantly striped as to its body, neck and head, but with legs that are almost white and free from stripes. The sub-species have legs that are striped about half as much as the mountain zebra and the Grevy species.

While there are Chapman zebras and Grant zebras in plenty, and of Crawshay's not a few, all these are forms that have developed northward of the range of the parent species, the original *Equus burchelli*. For half a century in South Africa the latter had been harried and driven and shot, and now it is gone, forever. Now, the museum people of the world are hungrily enumerating their mounted specimens, and live ones cannot be procured with money, because there are none! Already it is common talk that "the true Burchell zebra is extinct;" and unfortunately there is no good reason to doubt it. Even if there are a few now living in some

THYLACINE OR TASMANIAN WOLF
Now Being Exterminated by the Sheep Owners of Tasmania

remote nook of the Transvaal, or Zululand, or Portuguese East Africa, the chances are as 100 to 1 that they will not be suffered to bring back the species; and so, to Burchell's zebra, the world is to-day saying "Farewell!"

Species of Large Mammals Almost Extinct

The Thylacine or Tasmanian Wolf, (*Thylacinus cynocephalus*).—Four years ago, when Mr. W. H. D. Le Souef, Director of the Melbourne Zoological Garden (Australia), stood before the cage of the living thylacine in the New York Zoological Park, he first expressed surprise at the sight of the animal, then said:

"I advise you to take excellent care of that specimen; for when it is gone, you never will get another. The species soon will be extinct."

This opinion has been supported, quite independently, by a lady who is the highest authority on the present status of that species, Mrs. Mary G. Roberts, of Hobart, Tasmania. For nearly ten years Mrs. Roberts has been procuring all the living specimens of the thylacine that money could buy, and attempting to breed them at her private zoo. She states that the mountain home of this animal is now occupied by flocks of sheep, and because of the fact that the "Tasmanian wolves" raid the flocks and kill lambs, the sheep-owners and herders are systematically poisoning the thylacines as fast as possible. Inasmuch as the species is limited to

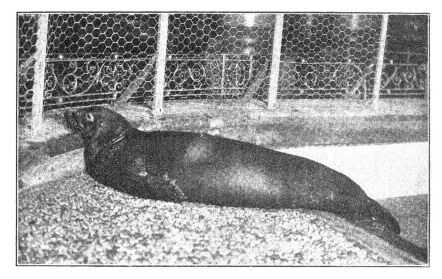

WEST INDIAN SEAL
In the New York Aquarium

Tasmania, Mrs. Roberts and others fear that the sheepmen will totally exterminate the remnant at an early date. This animal is the largest and also the most interesting carnivorous marsupial of Australia, and its untimely end will be a cause for sincere regret.

THE WEST INDIAN SEAL, (*Monachus tropicalis*).—For at least fifty years, all the zoologists who ever had heard of this species believed that the oil-hunters had completely exterminated it. In 1885, when the National Museum came into possession of one poorly-mounted skin, from Professor Poey, of Havana, it was regarded as a great prize.

Most unexpectedly, in 1886 American zoologists were startled by the discovery of a small herd on the Triangle Islands, in the Caribbean Sea, near Yucatan, by Mr. Henry L. Ward, now director of the Milwaukee Public Museum, and Professor Ferrari, of the National Museum of Mexico. They found about twenty specimens, and collected only a sufficient number to establish the true character of the species.

Since that time, four living specimens have been captured, and sent to the New York Aquarium, where they lived for satisfactory periods. The indoor life and atmosphere did not seem to injure the natural vitality of the animals. In fact, I think they were far more lively in the Aquarium than were the sluggish creatures that Mr. Ward saw on the Triangle reefs, and described in his report of the expedition.

It is quite possible that there are yet alive a few specimens of this odd species; but the Damocletian sword of destruction hangs over them suspended by a fine hair, and it is to be expected that in the future some

CALIFORNIA ELEPHANT SEAL
Photographed on Guadalupe Island by C H. Townsend.

roving sea adventurer will pounce upon the Remnant, and wipe it out of existence for whatever reason may to him seem good.

THE CALIFORNIA ELEPHANT SEAL, (*Mirounga angustirostris*).— This remarkable long-snouted species of seal was reluctantly stricken from the fauna of the United States several years ago, and for at least fifteen years it has been regarded as totally extinct. Last year, however (1911), the *Albatross* scientific expedition, under the control of Director C. H. Townsend of the New York Aquarium, visited Guadalupe Island, 175 miles off the Pacific coast of Lower California and there found about 150 living elephant seals. They took six living specimens, all of which died after a few months in captivity. Ever since that time, first one person and then another comes to the front with a cheerful proposition to go to those islands and "clean up" all the remainder of those wonderful seals. One hunting party could land on Guadalupe, and in one week totally destroy the last remnant of this almost extinct species. To-day the only question is, Who will be mean enough to do it?

Fortunately, those seals have no commercial value whatsoever. The little oil they would yield would not pay the wages of cook's mate. The proven impossibility of keeping specimens alive in captivity, even for one year, and the absence of cash value in the skins, even for museum purposes, has left nothing of value in the animals to justify an expedition to kill or to capture them. No zoological garden or park desires any of them, at any price. Adult males attain a length of sixteen feet, and females eleven feet. Formerly this species was abundant·in San Christobal Bay, Lower California.

At present, Mexico is in no frame of mind to provide real protection to a small colony of seals of no commercial value, 175 miles from her mainland, on an uninhabited island. It is wildly improbable that those seals will be permitted to live. It is a safe prediction that our next news of the elephant seals of Guadalupe will tell of the total extinction of those last 140 survivors of the species.

THE CALIFORNIA GRIZZLY BEAR, (*Ursus horribilis californicus*).—No one protects grizzly bears, except in the Yellowstone Park and other game preserves. For obvious reasons, it is impossible to say whether any individuals of this huge species now remain alive, or how long it will be until the last one falls before a .405 Winchester engine of extermination. We know that a living specimen can not be procured with money, and we believe that "Old Monarch" now in Golden Gate Park, San Francisco, is the last specimen of his species that ever will be exhibited alive.

I can think of no reason, save general Californian apathy, why the extinction of this huge and remarkable animal was not prevented by law. The sunset grizzly (on a railroad track) is the advertising emblem of the Golden State, and surely the state should take sufficient interest in the species to prevent its total extermination.

But it will not. California is hell-bent on exterminating a long list of her wild-life species, and it is very doubtful whether the masses can be reached and aroused in time to stop it. Name some of the species? Certainly; with all the pleasure in life: The band-tailed pigeon, the white-tailed kite, the sharp-tailed grouse, the sage grouse, the mountain sheep, prong-horned antelope California mule deer, and ducks and geese too numerous to mention.

CHAPTER V

THE EXTERMINATION OF SPECIES, STATE BY STATE

Early in 1912 I addressed to about 250 persons throughout the United States, three questions, as follows:

1. What species of birds have become totally extinct in your state?
2. What species of birds and mammals are threatened with early extinction?
3. What species of mammals have been exterminated throughout your state?

These queries were addressed to persons whose tastes and observations rendered them especially qualified to furnish the information de sired. The interest shown in the inquiry was highly gratifying. The best of the information given is summarized below; but this tabulation also includes much information acquired from other sources. The general summary of the subject will, I am sure, convince all thoughtful persons that the present condition of the best wild life of the nation is indeed very grave. This list is not submitted as representing prolonged research or absolute perfection, but it is sufficient to point forty-eight morals.

Birds and Mammals That Have Been Totally Exterminated in Various States and Provinces

ALABAMA:
Passenger pigeon, Carolina parrakeet; puma, elk, gray wolf, beaver.

ARIZONA:
Ridgway's quail (*Colinus ridgwayi*); Arizona elk (*Cervus merriami*), bison.

ARKANSAS:
Passenger pigeon, Carolina parrakeet, whooping crane; bison, elk, beaver.

CALIFORNIA:
No birds totally extinct, but several nearly so; grizzly bear (?), elephant seal.

COLORADO:
Carolina parrakeet, whooping crane; bison.

CONNECTICUT:
Passenger pigeon, Eskimo curlew, great auk, Labrador duck, upland plover, heath hen, wild turkey; puma, gray wolf, Canada lynx, black bear, elk.

DELAWARE
Wild turkey, ruffed grouse, passenger pigeon, heath hen, dickcissel, whooping crane, Carolina parrakeet; white-tailed deer, black bear, gray wolf, beaver, Canada lynx, puma.

FLORIDA:
Flamingo, roseate spoonbill, scarlet ibis, Carolina parrakeet, passenger pigeon.

GEORGIA:
Passenger pigeon, Carolina parrakeet, whooping crane, trumpeter swan; bison, elk, beaver, gray wolf, puma.—(Last 3, Craig D. Arnold.)

IDAHO:
Wood duck, long-billed curlew, whooping crane; bison.—(Dr. C. S. Moody.)

ILLINOIS:
Passenger pigeon, whooping crane, Carolina parrakeet, trumpeter swan, snowy egret, Eskimo curlew; bison, elk, white-tailed deer, black bear, puma, Canada lynx.

INDIANA:
Passenger pigeon, whooping crane, northern raven, wild turkey, ivory-billed woodpecker, Carolina parrakeet, trumpeter swan, snowy egret, Eskimo curlew; bison, elk, white-tailed deer, black bear, Canada lynx, beaver, porcupine.—(Amos W. Butler)

IOWA:
Wild turkey, Eskimo curlew, whooping crane, trumpeter swan, white pelican, passenger pigeon; bison, elk, antelope, white-tailed deer, black bear, puma, Canada lynx, gray wolf, beaver, porcupine.

KANSAS:
American scaup duck, woodcock, ruffed grouse, wild turkey, pileated woodpecker, parrakeet, white-necked raven, American raven (all Prof. L. L. Dyche); golden plover, Eskimo curlew, Hudsonian curlew, wood-duck (C. H. Smyth and James Howard, Wichita). Bison, elk, mule deer, white-tailed deer, gray wolf, beaver (?), otter, lynx (?) (L. L. D.)
(Reports as complete and thorough as these for other localities no doubt would show lists equally long for several other states.—(W. T. H.)

KENTUCKY:
Passenger pigeon, parrakeet; bison, elk, puma, beaver, gray wolf.

LOUISIANA:
Passenger pigeon, Carolina parrakeet, Eskimo curlew, flamingo, scarlet ibis, roseate spoonbill; bison, ocelot.

MAINE:
Great auk, Labrador duck, Eskimo curlew, oystercatcher, wild turkey, heath hen, passenger pigeon; puma, gray wolf, wolverine, caribou. —(All Arthur H. Norton, Portland.)

MARYLAND:
Sandhill crane, parrakeet, passenger pigeon; bison, elk, beaver, gray wolf, puma, porcupine.

MASSACHUSETTS:
Wild turkey, passenger pigeon, Labrador duck, whooping crane, sandhill crane, black-throated bunting, great auk, Eskimo curlew. — (William Brewster, W. P. Wharton); Canada lynx, gray wolf, black bear, moose, elk.

MICHIGAN:
Passenger pigeon, wild turkey, sandhill crane, whooping crane, bison, elk, wolverine.

MINNESOTA:
Whooping crane, white pelican, trumpeter swan, passenger pigeon, bison, elk, mule deer, antelope.
A strange condition exists in Minnesota, as will be seen by reference to the next list of states. A great many species are on the road to speedy extermination; but as yet the number of those that have become totally extinct up to date is small.

MISSISSIPPI:
Parrakeet, passenger pigeon; bison. (Data incomplete.)

MISSOURI:
Parrakeet, ivory-billed woodpecker, passenger pigeon, whooping crane, pinnated grouse; bison, elk, beaver.

MONTANA:
Although many Montana birds are on the verge of extinction, the only species that we are sure have totally vanished are the passenger pigeon and whooping crane. Mammals extinct, bison.

NEBRASKA:
Curlew, wild turkey, parrakeet, passenger pigeon, whooping crane, and no doubt *all* the other species that have disappeared from Kansas. Mammals: bison, antelope, elk, and mule deer.

NEVADA:
By a rather odd combination of causes and effects, Nevada retains representatives of nearly all her original outfit of bird and mammal species except the bison and elk; but several of them will shortly become extinct.

NEW HAMPSHIRE:
Wild turkey, heath hen, pigeon, whooping crane, Eskimo curlew, upland plover, Labrador duck; woodland caribou, moose.

NEW JERSEY:
Heath hen, wild turkey, pigeon, parrakeet, Eskimo curlew, Labrador duck, snowy egret, whooping crane, sandhill crane, trumpeter swan, pileated woodpecker; gray wolf, black bear, beaver, elk, porcupine, puma.

NEW MEXICO:
Notwithstanding an enormous decrease in the general volume of wild life in New Mexico, comparatively few species have been totally exterminated. The most important are the bison and Arizona elk.

NEW YORK:
Heath hen, passenger pigeon, wild turkey, great auk, trumpeter swan, Labrador duck, harlequin duck, Eskimo curlew, upland plover, golden plover, whooping crane, sandhill crane, purple martin, pileated woodpecker, moose, caribou, bison, elk, puma, gray wolf, wolverine, marten, fisher, beaver, fox, squirrel, harbor seal.

NORTH CAROLINA:
Ivory-billed woodpecker, parrakeet, pigeon, roseate spoonbill, long-billed curlew (*Numenius americanus*), Eskimo curlew; bison, elk, gray wolf, puma, beaver.—(E. L. Ewbank, T. Gilbert Pearson, *H. H.* and C. S. Brimley.)

NORTH DAKOTA:
Whooping crane, long-billed curlew, Hudsonian godwit, passenger pigeon; bison, elk, mule deer, mountain sheep.—(W. B. Bell and Alfred Eastgate.)

OHIO:
Pigeon, wild turkey, pinnated grouse, northern pileated woodpecker, parrakeet; white-tailed deer, bison, elk, black bear, puma, gray wolf, beaver, otter, puma, lynx.

OKLAHOMA:
Records for birds insufficient. Mammals: bison, elk, antelope, mule deer, puma, black bear.

OREGON:
The only species known to have been wholly exterminated during recent times is the California condor and the bison, both of which were rare stragglers into Oregon; but a number of species are now close to extinction.

PENNSYLVANIA:
Heath hen, pigeon, parrakeet, Labrador duck; bison, elk, moose, puma, gray wolf,

Canada lynx, wolverine, beaver. —(Witmer Stone, Dr. C. B. Penrose and Arthur Chapman.)

RHODE ISLAND:
Heath hen, passenger pigeon, wild turkey, least tern, eastern willet, Eskimo curlew, marbled godwit, long-billed curlew.—(Harry S. Hathaway); puma, black bear, gray wolf, beaver, otter, wolverine.

SOUTH CAROLINA
Ivory-billed woodpecker, Carolina parrakeet; bison, elk, puma, gray wolf.—(James H. Rice, Jr.)

SOUTH DAKOTA:
Whooping crane, trumpeter swan, pigeon, long-billed curlew; bison, elk, mule deer, mountain sheep.

TENNESSEE:
Records insufficient.

TEXAS:
Wild turkey, passenger pigeon, ivory-billed woodpecker, flamingo, roseate spoonbill, American egret, whooping crane, wood-duck; bison, elk, mountain sheep, antelope, "a small, dark deer that lived 40 years ago." (Capt. M. B. Davis.)

UTAH:
Records insufficient.

VERMONT:
Wild turkey, heath hen, pigeon, whooping crane, Eskimo curlew, upland plover, Labrador duck; caribou, moose, beaver, white-tailed deer in 1875, but successfully reintroduced.

VIRGINIA:
Records insufficient.

WASHINGTON:
Very few species have become totally extinct, but a number are on the verge, and will be named in the next state schedule.

WEST VIRGINIA:
Pigeon, parrakeet; bison, elk, beaver, puma, gray wolf.

WISCONSIN:
Whooping crane, passenger pigeon, American egret, wild turkey, Carolina parrakeet; bison, moose, elk, woodland caribou, puma, wolverine.

WYOMING·
Whooping crane, trumpeter swan, wood-duck; mountain goat.

CANADA

ALBERTA:
Passenger pigeon, whooping crane; bison.

BRITISH COLUMBIA·
A. Bryan Williams reports: "Do not know of any birds having become extinct."

MANITOBA:
Pigeon; bison, antelope, gray wolf.

NEW BRUNSWICK:
Pigeon.

NOVA SCOTIA:
Labrador duck, Eskimo curlew, passenger pigeon.

ONTARIO:
Wild turkey, pigeon, Eskimo curlew.

PRINCE EDWARD ISLAND:
  (Reported by E. T. Carbonell): Eskimo curlew, horned grebe, ring-billed gull, Caspian tern, passenger pigeon, Wilson's petrel, wood-duck, Barrow's golden-eye, whistling swan, American eider, white-fronted goose, purple sandpiper, Canada grouse, long-eared owl, screech owl, black-throated bunting, pine warbler, red-necked grebe, purple martin and catbird; beaver, black fox, silver gray fox, marten and black bear.

QUEBEC:
  Pigeon.

SASKATCHEWAN:
  Pigeon; bison.

BIRDS AND MAMMALS THREATENED WITH EXTINCTION

The second question submitted in my inquiry produced results even more startling than the first. None of the persons reporting can be regarded as alarmists, but some of the lists of species approaching extinction are appallingly long. To their observations I add other notes and observations of interest at this time.

ALABAMA:
  Wood-duck, snowy egret, woodcock. "The worst enemy of wild life is the pot-hunter and game hog. These wholesale slaughterers of game resort to any device and practice, it matters not how murderous, to accomplish the pernicious ends of their nefarious campaign of relentless extermination of fur and feather. They cannot be controlled by local laws, for these after having been tried for several generations have proven consummate failures, for the reason that local authorities will not enforce the provisions of game and bird protective statutes. Experience has demonstrated the fact that no one desires to inform voluntarily on his neighbors, and since breaking the game law is not construed to involve moral turpitude, even to an infinitesimal degree, by many of our citizens, the plunderers of nature's storehouse thus go free, it matters not how great the damage done to the people as a whole."—(John *H*. Wallace, Jr., Game Commissioner of Alabama.)

ALASKA:
  Thanks to geographic and climatic conditions, the Alaskan game laws and $15,000 with which to enforce them, the status of the wild life of Alaska is fairly satisfactory. I think that at present no species is in danger of extinction in the near future. When it was pointed out to Congress in 1902, by Madison Grant, T. S. Palmer and others that the wild life of Alaska was seriously threatened, Congress immediately enacted the law that was recommended, and now appropriates yearly a fair sum for its enforcement. I regard the Alaskan situation as being, for so vast and difficult a region, reasonably well in hand, even though open to improvement.

  There is one fatal defect in our Alaskan game law, in the perpetual and sweeping license to kill, that is bestowed upon "natives" and "prospectors." Under cover of this law, the Indians can slaughter game to any extent they choose; and they are great killers. For example: In 1911 at Sand Point, Kenai Peninsula, Frank E. Kleinschmidt saw 82 caribou tongues in the boat of a native, that had been brought in for sale at 50 cents, while the carcasses were left where they fell, to poison the air of Alaska. Thanks to the game law, and five wardens, the number of big game animals killed last year in Alaska by sportsmen was reasonably small,—just as it sh:uld have been.—(W. T. *H*.)

ARIZONA:
  During an overland trip made by Dr. MacDougal and others in 1907 from Tucson to Sonoyta, on the international boundary, 150 miles and back again, we saw not one antelope or deer.—(W. T. *H*.)

CALIFORNIA:
Swan, white heron, bronze ibis.   California valley quail are getting very scarce, and unless adequate protection is afforded them shortly, they will be found hereafter only in remote districts.   Ducks also are decreasing rapidly.—(H. W. Keller, Los Angeles.)

Sage grouse and Columbian sharp-tailed grouse are so nearly extinct that it may practically be said that they *are* extinct.   Among species likely to be exterminated in the near future are the wood-duck and band-tailed pigeon.—(W. P. Taylor, Berkeley.)

COLORADO:
Sage grouse and sharp-tailed grouse; nearly all the shore birds.

CONNECTICUT:
All the shore birds; quail, purple martin.

DELAWARE:
Wood duck, upland plover, least tern, Wilson tern, roseate tern, black skimmer, oystercatcher, and numerous other littoral species.   Pileated woodpeckers, bald eagles and all the ducks are much more rare than formerly.   Swan are about gone, geese scarce.   The list of ducks, geese and shore-birds, as well as of terns and gulls that are nearing extinction is appalling.—(C. J. Pennock, Wilmington.)

Wood-duck, woodcock, turtle dove and bob-white.—(A. R. Spaid, Wilmington.)

FLORIDA:
Limpkin, ivory-billed woodpecker, wild turkey (?).

GEORGIA:
Ruffed grouse, wild turkey.

IDAHO:
Harlequin duck, mountain plover, dusky grouse, Columbian sharp-tailed grouse, sage grouse.   Elk, goats and grizzly bears are becoming very scarce.   Of the smaller animals I have not seen a fisher for years, and marten are hardly to be found.   The same is true of other species.—(Dr. Charles S. Moody, Sand Point.)

ILLINOIS:
Pinnated grouse, except where rigidly protected.   In Vermillion County, by long and persistent protection Harvey J. Sconce has bred back upon his farm about 400 of these birds.

INDIANA:
Pileated woodpecker, woodcock, ruffed grouse, pigeon hawk, duck hawk.—(*A*mos W. Butler, Indianapolis.)

In northern and northwestern Indiana, a perpetual close season and rigid protection have enabled the almost-extinct pinnated grouse to breed up to a total number now estimated by Game Commissioner Miles and his wardens at 10,000 birds.   This is a gratifying illustration of what can be done in bringing back an almost-vanished species.   The good example of Indiana should be followed by every state that still possesses a remnant of prairie-chickens, or other grouse.

IOWA:
Pinnated grouse, wood-duck.   Notwithstanding an invasion of Jasper County, Iowa, in the winter of 1911-12 by hundreds of pinnated grouse, such as had not been known in 20 years, this gives no ground to hope that the future of the species is worth a moment's purchase.   The winter migration came from the Dakotas, and was believed to be due to the extra severe winter, and the scarcity of food.   Commenting on this unprecedented occurrence, J. L. Sloanaker in the "Wilson Bulletin" No. 78, says:

"In the opinion of many, the formerly abundant prairie chicken is doomed to early extinction.   Many will testify to their abundance in those years [in South Dakota, 1902] when the great land movement was taking place.   The influx of hungry settlers, together with an occasional bad season, decimated their ranks. They were eaten by the farmers, both in and out of season. Driven from pillar to post, with no friends and insufficient food,—what else then can be expected?"

Mr. F. C. Pellett, of Atlantic, Iowa, says: "Unless ways can be devised of rearing these birds in the domestic state, the prairie hen in my opinion is doomed to early extinction."

The older inhabitants here say that there is not one song-bird in summer where there used to be ten.—(G. *H.* Nicol, in *Outdoor Life* March, 1912.)

KANSAS:

To all of those named in my previous list that are not actually extinct, I might add the prairie hen, the lesser prairie hen, as well as the prairie sharp-tailed grouse and the wood-duck. Such water birds as the avocets, godwits, greater yellow-legs, long-billed curlew and Eskimo curlew are becoming very rare. All the water birds that are killed as game birds have been greatly reduced in numbers during the past 25 years. I have not seen a wood-duck in 5 years. *The prairie chicken* has entirely disappeared from this locality. *A* few are still seen in the sand hills of western Kansas, and they are still comparatively abundant along the extreme southwestern line, and in northern Oklahoma and the Texas panhandle.—(C. H. Smyth, Wichita.)

Yellow-legged plover, golden plover; Hudsonian and Eskimo curlew, prairie chicken.—(James Howard, Wichita.)

LOUISIANA:

Ivory-billed woodpecker, butterball, bufflehead. The wood-duck is greatly diminishing every year, and if not completely protected, ten years hence no wood-duck will be found in Louisiana.—(Frank M. Miller, and **G.** E. Beyer, New Orleans.)

Ivory-billed woodpecker, sandhill crane, whooping crane, pinnated grouse, American and snowy egret where unprotected.—(E. A. McIlhenny, Avery Island.)

MAINE:

Wood-duck, upland plover, purple martin, house wren, pileated woodpecker, bald eagle, yellow-legs, great blue heron, Canada goose, redhead and canvasback duck.—(John F. Sprague, Dover.)

Puffin, Leach's petrel, eider duck, laughing gull, great blue heron, fish-hawk and bald eagle.—(Arthur *H.* Norton, Portland.)

MARYLAND:

Curlew, pileated woodpecker, summer duck, snowy heron. No record of sandhill crane for the last 35 years. Greater yellow-leg is much scarcer than formerly, also Bartramian sandpiper. The only two birds which show an *increase* in the past few years are the robin and lesser scaup. General protection of the robin has caused its increase; stopping of spring shooting in the North has probably caused the increase of the latter. As a general proposition I think I can say that all birds are becoming scarcer in this state, as we have laws that do not protect, little enforcement of same, no revenue for bird protection and too little public interest. We are working to change all this, but it comes slowly. *The public fails to respond until the birds are 'most gone,* and we have a pretty good lot of game still left. The members of the Order Gallinæ are only holding their own where privately protected. The members of the Plover Family and what are known locally as shore birds are still plentiful on the shores of Chincoteague and Assateague, and although they do not breed there as formerly, so far as I know there are no species exterminated.—(Talbott Denmead, Baltimore.)

MASSACHUSETTS:

Wood-duck, hooded merganser, blue-winged teal, upland plover; curlew (perhaps already gone); red-tailed hawk (I have not seen one in Middlesex County for several years); great horned owl (almost gone in my county, Middlesex); house wren. The cave swallows and purple martins are fast deserting eastern Massachusetts and the barn swallows steadily diminishing in numbers. The bald eagle should perhaps be included here. I seldom see or hear of it now.—(William Brewster, Cambridge.)

Upland plover, woodcock, wood-duck (recent complete protection is helping these somewhat), heath hen, piping plover, golden plover, a good many song and insectivorous birds are apparently decreasing rather rapidly; for instance, the eave swallow.—(William P. Wharton, Groton.)

MICHIGAN:
Wood-duck, limicolae, woodcock, sandhill crane. The great whooping crane is not a wild bird, but I think it is now practically extinct. Many of our warblers and song birds are now exceedingly rare. Ruffed grouse greatly decreased during the past 10 years.—(W. B. Mershon, Saginaw.)

MINNESOTA:
The sandhill crane has been killed by sportsmen. I have not seen one in three years. Where there were, a few years ago, thousands of blue herons, egrets, wood ducks, redbirds, and Baltimore orioles, all those birds are now almost extinct in this state. They are being killed by Austrians and Italians, who slaughter everything that flies or moves. Robins, too, will be a rarity if more severe penalties are not imposed. I have seized 22 robins, 1 pigeon hawk, 1 crested log-cock, 4 woodpeckers and 1 grosbeak in one camp, at the Lertonia mine, all being prepared for eating. I have also caught them preparing and eating sea gulls, terns, blue heron, egret and even the bittern. I have secured 128 convictions since the first of last September.—(George E. Wood, Game Warden, Hibbing, Minnesota.)

From Robert Page Lincoln, Minneapolis.—Partridge are waning fast, quail gradually becoming extinct, prairie chickens almost extinct. Duck-shooting is rare. The gray squirrel is fast becoming extinct in Minnesota. Mink are going fast, and fur-bearing animals generally are becoming extinct. The game is passing so very rapidly that it will soon be a thing of the forgotten past. The quail are suffering most. The falling off is amazing, and inconceivable to one who has not looked it up. Duck-shooting is rare, the clubs are idle for want of birds. What ducks come down fly high, being harassed coming down from the north. I consider the southern Minnesota country practically cleaned out.

MISSOURI:
The birds threatened with extermination are the American woodcock, wood-duck, snowy egret, pinnated grouse, wild turkey, ruffed grouse, golden eagle, bald eagle, pileated woodpecker.

MONTANA:
Blue grouse.—(Henry Avare, Helena.)

Sage grouse, prairie and Columbian sharp-tailed grouse, trumpeter swan, Canada goose, in fact, most of the water-fowl. The sickle-billed curlew, of which there were many a few years ago, is becoming scarce. There are no more golden or black-bellied plover in these parts.—(Harry P. Stanford, Kalispell.)

Curlew, Franklin grouse (fool hen) and sage grouse.—W. R. Felton, Miles City.

Sage grouse.—(L. A. Huffman, Miles City.)

Ptarmigan, wood-duck, sharp-tailed grouse, sage grouse, fool hen and plover. All game birds are becoming scarce as the country becomes settled and they are confined to uninhabited regions.—(Prof. M. J. Elrod, Missoula.)

NEBRASKA:
Grouse, prairie chicken and quail.—(H. N. Miller, Lincoln.)

Whistling swan.—(Dr. S. G. Towne, Omaha.)

NEW HAMPSHIRE:
Wood-duck and upland plover.

NEW YORK:
Quail, woodcock, upland plover, golden plover, black-bellied plover, willet, dowitcher, red-breasted sandpiper, long-billed curlew, wood-duck, purple martin, red headed woodpecker, mourning dove; gray squirrel, otter.

NEW JERSEY:
Ruffed grouse, teal, canvasback, red-head duck, widgeon, and all species of shore birds, the most noticeable being black-bellied plover, dowitcher, golden plover, killdeer,

sickle-bill curlew, upland plover and English snipe; also the mourning dove.—(James M. Stratton and Ernest Napier, Trenton.)

Upland plover, apparently killdeer, egret, wood-duck, woodcock, and probably others.—(B. S. Bowdish, Demarest.)

NORTH CAROLINA:

Forster's tern, oystercatcher, egret and snowy egret.—(T. Gilbert Pearson, Sec. Nat. Asso. Audubon Societies.)

Ruffed grouse rapidly disappearing; bobwhite becoming scarce.—(E. L. Ewbank, Hendersonville.)

Perhaps American and snowy egret. If long-billed curlew is not extinct, it seems due to become so. No definite, reliable record of it later than 1885.—(H. H. Brimley, Raleigh.)

NORTH DAKOTA:

Wood-duck, prairie hen, upland plover, sharp-tailed grouse, canvas-back, pinnated and ruffed grouse, double-crested cormorant, blue heron, long-billed curlew, whooping crane and white pelican.—(W. B. Bell, Agricultural College.)

Upland plover, marbled godwit, Baird's sparrow, chestnut-collared longspur. (Alfred Eastgate, Tolna.)

OHIO:

White heron, pileated woodpecker (if not already extinct). White heron reported a number of times last year; occurrences in Sandusky, Huron, Ashtabula and several other counties during 1911. These birds would doubtless rapidly recruit under a proper federal law.—(Paul North, Cleveland.)

Turtle dove, quail, red-bird, wren, hummingbird, wild canary [goldfinch] and blue bird.—(Walter C. Staley, Dayton.)

OKLAHOMA:

Pinnated grouse.—(J. C. Clark); otter, kit fox, black-footed ferret.—(G. W. Stevens.)

OREGON:

American egret, snowy egret.—(W. L. Finley, Portland.)

PENNSYLVANIA:

Virginia partridge and woodcock.—(Arthur Chapman.)

Wood-duck, least bittern, phalarope, woodcock, duck hawk and barn swallow.—(Dr. Chas. B. Penrose.)

Wild turkey; also various transient and straggling water birds.—(Witmer Stone.)

RHODE ISLAND:

Wood-duck, knot, greater yellow-legs, upland plover, golden plover, piping plover, great horned owl.—(Harry S. Hathaway, South Auburn.)

SOUTH CAROLINA:

Wood duck, abundant 6 years ago, now almost gone. Wild turkey (abundant up to 1898); woodcock, upland plover, Hudsonian curlew Carolina rail, Virginia rail, clapper rail and coot. Black bear verging on extinction, opossum dwindling rapidly. (James H. Rice Jr., Summerville.)

SOUTH DAKOTA:

Prairie chicken and quail are most likely to become extinct in the near future. (W. F. Bancroft, Watertown.)

TEXAS:

Wild turkey and prairie chickens.—(J. D. Cox, Austin)

Plover, all species; curlew, cardinal, road-runner, woodcock, wood-duck, canvas-back, cranes, all the herons; wild turkey; quail, all varieties; prairie chicken and Texas guan.—(Capt. M. B. Davis, Waco.)

Curlew, very rare; plover, very rare; antelope. (Answer applies to the Panhandle of Texas.—Chas. Goodnight.)

Everything [is threatened with extinction] save the dove, which is a migrating bird. Antelope nearly all gone.—(Col. O. C. Guessaz, San Antonio.)

UTAH:

Our wild birds are well protected, and there are none that are threatened with extinction. They are increasing.—(Fred. W. Chambers, State Game Warden, Salt Lake City.)

VERMONT:

If all states afforded as good protection as does Vermont, none; but migrating birds like woodcock are now threatened.—(John W. Tilcomb, State Game Warden, Lyndonville.)

VIRGINIA:

Pheasants (ruffed grouse), wild turkey and other game birds are nearly extinct. *A* few bears remain, and deer in small numbers in remote sections. In fact, all animals show great reduction in numbers, owing to cutting down forests, and constant gunning.—(L. T. Christian, Richmond.)

WEST VIRGINIA:

Wood-duck, wild turkey, northern raven, dickcissel.—(Rev. Earle *A*. Brooks, Weston.)

Wild turkeys are very scarce, also ducks. Doves, once numerous, now almost *nil*. Eagles, except a few in remote fastnesses. Many native song-birds are retreating before the English sparrow.—(William Perry Brown, Glenville.)

Wood-duck and wild turkey.—(J. A. Viquesney, Belington.)

WISCONSIN:

Double-crested cormorant, upland plover, white pelican, long-billed curlew, lesser snow goose, Hudsonian curlew, sandhill crane, golden plover, woodcock, dowitcher and long-billed duck; spruce grouse, knot, prairie sharp-tailed grouse, marbled god wit and bald eagle. All these, formerly abundant, must now be called rare in Wisconsin.—(Prof. George E. Wagner, Madison.)

Common tern, knot, American white pelican, Hudsonian godwit, trumpeter swan, long-billed curlew, snowy heron, Hudsonian curlew, American avocet, prairie sharp-tailed grouse, dowitcher, passenger pigeon. Long-billed dowitcher and northern hairy woodpecker.—(*Henry L. Ward, Milwaukee Public Museum.*)

Wood-duck, ruddy duck, black mallard, grebe or hell-diver, tern and woodcock.—(Fred. Gerhardt, Madison.)

WYOMING:

Sage grouse and sharp-tailed grouse are becoming extinct, both in Wyoming and North Dakota. Sheridan and Johnson Counties (Wyoming) have sage grouse protected until 1915. The miners (mostly foreigners) are out after rabbits at all seasons. To them everything that flies, walks or swims, large enough to be seen, is a "rabbit." They are even worse than the average sheep-herder, as he will seldom kill a bird brooding her young, but to one of those men, a wren or creeper looks like a turkey. Antelope, mountain sheep and grizzly bears are *going*, fast! The moose season opens in 1915, for a 30 days open season, then close season until 1920.—(Howard Eaton, Wolf.)

Sage grouse, blue grouse, curlew, sandhill crane, porcupine practically extinct; wolverine and pine marten nearly all gone.—(S. N. Leek, Jackson's Hole.)

CANADA

ALBERTA:

Swainson's buzzard and sandhill crane are now practically extinct. Elk and antelope will soon be as extinct as the buffalo.—(Arthur G. Wooley-Dod, Calgary.)

BRITISH COLUMBIA:

Wild fowl are in the greatest danger in the southern part of the Province, especially the wood-duck. Otherwise birds are increasing rather than otherwise, especially the small non-game birds. The sea otter is almost extinct.—(A. Bryan Williams, Provincial Game Warden, Vancouver.)

MANITOBA:

Whooping crane, wood-duck and golden plover. Other species begin to show a marked increase, due to our stringent protective measures. For example, the pinnated grouse and sharp-tailed grouse are more plentiful than in 15 years. Prong-horned antelope and wolf are threatened with extinction.—(J. P. Turner, Winnipeg.)

The game birds indigenous to this Province are fairly plentiful. Though the prairie chicken was very scarce some few years ago, these birds have become very plentiful again, owing to the strict enforcement of our present "Game Act." The elk are in danger of becoming extinct if they are not stringently guarded. Beaver and otter were almost extinct some few years ago, but are now on the increase, owing to a strict enforcement of the "Game Act."—(Charles Barber, Winnipeg.)

NEW BRUNSWICK:

Partridge, plover and woodcock. Moose and deer are getting more plentiful every year.—(W. W. Gerard, St. John.)

NOVA SCOTIA:

The Canada grouse may possibly become extinct in Nova Scotia, unless the protection it now enjoys can save it. The American golden plover, which formerly came in immense flocks, is now very rare. Snowflakes are very much less common than formerly, but I think this is because our winters are now usually much less severe. The caribou is almost extinct on the mainland of Nova Scotia, but is still found in North Cape Breton Island. The wolf has become excessively rare, but as it is found in New Brunswick, it may occur here at any time again. The beaver had been threatened with extinction; but since being protected, it has multiplied, and is now on a fairly safe footing again.—(Curator of Museum, Halifax.)

ONTARIO:

Quail are getting scarce.—(E. Tinsley, Toronto.)

Wood-duck, bob white, woodcock, golden plover, Hudsonian curlew, knot and dowitcher [are threatened with extinction.]—(C. W. Nash, Toronto.)

PRINCE EDWARD ISLAND:

The species threatened with extinction are the golden plover, American woodcock, pied-billed grebe, red-throated loon, sooty shearwater, gadwall, ruddy duck, black-crowned night heron, Hudsonian godwit, kildeer, northern pileated woodpecker, chimney swift, yellow-bellied flycatcher, red-winged blackbird, pine finch, magnolia warbler, ruby-crowned kinglet.—(E. T. Carbonell, Charlottetown.)

In closing the notes of this survey, I repeat my assurance that they are not offered on a basis of infallibility. It would require years of work to obtain answers from forty-eight states to the three questions that I have asked that could be offered as absolutely exact. All these reports are submitted on the well-recognized court-testimony basis,—"to the best of our knowledge and belief." Gathered as they have been from persons whose knowledge is good, these opinions are therefore valuable; and they furnish excellent indices of wild-life conditions as they exist in 1912 in the various states and provinces of North America north of Mexico.

CHAPTER VI

THE REGULAR ARMY OF DESTRUCTION

In order to cure any disease, the surgeon must make of it a correct diagnosis. It is useless to try to prescribe remedies without a thorough understanding of the trouble.

That the best and most interesting wild life of America is disappearing at a rapid rate, we all know only too well. That proposition is entirely beyond the domain of argument. The fact that a species or a group of species has made a little gain here and there, or is stationary, does not sensibly diminish the force of the descending blow. The wild-life situation is full of surprises. For example, in 1902 I was astounded by the extent to which bird life had decreased over the 130 miles between Miles City, Montana, and the Missouri River since 1886; for there was no reason to expect anything of the kind. Even the jack rabbits and coyotes had almost totally disappeared.

The duties of the present hour, that fairly thrust themselves into our faces and will not be put aside, are these:

First,—To save valuable species from extermination!

Second,—To preserve a satisfactory representation of our once rich fauna, to hand down to Posterity.

Third,—To protect the farmer and fruit grower from the enormous losses that the destruction of our insectivorous and rodent-eating birds is now inflicting upon both the producer and consumer.

Fourth,—To protect our forests, by protecting the birds that keep down the myriads of insects that are destructive to trees and shrubs.

Fifth,—To preserve to the future sportsmen of America enough game and fish that they may have at least a taste of the legitimate pursuit of game in the open that has made life so interesting to the sportsmen of to-day.

For any civilized nation to exterminate valuable and interesting spe cies of wild mammals, birds or fishes is more than a disgrace. It is a crime! We have no right, legal, moral or commercial, to exterminate any valu able or interesting species; because none of them belong to us, to exter minate or not, as we please.

For the people of any civilized nation to permit the slaughter of the wild birds that protect its crops, its fruits and its forests from the insect hordes, is worse than folly. It is sheer orneryness and idiocy. People who are either so lazy or asinine as to permit the slaughter of their best friends deserve to have their crops destroyed and their forests ravaged. They deserve to pay twenty cents a pound for their cotton when the boll weevil has cut down the normal supply.

It is very desirable that we should now take an inventory of the forces that have been, and to-day are, active in the destruction of our wild birds, mammals, and game fishes. During the past ten years a sufficient quantity of facts and figures has become available to enable us to secure a reasonably full and accurate view of the whole situation. As we pause on our hill-top, and survey the field of carnage, we find that we are reviewing the *Army of Destruction!*

It is indeed a motley array. We see true sportsmen beside ordinary gunners, game-hogs and meat hunters; handsome setter dogs are mixed up with coyotes, cats, foxes and skunks; and well-gowned women and ladies' maids are jostled by half-naked "poor-white" and black-negro "plume hunters."

Verily, the destruction of wild life makes strange companions.

Let us briefly review the several army corps that together make up the army of the destroyers. Space in this volume forbids an extended notice of each. Unfortunately it is impossible to segregate some of these classes, and number each one, for they merge together too closely for that; but we can at least describe the several classes that form the great mass of destroyers.

THE GENTLEMEN SPORTSMEN.—These men are the very bone and sinew of wild life preservation. These are the men who have red blood in their veins, who annually hear the red gods calling, who love the earth, the mountains, the woods, the waters and the sky. These are the men to whom "the bag" is a matter of small importance, and to whom "the bag-limit" has only academic interest; because in nine cases out of ten they do not care to kill all that the law allows. The tenth and exceptional time is when the bag limit is "one." A gentleman sportsman is a man who protects game, stops shooting when he has "enough"—without reference to the legal bag-limit, and whenever a species is threatened with extinction, he conscientiously refrains from shooting it.

The true sportsmen of the world are the men who once were keen in the stubble or on the trail, but who have been halted by the general slaughter and the awful decrease of game. Many of them, long before a hair has turned gray, have hung up their guns forever, and turned to the camera. These are the men who are willing to hand out checks, or to leave their mirth and their employment and go to the firing line at their state capitols, to lock horns with the bull-headed killers of wild life who recognize no check or limit save the law.

These are the men who have done the most to put upon our statute books the laws that thus far have saved some of our American game from total annihilation, and who (so we firmly believe) will be chiefly instrumental in tightening the lines of protection around the remnant. These are the men who are making and stocking game preserves, public and private, great and small.

Drawn by Dan Beard

THE REGULAR ARMY OF DESTRUCTION, WAITING FOR THE FIRST OF OCTOBER

Each Year 2,642,274 Well-Armed Men Take the Field Against the Remnant of Wild Birds and Mammals in the United States

If you wish to know some of these men, I will tell you where to find a goodly number of them; and when you find them, you will also find that they are men you would enjoy camping with! Look in the membership lists of the Boone and Crockett Club, Camp-Fire Club of America, the Lewis and Clark Club of Pittsburgh, the New York State League, the Shikar Club of London, the Society for the Preservation of the Wild Fauna of the British Empire, the Massachusetts Fish and Game Protective Association, the Springfield (Mass.) Sportsmen's Association, the Camp-Fire Clubs of Detroit and Chicago, and the North American Fish and Game Protective Association.

There are other bodies of sportsmen that I would like to name, were space available, but to set down here a complete list is quite impossible.

The best and the most of the game-protective laws now in force in the United States and Canada were brought into existence through the initiative and efforts of the real sportsmen of those two nations. But for their activity, exerted on the right side, the settled portion of North America would to-day be an utterly gameless land! Even though the sportsmen have taken their toll of the wilds, they have made the laws that have saved a remnant of the game until 1912.

For all that, however, every man who still shoots game is a soldier in the Army of Destruction! There is no blinking that fact. Such men do not stand on the summit with the men who now protect the game *and do not shoot at all!* The millions of men who do not shoot, and who also *do nothing to protect or preserve wild life,* do not count! In this warfare they are merely ciphers in front of the real figures.

THE GUNNERS, WHO KILL TO THE LIMIT.—Out of the enormous mass of men who annually take up arms against the remnant of wild life, *and are called "sportsmen,"* I believe that only one out of every 500 *conscientiously* stops shooting when game becomes scarce, and extinction is impending. All of the others feel that it is right and proper to kill all the game that they can kill *up to the legal bag limit.* It is the reasoning of Shylock:

"Justice demands it, and *the law* doth give it!"

Especially is this true of the men who pay their *one dollar* per year for a resident hunting license, and feel that in doing so they have done a great Big Thing!

This is a very deadly frame of mind. Ethically it is *entirely wrong;* and at least two million men and boys who shoot American game must be shown that it is wrong! This is the spirit of Extermination, clothed in the robes of Law and Justice.

Whenever and wherever game birds are so scarce that a good shot who hunts hard during a day in the fields finds only three or four birds, he should *stop shooting at once, and devote his mind and energies to the problem of bringing back the game!* It is strange that conditions do not make this duty clear to every conscientious citizen.

The Shylock spirit which prompts a man to kill all that "the law allows" is a terrible scourge to the wild life of America, and to the world at large. It is the spirit of extermination according to law. Even the killing of game for the market is not so great a scourge as this; for this spirit searches out the game in every nook and cranny of the world, and spares not. In effect it says: "If the law is defective, it is right for me to take every advantage of it! I do not need to have any conscience in the matter outside *the letter of the law.*"

The extent to which this amazing spirit prevails is positively awful. You will find it among pseudo game-protectors to a paralyzing extent! It is the great gunner's paradox, and it pervades this country from corner to corner. No: there is no use in trying to "educate" the mass of the hunters of America out of it, as a means of saving the game; for positively it can not be done! Do not waste time in trying it. If you rely upon it, you will be doing a great wrong to wild life, and promoting extermination. The only remedy is *sweeping laws, for long close seasons, for a great many species.* Forget the paltry dollar-a-year license money. The license fees never represent more than a tenth part of the value of the game that is killed under licenses.

The savage desire to kill "all that the law allows" often is manifested in men in whom we naturally expect to find a very different spirit. By way of illumination, I offer three cases out of the many that I could state.

Case No. 1. *The Duck Breeder.*—A gentleman of my acquaintance has spent several years and much money in breeding wild ducks. From my relations with him, I had acquired the belief that he was a great lover of ducks, and at least wished all species well. One whizzing cold day in winter he called upon me, and stated that he had been duck-hunting; which surprised me. He added, "I have just spent two days on Great South Bay, and I made a great killing. *In the two days I got ninety-four ducks!*"

I said, "How *could* you do it,—caring for wild ducks as you do?"

"Well, I had hunted ducks twice before on Great South Bay and didn't have very good luck; but this time the cold weather drove the ducks in, and I got square with them!"

Case No. 2. *The Ornithologist.*—A short time ago the news was published in *Forest and Stream* that a well-known ornithologist had distinguished himself in one of the mid-western states by the skill he had displayed in bagging thirty-four ducks in one day, greatly to the envy of the natives; and if this shoe fits any American naturalist, he is welcome to put it on and wear it.

Case No. 3. *The Sportsman.*—A friend of mine in the South is the owner of a game preserve in which wild ducks are at times very numerous. Once upon a time he was visited by a northern sportsmen who takes a deep and abiding interest in the preservation of game. The sportsman was invited to go out duck-shooting; ducks being then in season there. He said:

"Yes, I will go; and I want you to put me in a place where I can kill

G. O. SHIELDS
A Notable Defender of Wild Life

a *hundred ducks in a day!* I never have done that yet, and I would like to do it, once!'"

"All right," said my friend, "I can put you in such a place; and if you can shoot well enough, you can kill a hundred ducks in a day."

The effort was made in all earnestness. There was much shooting, but few were the ducks that fell before it. In concluding this story my friend remarked in a tone of disgust:

"All the game-preserving sportsmen that come to me are just like that! *They want to kill all they can kill!*"

There is a blood-test by which to separate the conscientious sportsmen from the mere gunners. Here it is:

A *sportsman* stops shooting when game becomes scarce; and he does not object to long-close-season laws; but

A *gunner* believes in killing "all that the law allows;" and *he objects to long close seasons!*

I warrant that whenever and wherever this test is applied it will separate the sheep from the goats. It applies in all America, all Asia and Africa, and in Greenland, with equal force.

THE GAME-HOG.—This term was coined by G. O. Shields, in 1897, when he was editor and owner of *Recreation Magazine*, and it has come into general use. It has been recognized by a judge on the bench as being an appropriate term to apply to all men who selfishly slaughter wild game beyond the limits of decency. Although it is a harsh term, and was mercilessly used by Mr. Shields in his fierce war on the men who slaughtered game for "sport," it has jarred at least a hundred thousand men into their first realization of the fact that to-day there is a difference between decency and indecency in the pursuit of game. The use of the term has done *very great good;* but, strange to say, it has made for Mr. Shields a great many enemies *outside* the ranks of the game-hogs themselves! From this one might fairly suppose that there is such a thing as a sympathetic game-hog!

One thing at least is certain. During a period of about six years, while his war with the game-hogs was on, from Maine to California, Mr. Shields's name became a genuine terror to excessive killers of game; and it is reasonably certain that his war saved a great number of game birds from the slaughter that otherwise would have overtaken them!

The number of armed men and boys who annually take the field in the United States in the pursuit of birds and quadrupeds, is enormous.

People who do not shoot have no conception of it; and neither do they comprehend the mechanical perfection and fearful deadliness of the weapons used. This feature of the situation can hardly be realized until some aspect of it is actually seen.

I have been at some pains to collect the latest figures showing the number of hunting licenses issued in 1911, but the total is incomplete. In some states the figures are not obtainable, and in some states there are no hunters' license laws. The figures of hunting licenses issued in 1911 that I have obtained from official sources are set forth below.

THE UNITED STATES ARMY OF DESTRUCTION
Hunting Licenses issued in 1911

Alabama	5,090	Montana	59,291
California	138,689	Nebraska	39,402
Colorado	41,058	New Hampshire	33,542
Connecticut	19,635	New Jersey	61,920
Idaho	50,342	New Mexico	7,000
Illincis	192,244	New York	150,222
Indiana	54,813	Rhode Island	6,541
Iowa	91,000	South Dakota	31,054
Kansas	44,069	Utah	27,800
Louisiana	76,000	Vermont	31,762
Maine	2,552	Washington, about	40,000
Massachusetts	45,039	Wisconsin	138,457
Michigan	22,323	Wyoming	9,721
Missouri	66,662		

Total number of regularly licensed gunners 1,486,228

The average for the twenty-seven states that issued licenses as shown above is 55,046 for each state.

Now, the twenty-one states issuing no licenses, or not reporting, produced in 1911 fully as many gunners per capita as did the other twenty-seven states. Computed fairly on existing averages they must have turned out a total of 1,155,966 gunners, making for all the United States **2,642,194** armed men and boys warring upon the remnant of game in 1911. We are not counting the large number of lawless hunters who never take out licenses. Now, is Mr. Beard's picture a truthful presentation, or not?

New York with only deer, ruffed grouse, shore-birds, ducks and a very few woodcock to shoot annually puts into the field 150,222 armed men. In 1909 they killed about *9,000 deer!*

New Jersey, spending $30,000 in 1912 in efforts to restock her covers with game, and with a population of 2,537,167, sent out in 1911 a total army of 61,920 well-armed gunners. How can any of her game survive?

New Hampshire, with only 430,572 population, has 33,542 licensed hunters,—equal to *thirty-three regiments of full strength!*

Vermont, with 355,956 people, sends out annually an army of 31,762 men who hunt according to law; and in 1910 they killed 3,649 deer.

Utah, with only 373,351 population, had 27,800 men in the field after her very small remnant of game! How can any wild thing of Utah escape?

Montana, population 376,053, had in 1911 an army of 59,291 well-armed men, warring chiefly upon the big game, and swiftly extermi nating it.

How long can any of the big game stand before the army of *two and one-half million well-armed men*, eager and keen to kill, and out to get an equivalent for their annual expenditure in guns, ammunition and other expenses?

In addition to the hunters themselves, they are assisted by thousands of expert guides, thousands of horses, thousands of dogs, hundreds of automobiles and hundreds of thousands of tents. Each big-game hunter has an experienced guide who knows the haunts and habits of the game, the best feeding grounds, the best trails, and everything else that will aid the hunter in taking the game at a disadvantage and destroying it. The big-game rifles are of the highest power, the longest range, the greatest accuracy and the best repeating mechanism that modern inventive genius can produce. It is said that in Wyoming the Maxim silencer is now being used. England has produced a weapon of a new type, called "the scatter rifle," which is intended for use on ducks. The best binoculars are used in searching out the game, and horses carry the hunters and guides as near as possible to the game. For bears, baits are freely used, and in the pursuit of pumas, dogs are employed to the limit of the available supply.

The deadliness of the automobile in hunting already is so apparent that North Dakota has wisely and justly forbidden their use by law, (1911). The swift machine enables city gunmen to penetrate game regions they could not reach with horses, and hunt through from four to six localities per day, instead of one only, as formerly. The use of automobiles in hunting should be everywhere prohibited.

Every appliance and assistance that money can buy, the modern sportsman secures to help him against the game. The game is beset during its breeding season by various wild enemies,—foxes, cats, wolves, pumas, lynxes, eagles, and many other predatory species. The only help that it receives is in the form of an annual close season—*which thus far has saved in America only a few local moose, white-tailed deer and a few game birds, from steady and sure extermination.*

The bag limits on which vast reliance is placed to preserve the wild game, are a fraud, a delusion and a snare! The few local exceptions only prove the generality of the rule. In every state, without one single exception, the bag limits are far too high, and the laws are of deadly liberality. In many states, the bag limit laws on birds are an absolute dead letter. Fancy the 125 wardens of New York enforcing the bag-limit laws on 150,-000 gunners! It is this horrible condition that is enabling the licensed army of destruction to get in its deadly work on the game, all over the world. In America, the over-liberality of the laws are to blame for two-thirds of the carnival of slaughter, and the successful evasions of the law are responsible for the other third.

TWO GUNNERS OF KANSAS CITY

WHY THE SANDHILL CRANE IS BECOMING EXTINCT
Ninteen of Them Killed as "Game" by Three Gunners. (Note the Machine Gun.)

The only remedy for the present extermination of game according to law that so rapidly and so furiously is proceeding all over the United States, Canada, Alaska, and Africa, is ten-year close seasons on all the species threatened with extinction, and immensely reduced open seasons and bag limits on all the others.

Will the people who still have wild game take heed now, and clamp down the brakes, hard and fast before it is too late, or will they have their game exterminated?

Shall we have five-year close seasons, or close seasons of 500 years? We must take our choice.

Shall we hand down to our children a gameless continent, with all the shame that such a calamity will entail?

We have *got* to answer these questions like men, or they will soon be answered for us by the extermination of the wild life. For twenty-five years we have been smarting under the disgrace of the extermination of our bison millions. Let us not repeat the dose through the destruction of other species.

CHAPTER VII

THE GUERRILLAS OF DESTRUCTION

We have now to deal with THE GUERRILLAS OF DESTRUCTION.

In warfare, a *guerrilla, or bushwhacker,* is an armed man who recognizes none of the rules of civilized warfare, and very often has no com mander. In France he is called a "franc-tireur," or free-shooter. The guerrilla goes out to live on the country, to skulk, to war on the weak, and never attack save from ambush, or when the odds clearly are on his side. His military status is barely one remove from that of the spy.

The meat-shooters who harry the game and other wild life in order to use it as a staple food supply; the Italians, negroes and others who shoot song-birds as food; the plume-hunters and the hide-and-tusk hunters all over the world are the guerrillas of the Army of Destruction. Let us consider some of these grand divisions in detail.

Here is an inexorable law of Nature, to which there are no exceptions:

No wild species of bird, mammal, reptile or fish can withstand exploita tion for commercial purposes.

The men who pursue wild creatures for the money or other value there is in them, never give up. They work at slaughter when other men are enjoying life, or are asleep. If they are persistent, no species on which they fix the Evil Eye escapes extermination at their hands. ✔

Does anyone question this statement? If so let him turn backward and look at the lists of dead and dying species.

THE DIVISION OF MEAT-SHOOTERS contains all men who sordidly shoot for the frying-pan,—to save bacon and beef at the expense of the public, or for the markets. There are a few wilderness regions so remote and so difficult of access that the transportation of meat into them is a matter of much difficulty and expense. There are a very few men in North America who are justified in "living off the country," *for short periods.* The genuine prospectors always have been counted in this class; but all miners who are fully located, all lumbermen and railway-builders certainly are not in the prospector's class. They are abundantly able to maintain continuous lines of communication for the transit of beef and mutton.

Of all the meat-shooters, the market-gunners who prey on wild fowl and ground game birds for the big-city markets are the most deadly to wild life. Enough geese, ducks, brant, quail, ruffed grouse, prairie chickens, heath hens and wild pigeons have been butchered by gunners and netters for "the market" to have stocked the whole world. No section

A MARKET GUNNER AT WORK ON MARSH ISLAND
Killing Mallards for the New Orleans Market.   The Purchase of This Island by Mrs. Russell Sage has now
Converted it Into a Bird Sanctuary.

containing a good supply of game has escaped.   In the United States the great slaughtering-grounds have been Cape Cod; Great South Bay, New York; Currituck Sound, North Carolina; Marsh Island, Louisiana; the southwest corner of Louisiana; the Sunk Lands of Arkansas; the lake regions of Minnesota; the prairies of the whole middle West; Great Salt Lake; the Klamath Lake region (Oregon) and southern California.

The output of this systematic bird slaughter has supplied the greedy game markets of Boston, New York, Philadelphia, Washington, Baltimore, Chicago, New Orleans, St. Louis, Salt Lake City, San Francisco, Portland, and Seattle.   The history of this industry, its methods, its carnage, its profits and its losses would make a volume, but we can not enter upon it here.   Beyond reasonable doubt, this awful traffic in dead game is responsible for at least three-fourths of the slaughter that has reduced our game birds to a mere remnant of their former abundance. There is no influence so deadly to wild life as that of the market gunner who works six days a week, from sunrise until sunset, hunting down and killing every game bird that he can reach with a choke-bore gun.

During the past five years, several of the once-great killing grounds have been so thoroughly "shot out" that they have ceased to hold their former rank.   This is the case with the Minnesota Lakes, the Sunk Lands of Arkansas, the Klamath Lakes of Oregon, and I think it is also true of southern California.   The Klamath Lakes have been taken over by the Government as a bird refuge.   Currituck Sound, at the northeastern corner of North Carolina, has been so bottled up by the Bayne law of New

RUFFED GROUSE
A Common Victim of Illegal Slaughter

York State that Currituck's greatest market has been cut off. Last year only one-half the usual number of ducks and geese were killed; and already many "professional" duck and brant shooters have abandoned the business because the commission merchants no longer will buy dead birds.

Very many enormous bags of game have been made in a day by market gunners: but rarely have they published any of their records. The greatest kill of which I ever have heard occurred under the auspices of the Glenn County Club, in southern California, on February 5, 1906. Two men, armed with automatic shot-guns, fired five shots apiece, and got ten geese out of one flock. In one hour they killed *two hundred and eighteen geese*, and their bag for the day was *four hundred and fifty geese!* The shooter who wrote the story for publication (on February 12, at Willows, Glenn County, California) said: "It being warm weather, the birds had to be shipped at once in order to keep them from spoiling." A photograph was made of the "one hour's slaughter" of two hundred and eighteen geese, and it was published in a western magazine with "C. H. B.'s" story, nearly all of which will be found in Chapter XV.

The reasons why market shooting is so deadly destructive to wild life are not obscure

The true sportsman hunts during a very few days only each year. The market gunners shoot early and late, six days a week, month after month. When game is abundant, the price is low, and a great quantity must be killed in order to make it pay well. When game is scarce, the market prices are high, and the shooter makes the utmost exertions to find the last of the game in order to secure the "big money."

When game is protected by law, thousands of people with money desire it for their tables, just the same, and are willing to pay fabulous prices for what they want, when they want it. Many a dealer is quite willing to run the risk of fines, because fines don't really hurt; they are only annoying. The dealer wishes to make the big profit, and *retain his customers;* "and besides," he reasons, "if I don't supply him some one else will; so what is the difference?"

When game is scarce, prices high and the consumer's money ready, there are a hundred tricks to which shooters and dealers willingly resort to ship and receive unlawful game without detection. It takes the very

From "Rod and Gun in Canada"

A PERFECTLY LAWFUL BAG OF 58 RUFFED GROUSE FOR TWO MEN

best kind of game wardens,—genuine detectives, in fact,—to ferret out these cunning illegal practices, and catch lawbreakers "with the goods on them," so that they can be punished. Mind you, convictions can not be secured at *both* ends of the line save by the most extraordinary good fortune, and usually the shooter and shipper escape, even when the dealer is apprehended and fined.

Here are some of the methods that have been practiced in the past in getting illegal game into the New York market:

Ruffed grouse and quail have both been shipped in butter firkins, marked "butter"; and latterly, butter has actually been packed solidly on top of the birds.

Ruffed grouse and quail very often have been shipped in egg crates, marked "eggs." They have been shipped in trunks and suit cases,—a very common method for illegal game birds, all over the United States. In Oklahoma when a man refuses to open his trunk for a game warden, the warden joyously gets out his brace and bitt, and bores an inch hole into the lower story of the trunk. If dead birds are there, the tell-tale auger quickly reveals them.

Three years ago, I was told that certain milk-wagons on Long Island made daily collections of dead ducks intended for the New York market, and the drivers kindly shipped them by express from the end of the route.

Once upon a time, a New York man gave notice that on a certain date he would be in a certain town in St. Lawrence County, New York, with a palace horse-car, "to buy horses." Car and man appeared there as advertised. Very ostentatiously, he bought one horse, and had it taken aboard the car before the gaze of the admiring populace. At night, when the A. P. had gone to bed, many men appeared, and into the horseless end of that car, they loaded thousands of ruffed grouse. The game warden who described the incident to me said: "That man pulled out for New York with one horse and *half a car load of ruffed grouse!*"

Whenever a good market exists for the sale of game, as sure as the world that market will be supplied. Twenty-six states forbid by law the sale of *their own* "protected" game, but twenty of them do *not* expressly prohibit the sale of game stolen from neighboring states! That is *a very, very weak point in the laws of all those states.* A child can see how it works. Take Pittsburgh as a case in point.

In the winter and spring of 1912 the State Game Commission of Pennsylvania found that quail and ruffed grouse were being sold in Pittsburgh, in large quantities. The state laws were well enforced, and it was believed that the birds were not being killed in Pennsylvania. Some other state was being *robbed!*

The Game Commission went to work, and in a very short time certain game-dealers of Pittsburgh were arrested. At first they tried to bluff their way out of their difficulty, and even went as far as to bring charges against the game-warden whom the Commission had instructed to buy some of their illegal game, and pay for it. But the net of the law tightened upon them so quickly and so tightly that they threw up their hands and begged for mercy.

It was found that those Pittsburgh game-dealers were selling quail and grouse that had been stolen in thousands, from the state of Kentucky! Between the state game laws, working in lovely harmony with the Lacey federal law that prohibits the shipment of game illegally killed or sold, the whole bad business was laid bare, and signed confessions were promptly obtained from the shippers in Kentucky.

At that very time, a good bill for the better protection of her game was before the Kentucky legislature; and a certain member was vigorously opposing it, as he had successfully done in previous years. He was told that the state was being robbed, but refused to believe it. Then a signed confession was laid before him, bearing the name of the man who was instigating his opposition,—his friend,—who confessed that he had

SNOW BUNTING

A Great " Game Bird " ! Of These, 8,058 Were Found in 1902
in one New York Cold-Storage Warehouse

illegally bought and shipped to Pittsburgh over 5,000 birds. The objector literally threw up his hands, and said, "I have been *wrong!* Let the bill go through!" And it went.

Before the passage of the Bayne law, New York City was a "fence" for the sale of grouse illegally killed in Massachusetts, Connecticut, Pennsylvania, New Jersey and I know not how many other states. The Bayne law stopped all that business, abruptly and forever; and if the ruffed grouse, quail and ducks of the Eastern States are offered for sale in Chicago, Cincinnati, Baltimore and Washington, the people of New York and Massachusetts can at least be assured that they are not to blame. Those two states now maintain no "fences" for the sale of game that has been stolen from other states. They have both set their houses in order, and set two examples for forty other states to follow.

The remedy for all this miserable game-stealing, law-breaking business is simple and easily obtained. Let each state of the United States and each province and Canada *enact a Bayne law, absolutely prohibiting the sale of all wild native game*, and the thing is done! But nothing short of that will be really effective. It will not do at all to let state laws rest with merely forbidding the sale of game "protected by the State;" for that law is full of loop-holes. It does much good service, yes; but what earthly *objection* can there be in any state to the enactment of a law that is sweepingly effective, and which can not be evaded, save through the criminal connivance of officers of the law?

By way of illustration, to show what the sale of wild game means to the remnant of our game, and the wicked slaughter of non-game birds to which it leads, consider these figures:

DEAD BIRDS FOUND IN ONE COLD STORAGE HOUSE IN NEW YORK IN 1902.

Snow Buntings	8,058	Grouse	7,560
Sandpipers	7,607	Quail	4,385
Plover	5,218	Ducks	1,756
Snipe	7,003	Bobolinks	288
Yellow-legs	788	Woodcock	96

The fines for this lot, if imposed, would have amounted to $1,168,315

Shortly after that seizure American quail became so scarce that in effect they totally disappeared from the banquet tables of New York. I can not recall having been served with one since 1903, but the little Egyptian quail can be legally imported and sold when officially tagged.

Few persons away from the firing line realize the far-reaching effects of the sale of wild game. Here are a few flashes from the searchlight:

At Hangkow, China, Mr. C. William Beebe found that during his visit in 1911, over 46,000 pheasants of various species were shipped from that port on one cold-storage steamer to the London market. And this when English pheasants were selling in the Covent Garden market at from two to three shillings each, for *fresh* birds!

In 1910, 1,200 ptarmigan from Norway, bound for the Chicago market, passed through the port of New York,—not by any means the first or the last shipment of the kind. The epicures of Chicago are being permitted to comb the game out of Norway.

In 1910, 70,000 *dozen* Egyptian quail were shipped to Europe from Alexandria, Egypt. Just why that species has not already been exterminated, is a zoological mystery; but extermination surely will come some day, and I think it will be in the near future.

The coast of China has been raked and scraped for wild ducks to ship to New York,—prior to the passage of the Bayne law! I have forgotten the figures that once were given me, but they were an astonishing number of thousands for the year.

The Division of Negroes and Poor Whites who kill song and other birds indiscriminately will be found in a separate chapter.

THE DIVISION OF "RESIDENT" GAME-BUTCHERS.—This refers to the men who live in the haunts of big game, where wardens are the most of the time totally absent, and where bucks, does and fawns of hoofed big game may be killed in season and out of season, with impunity. It includes guides, ranchmen, sheep-herders, cowboys, miners, lumbermen and floaters generally. In times past, certain taxidermists of Montana promoted the slaughter of wild bison in the Yellowstone Park, and it was a pair of rascally taxidermists who killed, or caused to be killed in Lost Park, in 1897, the very last bison of Colorado.

It seems to be natural for the minds of men who live in America in the haunts of big game to drift into the idea that the wild game around them is all theirs. Very few of them recognize the fact that every other man, woman and child in a given state or province has vested rights in its wild game. It is natural for a frontiersman to feel that because he is in the wilds he has a God-given right to live off the country; but to-day *that idea is totally wrong!* If some way can not be found to curb that all-pervading propensity among our frontiersmen, then we may as well bid all our open-field big game a long farewell; for the deadly "residents" surely will exterminate it, outside the game preserves. The "residents" are, in my opinion, about ten times more destructive than the sportsmen. A sportsman in quest of large game is in the field only from ten to thirty days; all his movements are known, and all his trophies are seen and counted. His killing is limited by law, and upon him the law is actually enforced. Often a resident hunts the whole twelve months of the year,— for food, for amusement, and for trophies to sell. Rarely does a game warden reach his cabin; because the wardens are few, the distances great and the frontier cabins are widely scattered.

Mr. Carl Pickhardt told me of a guide in Newfoundland who had a shed in the woods hanging full of bodies of caribou, and who admitted to him that while the law allowed him five caribou each year, he killed each year about twenty-five.

Mr. J. M. Phillips knows of a mountain in British Columbia, once well stocked with goats, on which the goats have been completely exterminated by one man who lives within easy striking distance of them, and who finds goat meat to his liking.

I have been reliably informed that in 1911, at Haha Lake, near Grande Bay, Saguenay District, P. Q., one family of six persons killed thirty-four woodland caribou and six moose. This meant the waste of about 14,000 pounds of good meat, and the death of several female animals.

In 1886 I knew a man named Owens who lived on the head of Sunday Creek, Montana, who told me that in 1884-5 he killed thirty-five mule deer for himself and family. The family ate as much as possible, the dogs ate all they could, and in the spring the remainder spoiled. Now there is not a deer, an antelope, or a sage grouse within fifty miles of that lifeless waste.

Here is a Montana object lesson on the frame of mind of the "resident" hunter, copied from *Outdoor Life* Magazine (Denver) for Pebruary, 1912. It is from a letter to the Editor, written by C. B. Davis.

November 27, 28, 29, and 30, 1911, will remain a red letter day with a half thousand men for years to come. These half thousand men gathered along the border of the Yellowstone National Park, near Gardiner, Montana, at a point known as Buffalo Flats, to exterminate elk. The snow had driven the elk down to the foothills, and Buffalo Flats is on the border of the park and outside the park. The elk entered this little valley for food. Like hungry wolves, shooters, not hunters, gathered along the border waiting to catch an elk off the "reservation" and kill it.

On November 27th about 1500 elk crossed the line, and the slaughter began. I have not the data of the number killed this day, but it was hundreds.

On the 28th, twenty-two stepped over and were promptly executed. Like Custer's band, not one escaped. On the evening of the 28th, 600 were sighted just over the line, and the army of 125 brave men entrenched themselves for the battle which was expected to open next morning. Before daylight of the 29th the battle began. The elk were over the line, feeding on Buffalo Flats. One hundred and twenty-five men poured bullets into this band of 600 elk till the ground was red with blood and strewn with carcasses, and in their madress they shot each other. One man was shot through the ear,—a close call; another received a bullet through his coat sleeve, and another was shot through the bowels and can't live.

My informer told me he participated in the slaughter, and while he would not take fifty dollars for what he saw, and the experience he went through, yet he would not go through it again for $1,000. When my informer got back to Gardiner that day there were four sleigh loads of elk, each load containing from twenty to thirty-five elk, besides thirty-two mules and horses carrying one to two each. This was only a part of the slaughter. Hundreds more were carried to other points; and this was only one day's work.

Hundreds of wounded elk wandered back into the park to die, and others died outside the park. The station at Livingston, Montana, for a week looked like a packing house. Carcasses were piled up on the trucks and depot platform. The baggage cars were loaded with elk going to points east and west of Livingston.

Maybe this is all right. Maybe the government can't stop the elk from crossing the line. Maybe the elk were helped over; but it strikes me there is something wrong somewhere.

THE DIVISION OF HIRED LABORERS.—The scourge of lumber-camps in big-game territory, the mining camps and the railroad-builders is a long story, and if told in detail it would make several chapters. Their awful destructiveness is well known. It is a common thing for "the boss" to hire a hunter to kill big game to supply the hungry outfit, and save beef and pork.

The abuses arising from this source easily could be checked, and finally suppressed. A ten-line law would do the business,—forbidding any person employed in any camp of sheep men, cattle men, lumbermen, miners, railway laborers or excavators to own or use a rifle in hunting wild game; and forbidding any employer of labor to feed those laborers, or permit them to be fed, on the flesh of wild game mammals or birds. "Camp" laborers are not "pioneers;" not by a long shot! They are soldiers of Commerce, and makers of money.

A MOUNTAIN SHEEP CASE IN COLORADO.—The state of Colorado sincerely desires to protect and perpetuate its slender remnant of mountain sheep, but as usual the Lawless Miscreant is abroad to thwart the efforts of the guardians of the game. Every state that strives to protect its big game has such doings as this to contend with:

In the winter of 1911-12, a resident poacher brought into Grant, Colorado, a lot of mountain sheep meat *for sale;* and he actually sold it to residents of that town! The price was *six cents per pound.* A lot of it was purchased by the railway station-agent. I have no doubt that the same man who did that job, which was made possible only by the co-operation of the citizens of Grant, will try the same poaching-and-selling game next winter, unless the State Game Commissioner is able to bring him to book.

A WYOMING CASE IN POINT.—As a fair sample of what game wardens, and the general public, are sometimes compelled to endure through the improper decisions of judges, I will cite this case:

In the Shoshone Mountains of northern Wyoming, about fifty miles or so from the town of Cody, in the winter of 1911-12 a man was engaged in trapping coyotes. It was currently reported that he had been "driven out of Montana and Idaho." He had scores of traps. He baited his traps with the flesh of deer, elk calves and grouse, all illegally killed and illegally used for that purpose. A man of my acquaintance saw some of this game meat actually used as described.

The man was a notorious character, and cruel in the extreme. Finally a game warden caught him red-handed, arrested him, and took him to Cody for trial. It happened that the judge on the bench had once trapped with him, and therefore "he set the game-killer free, while the game-warden was roasted."

That wolf-trapper once took into the mountains a horse, to kill and use as bear-bait. The animal was blind in one eye, and because it would not graze precisely where the wolfer desired it to remain, he deliberately destroyed the sight of its good eye, and left it for days, without the ability to find water.

Think of the fate of any wild animal that unkind Fate places at the mercy of such a man!

CHAPTER VIII

UNSEEN FOES OF WILD LIFE

Quite unintentionally on his part, Man, the arch destroyer and the most predatory and merciless of all animal species except the wolves, has rendered a great service to all the birds that live or nest upon the ground. His relentless pursuit and destruction of the savage-tempered, strong-jawed fur-bearing animals is in part the salvation of the ground birds of to-day and yesterday. If the teeth and claws had been permitted to multiply unchecked down to the present time, with man's warfare on the upland game proceeding as it has done, scores upon scores of species long ere this would have been exterminated.

But the slaughter of the millions of North American foxes, wolves, weasels, skunks, and mink has so overwhelmingly reduced the four-footed enemies of the birds that the balance of wild Nature has been preserved. As a rule, the few predatory wild animals that remain are not slaughtering the birds to a serious extent; and for this we may well be thankful.

THE DOMESTIC CAT.—In such thickly settled communities as our northern states, from the Atlantic coast to the sandhills of Kansas and Nebraska, the domestic cat is probably the greatest four-footed scourge of bird life. Thousands of persons who never have seen a hunting cat in action will doubt this statement, but the proof of its truthfulness is only too painfully abundant.

Unhappily it is the way of the hunting cat to stalk unseen, and to kill the very birds that are most friendly with man, and most helpful to him in his farming and fruit-growing business. The quail is about the only game bird that the cat affects seriously, and to it the cat is very destructive. It is the robin, catbird, thrush, bluebird, dove, woodpecker, chickadee, phoebe, tanager and other birds of the lawn, the garden and orchard that afford good hunting for sly and savage old Thomas.

When I was a boy in my 'teens, I had a lasting series of object lessons on the cat as a predatory animal. Our "Betty" was the most ambitious and successful domestic-cat hunter of wild mammals of which I ever have heard. To her, rats and mice were mere child's-play, and after a time their pursuit offered such tame sport that she sought fresh fields for her prowess. Then she brought in young rabbits, chipmunks and thirteen-lined spermophiles, and once she came in, quite exhausted, half dragging and half carrying a big, fat pocket gopher. With her it seemed to be a point of honor that she should bring in her game and display it. Little did we realize then that in course of time the wild birds would become so scarce that their slaughter by house cats would demand legislative action in the states.

In considering the hunting cat, let us call in a credible witness of the effects of domestic cats on the bob white. The following is an eye-witness report, by Ernest B. Beardsley, in *Outdoor Life* for April, 1912. The locality was Wellington, Sumner County, Kansas.

In the meantime, old Queen was having a high old time up ahead, some hundred feet by then, running up the bank and back down in the draw. We had hardly caught up when up goes Mr. Savage's gun and he gives both barrels. I had seen nothing up to date, but I didn't have long to wait, for by the time I got up to him and the dog, they were both in the high grass and had a great, big, common gray maltese house-cat; and Queen had a half-eaten quail that Mr. Cat was busy with when disturbed.

Well, we followed the draw across the field and got nine of a covey of sixteen that had been ahead of Mr. Cat; and about four o'clock that evening we killed another white-and-gray cat. While driving home that night, Mr. Savage told me that he had killed fifty or more in three or four years. They will get in a draw full of tumble-grass, on a cold day when quail don't like to fly, and stay right with them; and even after feeding on two or three, they will lie and watch, and when the covey moves, they move. When eating time comes around they are at it again, and to a covey of young birds they are sure death to the whole covey.

Well, Will told me never to overlook a house-cat that I found as far as a quarter of a mile from a farm or ranch, for if they have not already turned wild, they are learning how easy it is to hunt and live on game, and are almost as bad. We found Mr. Black-and-White Hunter had eaten two quail just before we killed him that evening. I would rather not write what Mr. Savage said when we found the remains of a partly-eaten bird.

My advice is, don't let tame cats get away when found out hunting; for the chances are they have not seen a home in months, and maybe years,—and say! but they do get big and bad. When you meet one, give it to him good, and don't let your dog run up to him until he is out for keeps. I learned afterwards that was how Will knew it was a cat. Queen had learned to back off and call for help on cats some years before.

In the New York Zoological Park, we have had troubles of our own with marauding cats. They establish themselves in a day, and quickly learn where to seek easy game and good cover. In the daytime they lie close in the thick brush, exactly as tigers do in India, but if not molested for a period of days, they become bold and attack game in open view. One bird-killing cat was so shy of man that it was only after two weeks of hard hunting (mornings and evenings) that it was killed.

We have seen cats catch and kill gray squirrels, chipmunks, robins and thrushes, and have found the feathers of slaughtered quail. Once we had gray rabbits breeding in the park, and their number reached between eighty and ninety. For a time they fearlessly hopped about in sight from our windows. and they were of great interest to visitors and to all of us. Then the cats began upon them; and in one year there was not a rabbit to be seen, save at rare intervals. At the same time the chipmunks of the park were almost exterminated.

That was the last straw, and we began a vigorous war upon those wild and predatory cats. The cats came off second best. We killed every cat that was found hunting in the park, and we certainly got some that were big and bad. We eliminated that pest, and we are keeping it eliminated. And with what result?

In 1911 a covey of eleven quail came and settled in our grounds, and have remained there. Twenty times at least during the past eight months (winter and spring) I have seen the flock on the granite ledge not more than forty feet from the rear window of my office. Last spring when I left the Administration Building at six o'clock, after the visitors had gone, I found two half-grown rabbits calmly roosting on the door-mat. The rabbits are slowly coming back, and the chipmunks are visibly increasing in number. The gray squirrels now chase over the walks without fear of any living thing, and our ducklings and young guineas and peacocks are safe once more.

That cats destroy annually in the United States several *millions* of very valuable birds, seems fairly beyond question. I believe that in settled regions they are worse than weasels, foxes, skunks and mink *combined;* because there are about one hundred times as many of them, and those that hunt are not afraid to hunt in the daytime. Of course I am not saying that *all* cats hunt wild game; but in the country I believe that fully one-half of them do.

I am personally acquainted with a cat in Indiana, on the farm of relatives, which is notorious for its hunting propensities, and its remarkable ability in capturing game. Even the lady who is joint owner of the cat feels very badly about its destructiveness, and has said, over and over again, that it ought to be killed; but the cat is such a family-pet that no one in the family has the heart to destroy it, and as yet no stranger has come forward to play the part of executioner. The lady in question assured me that to her certain knowledge that particular cat would watch a nestful of young robins week after week until they had grown up to such a size that they were almost ready to fly; then he would kill them and devour them. Old "Tommy" was too wise to kill the robins when they were unduly small.

In a great book entitled *Useful Birds and Their Protection*, by E. H. Forbush, State Ornithologist of Massachusetts, and published by the Massachusetts State Board of Agriculture in 1905, there appears, on page 362, many interesting facts on this subject. For example:

Mr. William Brewster tells of an acquaintance in Maine, who said that his cat killed about fifty birds a year. Mr. A. C. Dike wrote [to Mr. Forbush] of a cat owned by a family, and well cared for. They watched it through one season, and found that it killed fifty-eight birds, including the young in five nests.

Nearly a hundred correspondents, scattered through all the counties of the state, report the cat as one of the greatest enemies of birds. The reports that have come in of the torturing and killing of birds by cats are absolutely sickening. The number of birds killed by them in this state is appalling.

Some cat lovers believe that each cat kills on the average not more than ten birds a year; but I have learned of two instances where more than that number were killed in a single day, and another where seven were killed. If we assume, however, that the average cat on the farm kills but ten birds per year, and that there is one cat to each farm in Massachusetts, we have, in round numbers, seventy thousand cats, killing seven hundred thousand birds annually.

In Mr. Forbush's book there is an illustration of the cat which killed fifty-eight birds in one year, and the animal was photographed with a dead robin in its mouth. The portrait is reproduced in this chapter.

Last year, a strong effort was made in Massachusetts to enact a law requiring cats to be licensed. On account of the amount of work necessary in passing the no-sale-of-game bill, that measure was not pressed, and so it did not become a law; but another year it will undoubtedly be passed, for it is a good bill, and extremely necessary at this time. *Such a law is needed in every state!*

There is a mark by which you may instantly and infallibly know the worst of the wild cats—by their presence *away from home, hunting in the open.* Kill all such, wherever found. The harmless cats are domestic

A HUNTING CAT AND ITS VICTIM

This Cat had fed so bountifully on the Rabbits and Squirrels of the Zoological Park, that it ate only the Brain of this Gray Rabbit

in their tastes, and stay close to the family fireside and the kitchen. Being properly fed, they have no temptation to become hunters. There are cats and cats, just as there are men and men: some tolerable, many utterly intolerable. No sweeping sentiment for *all* cats should be allowed to stand in the way of the abatement of the hunting-cat nuisances.

Of all men, the farmer cannot afford the luxury of their existence! It is too expensive. With him it is a matter of dollars, and cash out of pocket for every hunting cat that he tolerates in his neighborhood. There are two places in which to strike the hunting cats: in the open, and in the state legislature.

While this chapter was in the hands of the compositors, the hunting cat and gray rabbit shown in the accompanying illustration were brought in by a keeper.

DOGS AS DESTROYERS OF BIRDS.—I have received many letters from protectors of wild life informing me that the destruction of ground-nesting birds, and especially of upland game birds, by roaming dogs, has in some localities become a great curse to bird life. Complaints of this kind have come from New York, Massachusetts, Connecticut, Pennsylvania and elsewhere. Usually the culprits are *hunting dogs*—setters, pointers and hounds.

Now, surely it is not necessary to set forth here any argument on this subject. It is not open to argument, or academic treatment of any kind. The cold fact is:

In the breeding season of birds, and while the young birds are incapable of quick and strong flight, all dogs, of every description, should be restrained from free hunting; and all dogs found hunting in the woods during the season referred to should be arrested, and their owners should be fined twenty dollars for each offense. Incidentally, one-half the fine should go to the citizen who arrests the dog. The method of restraining hunting dogs should devolve upon dog owners; and the law need only prohibit or punish the act.

Beyond a doubt, in states that still possess quail and ruffed grouse, free hunting by hunting dogs leads to great destruction of nests and broods during the breeding season.

TELEGRAPH AND TELEPHONE WIRES.—Mr. Daniel C. Beard has strongly called my attention to the slaughter of birds by telegraph wires that has come under his personal observation. His country home, at Redding, Connecticut, is near the main line of the New York, New Haven and Hartford Railway, along which a line of very large poles carries a great number of wires. The wires are so numerous that they form a barrier through which it is difficult for any bird to fly and come out alive and unhurt.

Mr. Beard says that among the birds killed or crippled by flying against those wires near Redding he has seen the following species: olive-backed thrush, white-throated sparrow and other sparrows, oriole, blue jay, rail, ruffed grouse, and woodcock. It is a common practice for employees of the railway, and others living along the line, to follow the line and pick up on one excursion enough birds for a pot-pie.

Beyond question, the telegraph and telephone wires of the United States annually exact a heavy toll in bird life, and claim countless thousands of victims. They may well be set down as one of the unseen forces destructive to birds.

Naturally, we ask, what can be done about it?

I am told that in Scotland such slaughter is prevented by the attachment of small tags or discs to the telephone wires, at intervals of a few rods, sufficiently near that they attract the attention of flying birds, and reveal the line of an obstruction. This system should be adopted in all regions where the conditions are such that birds kill themselves against telegraph wires, and an excellent place to begin would be along the line of the N. Y., N. H. & H. Railway.

WILD ANIMALS.—Beyond question, it is both desirable and necessary that any excess of wild animals that prey upon our grouse, quail, pheasants, woodcock, snipe, mallard duck, shore birds and other species that nest on the ground, should be killed. Since we must choose between the two, the birds have it! Weasels and foxes and skunks are interesting, and they do much to promote the hilarity of life in rural districts, but they do not destroy insects, and are of comparatively little value as destroyers of the noxious rodents that prey upon farm crops. While a few persons may dispute the second half of this proposition, the burden of proof that my view is wrong will rest upon them; and having spent eighteen years "on the farm," I think I am right. If there is any positive evidence tending to prove that the small carnivores that we class as "vermin" are industrious and persistent destroyers of noxious rodents—pocket gophers, moles, field-mice and rats—or that they do not kill wild birds numerously, now is the time to produce it, because the tide of public sentiment is strongly setting against the weasels, mink, foxes and skunks. (Once upon a time, a shrewd young man in the Zoological Park discovered a weasel hiding behind a stone while devouring a sparrow that it had just caught and killed. He stalked it successfully, seized it in his bare hand, and, even though bitten, made good the capture.)

The State of Pennsylvania is extensively wooded, with forests and with brush which affords excellent home quarters and breeding grounds for mammalian "vermin." The small predatory mammals are so seriously destructive to ruffed grouse and other ground birds that the State Game Commission is greatly concerned. When the hunter's license law is enacted, as it very surely will be at the next session of the legislature (1913), a portion of the $70,000 that it will produce each year will be used by the commission in paying bounties on the destruction of the surplus of vermin. Through the pursuit of vermin, any farmer can easily win enough bounties to more than pay the cost of his annual hunting license (one dollar), and the farmers' boys will find a new interest in life.

In some portions of the Rocky Mountain region, the assaults of the large predatory mammals and birds on the young of the big-game species occasionally demand special treatment. In the Yellowstone Park the pumas multiplied to such an extent and killed so many young elk that their number had to be systematically reduced. To that end "Buffalo" Jones was sent out by the Government to find and destroy the intolerable surplus of pumas. In the course of his campaign he killed about forty, much to the benefit of the elk herds. Around the entrance to the den of a big old male puma, Mr. Jones found the skulls and other remains of nine elk calves that "the old Tom" had killed and carried there.

Pumas and lynxes attack and kill mountain sheep; and the golden eagle is very partial to mountain sheep lambs and mountain goat kids. It will not answer to permit birds of that bold and predatory species to become too numerous in mountains inhabited by goats and sheep; and the fewer the mountain lions the better, for they, like the lynx and eagle, have nothing to live upon save the game.

The wolves and coyotes have learned to seek the ranges of cattle, horses and sheep, where they still do immense damage, chiefly in killing young stock. In spite of the great sums that have been paid out by western states in bounties for the destruction of wolves, in many, many places the gray wolf still persists, and can not be exterminated. To the stockmen of the west the wolf question is a serious matter. The stockmen of Montana say that a government expert once told them how to get rid of the gray wolves. His instructions were: "Locate

THE EASTERN RED SQUIRREL
A Great Destroyer of Birds

the dens, and kill the young in the dens, soon after they are born!" "All very easy to *say*, but a trifle difficult to *do!*" said my informant; and the ranchman seem to think they are yet a long way from a solution of the wolf question.

During the past year the destruction of noxious predatory animals in the national forest reserves has seriously occupied the attention of the United States Bureau of Forestry. By the foresters of that bureau the following animals were destroyed in fifteen western states·

213	Bears	6,487	Coyotes
88	Mountain Lions	870	Wild-Cats
172	Gray Wolves	72	Lynxes
69	Wolf Pups		
		7,971	

In 1910 the total was 9,103.

THE RED SQUIRREL.—Once in a great while, conditions change in subtle ways, wild creatures unexpectedly increase in number, and a community awakens to the fact that some wild species has become a public nuisance. In a small city park, even gray squirrels may breed and become so fearfully numerous that, in their restless quest for food, they may ravage the nests of the wild birds, kill and devour the young, and become a pest. In the Zoological Park, in 1903, we found that the red squirrels had increased to such a horde that they were driving out all our nesting wild birds, driving out the gray squirrels, and making themselves intolerably obnoxious. We shot sixty of them, and brought the total down to a reasonable number. Wherever he is or whatever his numerical strength, the red squirrel is a bad citizen, and, while we do not by any means favor his extermination, he should resolutely be kept within bounds by the rifle.

When a crow nested in our woods, near the Beaver Pond, we were greatly pleased; but with the feeding of the first brood, the crows began to carry off ducklings from the wild-fowl pond. After one crow had been seen to seize and carry away *five* young ducks in one forenoon, we decided that the constitutional limit had been reached, for we did not propose that all our young mallards should be swept into the awful vortex of that crow nest. We took those young crows and reared them by hand; but the old one had acquired a bad habit, and she persisted in carrying off young ducks until we had to end her existence with a gun. It was a painful operation, but there was no other way.

COOPER'S HAWK
A Species to be Destroyed

BIRD-DESTROYING BIRDS.—There are several species of birds that may at once be put under sentence of death for their destructiveness of useful birds, without any extenuating circumstances worth mentioning. Four of these are *Cooper's Hawk*, the *Sharp-Shinned Hawk*, *Pigeon Hawk* and *Duck Hawk*. Fortunately these species are not so numerous that we need lose any sleep over them. Indeed, I think that today it would be a mighty good collector who could find one specimen in seven days' hunting. Like all other species, these, too, are being shot out of of our bird fauna.

Several species of bird-eating birds are trembling in the balance, and under grave suspicion. Some of them are the *Great Horned Owl*, *Barred Owl*, *Screech Owl*, *Butcher Bird* or *Great Northern Shrike*. The only circumstance that saves these birds from instant condemnation is the delightful amount of rats, mice, moles, gophers and noxious insects that they annually consume. In view of the awful destructiveness of the accursed bubonic-plague-carrying rat, we are impelled to think long before placing in our killing list even the great horned owl, who really

SHARP-SHINNED HAWK
A Species to be Destroyed

does levy a heavy tax on our upland game birds. As to the butcher bird, we feel that we ought to kill him, but in view of his record on wild mice and rats, we hesitate, and finally decline.

SNAKES.—Mr. Thomas M. Upp, a close and long observer of wild things wishes it distinctly understood that while the common black-snakes and racers are practically harmless to birds, the *Pilot Black-Snake*,—long, thick and truculent,—is a great scourge to nesting birds. It seems to be deserving of death. Mr. Upp speaks from personal knowledge, and his condemnation of the species referred to is quite sweeping. At the same time Mr. Raymond L. Ditmars points out the fact that this serpent feeds during 6 months of the year on mice, and in doing so renders good service. In the South it is called the "Mouse Snake."

Photo by A. C. Dyke

THE CAT THAT KILLED 58 BIRDS IN ONE YEAR
From Mr. Forbush's Book

CHAPTER IX

THE DESTRUCTION OF WILD LIFE BY DISEASES

Every cause that has the effect of reducing the total of wild-life population is now a matter of importance to mankind. The violent and universal disturbance of the balance of Nature that already has taken place throughout the temperate and frigid zone offers not only food for thought, but it calls for vigorous action.

There are vast sections in the populous centres of western civilization where the destruction of species, even to the point of extermination, is fairly inevitable. It is the way of Christian man to destroy all wild life that comes within the sphere of influence of his iron heel. With the exception of the big game, this destruction is largely a temperamental result, peculiar to the highest civilization. In India where the same fields have been plowed for wheat and dahl and raggi for at least 2,000 years, the Indian antelope, or "black buck," the saras crane and the adjutant stalk through the crops, and the nilgai and gazelle inhabit the eroded ravines in an agricultural land that averages 1,200 people to the square mile!

We have seen that even in farming country, where mud villages are as thick as farm houses in Nebraska, wild animals and even hoofed game can live and hold their own through hundreds of years of close association with man. The explanation is that the Hindus regard wild animals as creatures entitled to life, liberty and the pursuit of happiness, and they are not anxious to shoot every wild animal that shows its head. In the United States, nearly every game-inhabited community is animated by a feeling that every wild animal must necessarily be killed as soon as seen; and this sentiment often leads to disgraceful things. For instance, in some parts of New England a deer straying into a town is at once beset by the hue and cry, and it is chased and assaulted until it is dead, by violent and disgraceful means. New York State, however, seems to have outgrown that spirit. During the past ten years, at least a dozen deer in distress have been rescued from the Hudson River, or in inland towns, or in barnyards in the suburbs of Yonkers and New York, and carefully cared for until "the zoo people" could be communicated with. Last winter about 13 exhausted grebes and one loon were picked up, cared for and finally shipped with tender care to the Zoological Park. One distressed dovekie was picked up, but failed to survive.

The sentiment for the conservation of wild life has changed the mental attitude of very many people. The old Chinese-Malay spirit which cries "Kill! Kill!" and at once runs amuck among suddenly discovered wild animals, is slowly being replaced by a more humane and intelligent sentiment. This is one of the hopeful and encouraging signs of the times.

The destruction of wild animals by natural causes is an interesting subject, even though painful. We need to know how much destruction is wrought by influences wholly beyond the control of man, and a few cases must be cited.

RINDERPEST IN AFRICA.—Probably the greatest slaughter ever wrought upon wild animals by diseases during historic times, was by rinderpest, a cattle plague which afflicted Africa in the last decade of the previous century. Originally, the disease reached Africa by way of Egypt, and came as an importation from Europe. From Egypt it steadily traveled southward, reaching Somaliland in 1889. In 1896 it reached the Zambesi River and entered Rhodesia. From thence it went on southward almost to the Cape. Not only did it sweep away ninety per-cent of the native cattle but it also destroyed more than seventy-five per cent of the buffalos, antelopes and other hoofed game of Rhodesia. It was feared that many species would be completely exterminated, but happily that fear was not realized. The buffalo and antelope herds were fifteen years in breeding up again to a reasonable number, but thanks to the respite from hunters which they enjoyed for several years, finally they did recover. Throughout British East Africa the supply of big game in 1905 was very great, but since that time it has been very greatly diminished by shooting.

CARIBOU DISEASE.—From time to time reports have come from the Province of Quebec, and I think from Maine and New Brunswick also, of many caribou having died of disease. The nature of that disease has remained a mystery, because it seems that no pathologist ever has had an opportunity to investigate it. Fortunately, however, the alleged disease never has been sufficiently wide-spread or continuous to make appreciable inroads on the total number of caribou, and apparently the trouble has been local.

SCAB IN MOUNTAIN SHEEP.—"Scab" is a contagious and persistent skin disease that affects sheep, and is destructive when not controlled. Fifteen years ago it prevailed in some portions of the west. In Colorado it has several times been reported that many bighorn mountain sheep were killed by "scab," which was contracted on wild mountain pastures that had been gone over by domestic sheep carrying that disease. From the reports current at that time, we inferred that about 200 mountain sheep had been affected. It was feared that the disease would spread through the wild flocks and become general, but this did not occur. It seems that the remnant flocks had become so isolated from one another that the isolation of the affected flocks saved the others.

LUMPY-JAW IN ANTELOPE AND SHEEP.—It is a lamentable fact that some, at least, of the United States herds of prong-horned antelope are afflicted with a very deadly chronic infective disease known as actinomycosis, or lumpy-jaw.   It has been brought into the Zoological Park five times, by specimens shipped from Colorado, Texas, Wyoming and Montana.   I think our first cases came to us in 1902.

In its early stage this disease is so subtle and slow that it is months in developing; and this feature renders it all the more deadly, through the spread of infection long before the ailment can be discovered.

One of our antelope arrivals, apparently in perfect health when received, was on general principles kept isolated in rigid quarantine for two months.   At the expiration of that period, no disease of any kind having become manifest, the animal was placed on exhibition, with two others that had been in the Park for more than a year, in perfect health.

In one more week the late arrival developed a swelling on its jaw, drooled at the corner of the mouth, and became feverish,—sure symptoms of the dread disease.   At once it was removed and isolated, but in about 10 days it died.   The other two antelopes were promptly attacked, and eventually died.

The course of the disease is very intense, and thus far it has proven incurable in our wild animals.   We have lost about 10 antelopes from it, and one deer, usually, in each case, within ten days or two weeks from the discovery of the first outward sign,—the well known swelling on the jaw.   One case that was detected immediately upon arrival was very persistently treated by Dr. Blair, and the animal actually survived for four months, but finally it succumbed.   From first to last not a single case was cured.

In 1912, the future of the prong-horned antelope in real captivity seems hopeless.   We have decided not to bring any more specimens to our institution, partly because all available candidates seem reasonably certain to be affected with lumpy-jaw, and partly because we are unwilling to run further risks of having other hoofed animals inoculated by them.   Today we are anxiously wondering whether the jaw disease of the prong-horn is destined to exterminate the species.   Such a catastrophe is much to be feared.   This is probably one of the reasons why the antelope is steadly disappearing, despite protection.

In 1906 we discovered the existence of actinomycosis among the black mountain sheep of northern British Columbia.   Two specimens out of six were badly affected, the bones of the jaws being greatly enlarged, and perforated by deep pits.   The black sheep of the Stickine and Iskoot regions are so seldom seen by white men, save when a sportsman kills his allotment of three specimens, we really do not know anything about the extent to which actinomycosis prevails in those herds, or how deadly are its effects.   One thing seems quite certain, from the appearance of the diseased skulls found by the writer in the taxidermic laboratory of Frederick Sauter, in New York.   The enormous swelling of the diseased jaw bones clearly indicates a disease that in some cases affects its victim throughout many months.   Such a condition as we found in those sheep could not have been reached in a few days after the disease became, apparent. Now, in our antelopes, the collapse and death of the victim usually occured in about 10 days from the time that the first swelling was observed: which means a very virulent disease, and rapid progress at the climax. The jaw of one of our antelopes, which was figured in Dr. Blair's paper in the Eleventh Annual Report of the New York Zoological Society (1906) shows only a very slight lesion, in comparison with those of the mountain sheep.

The conclusion is that among the sheep, this disease does not carry off its victims in any short period like 10 days. The animal must survive for some months after it becomes apparent. At least two parties of American sportsmen have shot rams afflicted with this disease, but I have no reports of any sheep having been found dead from this cause.

This disease is well known among domestic cattle, but so far as we are aware it never before has been found among wild animals. The black sheep herds wherein it was found in British Columbia are absolutely isolated from domestic cattle and all their influences, and therefore it seems quite certain that the disease developed among the sheep spontaneously,—a remarkable episode, to say the least. Whether it will exterminate the black mountain sheep species, and in time spread to the white sheep of the northwest, is of course a matter of conjecture; but there is nothing in the world to prevent a calamity of that kind. The white sheep of Yukon Territory range southward until in the Sheslay Mountains they touch the sphere of influence of the black sheep, where the disease could easily be transmitted. It would be a good thing if there existed between the two species a sheepless zone about 200 miles wide.

I greatly fear that actinomycosis is destined to play an important part in the final extinction that seems to be the impending fate of the beautiful and valuable prong-horned antelope. In view of our hard experiences, extending through ten years (1902-1912), I think this fear is justified. All persons who live in country still inhabited by antelope are urged to watch for this disease. If any antelopes are found dead, see if the lower jaw is badly swollen and discharging pus. If it is, bury the body quickly, burn the ground over, and advise the writer regarding the case.

THE RABBIT PLAGUE.—One of the strangest freaks of Nature of which we know as effecting the wholesale destruction of wild animals by disease is the rabbit plague. In the northern wilderness, and particularly central Canada, where rabbits exist in great numbers and supply the wants of a large carnivorous population, this plague is well known, and among trappers and woodsmen is a common topic of conversation. The best treatment of the subject is to be found in Ernest T. Seton's "Life Histories of Northern Animals", Vol. 1, p. 640 et seq. From this I quote:

"Invariably the year of greatest numbers [of rabbits] is followed by a year of plague, which sweeps them away, leaving few or no rabbits in the land. The denser the rabbit population, the more drastically is it ravaged by the plague. They are wiped out in a single spring by epidemic diseases usually characterized by swellings of the throat, sores under the armpits and groins, and by diarrhea."

"The year 1885 was for the country around Carberry 'a rabbit year.' the greatest ever known in that country. The number of rabbits was incredible. W. R. Hine killed 75 in two hours, and estimated that he could have killed 500 in a day. The farmers were stricken with fear that the rabbit pest of Australia was to be repeated in Manitoba. But the years 1886-7 changed all that. The rabbits died until their bodies dotted the country in thousands. The plague seemed to kill all the members of the vast host of 1885."

The strangest item of Mr. Seton's story is yet to be told. In 1890 Mr. Seton stocked his park at Cos Cob, Conn., with hares and rabbits from several widely separated localities. In 1903, the plague came and swept them all away. Mr. Seton sent specimens to the Zoological Park for examination by the Park veterinary surgeon, Dr. W. Reid Blair. They were found to be infested by great numbers of a dangerous bloodsucking parasite known as *Strongylus strigosus*, which produces death by anemia and emaciation. There were hundreds of those parasites in each animal. I assisted in the examination, and was shown by Dr. Blair, under the microscope, that *Strongylus* puts forth eggs literally by hundreds of thousands!

The life history of that parasite is not well known, but it may easily develop that the cycle of its maximum destructiveness is seven years, and therefore it may be accountable for the seven-year plague among the hares and rabbits of the northern United States and Canada.

Possibly *Strongylus strigosus* is all that stands between Canada and a pest of rabbits like that of Australia. Just why this parasite is inoperative in Australia, or why it has not been introduced there to lessen the rabbit evil, we do not know. Mr. Seton declares that the rabbits of his park were "subject to all the ills of the flesh, except possibly writer's paralysis and housemaid's knee."

PARASITIC INFECTION OF WILD DUCKS.—The diseases of wild game, especially waterfowl, grouse and quail, have caused heavy losses in America as well as in European countries, and scientists have been carefully investigating the cause and the general nature of the maladies, as well as probable methods of prevention and cure. Mr. Geo. Atkinson, a well-known practical naturalist of Portage la Prairie, Manitoba, writes as follows to a local paper on this subject, which I find quoted in the *National Sportsman:*

The question which has developed these important proportions during the past year is that of the extent of the parasitic infection of our wild ducks and other game, and the possibilities of the extended transmission of these parasites to domestic stock, or even humanity, by eating.

The parasites in question are contained in small elliptical cases found underlying the surface muscles of the breast, and in advanced cases extending deeper into the flesh and the muscular tissues of the legs and wings. They are not noticeable in the ordinary process of plucking the bird for the table, and are not found internally, so that the only method of discovering their presence is by slitting the skin of the breast and paring it back a few inches when the worm-like sacs will be seen buried in the flesh.

These parasites have come to my notice periodically during the process of skinning birds for mounting during the past number of years, but it was only when they appeared in unusual numbers last fall that I made inquiries of the biological bureaus of Washington and Ottawa for information of their life history and the possibilities of their transmission to other hosts.

Replies from these sources surprised me with the information that very little was known of the life history of any of the Sarcosporidia, of which group this was a species. Nothing was known of the method of infection or the transference from host to host or species to species, and both departments asked for specimens for examination.

Authorities are a unit in opinion that the question is one of great importance to game conservation, and although opinions of the dangers from eating differ somewhat, a record is given of a hog fed upon affected flesh developing parasites in the muscles in six weeks' time, while a case of a man's death from dropsy was found to be the result of development of these parasites in the valves of the heart.

The ability of these low forms of life to withstand extremes of heat makes it necessary for more than ordinary cooking to be assured of killing them, and since their presence is unnoted in the ordinary course of dressing the birds for the table, there is little doubt that very considerable numbers of these parasites are consumed at our tables every season, with results at present unknown to us.

The species I have found most particularly infected have been mallards, shovellers, teal, gadwall and pintails, and the birds, outwardly in the best condition, have frequently been found loaded with sacs of these parasites and only the turning back of the breast skin can disclose their presence.

The greatest slaughter of wild ducks by disease occured on Great Salt Lake, Utah. Until the "duck disease" (intestinal coccidiosis) broke out there, in the summer of 1910, the annual market slaughter of ducks at the mouth of Bear River had been enormous. When at Salt Lake City in 1888 I made an effort to arouse the sportsmen whom I met to the necessity of a reform, but my exhortations fell on deaf ears. Naturally, the sweeping away of the remaining ducks by disease would suggest a heaven-sent judgment upon the slaughterers were it not for the fact that the last state of the unfortunate ducks is if anything worse than the first.

On Oct. 17, 1911, the annual report of the chief of the Biological Survey contained the following information on this subject:

Epidemic Among Wild Ducks on Great Salt Lake.—Following a long dry season, which favored the rearing of a large number of wild ducks, but materially reduced the area of the feeding ponds, resulting in great overcrowding, a severe epidemic broke out about August 1, 1910, among the wild ducks about Great Salt Lake, Utah. Dead ducks could be counted by thousands along the shores and the disease raged unabated until late fall. Shooting clubs found it necessary to declare a closed season. Some of the dead ducks were forwarded to the Biological Survey and were turned over for examination to the Bureau of Animal Industry, by the experts of which the disease was diagnosed as intestinal coccidiosis.

Various plans of relieving the situation were tried. The irrigation ditches were closed, thus providing the sloughs and ponds with fresh water, and lime was sprinkled on the mud flats and duck trails. Great improvement followed this treatment, and experiments proved that ducks provided with abundant fresh water and clean food began to recover immediately. These methods promised success, but later it was proposed that the marshes be drained and exposed to the sun's rays—a course which cannot be recommended. That coccidia are not always killed by exposure to the sun is shown by their survival on the sites of old chicken yards. An added disadvantage of the plan is that draining and drying the marshes would have a bad effect on the natural duck food, and upon the birds themselves.

CHAPTER X

DESTRUCTION OF WILD LIFE BY THE ELEMENTS

It is a fixed condition of Nature that whenever and wherever a wild species exists in a state of nature, free from the trammels and limitations that contact with man always imposes, the species is fitted to survive all ordinary climatic influences. Freedom of action, and the exercise of several options in the line of individual maintenance under stress, is essential to the welfare of every wild species.

A prong-horned antelope herd that is free can drift before a blizzard, can keep from freezing by the exercise, and eventually come to shelter. Let that same herd drift against a barbed-wire fence five miles long, and its whole scheme of self-preservation is upset. The herd perishes then and there.

Cut out the undergrowth of a given section, drain the swamps and mow down all the weeds and tall grass, and the next particularly hard winter starves and freezes the quail.

Naturally the cutting of forests, clearing of brush and drainage of marshes is more or less calamitous to all the species of birds that inhabit such places and find there winter food and shelter. Red-winged blackbirds and real estate booms can not inhabit the same swamps contemporaneously. Before the relentless march of civilization, the wild Indian, the bison and many of the wild birds must inevitably disappear. We cannot change conditions that are as inexorable as death itself. The wild life must either adjust itself to the conditions that civilized man imposes upon it, or perish. I say "civilized man," for the reason that the primitive races of man are not deadly exterminators of species, as we are. I know of not one species of wild life that has been exterminated by savage man without the aid of his civilized peers.

As civilization marches ever onward, over the prairies, into the bad lands and the forests, over the mountains and even into the farthest corner of Death Valley, the desert of deserts, the struggle of the wild birds, mammals and fishes is daily and hourly intensified. Man must help them to maintain themselves, or accept a lifeless continent. The best help consists in letting the wild creatures throughly alone, so that they can help themselves; but quail often need to be fed in critical periods. The best food is wheat screenings placed under little tents of straw, bringing food and shelter together.

In the well settled portions of the United States, such species as quail, ruffed grouse, wild turkey, pinnated grouse and sage grouse hang to life by slender threads. A winter of exceptionally deep snows, much sleet, and a late spring always causes grave anxiety among the state game wardens. In Pennsylvania a very earnest movement is in progress to educate and persuade farmers to feed the quail in winter, and much good is being done in that direction.

Mr. Erasmus Wilson, of the *Pittsburgh Gazette-Times* is the apostle of that movement.

Quail should be fed every winter, in every northern state. The methods to be pursued will be mentioned elsewhere.

By way of illustration, here is a sample game report, from Las Animas, Colorado, Feb. 22, 1912:

"After the most severe winter weather experienced for twenty years we are able to compute approximately our loss of feathered life. It is seventy-five per cent of the quail throughout the irrigated district, and about twenty per cent of meadow-larks. In the rough cedar-covered sections south of the Arkansas River, the loss among the quail was much lighter. The ground sparrows suffered severely, while the English sparrow seems to have come through in good shape. Many cotton-tail rabbits starved to death, while the deep, light snow of January made them easy prey for hawks and coyotes." (F. T. Webber).

It would be possible to record many instances similar to the above, but why multiply them? And now behold the cruel corollary

At least twenty-five times during the past two years I have heard and read arguments by sportsmen against my proposal for a 5-year close season for quail, taking the ground that "The sportsmen are not wholly to blame for the scarcity of quail. It is the cold winters that kill them off!"

So then, *because the fierce winters murder the bob white, wholesale, they should not have a chance to recover themselves!* Could human beings possibly assume a more absurd attitude?

Yes, it is coldly and incontestably true, that even after such winter slaughter as Mr. Webber has reported above, the very next season will find the quail hunter joyously taking the field, his face beaming with health and good living, to hunt down and shoot to death as many as possible of the pitiful 25 per cent remnant that managed to survive the pitiless winter. How many quail hunters, think you, ever stayed their hands because of "a hard winter on the quail?" I warrant not one out of every hundred! How many states in this Union ever put on a close season because of a hard winter? I'll warrant that not one ever did; and I think there is only one state whose game commissioners have the power to act in that way without recourse to the legislature. This situation is intolerable.

Thanks to the splendid codified game laws enacted in New York state in 1912, our Conservation Commission can declare a close season in any locality, for any length of time, when the state of the game demands an emergency measure. This act is as follows; and it is a model law, which every other state should speedily enact:

THE NEW YORK CLOSE-SEASON LAW.

152. Petition for additional protection; notice of hearings; power to grant additional protection; notice of prohibition or regulation; penalties.

1. Petition for additional protection. Any citizen of the state may file with the commission a petition in writing requesting it to give any species of fish, other than migratory food fish of the sea, or game protected by law, additional or other protection than that afforded by the provisions of this article. Such petition shall state the grounds upon which such protection is considered necessary, and shall be signed by the petitioner with his address.

2. Notice of hearings. The commission shall hold a public hearing in the locality or county to be affected upon the allegations of such petition within twenty days from the filing thereof. At least ten days prior to such hearing notice thereof, stating the time and place at which such hearing shall be held, shall be advertised in a newspaper published in the county to be affected by such additional or other protection. Such notice shall state the name and the address of the petitioner, together with a brief statement of the grounds upon which such application is made, and a copy thereof shall be mailed to the petitioner at the address given in such petition at least ten days before such hearing.

3. Power to grant additional protection. If upon such hearing the commission shall determine that such species of fish or game, by reason of disease, danger of extermination, or from any other cause or reason, requires such additional or other protection, in any locality or throughout the state, the commission shall have power to prohibit or regulate, during the open season therefor, the taking of such species of fish or game. Such prohibition or regulation may be made general throughout the state or confined to a particular part or district thereof.

4. Notice of prohibition or regulation. Any order made by the commission under the provisions of this section shall be signed by it, and entered in its minute book. At least thirty days before such prohibition or regulation shall take effect, copies of the same shall be filed in the office of the clerk issuing hunting and trapping licenses for the district to which the prohibition or regulation applies. It shall be the duty of said clerks to issue a copy of said prohibition or regulation to each person to whom a hunting or trapping license is issued by them; to mail a copy of such prohibition or regulation to each holder of a hunting and trapping license theretofore issued by them and at that time in effect, and to post a copy thereof in a conspicuous place in their office. At least thirty days before such prohibition or regulation shall take effect the commission shall cause a notice thereof to be advertised in a newspaper published in the county wherein such prohibition or regulation shall take effect.

5. Penalties. Any person violating the provisions of such prohibition, rule or regulation shall be guilty of a misdemeanor and shall, upon conviction, be subject to a fine of not to exceed one hundred dollars, or shall be imprisoned for not more than thirty days, or both, for each offense, in addition to the penalties hereinafter provided for taking fish, birds or quadrupeds in the close season.

I want all sensible, honest sportsmen to stop citing the killing of game birds by severe winters *as a reason* why long close seasons are not necessary, and why automatic guns "don't matter." And I want sportsmen to consider their duty, and not go out hunting any game species that has been slaughtered by a hard winter, until it has had at least five years in which to recover. Any other course is cruel, selfish, and shortsighted; and a word to the humane should be sufficient.

The worst exhibitions ever made of the wolfish instinct to slay that springs eternal in some human (!) breasts are those brought about through the distress or errors of wild animals. By way of illustration, consider the slaughter of half-starved elk that took place in the edge of Idaho in the winter of 1909 and 1910, when about seven hundred elk that were driven out of the Yellowstone Park at its northwestern corner by the deep snow, fled into Idaho in the hope of finding food. The inhabitants met the starving herds with repeating rifles, and as the unfortunate animals struggled westward through the snow and storm, they were slaughtered without mercy. Bulls and cows, old and young, all of the seven hundred, went down; and Stoney Indians could not have acted any worse than did those "settlers."

On another occasion, it is recorded that the prong-horned antelope herd of the Mammoth Hot Springs wandered across the line into Gardiner, and quickly met a savage attack of gunners with rifles. A number of those rare and valuable animals were killed, and others fled back into the Park with broken legs dangling in the air.

In the interest of public decency, and for the protection of the reputation of American citizenship, one of two things should be done. The northern boundary of the Park should be extended northward beyond Gardiner, or else the deathtrap should be moved elsewhere. The case of the town of Gardiner is referred to the legislature of Montana for treatment.

Beyond question, the highest sentiments of humanity are those that are stirred by the misfortunes of killable game. During the past thirty years, I have noticed some interesting manifestations of the increased sympathy for wild creatures that steadily is growing in a large section of the public mind. Thirty years ago, the appearance of a deer or moose in the streets of any eastern village nearly always was in itself a signal for a grand chase of the unfortunate creature, and its speedy slaughter. Today, in the eastern states, the general feeling is quite different. The appearance of a deer in the Hudson River itself, or a moose in a Maine village is a signal, not for a wild chase and cruel slaughter, but for a general effort to save the animal from being hurt, or killed. I know this through ocular proof, at least half a dozen lost and bewildered deer having been carefully driven into yards, or barns, and humanely kept and cared for until they could be shipped to us. Several have been caught while swimming in the Hudson, bewildered and panic-stricken. The latest capture occurred in New York City itself.

A puma that escaped (about 1902) from the Zoological Park, instead of being shot was captured by sensible people in the hamlet of Bronxdale, alive and unhurt, and safely returned to us.

In some portions of the east, though not all, the day of the hue and cry over "a wild animal in town" seems to be about over. On Long Island some humane persons found an injured turkey vulture, and took it in and cared for it,—only to be persecuted by ill-advised game wardens, because they had a forbidden wild bird "in their possession!" There are times when it is the highest (moral) duty of a game warden to follow the advice of Private Mulvaney to the "orficer boy," and "Shut yer oye to the rigulations, sorr!"

Such occurrences as these are becoming more and more common. *The desire of "the great silent majority" is to SAVE the wild creatures;*

and it is in response to that sentiment that thousands of people are to-day in the field against the Army of Destruction.

It is the duty of every sportsman to assist in promoting the passage of a law like our New York law which empowers the State Game Commission to throw extra protection around any species that has been slaughtered too much by snow or by firearms, by closing the open season as long as may be necessary. Can there be in all America even one thinking, reasoning being who can not see the justice and also the imperative necessity of this measure? It seems impossible.

Give the game the benefit of every doubt! If it becomes too thick, your gun can quickly thin it out; but if it is once exterminated, it will be impossible to bring it back. Be wise; and take thought for the morrow. Remember the heath hen.

SLAUGHTER OF BLUEBIRDS.—In the late winter and early spring of 1896 the wave of bluebirds was caught on its northward migration by a period of unseasonably cold and fearfully tempestuous weather, involving much icy-cold rain and sleet. Now, there is no other climatic condition that is so hard for a wild bird or mammal to withstand as rain at the freezing point, and a mantle of ice or frozen snow over all supplies of food.

The bluebirds perished by thousands. The loss occured practically all along their east-and-west line of migration, from Arkansas to the Atlantic Coast. In places the species seemed almost exterminated; and it was several years ere it recovered to a point even faintly approximating its original population. I am quite certain that the species never has recovered more than 50 per cent of the number that existed previous to the calamity.

DUCK CHOLERA IN THE BRONX RIVER.—In 1911, some unknown but new and particularly deadly element, probably introduced in sewage, contaminated the waters of Bronx River where it flows through New York City, with results very fatal in the Zoological Park. The large flock of mallard ducks, Canada geese, and snow geese on Lake Agassiz was completely wiped out. In all about 125 waterfowl died in rapid sucession, from causes commonly classed under the popular name of "duck cholera." The disease was carried to other bodies of water in the Park that were fed from other sources, but made no headway elsewhere than on lakes fed by the polluted Bronx River.

Fortunately the work of the Bronx River Parkway Commission soon will terminate the present very unsanitary condition of that stream.

WILD DUCKS IN DISTRESS.—In the winter of 1911-12, many flocks of wild ducks decided to winter in the North. Many persons believe that this was largely due to the prevention of late winter and spring shooting; which seems reasonable. Unfortunately the winter referred to proved exceptionally severe and formed vast sheets of thick ice over the feeding-grounds where the ducks had expected to obtain their food. On Cayuga, Seneca and other lakes in central New York, and on the island of Martha's Vineyard, the flocks of ducks suffered very severely, and many perished of hunger and cold. *But for the laws prohibiting late winter shooting undoubtedly all of them would have been shot and eaten, regardless of their distress.*

Game wardens and humane citizens made numerous efforts to feed the starving flocks and many ducks were saved in that way. An illustrated article on the distressed ducks of Keuka Lake, by C. William Beebe and Verdi Burtch, appeared in the *Zoological Society Bulletin* for May, 1912. Fortunately there is every reason to believe that such occurrences will be rare.

WILD SWANS SWEPT OVER NIAGARA FALLS.—During the past ten years, several winter tragedies to birds have occurred on a large scale at Niagara Falls. Whole flocks of whistling swans of from 20 up to 70 individuals alighting in the Niagara River above the rapids have permitted themselves to float down into the rapids, and be swept over the Falls, en masse. On each occasion, the great majority of the birds were drowned, or killed on the rocks. Of the very few that survived, few if any were able to rise and fly out of the gorge below the Falls to safety. It is my impression that about 200 swans recently have perished in this strange way.

CHAPTER XI

SLAUGHTER OF SONG-BIRDS BY ITALIANS

In these days of wild-life slaughter, we hear much of death and destruction. Before our eyes there continually arise photographs of hanging masses of waterfowl, grouse, pheasants, deer and fish, usually supported in true heraldic fashion by the men who slew them and the implements of slaughter. The world has become somewhat hardened to these things, because the victims are classed as game; and in the destruction of game, one game-bag more or less "Will not count in the news of the battle."

The slaughter of song, insectivorous and all other birds by Italians and other aliens from southern Europe has become a scourge to the bird life of this country. The devilish work of the negroes and poor whites of the South will be considered in the next chapter. In Italy, linnets and sparrows are "game"; and so is everything else that wears feathers! Italy is a continuous slaughtering-ground for the migratory birds of Europe, and as such it is an international nuisance and a pest. The way passerine birds are killed and eaten in that country is a disgrace to the government of Italy, and a standing reproach to the throne. Even kings and parliaments have no right in moral or international law to permit year after year the wholesale slaughter of birds of passage of species that no civilized man has a right to kill.

There are some tales of slaughter from which every properly-balanced Christian mind is bound to recoil with horror. One such tale has recently been given to us in the pages of the *Avicultural Magazine*, of London, for January, 1912, by Mr. Hubert D. Astley, F. Z. S., whose word no man will dispute. In condensing it, let us call it

THE ITALIAN SLAUGHTER OF THE INNOCENTS

This story does not concern game birds of any kind. Quite the contrary. That it should be published in America, a land now rapidly filling up with Italians, is a painful necessity in order that the people of America may be enabled accurately to measure the fatherland traditions and the fixed mental attitude of Italians generally toward our song birds. I shall now hold a mirror up to Italian nature. If the image is either hideous or grotesque, the fault will not be mine. I specially commend the picture to the notice of American game wardens and judges on the bench.

The American reader must be reminded that the Italian peninsula reaches out a long arm of land into the Mediterranean Sea for several

A ROCCOLO.
LAKE COMO

AN ITALIAN ROCCOLO, ON LAKE COMO

A Death-Trap for Song-Birds. From the Avicultural Magazine

hundred miles toward the sunny Barbary coast of North Africa. This great southward highway has been chosen by the birds of central Europe as their favorite migration route. Especially is this true of the small song-birds with weak wings and a minimum of power for long-sustained flight. Naturally, they follow the peninsula down to the Italian Land's End before they launch forth to dare the passage of the Mediterranean.

Italy is the narrow end of a great continental funnel, into the wide northern end of which Germany, Austria, France and Switzerland annually pour their volume of migratory bird life. And what is the result? For answer let us take the testimony of two reliable witnesses, and file it for use on the day when Tony Macchewin, gun in hand and pockets bulging with cartridges, goes afield in our country and opens fire on our birds.

The linnet is one of the sweet singers of Europe. It is a small, delicately formed, weak-winged little bird, about the size of our phoebe-bird. It weighs only a trifle more than a girl's love-letter. Where it breeds and rears its young, in Germany for example, a true sportsman would no more think of shooting a linnet than he would of killing and eating his daughter's dearest canary.

To the migrating bird, the approach to northern Italy, either going or returning, is not through a land of plenty. The sheltering forests have mostly been swept away, and safe shelters for small birds are very rare. In the open, there are owls and hawks; and the only refuge from either is the thick-leafed grove, into which linnets and pipits can dive at the approach of danger and quickly hide.

A linnet from the North after days of dangerous travel finally reached Lake Como, southward bound. The country was much too open for safety, and its first impulse was to look about for safe shelter. The low bushes that sparsely covered the steep hillsides were too thin for refuge in times of sudden danger.

Ah! Upon a hilltop is a little grove of trees, green and inviting. In the grove a bird is calling, calling, insistently. The trees are very small; but they seem to stand thickly together, and their foliage should afford a haven from both hawk and gunner. To it joyously flits the tired linnet. As it perches aloft upon a convenient whip-like wand, it notices for the first time a queer, square brick tower of small dimensions, rising in the center of a court-yard surrounded by trees. The tower is like an old and dingy turret that has been shorn from a castle, and set on the hilltop without apparent reason. It is two stories in height, with one window, dingy and uninviting. A door opens into its base.

Several birds that seem very near, but are invisible, frequently call and chirp, as if seeking answering calls and companionship. Surely the grove must be a safe place for birds, or they would not be here.

Hark! A whirring, whistling sound fills the air, like the air tone of a flying hawk's wings. A hawk! A hawk!

Down plunges the scared linnet, blindly, frantically, into the space sheltered by the grove!

Horrors! What is this?

Threads! Invisible, interlacing threads; tangled and full of pockets, treacherously spanning the open space. It is a fowler's net! The linnet is entangled. It flutters frantically but helplessly, and hangs there, caught. Its alarm cry is frantically answered by the two strange, invisible bird voices that come from the top of the tower!

The grove and the tower are A ROCCOLO! A huge, permanent, merciless, deadly *trap*, for the wholesale capture of songbirds! The tower is the hiding place of the fowler, and the calling birds are decoy birds whose eyes have been totally blinded by red-hot wires in order that they will call more frantically than birds with eyes would do. The whistling wings that seemed a hawk were a sham, made by a racquet thrown through the air by the fowler, through a slot in his tower. He keeps by him many such racquets.

The door of the tower opens, and out comes the fowler. He is low-browed, swarthy, ill kept, and wears rings in his ears. A soiled hand seizes the struggling linnet, and drags it violently from the threads that entangled it. A sharp-pointed twig is thrust straight through the head of the helpless victim *at the eyes*, and after one wild, fluttering agony—it is dead.

The fowler sighs contentedly, re-enters his dirty and foul-smelling tower, tosses the feathered atom upon the pile of dead birds that lies upon the dirty floor in a dirty corner,—and is ready for the next one.

Ask him, as did Mr. Astley, and he will tell you frankly that there are about 150 dead birds in the pile,—starlings, sparrows, linnets, greenfinches, chaffinches, goldfinches, hawfinches, redstarts, blackcaps, robins, song thrushes, blackbirds, blue and coal tits, fieldfares and redwings. He will tell you also, that there are *seven other roccolos within sight and twelve within easy walking distance*. He will tell you, as he did Mr. Astley, that during that week he had taken about 500 birds, and that that number was a fair average for each of the 12 other roccolos.

This means the destruction of about 5,000 songbirds per week *in that neighborhood alone!* Another keeper of a roccolo told Mr. Astley that during the previous autumn he took about 10,000 birds at his small and comparatively insignificant roccolo.

And above that awful roccolo of slaughtered innocents rose a *wooden cross*, in memory of Christ, the Merciful, the Compassionate!

Around the interior of the entwined sapling tops that formed the fatal bower of death there hung a semicircle of tiny cages containing live decoys,—chaffinches, hawfinches, titmice and several other species. "The older and staider ones call repeatedly," says Mr. Astley, "and the chaffinches break into song. It is the only song to be heard in Italy at the time of the autum migration."

And the King of Italy, the Queen of Italy, the Parliament of Italy and His Holiness the Pope permit these things, year in and year out. It is now said, however, that through the efforts of a recently organized bird-lovers' society in Italy, the blinding of decoy birds for roccolos is to be stopped.

In Germany, Austria, and Switzerland, the protection of these birds during their breeding season must be very effective, for otherwise the supply for the Italian slaughter of the Innocents would long ago have fallen to nothing.

The Germans love birds, and all wild life. I wonder how they like the Italian roccolo. I wonder how France regards it; and whether the nations of Europe north of Italy will endure this situation forever.

To the American and English reader, comment on the practices recorded above is quite unnecessary, except the observation that they betoken a callousness of feeling and a depth of cruelty and destructiveness to which, so far as known, no savages ever yet have sunk. As an exhibit of the groveling pusillanimity of the human soul, the roccolo of northern Italy reveals minus qualities which can not be expressed either in words or in figures.

And what is the final exhibit of the gallant knight of the roccolo, the feudal lord of the modern castle and its retainers?

The answer is given by Dr. Louis B. Bishop, in an article on "Birds in the Markets of Southern Europe."

In Venice, which was visited in October and November, during the fall migration, he found on sale in the markets, as food, thousands of songbirds.

"Birds were there in profusion, from ducks to kites, in the early morning, hung in great bunches above the stalls, but by 9 A. M. most of them had been sold. Ducks and shorebirds occurred in some numbers, but the vast majority were small sparrows, larks and thrushes. These were there during my visit by the thousands, if not ten thousands. To the market they were brought in large sacks, strung in fours on twigs which had been passed through the eyes and then tied. Most of these small birds had been trapped, and on skinning them I often could find no injury except at their eyes.* One of these sacks which I examined on November 3, contained hundreds of birds, largely siskins, skylarks and bramblings. As a rule the small birds that were not sold in the early morning were skinned or picked, and their tiny bodies packed in regular order, breasts up, in shallow tin boxes, and exposed for sale."

"During these visits to the Venetian markets, I identified 60 species, and procured specimens of most. As nearly as I can remember, small birds cost from two to five cents apiece. For example I paid $2.15 on Nov. 8, for

1 Woodcock,	1 Skylark,
1 Jay,	1 Greenfinch,
2 Starlings,	1 Bullfinch,
2 Spotted Crakes,	1 Redpoll,
1 Song Thrush,	3 Linnets,
1 Gold-Crest,	2 Goldfinches

It is probable that these birds were killed by piercing the head through the eyes.

1 Long-Tailed Titmouse,
1 Great Titmouse,
1 Pipit,
1 Redstart,

6 Siskins,
3 Reed Buntings,
3 Bramblings,
and 5 Chaffinches.

'On November 10, I paid $3.25 for

2 Coots,
1 Water Rail,
1 Spotted Crake,
1 Sparrow Hawk,
2 Woodcock,
1 Common Redshank,
1 Dusky Redshank,

1 European Curlew,
2 Kingfishers,
2 Greenfinches,
2 Wrens,
1 Great Titmouse,
1 Blue Titmouse,
1 Redbreast, and

2 Dunlins."

Of course there were various species of upland game birds, shore-birds and waterfowl,—everything, in fact, that could be found and killed. In addition to the passerine birds listed above, Dr. Bishop noted the following, all in Venice alone:

Skylark ("in great numbers"),
Crested Lark,
Calandra,
Tree Sparrow,
Hawfinch,
Yellow-Hammer,
Blackbird,
Fieldfare,
Song Thrush,

Crossbill,
House Sparrow,
Stonechat,
Coal,
Goldcrest,
Rock Pipit,
White Wagtail,
Redwing.

"In Florence," says Dr. Bishop, "I visited the central market on November 26, 28, 29, 30, December 1, 2, 3, 5, 6, 7, 8 and 9, and found birds even more plentiful than in Venice." Besides a variety of game birds, he found quantities of the species mentioned above, seen in Venice, and also the following:

Green Sandpiper,
Dotterel,
Magpie,
Corn Bunting,
Migratory Quail,
Green Woodpecker,
Spotted Woodpecker,
Wood Lark,

Brown Creeper,
Nuthatch,
Black-Cap Warbler,
Black-Headed Warbler,
Fantail Warbler,
Missel Thrush,
Ring Ouzel,
Rock Sparrow, and

Gray Wagtail.

"Here, too [at Florence] we saw often, bunches and baskets of small birds, chiefly redbreasts, hawked through the streets. . . . Every Sunday that we went into the country we met numbers of Italians out shooting, and their bags seemed to consist wholly of small birds.

"At Genoa, San Remo, Monte Carlo and Nice, between December 13 and 29, I did not visit the central markets, if such exist, but saw frequently bunches of small birds hanging outside stores. . . . A gentleman who spent the fall on an automobile trip through the west of FRANCE *from Brittany to the Pyrenees, tells me he noticed these bunches of small birds on sale in every town he visited.*

"That killing song-birds for food," continues Dr. Bishop, "is not confined to the poor Italians I learned on October 27, when one of the most prominent and wealthy Italian *ornithologists*—a delightful man— told me he had shot 180 skylarks and pipits the day before, and that his family liked them far better than other game. Our prejudice against selling game does not exist in Europe, and this same ornithologist told me he often shot 200 ducks in a day at his shooting-box, sending to the market what he could not use himself. On November 1, 1910, he shot 82 ducks, and on November 8, 103, chiefly widgeon and teal."

An "ornithologist" indeed! A "sportsman" also, is he not? He belongs with his brother "ornithologists" of the roccolos, who net their "game" with the aid of *blind* birds! Brave men, gallant "sportsmen," are these men of Italy,—and western France also if the tale is true!

If the people of Europe can stand the wholesale, systematic slaughter of their song and insectivorous birds, *we can!* If they are too mean-spirited to rise up, make a row about it, and stop it, then let them pay the price; but, by the Eternal, Antonio shall not come to this country with the song-bird tastes of the roccolo and indulge them here!

The above facts have been cited, not at all for the benefit of Europe, but for our own good. The American People are now confronted by the Italian and Austrian and Hungarian laborer and saloon-keeper and mechanic, and all Americans should have an exact measure of the sentiments of southern Europe toward our wild life generally, especially the birds that we do not shoot at all, *and therefore are easy to kill.*

When a warden or a citizen arrests an alien for killing any of our non-game birds, show the judge these records of how they do things in Italy, and ask for the extreme penalty.

I have taken pains to publish the above facts from eye-witnesses in order that every game commissioner, game warden and state legis-lator who reads these pages may know exactly what he is "up against" in the alien population of our country from southern Europe. For un-numbered generations, the people of Italy have been taught to believe that it is *perfectly right* to shoot and devour every song-bird that flies. The Venetian is no respector of species; and when an Italian "ornithol-ogist" (!) can go out and murder 180 linnets and pipits in one day for the pot, it is time for Americans to think hard.

We sincerely hope that it will not require blows and kicks and fines to remove from Antonio's head the idea that America is not Italy, and that the slaughter of song birds "don't go" in this country. I strongly rec-ommend to every state the enactment of a law that will do these things:

1.—Prohibit the owning, carrying or use of firearms by aliens, and

2.—Prohibit the use of firearms in hunting by any naturalized alien from southern Europe until after a 10-years' residence in America.

From reports that have come to me at first hand regarding Italians in the East, Hungarians in Pennsylvania and Austrians in Minnesota, it seems absolutely certain that all members of the lower classes of southern Europe are a dangerous menace to our wild life.

On account of the now-accursed land-of-liberty idea, every foreigner who sails past the statue on Bedloe's Island and lands on our liberty-ridden shore, is firmly convinced that *now, at last*, he can do as he pleases! And as one of his first ways in which to show his newly-acquired personal liberty and independence in the Land of Easy Marks, he buys a gun and goes out to shoot "free game!"

If we, as a people, are so indolent and so somnolent that Antonio gets away with all our wild birds, then do we deserve to be robbed.

Italians are pouring into America in a steady stream. They are strong, prolific, persistent and of tireless energy. New York City now contains 340,000 of them. They work while the native Americans sleep. Wherever they settle, their tendency is to root out the native American and take his place and his income. Toward wild life the Italian laborer is a human mongoose. Give him power to act, and he will quickly exterminate every wild thing that wears feathers or hair. To our song-birds he is literally a "pestilence that walketh at noonday".

As we have shown, the Italian is a born pot-hunter, and he has grown up in the fixed belief that killing song-birds for food is right! To him all is game that goes into the bag. The moment he sets foot in the open, he provides himself with a shot-gun, and he looks about for things to kill. It is "a free country;" therefore, he may kill anything he can find, cook it and eat it. If anybody attempts to check him,—sapristi! beware his gun! He cheerfully invades your fields, and even your lawn; and he shoots robins, bluebirds, thrushes, catbirds, grosbeaks, tanagers, orioles, woodpeckers, quail, snipe, ducks, crows, and herons.

Down in Virginia, near Charlottesville, an Italian who was working on a new railroad once killed a turkey buzzard; and he selfishly cooked it and ate it, all alone. A pot-hunting compatriot of his heard of it, and reproached him for having dined on game in camera. In the quarrel that ensued, one of the "sportsmen" stabbed the other to death.

When the New York Zoological Society began work on its Park in 1899, the northern half of the Borough of the Bronx was a regular daily hunting-ground for the slaughter of song-birds, and all other birds that could be found. Every Sunday it was "bangetty!" "bang!" from Pelham Bay to Van Cortlandt. The police force paid not the slightest attention to these open, flagrant, shameless violations of the city ordinances and the state bird laws. In those days I never but once heard of a policeman *on his own initiative* arresting a birdshooter, even on Sunday; but whenever meddlesome special wardens from the Zoological Park have pointedly called upon the local police force for help, it has always been given with cheerful alacrity. In the fall of 1912 an appeal to the Police Commissioner resulted in a general order to stop all hunting and shooting in the Borough of the Bronx, and a reform is now on.

The war on the bird-killers in New York City began in 1900. It seemed that if the Zoological Society did not take up the matter, the slaughter would . continue indefinitely. The white man's burden was taken up; and the story of the war is rather illuminating. Mr. G. O.

Shields, President of the League of American Sportsmen, quickly became interested in the matter, and entered actively into the campaign. For months unnumbered, he spent every Sunday patroling the woods and thickets of northern New York and Westchester county, usually aecompanied by John J. Rose and Rudolph Bell of the Zoological Park force, for whom appointments as deputy game wardens had been secured from the State.

The adventures of that redoubtable trio of man-hunters would make an interesting chapter. They were shot at by poachers, but more frequently they shot at the other fellows. Just why it was that no one was killed, no one seems to know. Many Italians and several Americans were arrested while hunting, haled to court, prosecuted and fined. Finally, a reign of terror set in; and that was the beginning of the end. It became known that those three men could not be stopped by threats, and that they always got their man—unless he got into a human rabbit-warren of the Italian boarding-house species. That was the only escape that was possible.

The largest haul of dead birds was 43 robins, orioles, thrushes and woodpeckers, captured along with the five Italians who committed the indiscretion of sitting down in the woods to divide their dead birds. We saved all the birds in alcohol, and showed them in court. The judge fined two of the Italians $50 each, and the other three were sent to the penitentiary for two months each.

Even yet, however, at long intervals an occasional son of sunny Italy tries his luck at Sunday bird shooting; but if anyone yells at him to "Halt!" he throws away his gun and stampedes through the brush like a frightened deer. The birds of upper New York are now fairly secure; but it has taken ten years of fighting to bring it about.

Throughout New York State, Pennsylvania, New Jersey, Connecticut, Massachusetts, and even Minnesota, wherever there are large settlements of Italians and Hungarians, the reports are the same. They swarm through the country every Sunday, and shoot every wild thing they see. Wherever there are large construction works,—railroads, canals or aqueducts,—look for bird slaughter, and you are sure to find it. The exception to this rule, so far as I know, is along the line of the new Catskill aqueduct, coming to New York City. The contractors have elected not to permit bird slaughter, and the rule has been made that any man who goes out hunting will instantly be discharged. That is the best rule that ever was made for the protection of birds and game against gang-working aliens.

Let every state and province in America look out sharply for the bird-killing foreigner; for sooner or later, he will surely attack your wild life. The Italians are spreading, spreading, spreading. If you are without them to-day, to-morrow they will be around you. Meet them at the threshold with drastic laws, throughly enforced; for no half way measures will answer.

Pennsylvania has had the worst experience of alien slaughterers of any state,—thus far. *Six* of her game wardens have been *killed*, and eight or ten have been wounded, by shooting! Finally her legislature arose in wrath, and passed a law prohibiting the ownership or possession of guns of any kind by aliens. The law gives the right of domiciliary search, and it surely is enforced. Of course the foreign population "kicked" against the law, but the People's steam roller went over them just the same. In New York, we require from an alien a license costing $20, and it has saved a million (perhaps) of our birds; but the Pennsylvania law is the best. It may be taken as a model for every state and province in America. Its text is as follows:

Section 1. Be it enacted, &c., That from and after the passage of this act, it shall be unlawful for any unnaturalized foreign-born resident to hunt for or capture or kill, in this Commonwealth, any wild bird or animal, either game or otherwise, of any description, excepting in defense of person or property; and to that end it shall be unlawful for any unnaturalized foreign-born resident, within this Commonwealth, to either own or be possessed of a shotgun or rifle of any make. Each and every person violating any provision of this section shall, upon conviction thereof, be sentenced to pay a penalty of twenty-five dollars for each offense, or undergo imprisonment in the common jail of the county for the period of one day for each dollar of penalty imposed. Provided, That in addition to the before-named penalty, all guns of the before-mentioned kinds found in possession or under control of an unnaturalized foreign-born resident shall, upon conviction of such person, or upon his signing a declaration of guilt as prescribed by this act, be declared forfeited to the Commonwealth of Pennsylvania, and shall be sold by the Board of Game Commissioners as hereinafter directed.

Section 2. For the purpose of this act, any unnaturalized foreign-born person who shall reside or live within the boundaries of the Commonwealth of Pennsylvania for ten consecutive days shall be considered a resident and shall be liable to the penalties imposed for violation of the provisions of this act.

Section 3. That the possession of a shotgun or rifle at any place outside of a building, within this Commonwealth, by an unnaturalized foreign-born resident, shall be conclusive proof of a violation of the provisions of section one of this act, and shall render any person convicted thereof liable to the penalty as fixed by said section.

Section 4. That the presence of a shotgun or rifle in a room or house, or building or tent, or camp of any description, within this Commonwealth, occupied by or controlled by an unnaturalized foreign-born resident shall be prima facie evidence that such gun is owned or controlled by the person occupying or controlling the property in which such gun is found, and shall render such person liable to the penalty imposed by section one of this act.

Other sections provide for the full enforcement of this law.

It is now high time, and an imperative public necessity, that every state should act in this matter, before its bird life is suddenly attacked, and serious inroads made upon it. Do it NOW! The enemy is headed your way. Don't wait for him to strike the first blow!

Duty of the Italian Press and Clergy.—Now what is the best remedy for the troubles that will arise for Italians in America because of wrong principles established in Italy? It is not in the law, the police, the court and the punishment. It is in *educating the Italian into a knowledge of the duties of the good citizen!* The Italian press and clergy can do this; and *no one else can do it so easily, so quickly and so well!*

Those two powerful forces should enter seriously upon this task. In every other respect, the naturalized Italian tries to become a good citizen, and adjust himself to the laws and the customs of his new country. Why should he not do this in regard to bird life? It is not too much to ask, nor is it too much to *exact*. Does the Italian workman, or store-keeper who makes his living by honest toil *enjoy* breaking our bird laws, *enjoy* irritating and injuring those with whom he has come to live? Does he *enjoy* being watched, and searched, and chased, and arrested, —all for a few small birds that he *does not need* for food? He earns good. wages: he has plenty of good food; and he must be *educated* into protecting our birds instead of destroying them. The Italian newspapers and clergy have a serious duty to perform in this matter, and we hope they will diligently discharge it.

DEAD SONG-BIRDS

These jars contain the dead bodies of 43 valuable insectivorous birds that were taken from two Italians in October, 1905, in the suburbs of New York City, by game wardens of the New York Zoological Society.

CHAPTER XII

DESTRUCTION OF SONG BIRDS BY SOUTHERN NEGROES AND POOR WHITES

Before going farther, there is one point that I wish to make quite clear.

Whenever the people of a particular race make a specialty of some particular type of wrong-doing, anyone who pointedly rebukes the faulty members of that race is immediately accused of "race prejudice." On account of the facts I am now setting forth about the doings of Italian and negro bird-killers, I expect to be accused along that line. If I am, I shall strenuously deny the charge. The facts speak for themselves. Zoologically, however, I am strongly prejudiced against the people of any race, creed, club, state or nation who make a specialty of any particularly offensive type of bird or wild animal slaughter; and I do not care who knows it.

The time was, and I remember it very well, when even the poorest gunner scorned to kill birds that were not considered "game." In days lang syne, many a zoological collector has been jeered because the specimens he had killed for preservation were not "game."

But times have changed. In the wearing of furs, we have bumped down steps both high and steep. In 1880 American women wore sealskin, marten, otter, beaver and mink. To-day nothing that wears hair is too humble to be skinned and worn. To-day "they are wearing" skins of muskrats, foxes, rabbits, skunks, domestic cats, squirrels, and even rats. And see how the taste for game,—of some sections of our population,—also has gone down.

In the North, the Italians are fighting for the privilege of eating everything that wears feathers; but we allow no birds to be shot for food save game birds and cranes. In the South, the negroes and poor whites are killing song-birds, woodpeckers and doves for food; and in several states some of it is done under the authority of the laws. Look at these awful lists

IN THESE STATES, ROBINS ARE LEGALLY SHOT AND EATEN:

| Louisiana | North Carolina | Tennessee | Texas |
| Mississippi | South Carolina | Maryland | Florida |

IN THESE STATES, BLACKBIRDS ARE LEGALLY SHOT AND EATEN·

| Louisiana | Pennsylvania | Tennessee |
| | District of Columbia | South Carolina | |

CRANES ARE SHOT AND *EATEN* IN *THESE* STATES·

Colorado   North Dakota   Nevada   Oklahoma   Nebraska

In Mississippi, the *cedar bird* is legally shot and eaten!
In North Carolina, the meadow lark is shot and eaten.

IN THE FOLLOWING STATES, *DOVES ARE CONSIDERED* "GAME," AND
ARE SHOT IN AN "OPEN SEASON:"

Alabama	Georgia	Minnesota	Ohio
Arkansas	Idaho	Mississippi	Oregon
California	Illinois	Missouri	Pennsylvania
Connecticut	Kentucky	Nebraska	South Carolina
Delaware	Louisiana	New Mexico	Tennessee
Dist. of Columiba	Maryland	North Carolina	Texas
	Utah		Virginia

The killing of doves represents a great and widespread decline in the ethics of sportsmanship. In the twenty-six States named, a great many men who *call* themselves sportsmen indulge in the cheap and ignoble pastime of potting weak and confiding doves. It is on a par with the "sport" of hunting English sparrows in a city street. Of course this is, to a certain extent, a matter of taste; but there is at least one club of sportsmen into which no dove-killer can enter, provided his standard of ethics is known in advance.

With the killing of robins, larks, blackbirds and cedar birds for food, the case is quite different. No white man calling himself a sportsman ever indulges in such low pastimes as the killing of such birds for food. That burden of disgrace rests upon the negroes and poor whites of the South; but at the same time, it is a shame that respectable white men sitting in state legislatures should deliberately enact laws *permitting* such disgraceful practices, or permit such disgraceful and ungentlemanly laws to remain in force!

Here is a case by way of illustration, copied very recently from the Atlanta *Journal:*

Editor *Journal:*—I located a robin roost up the Trinity River, six miles from Dallas, and prevailed on six Dallas sportsmen to go with me on a torch-light bird hunt. This style of hunting was, of course, new to the Texans, but they finally consented to go, and I had the pleasure of showing them how it was done.

Equipped with torch lights and shot guns, we proceeded. After reaching the hunting grounds the sport began in reality, and continued for two hours and ten minutes, with a total slaughter of 10,157 birds, an average of 1,451 birds killed by each man.

But the Texans give me credit for killing at least 2,000 of the entire number. I was called 'the king of bird hunters' by the sportsmen of Dallas, Texas, and have been invited to command-in-chief the next party of hunters which go from Dallas to the Indian Territory in search of large game.—F. L. CROW, Dallas, Texas, former Atlantan.

Dallas, Texas, papers and Oklahoma papers, please copy!

As a further illustration of the spirit manifested in the South toward robins, I quote the following story from Dr. P. P. Claxton, of the University of Tennessee, as related in Audubon Educational Leaflet No. 46, by Mr. T. Gilbert Pearson:—

THE ROBIN OF THE NORTH

Our best-beloved Song Bird, now being legally shot as "game" in the South. In the North there is now only one robin for every ten formerly there.

"The roost to which I refer," says Professor Claxton, "was situated in what is locally known as a 'cedar glade,' near Forestville, Bedford Co., Tennessee. This is a great cedar country, and robins used to come in immense numbers during the winter months, to feed on the berries.

"The spot which the roost occupied was not unlike numerous others that might have been selected. The trees grew to a height of from five to thirty feet, and for a mile square were literally loaded at night with robins. Hunting them while they roosted was a favorite sport. A man would climb a cedar tree with a torch, while his companions with poles and clubs would disturb the sleeping birds on the adjacent trees. Blinded by the light, the suddenly awakened birds flew to the torch-bearer; who, *as he seized each bird would quickly pull off its head*, and drop it into a sack suspended from his shoulders.

"The capture of three of four hundred birds was an ordinary night's work. Men and boys would come in wagons from all the adjoining counties and camp near the roost for the purpose of killing robins. Many times, 100 or more hunters with torches and clubs would be at work in

THE MOCKING-BIRD OF THE SOUTH

This sweet singer of the South is NOT being shot in the North for food ! No northern lawmaker ever will permit such barbarity.

NORTHERN ROBINS READY FOR SOUTHERN SLAUGHTER

195 Birds at Avery Island, La. in January 1912, Photographed During the Annual
Slaughter, by E. A. McIlhenny

a single night. *For three years* this tremendous slaughter continued in winter,—and then the survivors deserted the roost."

No: these people were not Apache Indians, led by a Geronimo who knew no mercy, no compassion. We imagine that they were mostly poor white trash, of Tennessee. One small hamlet sent to market annually enough dead robins to return $500 at *five cents per dozen;* which means *120,000 birds!*

Last winter Mr. Edward A. McIlhenny of Avery Island, La. (south of New Iberia) informed me that every winter, during the two weeks that the holly berries are ripe thousands of robins come to his vicinity to feed upon them. "Then every negro man and boy who can raise a gun is after them. About 10,000 robins are slaughtered each day while they remain. Their dead bodies are sold in New Iberia at 10 cents each." The accompanying illustrations taken by Mr. McIlhenny shows 195 robins on one tree, and explains how such great slaughter is possible.

An officer of the Louisiana Audubon Society states that a conservative estimate of the number of robins annually killed in Louisiana for food purposes when they are usually plentiful, is *a quarter of a million!*

The food of the robin is as follows:

Insects, 40 per cent; wild fruit, 43 per cent; cultivated fruit, 8 per cent, miscellaneous vegetable food, 5 per cent.

SPECIAL WORK OF THE SOUTHERN NEGROES.—In 1912 a female colored servant who recently had arrived from country life in Virginia chanced to remark to me at our country home in the middle of August: "I wish I could find some birds' nests!"

"What for?" I asked, rather puzzled.

"Why, to get the aigs and *eat 'em!*" she responded with a bright smile and flashing teeth.

"Do you eat the eggs of *wild* birds?"

"Yes indeed! It's *fine* to get a pattridge nest! From them we nearly always git a whole dozen of aigs at once,—back where I live, in Virginia."

"Do the colored people of Virginia make a *practice* of hunting for the eggs of wild birds, and eating them?"

"Yes, indeed we do. In the spring and summer, when the birds are around, we used to get out every Sunday, and hunt all day. Some days we'd come back with a whole bucket full of aigs; and then we'd set up half the night, cookin' and eatin' 'em. They was *awful* good!"

Her face fairly beamed at the memory of it.

A few days later, this story of the doings of Virginia negroes was fully corroborated by a colored man who came from another section of that state. Three months later, after special inquiries made at my request, a gentleman of Richmond obtained further corroboration, from negroes. He was himself much surprised by the state of fact that was revealed to him.

In the North, the economic value of our song birds and other destroyers of insects and weed seeds is understood by a majority of the people, and as far as possible those birds are protected from all human enemies. But in the South, a new division of the Army of Destruction has risen into deadly prominence.

In *Recreation* Magazine for May, 1909, Mr. Charles Askins published a most startling and illuminating article, entitled "The South's Problem in Game Protection." It brought together in concrete form and with eye-witness reliability the impressions that for months previous had been gaining ground in the North. In order to give the testimony of a man who has seen what he describes, I shall now give numerous quotations from Mr. Askins' article, which certainly bears the stamp of truthfulness, without any "race prejudice" whatever. It is a calm, judicial, unemotional analysis of a very bad situation: and I particularly commend it alike to the farmers of the North and all the true sportsmen of the South.

In his opening paragraphs Mr. Askins describes game and hunting conditions in the South as they were down to twenty years ago, when the negroes were too poor to own guns, and shooting was not for them.

SPECIAL WORK OF THE SOUTHERN NEGROES.

It is all different now, says Mr. Askins, and the old days will only come back with the water that has gone down the stream. The master is with his fathers or he is whiling away his last days on the courthouse steps of the town. Perhaps a chimney or two remain of what was once the "big house" on the hill; possibly it is still standing, but as forlorn and lifeless as a dead tree. The muscadine grapes still grow in the swale and the persimmons in the pasture field, but neither 'possum nor 'coon is left to eat them. The last deer vanished years ago, the rabbits died in their baby coats and the quail were killed in June. Old "Uncle Ike" has gone across the "Great River" with his master, and his grandson glances at you askance, nods sullenly, whistles to his halfbreed bird dog, shoulders his three dollar gun and leaves you. He is typical of the change and has caused it, this grandson of dear old Uncle Ike.

In the same way the white man is telling the black to abide upon the plantation raising cotton and corn, and further than this nothing will be required of him. He can cheat a white man or a black, steal in a petty way anything that comes handy, live in marriage or out of it to please himself, kill another negro if he likes, and lastly shoot every wild thing that can be eaten, if only he raises the cotton and the corn. But the white sportsmen of the South have never willingly granted the shooting privilege in its entirety, and hence this story. They have told him to trap the rabbits, pot the robins, slaughter the doves, kill the song birds, but to spare the white sportsman's game, the aristocratic little bobwhite quail.

In the beginning not so much damage to southern game interests could be accomplished by our colored man and brother, however decided his inclinations. He had no money, no ammunition and no gun. His weapons were an ax, a club, a trap, and a hound dog; possibly he might own an old war musket bored out for shot. Such an outfit was not adapted to quail shooting and especially to wing shooting, with which knowledge Dixie's sportsmen were content. Let the negro ramble about with his hound dog and his war musket; he couldn't possibly kill the quail. And so Uncle Ike's grandson loafed and pottered about in the fields with his ax and his hound dogs, not doing so much harm to the quail but acquiring knowledge of the habits of the birds and skill as a still-hunting pot-hunter that would serve him well later on. The negro belongs to a primitive race of people and all such races have keener eyes than white men whose fathers have pored over lines of black and white. He learned to see the rabbit in its form, the squirrels in the leafy trees, and the quails huddled in the grass. The least shade of gray in the shadow of the creek bank he distinguished at once as a rabbit, a glinting flash from a tree top he knew instantly as being caused by the slight movement of a hidden squirrel, and the quiver of a single stem of sedge grass told him of a bevy of birds hiding in the depths. The pot-hunting negro has all the skill of the Indian, has more industry in his loafing, and kills without pity and without restraint. This grandson of Uncle Ike was growing sulky, too, with the knowledge that the white man was bribing him with half a loaf to raise cotton and corn when he might as well exact it all. And this he shortly did, as we shall see.

The time came when cotton went up to sixteen cents a pound and single breech-loading guns went down to five dollars apiece. The negro had money now, and the merchants—these men who had said let the nigger alone so long as he raises cotton and corn—sold him the guns, a gun for every black idler, man and boy, in all the South. Then shortly a wail went up from the sportsmen, "The niggers are killing our quail." They not only were killing them, but most of the birds were already dead. On the grounds of the Southern Field Club where sixty bevies were raised by the dogs in one day, within two years but three bevies could be found in a day by the hardest kind of hunting; and this story was repeated all over the South. Now the negro began to raise bird dogs in place of hounds, and he carried his new gun to church if services happened to be held on a week day. Finally the negro had grown up and had com-

Reproduced from Recreation Magazine.

THE SOUTHERN-NEGRO METHOD OF COMBING OUT THE WILD LIFE   By permission of the Outdoor World.

"Our colored sportsman is gregarious at all times, but especially so in the matter of recreation.   He may slouch about alone, and pot a bevy or two of quail when in actual need of something to eat, or when he has a sale for the birds, but when it comes to shooting for fun he wants to be with the 'gang'."—Charles Askins.

passed his ambition: he could shoot partridges flying just the same as a white man, was a white man except for a trifling difference in color; and he could kill more birds, too, three times as many. It was merely a change from the old order to the new in which a dark-skinned "sportsman" had taken the place in plantation life of-the dear old "Colonel" of loved memory. The negro had exacted his price for raising cotton and corn.

Our colored sportsman is gregarious at all times, but especially so in the matter of recreation. He may slouch about alone and pot a bevy or two of quail when in actual need of something to eat, or when he has a sale for the birds, but when it comes to shooting for fun he wants to be with the "gang." I have seen the darkies at Christmas time collect fifty in a drove with every man his dog, and spread out over the fields. Such a glorious time as he has then! A single cottontail will draw a half-dozen shots and perhaps a couple of young bucks will pour loads into a bunny after he is dead out of pure deviltry and high spirits. I once witnessed the accidental killing of a young negro on this kind of a foray. His companions loaded him into a wagon, stuck a cigar in his mouth, and tried to pour whiskey down him every time they took a drink themselves as they rode back to town. This army of black hunters and their dogs cross field after field, combing the country with fine teeth that leave neither wild animal nor bird life behind.

There comes a time toward the spring of the year after the quail season is over when the average rural darky is "between hay and grass." The merchants on whom he has depended for supplies make it a practice to refuse credit between January first and crop time. The black has spent his cotton money, his sweet potato pile has vanished, the sorghum barrel is empty, he has eaten the last of his winter's pork, and all that remains is a bit of meal and the meat his gun can secure. He is hunting in grim earnest now, using all the cunning and skill acquired by years of practice. He eats woodpeckers, jaybirds, hawks and skunks, drawing the line only at crows and buzzards. At this season of the year I have carried chicken hawks up to the cabins for the sake of watching the delight of the piccaninnies who with glowing eyes would declare, "Them's mos' as good as chicken." What happens to the robins, doves, larks, red birds, mocking birds and all songsters in this hungry season needs hardly to be stated.

It is also a time between hay and grass for the rabbits and the quail. The corn fields are bare and the weed seeds are exhausted. A spring cold spell pinches, they lose their vitality, become thin and quite lack their ordinary wariness. Then the figure-four trap springs up in the hedgerow and the sedge while the work of decimation goes more rapidly along. The rabbits can no longer escape the half-starved dogs, the thinning cover fails to hide the quail and the song birds betray themselves by singing of the coming spring.

With the growing scarcity of the game now comes the season of sedge and field burning. This is done ostensibly to prepare the land for spring plowing, but really to destroy the last refuge of the quail and rabbits so that they can be bagged with certainty. All the negroes of a neighborhood collect for one of these burnings, all their dogs, and of course all the boys from six years old up. They surround the field and set it on fire in many places, leaving small openings for the game to dash out among the motley assembly. I have seen quail fly out of the burning grass with flaming particles still attached to them. They alight on the burnt ground too bewildered to fly again and the boys and dogs pick them up. Crazed rabbits try the gauntlet amidst the barking curs, shouting negroes and popping guns, but death is sure and quick. The few quail that may escape have no refuge from the hawks and nothing to eat, so every battue of this kind marks the absolute end of the birds in one vicinity; and the next day the darkies repeat the performance elsewhere.

At this season of the year, the first of May, the blacks are putting in some of their one hundred working days while the single breech-loader rusts in the chimney corner. Surely the few birds that have escaped the foray of the "gang," lived through the hungry days, and survived their burned homes can now call "Bob White" and mate in peace. But school is out and the summer sun is putting new life into the bare feet of the half-grown boys, and the halfbreed bird dogs are busier than they were even in winter. The young rabbits are killed before they get out of the nest, and the quail eggs must be hidden rarely well that escape both the eyes of the boys and the noses of the dogs. After all it is not surprising that but three bevies remained of the sixty. Doubtless they would not, except that nature is very kind to her own in the sunny South.

Not every white man in the South is a sportsman or even a shooter; many are purely business men who have said let the "nigger" do as he likes so long as he raises cotton and buys our goods. But Dixie has her full share of true men of the out-of-doors and they have sworn in downright Southern fashion that this thing has got to end. Nevertheless their problem is deep and puzzling. In Alabama they made an effort and a beginning. They asked for a law requiring every man to obtain written permission before entering the lands of another to hunt and shoot; they asked for a resident license law taxing every gun not less than five dollars a year; for a shortened season, a bag limit, and a complete system of State wardens. Unfortunately, a lot of white farmers were in the same range as the blacks, and being hit, too, they raised a great outcry. The result was that the Alabama sportsmen got everything they asked for except the foundation of the structure they were trying to build, the high resident license or gun tax which alone could have shut out three dollar guns and saved the remnant of the game. Under the new law the sale of game was forbidden, neither could it be shipped out of the State alive or dead; the ever popular non-resident license was provided for; the season was shortened and the bag limited; the office of State game warden was created with deputies to be paid from fines; hunting upon the lands of another without written permission became a misdemeanor; and then the whole thing was nullified by reducing the resident license to nothing where a man shot upon his own land, one dollar in his own county, and two dollars outside of it. In its practical workings the new law amounts to this: A few northern gunners have paid the non-resident license fee, and enough resident licenses have been taken out by the city sportsmen to make up the handsome salary of the State warden. The negro still hunts upon his own land *or upon the land of the man who wants corn and cotton raised*, with perfect indifference to the whole thing. Who was to enforce the law against him? Not the one disgusted deputy with three big counties to patrol who depended for his salary upon the fines collected from the negroes. It would take one man to every three miles square to protect the game in the South.

The one effective way of dealing with the situation in Alabama was to have legislated three dollar guns out of existence with a five dollar tax, adding to this nearly a like amount on dogs. Hardly a sportsman in the South will disagree with this conclusion. But sportsmen never had a majority vote either in the South or in the North, and the South's grave problem is yet unsolved.

I do not favor depriving the black man of his natural human right to hunt and shoot. If he is the owner of land, or if he leases or rents it, or if he does not, he should have exactly the same privilege of hunting that the white man has. That is not the question now, however, but how to restrict him to legal shooting, to make him amenable to the law that governs the white man, to deprive him of the absolute license he now enjoys to kill throughout the year without mercy, without discrimination, without restraint. If only for selfish reasons, we of the North should reach to southern sportsmen a helping hand, for by and by the last of our migratory song birds will go down into Dixie and never return.

Mr. Askins has fairly stated a profoundly disturbing case. The remedy must contain at least three ingredients. The sportsmen of the South must stop the unjustifiable slaughter of their non-migratory game birds. As a matter of comity between states, the gentlemen of the South must pass laws to stop the killing of northern song-birds and all crop-protecting birds, for food. Finally, all men, North and South, East and West, must unite in the work that is necessary to secure the immediate enactment by Congress of a law for the federal protection of all migratory birds.

CHAPTER XIII

EXTERMINATION OF BIRDS FOR WOMEN'S HATS*

It is high time for the whole civilized world to know that many of the most beautiful and remarkable birds of the world are now being *exterminated* to furnish millinery ornaments for women's wear. The mass of new information that we have recently secured on this traffic from the headquarters of the feather trade is appalling. Previously, I had not dreamed that conditions are half as bad as they are.

It is entirely fitting that on this subject New York should send a message to London. New York is almost a Spotless Town in plume-free millinery, and London and Paris are the worst places in the world. We have cleaned house. With but extremely slight exceptions, the blood of the slaughtered innocents is no longer upon our skirts, and on the subject of plumage millinery we have a right to be just as Pharisaical as we choose.

Here in New York (and also in New Jersey) no man may sell, own for sale or offer for sale the plumage of any wild American bird other than a game bird. More than that, the plumage of no foreign bird belonging to any bird family represented in the fauna of North America can be sold here! There are only a few kinds of improper "millinery" feathers that it is possible to sell here under the law. Thanks to the long and arduous campaign of the National Association of Audubon Societies, founded and for ten years directed by gallant William Dutcher, you now see on the streets of New York very, very little wild-bird plumage save that from game birds.

It is true that a few servant girls are now wearing the cast-off aigrettes of their mistresses; but they are only as one in a thousand. At Atlantic City there is said to be a fine display of servant-girl and ladies-maid aigrettes. In New York and New Jersey, in Pennsylvania for everything save the sale of heron and egret plumes (a privilege obtained by a bunko game), in Massachusetts, and in many other of our States, the wild-birds'-plumage millinery business is dead. Two years ago, when the New York legislature refused to repeal the Dutcher law, the Millinery Association asserted, and brought a cloud of witnesses to Albany to prove, that the enforcement of the law would throw thousands of operatives out of employment.

The law is in effect; and the aigrette business is dead in this state. Have any operatives starved, or been thrown out of employment? We

*In the preparation of this chapter and its illustrations, I have had much valuable assistance from Mr. C. William Beebe, who recently has probed the London feather trade almost to the bottom.

BEAUTIFUL AND CURIOUS BIRDS NOW BEING DESTROYED
FOR THE FEATHER TRADE—(I)

Belted Kingfisher
Victoria Crowned Pigeon
S   h

Greater Bird of Paradise
Common Tern

1600 HUMMINGBIRD SKINS AT 2 CENTS EACH!
Part of a Lot Purchased by the Zoological Society at the Regular Quarterly
London Millinery Feather Sale, August, 1912.

have heard of none. They are now at work making very pretty hat ornaments of silk and ribbons, and gauze and lace; and "*They* are wearing
them."

But even while these words are being written, there is one large fly
in the ointment. The store-window of E. &. S. Meyers, 688 Broadway,
New York, contains about *six hundred plumes and skins of birds of
paradise, for sale for millinery purposes.* No wonder the great bird of
paradise is now almost extinct! Their sale here is possible because the
Dutcher law protects from the feather dealers only the birds that belong
to avian families represented in the United States. With fiendish cunning and enterprise, the shameless feather dealers are ferreting out the
birds whose skins and plumes may legally be imported into this country

and sold; but we will meet that with a law that will protect all foreign birds, so far as we are concerned. Now it is time for the universal enactment of a law which will prohibit the sale and use as ornaments of the plumage, feathers or skins of *any* wild bird that is not a legitimate game bird.

London is now the head of the giant octopus of the "feather trade" that has reached out its deadly tentacles into the most remote wildernesses of the earth, and steadily is drawing in the "skins" and "plumes" and "quills" of the most beautiful and most interesting *unprotected* birds of the world. The extent of this cold-blooded industry, supported by vain and hard-hearted women, will presently be shown in detail. Paris is the great manufacturing center of feather trimming and ornaments, and the French people obstinately refuse to protect the birds from extermination, because their slaughter affords employment to a certain numbers of French factory operatives.

All over the world where they have real estate possessions, the men of England know how to protect game from extermination. The English are good at protecting game—when they decide to set about it.

Why should London be the Mecca of the feather-killers of the world?

It is easily explained:

(1) London has the greatest feather market in the world; (2) the feather industry "wants the money"; and (3) the London feather industry is willing to spend money in fighting to retain its strangle-hold on the unprotected birds of the world.

Let us run through a small portion of the mass of fresh evidence before us. It will be easier for the friends of birds to read these details here than to procure them at first hand, as we have done.

The first thing that strikes one is the fact that the feather-hunters are scattered *all over the world where bird life is plentiful* and there are no laws to hinder their work. I commend to every friend of birds this list of the species whose plumage is to-day being bought and sold in large quantities every year in London. To the birds of the world this list is of deadly import, for it spells extermination.

The reader will notice that it is the way of the millinery octopus to reach out to the uttermost ends of the earth, and take everything that it can use. From the trackless jungles of New Guinea, round the world both ways to the snow-capped peaks of the Andes, no unprotected bird is safe. The humming-birds of Brazil, the egrets of the world at large, the rare birds of paradise, the toucan, the eagle, the condor and the emu, all are being *exterminated* to swell the annual profits of the millinery trade. The case is *far* more serious than the world at large knows, or even suspects. But for the profits, the birds would be safe; and no unprotected wild species can long escape the hounds of Commerce.

But behold the list of rare, curious and beautiful birds that are to-day in grave peril:

BEAUTIFUL AND CURIOUS BIRDS NOW BEING DESTROYED
FOR THE FEATHER TRADE—(II)

Lyre Bird   Resplendent Trogan
White Ibis   Silver Pheasant
Golden Eagle   Toco Toucan'

List of Birds Now Being Exterminated for the London and Continental Feather Markets:

Species.	*Locality.*
American Egret	Venezuela, S. America, Mexico, etc.
Snowy Egret	Venezuela, S. America, Mexico, etc.
Scarlet Ibis	Tropical South America.
"Green" Ibis	Species not recognizable by its trade name.
Herons, generally	All unprotected regions.
Marabou Stork	Africa.
Pelicans, all species	All unprotected regions.
Bustard	Southern Asia, Africa.
Greater Bird of Paradise	New Guinea; Aru Islands.
Lesser Bird of Paradise	New Guinea.
Red Bird of Paradise	Islands of Waigiou and Batanta.
Twelve-Wired Bird of Paradise	New Guinea, Salwatti.
Black Bird of Paradise	Northern New Guinea.
Rifle Bird of Paradise	New Guinea generally.
Jobi Bird of Paradise	Island of Jobi.
King Bird of Paradise	New Guinea.
Magnificent Bird of Paradise	New Guinea.
Impeyan Pheasant	Nepal and India.
Tragopan Pheasant	Nepal and India.
Argus Pheasant	Malay Peninsula, Borneo.
Silver Pheasant	Burma and China.
Golden Pheasant	China.
Jungle Cock	East Indies and Burma.
Peacock	East Indies and India.
Condor	South America.
Vultures, generally	Where not protected.
Eagles, generally	All unprotected regions.
Hawks, generally	All unprotected regions.
Crowned Pigeon, two species	New Guinea.
"Choncas"	Locality unknown.
Pitta	East Indies.
Magpie	Europe.
Touracou, or Plantain-Eater	Africa.
Velvet Birds	Locality uncertain.
"Grives"	Locality uncertain.
Mannikin	South America.
Green Parrot (now protected)	India.
"Dominos" (Sooty Tern)	Tropical Coasts and Islands.
Garnet Tanager	South America.
Grebe	All unprotected regions.
Green Merle	Locality uncertain.
"Horphang"	Locality uncertain.
Rhea	South America.

"Sixplet"........................Locality uncertain.
Starling........................Europe.
Tetras..........................Locality not determined.
Emerald-Breasted Hummingbird. . .West Indies, Cent. and S. America.
Blue-Throated Hummingbird   West Indies, Cent. and S. America.
Amethyst Hummingbird.   West Indies, Cent. and S. America.
Resplendent Trogon, several species. Central America.
Cock-of-the-Rock.................South America.
Macaw..........................South America!
Toucan.........................South America.
Emu............................Australia.
Sun-Bird.......................East Indies.
Owl............................All unprotected regions.
Kingfisher.....................All unprotected regions.
Jabiru Stork...................South America.
Albatross......................All unprotected regions.
Tern, all species..............All unprotected regions.
Gull, all species..............All unprotected regions.

In order to throw a spot-light on the most recent transactions in the London wild-birds'-plumage market, and to furnish a clear idea of what is to-day going on in London, Paris, Berlin and Amsterdam, I will set out in some detail the report of an agent whom I engaged to ascertain the London dealings in the plumage of wild birds that were killed especially to furnish that plumage. As one item, let us take the sales in London in February, May and October, 1911, because they bring the subject well down to date. My agent's explanatory note is as follows:

"These three sales represent six months. Very nearly double this quantity is sold by these four firms in a year. We must also take into consideration that all the feathers are not brought to the London market, and that *very large shipments are also made direct to the raw-feather dealers and manufacturers of Paris and Berlin, and that Amsterdam also gets large quantities from the West Indies.* For your purpose, I report upon three sales, at different periods of the year 1911, and as those sales do not vary much, you will be able to judge the consumption of birds in a year."

The "aigrettes" of the feather trade come from egrets, and, being very light, it requires the death of several birds to yield one ounce. In many catalogues, the word "albatross" stands for the jabiru, a nearly-exterminated species of giant stork, inhabiting South America. "Rhea" often stands for vulture plumage.

If the feather dealers had deliberately attempted to form an educational list of the most beautiful and the most interesting birds of the world, they could hardly have done better than they have done in the above list. If it were in my power to show the reader a colored plate of each species now being exterminated by the feather trade, he would be startled by the exhibit. That the very choicest birds of the whole avian world should be thus blotted out at the behest of vain and heartless women is a shame, a disgrace and world-wide loss.

LONDON FEATHER SALE OF FEBRUARY, 1911

Sold by Hale & Sons

Aigrettes....	.... 3,069 ounces
Herons..................	960 "
Birds of Paradise.	..... 1,920 skins

Sold by Figgis & Co.

Aigrettes.................	421 ounces
Herons..................	103 "
Paradise.................	414 skins
Eagles..................	2,600 "
Condors.................	1,580 "
Bustards.................	2,400 "

Sold by Dalton & Young

Aigrettes.	.... 1,606 ounces
Herons.................	250 "
Paradise......	.... 4,330 bodies

Sold by Lewis & Peat

Aigrettes.................	1,250 ounces
Paradise.................	362 skins
Eagles..................	384 "
Trogons.................	206 "
Hummingbirds............24,800 '

LONDON FEATHER SALE OF MAY, 1911

Sold by Hale & Sons

Aigrettes.................	1,390 ounces
Herons..................	178 "
Paradise.................	1,686 skins
Red Ibis.................	868 "
Junglecocks..............	1,550 "
Parrots..................	1,700 "
Herons..................	500 '

Sold by Figgis & Co.

Aigrettes	.... 201 ounces
Herons...	.... 248 "
Paradise.................	546 skins
Falcons, Hawks...........	1,500 "

Sold by Dalton & Young

Aigrettes.................	2,921 ounces
Herons..................	254 "
Paradise.................	5,303 skins
Golden Pheasants.........	1,000 "

Sold by Lewis & Peat

Aigrettes.................	590 ounces
Herons..................	190 "
Paradise.................	60 skins
Trogons.................	348 "
Hummingbirds	6,250 "

LONDON FEATHER SALE OF OCTOBER, 1911

Sold by Hale & Sons

Aigrettes.................	1,020 ounces
Paradise.................	2,209 skins
Hummingbirds............	10,040 "
Bustard.................	28,000 quills

Sold by Figgis & Co.

Aigrettes.......	..... 1,501 ounces
Herons..................	140 "
Paradise..	..... 318 skins

Sold by Dalton & Young

Aigrettes.................	5,879 ounces
Heron...................	1,608 "
Paradise.................	2,850 skins
Condors.................	1,500 "
Eagles..................	1,900 "

Sold by Lewis & Peat

Aigrettes.................	1,680 ounces
Herons.	.... 400 "
Birds of Paradise.........	700 skins

If I am correctly informed, the London feather trade admits that it requires six egrets to yield one "ounce" of aigrette plumes. This being the case, the 21,528 ounces sold as above stand for 129,168 egrets killed for nine months' supply of egret plumes, for London alone.

The total number of bird corpses auctioned during these three sales is as follows:

Aigrettes,	21,528 ounces	=	129,168 *Egrets*.
Herons,	2,683 "	=	13,598 *Herons*.
			20,698 Birds of Paradise
			41,090 Hummingbirds.
			9,464 Eagles, Condors, etc.
			9,472 Other Birds.

Total number of birds.....223,490

It is to be remembered that the sales listed above cover the transactions of four firms only, and do not in any manner take into account the direct importations from Paris, Berlin and Amsterdam of manufacturers and other dealers. The defenders of the feather trade are at great pains to assure the world that in the monthly, bi-monthly and quarterly sales, feathers often appear in the market twice in the same year; and this statement is made for them in order to be absolutely fair. Recent examinations of the plume catalogues for an entire year, marked with the price *paid* for each item, reveals very few which are blank, indicating no sale! The subtractions of the duplicated items would alter the result only very slightly.

The full extent of England's annual consumption of the plumage of wild birds slaughtered especially for the trade never has been determined. I doubt whether it is possible to ascertain it. The information that we have is so fragmentary that in all probability it reflects only a small portion of the whole truth, but for all that, it is sufficient to prove the case of the Defenders of the Birds *vs.* the London Chamber of Commerce.

IMPORTS OF *FEATHERS* AND *DOWN* (ORNAMENTAL) FOR THE
YEAR 1910

	Pounds.	Value.
Venezuela	8,398	$191,058
Brazil	787	5,999
Japan	2,284	3,830
China	6,329	16,308
Tripoli	345	900
Egypt	21,047	89,486
Java, Sumatra, and Borneo	15,703	186,504
Cape of Good Hope	709,406*	9,747,146
British India	18,359	22,137
Hong-Kong	310	3,090
British West Indies	30	97
Other British Colonies	10,438	21,938

* Chiefly Ostrich feathers.

The above does not take into account the feathers from game birds received in England from France, Germany, Austria-Hungary, Belgium and the Netherlands.

As a final side-light on the quantity of egret and heron plumes offered and sold in London during the twelve months ending in April, 1912, we offer the following exhibit:

"OSPREY" FEATHERS (*EGRET* AND *HERON* PLUMES) SOLD IN LONDON
DURING THE YEAR *ENDING* APRIL, 1912

	Offered.	Sold.
Venezuelan, long and medium	11,617 ounces	7,072 ounces
Venezuelan, mixed Heron	4,043 "	2,539 "
Brazilian	3,335 "	1,810 "
Chinese	641	576
	19,636 ounces	11,997 ounces
Birds of Paradise, plumes (2 plumes = 1 bird)	29,385	24,579

BEAUTIFUL AND CURIOUS BIRDS NOW BEING DESTROYED
FOR THE FEATHER TRADE—(III)

Under the head of "Hummingbirds Not Wanted," Mr. Downham is at great pains to convey* the distinct impression that to-day hummingbirds are scorned by the feather trade, and the demand for them is dead. *I believed him*—until my agent turned in the following statement:

Hummingbirds sold by Lewis & Peat, London, February, 1911....24,800
Hummingbirds sold by Lewis & Peat, London, May, 1911   . 6,250
Hummingbirds sold by Hale & Sons, London, October, 1911......10,040

Total..41,090

It is useless for anyone to assert that these birds were merely "offered," and not actually sold, as Mr. Downham so laboriously explains is the regular course with hummingbird skins; for that will deceive no intelligent person. The statement published above comes to me direct, from an absolutely competent and reliable source.

Undoubtedly the friends of birds, and likewise their enemies, will be interested in the prices at which the skins of the most beautiful birds of the world are sold in London, prior to their annihilation by the feather industry. I submit the following exhibit, copied from the circular of Messrs. Lewis & Peat. It is at least of academic interest.

PRICES OF RARE AND BEAUTIFUL BIRD SKINS IN *LONDON*

Condor skins.......................................$3.50 to $5.75
Condor wing feathers, each.............................   .05
Impeyan Pheasant......................................   .66 "   2.50
Argus Pheasant..   3.60   3.85
Tragopan Pheasant.....................................   2.70
Silver Pheasant.......................................   3.50
Golden Pheasant.......................................   .34 "   .46
Greater Bird of Paradise:
    Light Plumes: Medium to giants...................10.32 " 21.00
                  Medium to long, worn............... 7.20 " 13.80
                  Slight def. and plucked............ 2.40 "   6.72
    Dark Plumes: Medium to good long................ 7.20 " 24.60
12-Wired Bird of Paradise............................ 1.44 "   1.80
Rubra Bird of Paradise...............................   2.50
Rifle Bird of Paradise............................... 1.14 "   1.38
King Bird of Paradise................................   2.40
"Green" Bird of Paradise.............................   38 "   .44
East Indian Kingfisher...............................   .06 "   .07
East Indian Parrots..................................   .03
Peacock Necks, gold and blue.........................   ?4 "   .66
Peacock Necks, blue and green 36
Scarlet Ibis...   .14 "   .24
Toucan breasts.......................................   22 "   .26
Red Tanagers...   09
Orange Oriels..   05
Indian Crows' breasts................................   13
Indian Jays..   04
Amethyst Hummingbirds................................   .01½
Hummingbird, various.................................3/16 of .01   .02
Hummingbird, others..................................1/32 of .01 "   .01
Egret ("Osprey") skins............................... 1.08 "   2.78

* "The Feather Trade," by C. F. Downham, p. 63-4.

Egret ("Osprey") skins, long........................... 2.40
Vulture feathers, per pound........................... .36 " 4.56
Eagle, wing feathers, bundles of 100 09
Hawk, wing feathers, bundles of 100. 12
Mandarin Ducks, per skin............................. .15
Pheasant tail feathers, per pound...................... ².80
Crown Pigeon heads, Victoria......................... 1.68 " 2.50
Crown Pigeon heads, Coronatus....................... .84 " 1.20
Emu skins .... 4.56 " 4.80
Cassowary plumes, per ounce.......................... 3.48
Swan skins... .72 " .74
Kingfish skins...................................... .07 " .09
African golden Cuckoo............................... 1.68

Many thoughts are suggested by these London lists of bird slaughter and loot.

It will be noticed that the breast of the grebe has almost wholly disappeared from the feather market and from women's hats. The reason is that there are no longer enough birds of that group to hold a place in the London market! Few indeed are the Americans who know that from 1900 to 1908 the lake region of southern Oregon was the scene of the slaughter of uncountable thousands of those birds, which continued until the grebes were almost exterminated.

When the wonderful lyre-bird of Australia had been almost exterminated for its tail feathers, its open slaughter was stopped by law, and a heavy fine was imposed on exportation, amounting, I have been told, to $250 for each offense. My latest news of the lyre-bird was of the surreptitious exportation of 200 skins to the London feather market.

In India, the smuggling outward of the skins of protected birds is constantly going on. Occasionally an exporter is caught and fined; but that does not stop the traffic.

Bird-lovers must now bid farewell forever to all the birds of paradise. Nothing but the legal closing of the world's markets against their plumes and skins can save any of them. They never were numerous; nor does any species range over a wide area. They are strictly insular, and the island homes of some of them are very small. Take the great bird of paradise (*Paradisea apoda*) as an illustration. On Oct. 2, 1912, at Indianapolis, Indiana, a city near the center of the United States, in three show-windows within 100 feet of the headquarters of the Fourth National Conservation Congress, I counted 11 stuffed heads and 11 complete sets of plumes of this bird, displayed for sale. The prices ranged from $30 to $47.50 each! And while I looked, a large lady approached, pointed her finger at the remains of a greater bird of paradise, and with grim determination, said to her shopping companion: "There! I want one o' them, an' I'm agoin' to *have* it, too!"

Says Mr. James Buckland in "Pros and Cons of the Plumage Bill":

"Mr Goodfellow has returned within the last few weeks from a second expedition to new Guinea. * * One can now walk, he states, miles and miles through the former haunts of these birds [of paradise] without seeing or hearing even the commonest species. When I reflect on this sacrilege, I am lost in wonder at the apathy of the British public."

Mr. Carl Hagenbeck wrote me only three months ago that "the condors of the Andes are all being exterminated for their feathers, and these birds are now very difficult to obtain."

The egret and heron plumes, known under the trade name of "osprey, etc., feathers," form by far the most important item in each feather sale. There are *fifteen* grades! They are sold by the ounce, and the prices range all the way from twenty-eight cents per ounce for "mixed heron" to *two hundred and twenty-five shillings* ($45.60) per ounce for the best Brazilian "short selected," on February 7, 1912! Is it any wonder that in Philadelphia the prices of finished aigrettes, ready to be worn, runs from $20 to $125!

The plumes that run up into the big figures are the "short selected" coming from the following localities, and quoted at the prices set down here in shillings and pence. Count the shilling at twenty-four cents, United States money.

PRICES OF "SHORT SELECTED" EGRET AND HERON PLUMES, IN LONDON ON FEBRUARY 7, 1912

(Lewis & Peat's List)

East Indies.................per ounce,	117/6 to	207/6 =	$49.80 max.
Rangoon.................... "	" 150/0 "	192/6 =	46.20 "
China...................... "	" 130/0 "	245/0 =	58.80 "
Brazil..................... "	" 200/0 "	225/0 =	54.00 "
Venezuela................. "	" 165/0 "	222/6 =	53.40 "

The total offering of these "short selected" plumes in December 1911, was 689 ounces, and in February, 1912, it was 230 ounces.

Now with these enormous prices prevailing, is it any wonder that the egrets and herons are being relentlessly pursued to the uttermost ends of the earth? I think that any man who really knows the habits of egrets and herons, and the total impossibility of any quantity of their shed feathers being picked up in a marketable state, must know in his heart that if the London and continental feather markets keep open a few years longer, *every species* that furnishes "short selected" plumes will be utterly exterminated from off the face of the earth.

Let the English people make no mistake about this, nor be fooled by any fairy tales of the feather trade about Venezuelan "garceros," and vast quantities of valuable plumes picked off the bushes and out of the mud. Those carefully concocted egret-farm stories make lovely reading, but the reader who examines the evidence will soon decide the extent of their truthfulness. I think that they contain not even ten per cent of truth; and I shall not rest until the stories of Leon Laglaize and Maveul Grisol have been put to the test in the regions where they originated.

A *few* plumes may be picked out of the jungle, yes; but as for any *commercial quantity*, it is at present beyond belief. Besides, we have direct, eye-witness testimony to the contrary.

It must not be inferred that the friends of birds in England have been idle or silent in the presence of the London feather trade. On the contrary, the Royal Society for the Protection of Wild Birds and Mr. James Buckland have so strongly attacked the feather industry that the London Chamber of Commerce has felt called upon to come to its rescue. Mr. Buckland, on his own individual account, has done yeoman service to the cause, and his devotion to the birds, and his tireless energy, are both almost beyond the reach of praise in words. At the last moment before going to press I learn that the birds'-plumage bill has achieved the triumph of a "first reading" in Parliament, which looks as if success is at last in sight. The powerful pamphlet that he has written, published and circulated at his own expense, entitled "Pros and Cons of the Plumage Bill," is a splendid effort. What a pity it is that more individuals are not similarly inspired to make independent effort in the protection cause! But, strange to say, few indeed are the men who have either the nerve or the ability to "go it alone."

On the introduction in Parliament of the bill to save the birds from the feather trade, it was opposed (through the efforts of the Chamber of Commerce), on the ground that if any bill against the sale of plumes should pass, and plumes could not be sold, the London business in wild-bird skins and feathers "would immediately be transferred to the continent!"

In the face of that devastating and altogether horrible prospect, and because the London feather dealers "need the money," the bill was at first defeated—to the great joy of the Chamber of Commerce and Mr. Downham; but the cause of birds will win in the end, because it is Right.

The feather dealers have been shrewdly active in the defense of their trade, and the methods they have employed for influencing public opinion have quite outshone those put forth by their brethren in America. I have before me a copy of a booklet bearing the name of Mr. C. F. Downham as the author, and the London Chamber of Commerce has loaned its good name as publisher. Altogether it is a very shrewd piece of work, even though its arguments in justification of bird slaughter for the feather market are too absurd and weak for serious consideration.

The chief burden of the defender of bird slaughter for millinery purposes is on account of the destruction of egrets and herons, but particularly the former. To offset as far as possible the absolutely true charge that egrets bear their best plumes in their breeding season, when the helpless young are in the nest and the parent birds must be killed to obtain the plumes, the feather trade has obtained from three Frenchmen—Leon Laglaize, Mayeul Grisol, and F. Geay—a beautiful and plausible story to the effect that in Venezuela the enormous output of egret plumes has been obtained *by picking up, off the bushes and out of the water and mud, the shed feathers of those birds!* According to the story, Venezuela is full of *egret farms*, called "garceros,"—where the birds breed and moult under strict supervision, and kindly drop their feathers in such places that it is possible *to find them*, and to *pick them up*, in a

THE FIGHT IN ENGLAND AGAINST THE USE OF WILD BIRD'S PLUMAGE
IN THE MILLINERY TRADE

Sandwich-men Employed by the Royal Society for the Protection of Birds
that Patroled London Streets in July, 1911.

high state of preservation! And we are asked to believe that it is these very Venezuelan picked-up feathers that command in London the high price of *$44 per ounce.*

Mr. Laglaize is especially exploited by Mr. Downham, as a French traveler of high standing, and well known in the zoological museums of France; but, sad to say, when Prof. Henry Fairfield Osborn cabled to the Museum of Natural History in Paris, inquiring about Mr. Laglaize, the cable flashed back the one sad word: "*Inconnu!*" (Unknown!)

I think it entirely possible that enough shed feathers have been picked up in the reeking swamps of Venezuela, on the upper tributaries of the Orinoco, to afford *an excuse* for the beautiful story of Mr. Laglaize. Any shrewd individual with money, and the influence that money secures, could put up just such a "plant" as I firmly believe *has* been put up by some one in Venezuela. I will guarantee that I could accomplish such a job in Venezuela or Brazil, in four months' time, at an expense not exceeding one thousand dollars.

That the great supply of immaculately perfect egret plumes that annually come out of Venezuela could by any possibility be picked up in the swamps where they were shed and dropped by the egrets, is entirely preposterous and incredible. The whole proposition is denounced by several men of standing and experience, none of whom are *"inconnu."*

As a sweeping refutation of the fantastic statements regarding "garceros," published by Mr. Downham as coming from Messrs. Laglaize, Grisol and Geay, I offer the written testimony of an American gentleman who at this moment owns and maintains within a few yards of his residence a large preserve of snowy egrets and herons, the former representing the species which furnishes egret plumes exactly similar to those shipped from Venezuela and Brazil. If the testimony of Mr. McIlhenny is not sufficient to stamp the statements of the three Frenchmen quoted by Mr. Downham as absolute and thoroughly misleading falsehoods, then there is no such thing in this world as evidence. I suggest a perusal of the statements of the three Frenchmen who are quoted with such confidence by Mr. Downham and published by the Hon. Chamber of Commerce at London, and then a careful reading of the following letter :

Avery Island, La., June 17, 1912.

DEAR MR. HORNADAY:—

I have before me your letter of June 8th, asking for information as to whether or no egrets shed their plumes at their nesting places in sufficient quantities to enable them to be gathered commercially. I most emphatically wish to state that it is impossible to gather at the nesting places of these birds any quantity of their plumes. I have nesting within 50 yards of where I am now sitting dictating this letter not less than 20,000 pairs of the various species of herons and egrets, and there are fully 2,500 pairs of snowy herons nesting within my preserve.

During the nesting season, which covers the months of April, May and June, I am through this heronry in a small canoe almost every day, and often twice a day. I have had these herons under my close inspection for the past 17 years, and I have not in any one season picked up or seen more than half a dozen discarded plumes. Such plumes as I have picked up, I have kept on my desk, and given to the people who were interested. I remember that last year I picked up four plumes of the snowy heron that were in one bunch. I think these must have been plucked out by the birds fighting.

This year I have found only one plume so far. I enclose it herewith. You will notice that it is one of the shorter plumes, and is badly worn at the end, as have been all the plumes which I have picked up in my heronry.

I am positive that it is not possible for natural shed plumes to be gathered commercially. I have a number of times talked with plume hunters from Venezuela and other South American countries, and I have never heard of any egret feathers being gathered by their being picked up after the birds have shed them.

I have heard of a number of heronries in South America that are protected by the land owners for the purpose of gathering a yearly crop of egret plumes, but this crop is gathered always by shooting a certain percentage of the birds. This shooting is done by experts with 22-calibre rifles, and does not materially disturb the nesting colony. I have known of two men who have been engaged in killing the birds on large estates in South America, who were paid regular salaries for their services as egret hunters.

Very truly yours.

E. A. McILHENNY

I am more than willing to set the above against the fairy tale of Mr. Laglaize.

Here is the testimony of A. H. Meyer, an ex-plume-hunter, who for nine years worked in Venezuela. His sworn testimony was laid before the Legislature of the State of New York, in 1911, when the New York Milliners' Association was frantically endeavoring to secure the repeal of the splendid Dutcher law. This witness was produced by the National Association of Audubon Societies.

"My attention has been called to the fact that certain commercial interests in this city are circulating stories in the newspapers and elsewhere to the effect that the aigrettes used in the millinery trade come chiefly from Venezuela, where they are gathered from the ground in the large *garceros*, or breeding-colonies, of white herons.

"I wish to state that I have personally engaged in the work of collecting the plumes of these birds in Venezuela. This was my business for the years 1896 to 1905, inclusive. I am thoroughly conversant with the methods employed in gathering egret and snowy heron plumes in Venezuela, and I wish to give the following statement regarding the practices employed in procuring these feathers:

"The birds gather in large colonies to rear their young. They have the plumes only during the mating and nesting season. After the period when they are employed in caring for their young, it is found that the plumes are virtually of no commercial value, because of the worn and frayed condition to which they have been reduced. It is the custom in Venezuela to shoot the birds while the young are in the nests. A few feathers of the large white heron (American egret), known as the *Garza blanca*, can be picked up of a morning about their breeding places, but these are of small value and are known as "dead feathers." They are worth locally not over three dollars an ounce; while the feathers taken from the bird, known as "live feathers," are worth fifteen dollars an ounce.

"My work led me into every part of Venezuela and Colombia where these birds are to be found, and I have never yet found or heard of any *garceros* that were guarded for the purpose of simply gathering the feathers from the ground. No such condition exists in Venezuela. The story is absolutely without foundation, in my opinion, and has simply been put forward for commercial purposes.

"The natives of the country, who do virtually all of the hunting for feathers, are not provident in their nature, and their practices are of a most cruel and brutal nature. I have seen them frequently pull the plumes from wounded birds, leaving the crippled birds to die of starvation, unable to respond to the cries of their young in the nests above, which were calling for food. *I have known these people to tie and prop up wounded egrets on the marsh where they would attract the attention of other birds flying by. These decoys they keep in this position until they die of their wounds, or from the attacks of insects. I have seen the terrible red ants of that country actually eating out the eyes of these wounded, helpless birds that were tied up by the plume-hunters.* I could write you many pages of the horrors practiced in gathering aigrette feathers in Venezuela by the natives for the millinery trade of Paris and New York.

"To illustrate the comparatively small number of dead feathers which are collected, I will mention that in one year I and my associates shipped to New York eighty pounds of the plumes of the large heron and twelve pounds of the little recurved plumes of the snowy heron. In this whole lot there were not over five pounds of plumes that had been gathered from the ground—and these were of little value. The plume-birds have been nearly exterminated in the United States and Mexico, and the same condition of affairs will soon exist in tropical America. This extermination will come about because of the fact that the young are left to starve in the nest when the old birds are killed, any other statement made by interested parties to the contrary notwithstanding.

"I am so incensed at the ridiculously absurd and misleading stories that are being published on this question that I want to give you this letter, and, before delivering it to you, shall take oath to its truthfulness."

Here is the testimony of Mr. Caspar Whitney, of New York, formerly editor of *Outing* Magazine and *Outdoor America:*

"During extended travel throughout South America, from 1903 to 1907, inclusive, I journeyed, on three separate occasions, by canoe (1904-1907), on the Lower Orinoco and Apure rivers and their tributaries. This is the region, so far as Venezuela is concerned, in which is the greatest slaughter of white herons for their plumage, or more specifically for the marital plumes, which are carried only in the mating and breeding season, and are known in the millinery trade as 'aigrettes.'

"There is literally no room for question. The snowy herons are killed exactly as I describe. It is the custom of all those who hunt for the millinery trade, and is recognized by the natives as the usual method."

Here is the testimony of Mr. Julian A. Dimock, of Peekamose, N. Y., the famous outdoor photographer, and illustrator of "Florida Enchantments":

"I know a goodly number of the plume-hunters of Florida. I have camped with them, and talked to them. I have heard their tales, and even full accounts of the 'shooting-up' of an egret rookery. Never has a man in Florida suggested to me that plumes could be obtained without killing the birds. I have known the wardens, and have visited rookeries after they had been 'shot-up,' and the evidence all pointed to the everlasting use of the gun. *It is certainly not true that the plumes can be obtained without killing the birds bearing them.*

"Nineteen years ago, I visited the Cuthbert Rookery with one of the men who discovered the birds nesting in that lake. He and his partner had sold the plumes gathered there for more than a thousand dollars. He showed me how they hid in the bushes and shot the birds. He even gave me a chance to watch him kill two or three birds.

"I know personally the man chiefly responsible for the slaughter of the birds at Alligator Bay. *He laughed at the idea of getting plumes without killing the birds!* I well know the man who shot the birds up Rogers River, and even saw some of the empty shells left on the ground by him.

YOUNG EGRETS, UNABLE TO FLY, STARVING

The Parent Birds had Been Killed by Plume Hunters

SNOWY EGRET, DEAD ON HER NEST

Wounded in the Feeding-Grounds, and Came Home to Die. Photographed in a Florida Rookery
Protected by the National Association of Audubon Societies

I have camped with Seminoles, whites, blacks, outlaws, and those within the pale, connected with plume-hunting, and all tell the same story: *The birds are shot to get the plumes.* The evidence of my own eyes, and the action of the birds themselves, convinces me that there is not a shadow of doubt concerning this point."

This sworn testimony from Mr. T. J. Ashe, of Key West, Florida, is very direct and to the point:

"I have seen many moulted and dropped feathers from wild plumed birds. I have never seen a moulted or dropped feather that was fit for anything. It is the exception when a plumed bird drops feathers of any value while in flight. Whatever feathers are so dropped are those that are frayed, worn out, and forced out by the process of moulting. The moulting season is not during the hatching season, but is after the hatching season. The shedding, or moulting, takes place once a year; and during this moulting season the feathers, after having the hard usage of the year from wind, rain and other causes, when dropped are of absolutely no commercial value."

Mr. Arthur T. Wayne, of Mount Pleasant, S. C., relates in sworn testimony his experience in attempting to secure egret plumes without killing the birds:

"It is utterly impossible to get fifty egret plumes from any colony of breeding birds without shooting the birds. Last spring, I went twice a week to a breeding colony of American and snowy egrets, from early in April until June 8. Despite the fact that I covered miles of territory in a boat, I picked up but two American egret plumes (which I now have); but not a single snowy egret plume did I see, nor did my companion who accompanied me on every trip.

"I saw an American egret plume on the water, and left it, purposely, to see whether it would sink or not. Upon visiting the place a few days afterwards, the plume was not in evidence, undoubtedly having sunk. The plumes are chiefly shed in the air while the birds are going to or coming from their breeding grounds. If that millinery plume law is repealed, the fate of the American and snowy egrets is sealed, for the few birds that remain will be shot to the very last one."

Any man who ever has been in an egret rookery (and I have) knows that the above testimony is *true!* The French story of the beautiful and smoothly-running egret farms in Venezuela is preposterous, save for a mere shadow of truth. I do not say that *no* egret plumes could be picked up, but I do assert that the total quantity obtainable in one year in that way would be utterly trivial.

No; the "ospreys" of the British feather market come from slaughtered egrets and herons, *killed in the breeding season.* Let the British public and the British Parliament make no mistake about that. If they wish the trade to continue, let it be based on the impregnable ground that the merchants want the money, and not on a fantastic dream that is too silly to deceive even a child that knows birds.

The use or disuse of wild birds' plumage as millinery ornaments is another of those wild-life subjects regarding which there is no room for argument. To assert that the feather-dealers want the business for the money it brings them is not argument! We have seen many a steam roller go over Truth, and Right, and Justice, by main strength and red-hot power; but Truth and Right refuse to stay flat down. . There is on this earth not one wild-animal species—mammal, bird or reptile—that can long withstand exploitation for commercial purposes. Even the whales of the deep sea, the walrus of the arctic regions, the condors of the Andes and alligators of the Everglade morasses are no exception to the universal rule.

In Mr. Downham's book there is much fallacious reasoning, and many conclusions that are not borne out by the facts. For example, he says that no species of bird of paradise has been diminished in number by slaughter for the feather trade; that Florida still contains a supply of egrets; that the decrease in bird li˜e should be charged to the spread of cities, towns and farms, and not to the trade; that the trade was "in no way responsible" for the slaughter of three hundred thousand gulls and albatrosses on Laysan Island!

I have space to notice one other important erroneous conclusion that Mr. Downham publishes in his book, on page 105. He says:

"The destruction of birds in foreign countries is something that no trade can direct or control."

This is an amazing declaration; and absolutely contrary to experience. Let me prove what I say by a fresh and incontestable illustration:

Prior to April, 1911, when Governor Dix signed the Bayne law against the sale of wild native game in the State of New York, Currituck County, N. C., was a vast slaughter-pen for wild fowl. No power or persuasion had availed to induce the people of North Carolina to check, or regulate, or in any manner mitigate that slaughter of geese, ducks and swans. It was estimated that two hundred thousand wild fowl were annually slaughtered there.

We who advocated the Bayne law said: "Close the New York markets against Currituck birds, and you will stop a great deal of the slaughter."

We cleaned our Augean stable. The greatest game market in America was absolutely closed.

Last winter (1911) the annual killing of wild fowl was fully fifty per cent less than during previous years. In one small town, twenty professional duck shooters went entirely out of business—because they *couldn't sell their ducks!* The dealers refused to buy them. The result was exactly what we predicted it would be; and this year, it is reported over and over that ducks are more plentiful in New England than they have been in twenty years previously! The result is wonderful, because so quick.

Beyond all question, the feather merchants of London, Paris and Ber-

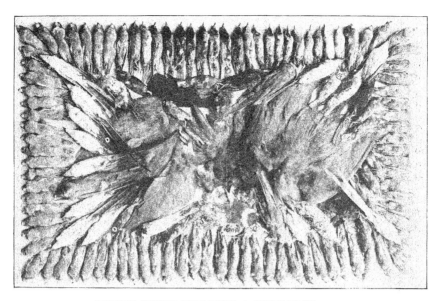

MISCELLANEOUS BIRD SKINS. 8 CENTS EACH
Purchased by the New York Zoological Society from the Quarterly Sale in London. August, 1912

lin absolutely control the bird-killers of Venezuela, China, New Guinea, Mexico and South America. Let the word go forth that "the trade" is no longer permitted to buy and sell egret and heron plumes, skins of birds of paradise and condor feathers, and presto! the killing industry falls dead the next moment.

Yes, indeed, members of the British Parliament: it is easily within *your power* to wipe out at a single stroke fully one-half of the bird slaughter for fancy feathers. It can be done just as we wiped out one-half the annual duck slaughter in wickedly-wasteful North Carolina!

The feather trade absolutely *does* control the killing situation! Now, will the people of England clean house by controlling the feather trade? If a hundred species of the most beautiful birds of the world must be exterminated for the feather trade, let the odium rest elsewhere than on the people of England.

The bird-lovers of America may rest assured that the bird-lovers of England—a mighty host—are neither careless nor indifferent regarding the wild-birds' plumage business. On the contrary, several bills have been brought before Parliament intended to regulate or prohibit the traffic, and a measure of vast importance to the birds of the world is now before the House of Commons. It is backed by Mr. Percy Alden, M.P., by the Royal Society for the Protection of Birds, by the Selbourne Society, and by Mr. James Buckland—a host in himself. For years past that splendidly-equipped and well-managed Royal Society has waged ceaseless warfare for the birds. Its activity has been tremendous, and its membership list contains many of the finest names in England. The address of the Honorary Secretary, Frank E. Lemon, Esq., is 23 Queen Anne's Gate, London, S.W.

Naturally, these influences are opposed by the Textile Trade Section of the London Chamber of Commerce, and their only argument consists of the plea that if London doesn't get the money out of the feather trade, the Continent will get it! A reasonable, logical, magnificent and convincing excuse for wholesale bird slaughter, truly!

Mr. Buckland has been informed from the Continent that the people of France, Germany, the Netherlands and Belgium are waiting and watching to see what England is going to do with the question, "To slaughter, or not to slaughter?" For England has no monopoly of the birds' plumage trade, not by any means. Says Mr. Buckland ("Pros and Cons of the Plumage Bill," page 17):

"As regards the vast majority of fancy feathers used in millinery, the Continent receives its own supplies. The feathers of the hundreds of thousands of albatrosses which are killed in the North Pacific all go to Paris. Of the untold thousands of 'magpies,' owls, and other species which come from Peru, not one skin or feather crosses the Channel. The white herons of the Upper Senegal and the Niger are being rapidly exterminated at the instigation of the feather merchants, but not one of the plumes reaches London. Paris receives direct a large supply of aigrettes from South America and elsewhere. * * * The millions of swallows and other migratory birds which are killed annually as they pass through Italy, France and Spain on their way north, supply the millinery trade of Europe with an incredible quantity of wings and other plumage, but none of it is distributed from London. * * * London, as a distributing center, has no monopoly of the trade in raw feathers."

Mr. Buckland's green-covered pamphlet is a powerful document, and both his facts and his conclusions seem to be unassailable. The author's address is Royal Colonial Institute, Northumberland Ave., London, W.C.

The duty of the civilized nations of Europe is perfectly plain. The savage and bloody business in feathers torn from wild birds should be stopped, completely and forever. If the commons will not arise and reform the odious business out of existence, then the kings and queens and presidents should do their plain duty. In the suppression of a world crime like this it is clearly a case of *noblesse oblige!*

CHAPTER XIV.

THE BIRD TRAGEDY ON LAYSAN ISLAND

This chapter is a curtain-dropper to the preceding chapter. As a clearly-cut, concrete case, the reader will find it unique and unsurpassed. It should be of lively interest to every American because the tragedy occurred on American territory.

In the far-away North Pacific Ocean, about seven hundred miles from Honolulu west-b'-north, lies the small island of Laysan. It is level, sandy, poorly planted by nature, and barren of all things likely to enlist the attention of predatory man. To the harassed birds of mid-ocean, it seemed like a secure haven, and for ages past it has been inhabited only by them. There several species of sea birds, large and small, have found homes and breeding places. Until 1909, the inhabitants consisted of the Laysan albatross, black-footed albatross, sooty tern, gray-backed tern, noddy tern, Hawaiian tern, white tern, Bonin petrel, two shearwaters, the red-tailed tropic bird, two boobies and the man-of-war bird.

Laysan Island is two miles long by one and one-half miles broad, and at times it has been literally covered with birds. Its bird life was first brought prominently to notice in 1891, by Henry Palmer, the agent of Hon. Walter Rothschild, and in 1902 and 1903 Walter K. Fisher and W. A. Bryan made further observations.

Ever since 1891 the bird life on Laysan has been regarded as one of the wonders of the bird world. One of the photographs taken prior to 1909 shows a vast plain, apparently a square mile in area, covered and crowded with Laysan albatrosses. They stand there on the level sand, serene, bulky and immaculate. Thousands of birds appear in one view—a very remarkable sight.

Naturally man, the ever-greedy, began to cast about for ways by which to convert some product of that feathered host into money. At first guano and eggs were collected. A tramway was laid down and small box-cars were introduced, in which the collected material was piled and pushed down to the packing place.

For several years this went on, and the birds themselves were not molested. At last, however, a tentacle of the feather-trade octopus reached out to Laysan. In an evil moment in the spring of 1909, a predatory individual of Honolulu and elsewhere, named Max Schlemmer, decided that the wings of those albatross, gulls and terns should be torn off and sent to Japan, whence they would undoubtedly be shipped to

By the Courtesy of Hon. Walter Rothschild.

LAYSAN ALBATROSSES BEFORE THE GREAT S AUGHTER

LAYSAN ALBATROSS ROOKERY, AFTER THE GREAT SLAUGHTER
The Same Ground as Shown in the Preceding Picture, Photographed in 1911 by Prof. Homer R. Dill

Paris, the special market for the wings of sea-birds slaughtered in the North Pacific.

Schlemmer the Slaughterer bought a cheap vessel, hired twenty-three phlegmatic and cold-blooded Japanese laborers, and organized a raid on Laysan. With the utmost secrecy he sailed from Honolulu, landed his bird-killers upon the sea-bird wonderland, and turned them loose upon the birds.

For several months they slaughtered diligently and without mercy. Apparently it was the ambition of Schlemmer to kill every bird on the island.

By the time the bird-butchers had accumulated between three and four car-loads of wings, and the carnage was half finished, William A. Bryan, Professor of Zoology in the College of Honolulu, heard of it and promptly wired the United States Government.

Without the loss of a moment the Secretary of the Navy despatched the revenue cutter *Thetis* to the shambles of Laysan. When Captain Jacobs arrived he found that in round numbers about *three hundred thousand* birds had been destroyed, and all that remained of them were several acres of bones and dead bodies, and about three carloads of wings, feathers and skins. It was evident that Schlemmer's intention was to kill all the birds on the island, and only the timely arrival of the *Thetis* frustrated that bloody plan.

The twenty-three Japanese poachers were arrested and taken to Honolulu for trial, and the *Thetis* also brought away all the stolen wings and plumage with the exception of one shedful of wings that had to be left behind on account of lack of carrying space. That old shed, with

ACRES OF GULL AND ALBATROSS BONES
Photographed on Laysan Island by H. R. Dill, 1911

one end torn out, and supposed to contain nearly fifty thousand pairs of wings, was photographed by Prof. Dill in 1911, as shown herewith.

Three hundred thousand albatrosses, gulls, terns and other birds were butchered to make a Schlemmer holiday! Had the arrival of the *Thetis* been delayed, it is reasonably certain that every bird on Laysan would have been killed to satisfy the wolfish rapacity of one money-grubbing white man.

In 1911, the Iowa State University despatched to Laysan a scientific expedition in charge of Prof. Homer R. Dill. The party landed on the island on April 24 and remained until June 5, and the report of Professor Dill (U. S. Department of Agriculture) is consumedly interesting to the friends of birds. Here is what he has said regarding the evidences of bird-slaughter:

"Our first impression of Laysan was that the poachers had stripped the place of bird life. An area of over 300 acres on each side of the buildings was apparently abandoned. Only the shearwaters moaning in their burrows, the little wingless rail skulking from one grass tussock to another, and the saucy finch remained. It is an excellent example of what Prof. Nutting calls the survival of the inconspicuous.

"Here on every side are bones bleaching in the sun, showing where the poachers had piled the bodies of the birds as they stripped them of wings and feathers. In the old open guano shed were seen the remains of hundreds and possibly thousands of wings which were placed there but never cured for shipping, as the marauders were interrupted in their work.

SHED FILLED WITH WINGS OF SLAUGHTERED BIRDS ON LAYSAN ISLAND

"An old cistern back of one of the buildings tells a story of cruelty that surpasses anything else done by these heartless, sanguinary pirates, not excepting the practice of cutting wings from living birds and leaving them to die of hemorrhage. In this dry cistern the living birds were kept by hundreds to slowly starve to death. In this way the fatty tissue lying next to the skin was used up, and the skin was left quite free from grease, so that it required little or no cleaning during preparation.

"Many other revolting sights, such as the remains of young birds that had been left to starve, and birds with broken legs and deformed beaks were to be seen. Killing clubs, nets and other implements used by these marauders were lying all about. Hundreds of boxes to be used in shipping the bird skins were packed in an old building. It was very evident they intended to carry on their slaughter as long as the birds lasted.

"Not only did they kill and skin the larger species but they caught and caged the finch, honey eater, and miller bird. Cages and material for making them were found."—(Report of an Expedition to Laysan Island in 1911. By Homer R. Dill, page 12.)

The report of Professor Bryan contains the following pertinent paragraphs:

"This wholesale killing has had an appalling effect on the colony. * * It is conservative to say that fully one-half the number of birds of both species of albatross that were so abundant everywhere in 1903 have been killed. The colonies that remain are in a sadly decimated condition. * * Over a large part of the island, in some sections a hundred acres in a place, that ten years ago were thickly inhabited by albatrosses not a single bird remains, while heaps of the slain lie as mute testimony of the awful slaughter of these beautiful, harmless, and without doubt beneficial inhabitants of the high seas.

"While the main activity of the plume-hunters was directed against the albatrosses, they were by no means averse to killing anything in the bird line that came in their way * * Fortunately, serious as were the depredations of the poachers, their operations were interrupted before any of the species had been completely exterminated."

But the work of the Evil Genius of Laysan did not stop with the slaughter of three hundred thousand birds. Mr. Schlemmer introduced rabbits and guinea-pigs; and these rapidly multiplying rodents now are threatening to consume every plant on the island. If the plants disappear, many of the insects will go with them; and this will mean the disappearance of the small insectivorous birds.

In February, 1909, President Roosevelt issued an executive order creating the Hawaiian Islands Reservation for Birds. In this are included Laysan and twelve other islands and reefs, some of which are inhabited by birds that are well worth preserving. By this act, we may feel that for the future the birds of Laysan and neighboring islets are secure from further attacks by the bloody-handed agents of the vain women who still insist upon wearing the wings and feathers of wild birds.

CHAPTER XV

UNFAIR FIREARMS, AND SHOOTING ETHICS

For considerably more than a century, the States of the American Union have enacted game-protective laws based on the principle that the wild game belongs to the People, and the people's senators, representatives and legislators generally may therefore enact laws for its protection, prescribing the manner in which it may and may not be taken and possessed. The soundness of this principle has been fully confirmed by the Supreme Court of the United States in the case of Geer *vs*. Connecticut, on March 2, 1896.

The tendency of predatory man to kill and capture wild game of all kinds by wholesale methods is as old as the human race. The days of the club, the stone axe, the bow and arrow and the flint-lock gun were contemporaneous with the days of great abundance of game. Now that the advent of breech-loaders, repeaters, automatics and fixed ammunition has rendered game scarce in all localities save a very few, the thoughtful man is driven to consider measures for the checking of destruction and the suppression of wholesale slaughter.

First of all, the deadly floating batteries and sail-boats were prohibited. To-day a punt gun is justly regarded as a relic of barbarism, and any man who uses one places himself beyond the pale of decent sportsmanship, or even of modern pot-hunting. Strange to say, although the unwritten code of ethics of English sportsmen is very strict, the English to this day permit wild-fowl hunting with guns of huge calibre, some of which are more like shot-cannons than shot-guns. And they say, "Well, there are still wild duck on our coast!"

Beyond question, it is now high time for the English people to take up the shot-gun question, and consider what to-day is fair and unfair in the killing of waterfowl. The supply of British ducks and geese can not forever withstand the market gunners and their shot-cannons. Has not the British wild-fowl supply greatly decreased during the past fifteen years? I strongly suspect that a careful investigation would reveal the fact that it has diminished. The Society for the Preservation of the Fauna of the Empire should look into the matter, and obtain a series of reports on the condition of the waterfowl to-day as compared with what it was twenty years ago.

In the United States we have eliminated the swivel guns, the punt guns and the very-big-bore guns. Among the real sportsmen the tendency is steadily toward shot-guns of small calibre, especially under 12-gauge. But, outside the ranks of sportsmen, we are now face to face with two automatic and five "pump" shotguns of deadly efficiency. Of these,

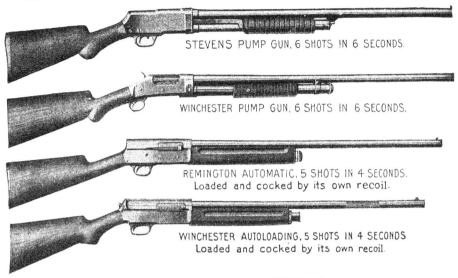

STEVENS PUMP GUN, 6 SHOTS IN 6 SECONDS.

WINCHESTER PUMP GUN, 6 SHOTS IN 6 SECONDS.

REMINGTON AUTOMATIC, 5 SHOTS IN 4 SECONDS.
Loaded and cocked by its own recoil.

WINCHESTER AUTOLOADING, 5 SHOTS IN 4 SECONDS
Loaded and cocked by its own recoil.

FOUR OF THE SEVEN MACHINE GUNS

more than one hundred thousand are being made and sold annually by the five companies that produce them. Recently the annual output has been carefully estimated from known facts to be about as follows:

Winchester Arms Co., New Haven, Conn.	
(1 Automatic and 1 Pump-gun)	50,000 guns.
Remington Arms Co., Ilion, N. Y.	
(1 Automatic and 1 Pump-gun)	25,000
Marlin Fire Arms Co., New Haven, Conn. 1 Pump-gun	12,000 "
Stevens Arms Co., Chicopee Falls, Mass. 1 Pump-gun	10,000 "
Union Fire Arms Co., 1 Pump-gun	5,000 '
	103,000 guns

THE ETHICS OF SHOOTING AND SHOT-GUNS.—Are the American people willing that their wild birds shall be shot by machinery?

In the ethics of sportsmanship, the anglers of America are miles ahead of the men who handle the rifle and shot-gun in the hunting field. Will the hunters ever catch up?

The anglers have steadily diminished the weight of the rod and the size of the line; and they have prohibited the use of gang hooks and nets. In this respect the initiative of the Tuna Club of Santa Catalina is worthy of the highest admiration. Even though the leaping tuna, the jewfish and the sword-fish are big and powerful, the club has elected to raise the standard of sportsmanship by making captures more difficult than ever before. A higher degree of skill, and nerve and judgment, is required in the angler who would make good on a big fish; and, incidentally, the fish has about double "the show" that it had fifteen years ago.

That is Sportsmanship!

But how is it with the men who handle the shot-gun?

By them, the Tuna Club's high-class principle has been exactly reversed! In the making of fishing-rods, commercialism plays small part; but in about forty cases out of every fifty the making of guns is solely a matter of dollars and profits.

Excepting the condemnation of automatic and pump guns, I think that few clubs of sportsmen have laid down laws designed to make shooting more difficult, and to give the game more of a show to escape. Thousands of gentlemen sportsmen have their own separate unwritten codes of honor, but so far as I know, few of them have been written out and adopted as binding rules of action. I know that among expert wing shots it is an unwritten law that quail and grouse must not be shot on the ground, nor ducks on the water. But, among the three million gunners who annually shoot in the United States how many, think you, are there who in actual practice observe any sentimental principles when in the presence of killable game? I should say about one man and boy out of every five hundred.

Up to this time, the great mass of men who handle guns have left it to the gunmakers to make their codes of ethics, and hand them out with the loaded cartridges, all ready for use.

For fifty years the makers of shot-guns and rifles have taxed their ingenuity and resources to make killing easier, especially for "amateur" sportsmen,—*and take still greater advantages of the game!* Look at this scale of progression:

FIFTY YEARS' INCREASE IN THE DEADLINESS OF FIREARMS.

KIND OF GUN.	ESTIMATED DEGREE OF DEADLINESS.
Single-shot muzzle loader	10
Single-shot breech-loader	30
Double-barrel breech-loader	50
Choke-bore breech-loader	60
Repeating rifle	60
Repeating rifle, with silencer	70
"Pump" shot-gun (6 shots)	90
Automatic or "autoloading" shot-guns, 5 shots	100

The Output of 1911.—At a recent hearing before a committee of the House of Representatives at Washington, a representative of the gun making industry reported that in the year 1911 ten American manufacturing concerns turned out the following:

> 391,875 shot-guns,
> 666,643 rifles, and
> 580,042 revolvers.

There are 66 factories producing firearms and ammunition, employing $39,377,000 of invested capital and 15,000 employees.

The sole and dominant thought of many gunmakers is to make the very deadliest guns that human skill can invent, sell them as fast as possible, and declare dividends on their stock. The Remington, Winchester, Marlin, Stevens and Union Companies are engaged in a mad race to see who can turn out the deadliest guns, and the most of them. On the market to-day there are five pump-guns, that fire six shots each, in about *six seconds*, without removal from the shoulder, by the quick sliding of a sleeve under the barrel, that ejects the empty shell and inserts a loaded one. There are two automatics that fire five shots each in *five seconds or less*, by five pulls on the trigger! *The autoloading gun is reloaded and cocked again wholly by its own recoil.* Now, if these are not machine guns, what are they?

In view of the great scarcity of feathered game, and the number of deadly machine guns already on the market, the production of the last and deadliest automatic gun (by the Winchester Arms Company), *already in great demand*, is a crime against wild life, no less.

Every human action is a matter of taste and individual honor.

It is natural for the duck-butchers of Currituck to love the automatic shot-guns as they do, because they kill the most ducks per flock. With two of them in his boat, holding *ten shots*, one expert duck-killer can,— and sometimes *actually does*, so it is said,—get every duck out of a flock, up to seven or eight.

It is natural for an awkward and blundering wing-shot to love the deadliest gun, in order that he may make as good a bag as an expert shot can make with a double-barreled gun. It is natural for the hunter who does not care a rap about the extermination of species to love the gun that will enable him to kill up to the bag limit, every time he takes the field. It is natural for men who don't think, or who think in circles, to say "so long as I observe the lawful bag limit, what difference does it make what kind of a gun I use?"

It is natural for the Remington, and Winchester, and Marlin gun makers to say, as they do, "Enforce the laws! Shorten the open seasons! Reduce the bag limit, and then it won't matter what guns are used! But,—DON'T touch autoloading guns! Don't hamper Inventive Genius!"

Is it not high time for American sportsmen to cease taking their moral principles and their codes of ethics from the gun-makers?

Here is a question that I would like to put before every hunter of game in America:

In view of the alarming scarcity of game, in view of the impending extermination of species by legal hunting, can any high-minded *sportsman*, can any *good citizen* either sell a machine shot-gun or use one in hunting?

A gentleman is incapable of taking an unfair advantage of any wild creature; therefore a gentleman cannot use punt guns for ducks, dynamite for game fish, or automatic or pump guns in bird-shooting. The machine guns and "silencers" are grossly unfair, and like gang-hooks, nets and dynamite for trout and bass, their use in hunting must every-

THE CHAMPION GAME SLAUGHTER CASE
One Hour's Slaughter (218 Geese) With Two Automatic Shot-Guns

where be prohibited by law.   Times have changed, and the lines for protection must be more tightly drawn.

The Supreme Court of Pennsylvania (Judge Orlady) has decided
that the Pennsylvania law against the use of automatic guns in hunting
is entirely constitutional, because every state has a right to say how its
game may and may not be killed.

It is up to the American People to say *now* whether their wild life
shall be slaughtered by machinery, or not.

If they are willing that it should be, then let us be consistent and say,
—away with all "conservation!"   The game conservators can endure a
gameless and birdless continent quite as well as the average citizen can.

How THEY WORK.—There are a few apologists for the automatic
and pump guns who cheerfully say, "So long as the bag limit is observed,
what difference does it make how the birds are killed?"

It is strange that a conscientious man should ask such a question,
when the answer is apparent.

We reply, "The difference is that an automatic or pump gun will kill
fully twice as many waterfowl as a double-barrel, *if not more;* and *it is
highly undesirable that every gunner should get the bag limit of birds, or any*

number near it! The birds can not stand it. Moreover, *the best states for ducks and geese have no bag limits on those birds!* To-day, on Currituck Sound, for example, the market hunters are killing all the waterfowl they can sell. On Marsh Island, Louisiana, one man has killed 369 ducks in one day, and another market gunner killed 430 in one day.

The automatic and the "pump" shot-guns are the favorite weapons of the game-hog who makes a specialty of geese and ducks. It is no uncommon thing for a gunner who shoots a machine gun to get, with one gun, as high as *eight* birds out of one flock. A man who has himself done this has told me so.

The Champion Game-Slaughter Case.—Here is a story from California that is no fairy tale. It was published, most innocently, in a western magazine, with the illustration that appears herewith, and in which please notice the automatic shot-gun:

"February 5th, I and a friend were at one of the Glenn County Club's camps. * * Neither of us having ever had the pleasure of shooting over live decoys, we were anxious, and could hardly wait for the sport to commence. On arriving at the scene we noticed holes which had been dug in the ground, just large enough for a man to crawl into. These holes were used for hiding places, and were deep enough so the sportsmen would be entirely out of sight of the game. The birds are so wild that to move a finger will frighten them. * *

"The decoys are wild geese which had been crippled and tamed for this purpose. They are placed inside of silk net fences which are located on each side of the holes dug for hiding places. These nets are the color of the ground and it is impossible for the wild geese flying overhead to detect the difference.

"After we had investigated everything the expert caller and owner of the outfit exclaimed: 'Into your holes!'

"We noticed in the distance a flock of geese coming. Our caller in a few seconds had their attention, and they headed towards our decoys. Soon they were directly over us, but out of easy range of our guns. We were anxious to shoot, but in obedience to our boss had to keep still, and soon noticed that the birds were soaring around and in a short time were within fifteen or twenty feet of us. At that moment we heard the command, 'Punch 'em!' and the bombardment that followed was beyond imagining. *We had fired five shots apiece and found we had bagged ten geese from this one flock.*

"At the end of one hour's shooting we had **218** birds to our credit and were out of ammunition.

"On finding that no more shells were in our pits we took our dead geese to the camp and returned with a new supply of ammunition. We remained in the pits during the entire day. When the sun had gone behind the mountains we summed up our kill and *it amounted to 450 geese!*

"The picture shown with this article gives a view of *the first hour's*

SLAUGHTERED ACCORDING TO LAW

A Result of a Faulty System. Such Pictures as this are Very Common in Sportsmen's Magazines
Note the Automatic Gun

shoot. A photograph would have been taken of the remainder of the shoot, but it being warm weather the birds had to be shipped at once in order to keep them from spoiling.

"Supper was then eaten, after which we were driven back to Willows; both agreeing that it was one of the greatest days of sport we ever had, and wishing that we might, through the courtesy of the Glenn County Goose Club, have another such day. C. H. B."

Another picture was published in a Canadian magazine, illustrating a story from which I quote:

"I fixed the decoys, hid my boat and took my position in the blind. My man started his work with a will and hustled the ducks out of every cove, inlet or piece of marsh for two miles around. I had barely time to slip the cartridges into my guns—*one a double and the other a five shot automatic*—when I saw a brace of birds coming toward me. They sailed in over my decoys. I rose to the occasion, and the leader up-ended and tumbled in among the decoys. The other bird, unable to stop quick enough, came directly over me. He closed his wings and struck the ground in the rear of the blind.

"More and more followed. Sometimes they came singly, and then in twos and threes. I kept busy and attended to each bird as quickly as possible. Whenever there was a lull in the flight I went out in the boat and picked up the dead, leaving the wounded to take chances with any gunner lucky enough to catch them in open and smooth water. A bird handy in the air is worth two wounded ones in the water. *Twice I took six dead birds out of the water for seven shots, and both guns empty.*

"The ball thus opened, the birds commenced to move in all directions. Until the morning's flight was over I was kept busy pumping lead, *first with the 10, then with the automatic*, reloading, picking up the dead, etc."

And the reader will observe that the harmless, innocent, inoffensive automatic shot gun, that "don't matter if you enforce the bag limit," figures prominently in both stories and both photographs.

A Story of Two Pump Guns and Geese:—It comes from Aberdeen, S. D. (Sand Lake), in the spring of 1911. Mr. J. J. Humphrey tells it, in *Outdoor Life* magazine for July, 1911.

"Smith and I were about a hundred yards from them [the flock of Canada geese], when Murphy scared them. They rose in a dense mass and came directly between Smith and me. We were about gunshot distance apart, and they were not over thirty feet in the air when we opened up on them with our pump guns and No. 5 shot. When the smoke cleared away and we had rounded up the cripples we found we had twenty-one geese. I have heard of bigger killings out in this country, but never positively knew of them."

So then: *those two gunners averaged 10½ wild geese per pump gun out of one flock!* And yet there are wise and reflective sportsmen who say, "What difference does the kind of gun make so long as you live up to the law?"

I think that the pump and automatic guns make about *75 per-cent of difference, against the game;* that is all!

The number of shot-guns now in use in the United States is almost beyond belief. About six years ago a gentleman interested in the manufacture of such weapons informed me, and his statement has never been disputed, that *every year* about 500,000 new shot-guns were sold in the United States. The number of shot cartridges annually produced by our four great cartridge companies has been reliably estimated as follows:

Winchester Arms Co	300,000,000
Union Metallic Cartridge Co	250,000,000
Peters Cartridge Co	150,000,000
Western Cartridge Co	75,000,000
	775,000,000

We must stop all the holes in the barrel, or eventually lose all the water. No group of bird-slaughterers is entitled to immunity. We will not "limit the bag, and enforce the laws," while we permit the makers and users of autoloading and pump guns to kill at will, as they demand.

Yes; we *will* "limit the bag" and "enforce the laws;" but the machine

National Association of Audubon Societies

FOUNDED 1901. INCORPORATED 1905.

For the Protection of Wild Birds and Animals

WILLIAM DUTCHER, President
JOHN E. THAYER, 1st Vice-President
THEO. S. PALMER, M. D., 2d Vice-President
T. GILBERT PEARSON, Secretary
FRANK M. CHAPMAN, Treasurer
SAMUEL T. CARTER, Jr., Attorney

OFFICES
525 Manhattan Avenue, New York City

141 Broadway.

Map showing (shaded) States having
Audubon Societies

Map showing (shaded) States which have adopted
the A. O. U. model law Protecting
the non-game birds

Feb. 26th 1906.

My dear Mr. Hornaday:—

It is with much surprise that I learn through your communication of even date that certain persons are claiming that the National Association of Audubon Societies for the Protection of Wild Animals and Birds is in favor of the use of automatic or pump guns, and consequently is not in favor of the passage of laws to prevent the use or sale of such firearms.

I beg officially to state that the National Association of Audubon Societies is absolutely opposed to either the manufacture, sale, or use of such firearms, and therefore hopes that the meritorious bill introduced by the New York Zoological Society will become a law.

I beg further to add that any statement contrary to the above in effect is unauthorized.

This society is working for the preservation of the wild birds and game of North America, and it sincerely should not stultify itself by advocating the use of one of the most potent means of destruction that has ever been devised.

You are at liberty to use this communication either publicly or privately.

Very sincerely yours,

Wm Dutcher, President.

A LETTER THAT TELLS ITS OWN STORY

guns and the alien shooters shall be eliminated at the same time! Each state has the power to regulate, absolutely, down to the smallest detail, the manner in which the game of The People shall be taken or not taken; and such laws are absolutely constitutional. If we can legislate punt guns and dynamite out of use, the machine guns and silencers can be treated similarly.

No immunity for wild-life exterminators.

The following unprejudiced testimony from a New York business man who is a sportsman, with a fine game preserve of his own, should be of general interest. It was written to G. O. Shields, March 21, 1906.

DEAR SIR:

Regarding the use of the automatic shot-gun, would say that I am a member of two southern ducking clubs where these guns are used very extensively. I have seen a flock of ducks come into a blind where one, two, or even three of these guns were in use, and have seen as many as eleven shots poured into a single flock.

We have considerable poaching on one of these clubs, the territory being so extensive that it is impossibe to prevent it. We own 60,000 acres, and these poachers, I am told, nearly all use the automatic guns. They frequently kill six or eight ducks out of one flock—first taking a raking shot on the water, and then getting in the balance of the magazine before the flock is out of range. In fact, some of them carry two guns, and are able to discharge a part of the second magazine into the same flock.

As I told you the other evening, I am not so much against the gun when in the hands of gentlemen and real sportsmen, but, on account of its terrible possibilities for market hunters, I believe that the only safe way is to abolish it entirely, and that the better class should be willing to give up this weapon as being the only means of putting a stop to this willful game slaughter.

                    Very truly yours,

                                    ARTHUR ROBINSON.

HOW *GENTLEMEN* SPORTSMEN REGARD AUTOMATIC AND PUMP GUNS

Each one of the following organizations, chiefly clubs of gentlemen sportsmen, have adopted strong resolutions condemning the use of automatic guns in hunting, and either requesting or recommending the enactment of laws against their use:

New York Zoological Society. . . . . Henry Fairfield Osborn, President
The Camp-Fire Club of America. . . . . Daniel C. Beard, President
Boone and Crockett Club. . . . . W. Austin Wadsworth, President
New York State Fish, Game and Forest League. . . . . 81 Clubs and Associations
New York Association for the Protection of Fish and Game. . Alfred Wagstaff, President
Lewis and Clark Club. . . . . John M. Phillips, President
League of American Sportsmen. .   . . . G. O. Shields, President
Wild Life Protective Association. . . . . W. T. Hornaday, President

WHERE AUTOMATIC GUNS ARE BARRED OUT BY LAW

PENNSYLVANIA, 1907	BRITISH COLUMBIA, 1911
NEW JERSEY, 1912	ONTARIO, 1907
SASKATCHEWAN, 1906	MANITOBA, 1909
NEW BRUNSWICK, 1907	ALBERTA, 1907
PRINCE EDWARD ISLAND, 1906	

SPORTSMEN'S CLUBS WHEREIN THEY ARE BARRED BY CODES OF ETHICS AND RULES

Adirondack League Club, New York
Blooming Grove Park Hunting
and Fishing Club, Penn.
Greenwing Gun Club, Ottawa, Ill
Western Ducking Club, Detroit, Minn.
Bolsa Chica Club, Los Angeles, Cal.
Westminster Club, Los Angeles, Cal.
Los Patos Club, Los Angeles, Cal.
Pocahontas Club, Va.

Tobico Hunting Club, Kawkawlin, Mich.
Turtle Lake Club, Turtle Lake, Mich.
Au Sable Forest Farm Club, Mich.
Wallace Ducking Club, Wild Fowl Bay,
Mich.
Lomita Club, Los Angeles, Cal.
Golden West Club, Los Angeles, Cal.
Recreation Club, Los Angeles, Cal.

A MODEL BILL TO PROHIBIT THE USE OF AUTOMATIC AND REPEATING SHOT GUNS IN HUNTING

Section 1. It shall be unlawful to use in hunting or shooting birds or animals of any kind, any automatic or repeating shot gun or pump gun, or any shot-gun holding more than two cartridges at one time, or that may be fired more than twice without removal from the shoulder for reloading.

Section 2. Violation of any provision of this act shall be punished by a fine of not less than twenty-five nor more than one hundred dollars for each offence; and the carrying, or possession in the woods, or in any field, or upon any water of any gun or other weapon the use of which is prohibited, as aforesaid, shall be prima facie evidence of the violation of this act.

The English 3-barrel "Scatter Rifle," for Ducks.—All gunners who find machine guns good enough for them will be delighted by the news that an Englishman whose identity is concealed under the initials "F. M. M." has invented and manufactured a 3-barreled rifle specially intended to kill ducks that are beyond the reach of a choke-bore shotgun. The weapon discharges all three barrels simultaneously. In the *London Field*, of Dec. 9, 1911, it is described by a writer who also thoughtfully conceals his identity under a nom-de-plume. After a trial of 48 shots, the writer declares that "the 3-barreled is a really practicable weapon," and that with it one could bag wild-fowl that were quite out of reach of any shot-gun. Just why a Gatling gun or a Maxim should not be employed for the same purpose, the writer fails to state. The use of either would be quite as sportsmanlike, and as fair to the game. There are great possibilities in ducking mortars, also.

The "Sunday Gun."—A new weapon of peculiar form and great deadliness to song birds, has recently come into use. Because of the manner of its use, it is known as the "Sunday gun." It is specially adapted to concealment on the person. A man could go through a reception with one of these deadly weapons absolutely concealed under his dress coat! It is a weapon with two barrels, rifle and shot; and it enables the user to kill anything from a humming-bird up to a deer. What the shot-barrel can not kill, the rifle will. It is not a gun that any sportsman would own, save as a curiosity, or for target use.

The State Ornithologist of Massachusetts, Mr. E. H. Forbush, informs me that already the "Sunday gun" has become a scourge to the bird life of that state. Thousands of them are used by men and boys who live in cities and towns, and are able to get into the country only on

Sundays. They conceal them under their coats, on Sunday mornings, go out into the country, and spend the day in shooting small birds and mammals. The dead birds are concealed in various pockets, the Sunday gun goes under the coat, and at nightfall the guerrilla rides back to the city with an innocent smile on his face, as if he had spent a day in harmless enjoyment of the beauties of nature.

The "Sunday gun" is on sale everywhere, and it is said to be in use both by American and Italian killers of song-birds. It weighs only two pounds, eight ounces, and its cost is so trifling that any guerrilla who wishes one can easily find the money for its purchase. There are in the United States at least a million men and boys quite mean enough to use this weapon on song-birds, swallows, woodpeckers, nuthatches, rabbits and squirrels, and like other criminals, hide both weapon and loot in their clothing. So long as this gun is in circulation, no small bird is safe, at any season, near any city or town.

Now, what are the People going to do about it?

My recommendation is that each state enact a law in the following terms:

Be it enacted, etc.—That from and after the passage of this act it shall be unlawful for any person to use in hunting, or to carry concealed on the person, any shotgun, or rifle, or combination of shotgun and rifle, with a barrel or barrels less than twenty-eight inches in length, or with a skeleton stock fixed on a hinge.

The carrying of any rifle or shotgun concealed on the person shall constitute a felony.

The penalties for hunting with any gun specially adapted to concealment should be not less than $50 fine or two months imprisonment at hard labor, and the carrying of such weapons concealed should be $100 or four months at hard labor.

Incidentally, we wonder what will be the next devilish device for the destruction of wild life that American inventive genius will produce.

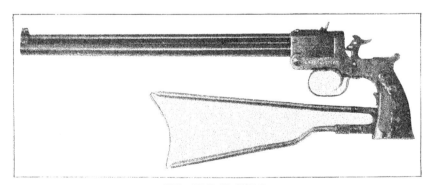

THE "SUNDAY GUN!"
A Deadly Combination of Concealable Rifle-and-Shot-Gun.

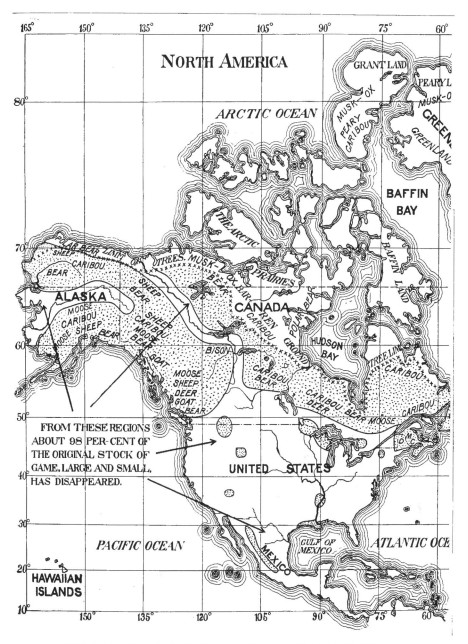

THE WILDERNESS OF NORTH AMERICA (SHADED) AND THE ARCTIC
PRAIRIES, WELL STOCKED WITH BIG GAME

CHAPTER XVI

THE PRESENT AND FUTURE OF NORTH AMERICAN BIG GAME

The subject of this chapter opens up a vast field of facts and conclusions, quite broad enough to fill a whole volume. In the space at our disposal here it is possible to offer only a summary of the subject, without attempting to prove our statements by the production of detailed evidence.

To say that all over the world, the large land mammals are being destroyed more rapidly than they are breeding, would not be literally true, for the reason that there are yet many areas that are almost untouched by the destroying hand of civilized man. It is true, however, that all the unspoiled areas rapidly are growing fewer and smaller. It is also true that in all the regions of the earth that ar easily penetrable by civilized man, the wild life is being killed faster than it breeds, and of necessity it is disappearing. This is why the British are now so urgently bestirring themselves to create game preserves in all the countries that they own.

It is one of the inexorable laws of Nature, to which I know of not one exception, that large hoofed animals which live on open plains, on open mountains, or in regions that are thinly forested, always are easily found and easily exterminated. All such animals have a weak hold on life. This is because it is so difficult for them to hide, and so very easy for man to creep up within the killing range of modern, high-power, long-range rifles. Is it not pitiful to think of animals like the caribou, moose, white sheep and bear trying to survive on the naked ridges and bald mountains of Yukon Territory and Alaska! With a modern rifle, the greatest duffer on earth can creep up within killing distance of any of the big game of the North.

The gray wolf is practically the only large animal that is able to hide successfully and survive in the treeless regions of the North; but his room is always preferable to his company, because he, too, is a destroyer of big game.

I am tempted to try to map out roughly what are to-day the unopened and undestroyed wild haunts of big game in North America. In doing this, however, I warn the reader not to be deceived into thinking that because game still exists in those regions, those areas therefore constitute a permanent preserve and safe breeding-ground for large mammals. That is very, very far from being the case. The further "opening up" of the wilderness areas, as I shall call them for convenience, can and surely will quickly wipe out their big game; for throughout nine-tenths of those areas it holds to life by very slender threads.

To-day the unopened and undestroyed wilderness areas of North America, wherein large mammals still live in a normal wild state, are in general as follows:

THE ARCTIC BARREN GROUNDS, or Arctic Prairies, north of the limit of trees, embracing the Barren Grounds of northern Canada, the great arctic archipelago, Ellesmere, Melville and Grant Lands and Greenland. This region is the home of the musk-ox and three species of arctic caribou.

THE ALASKA-YUKON REGION, inhabited by the moose, white mountain sheep, mountain goat, four species of caribou, and half a dozen species of Alaska brown, grizzly and black bears.

NORTHERN ONTARIO, QUEBEC, LABRADOR AND NEWFOUNDLAND, inhabited by moose, woodland caribou, white-tailed deer and black bear.

BRITISH COLUMBIA, inhabited by a magnificent big-game fauna embracing the moose, elk, caribou of two species, white sheep, black sheep, big-horn sheep, mule deer, white-tailed deer, mountain goat, grizzly, black and inland white bears.

THE SIERRA MADRE OF MEXICO, containing jaguar, puma, grizzly and black bears, mule deer, white-tailed deer, antelope, mountain sheep and peccaries.

I have necessarily omitted all those regions of the United States and Canada that still contain a remnant of big game, but have been literally "shot to pieces" by gunners.

In the United States and southern Canada there are about fifteen localities which contain a supply of big game sufficient that a conscientious sportsman might therein hunt and kill one head per year with a clear conscience. *All others should be closed for five years!* Here is the list of availables; and regarding it there will be about as many opinions as there are big-game sportsmen:

HUNTING GROUNDS IN AND NEAR THE UNITED STATES AND
SOUTHERN CANADA WHEREIN IT IS RIGHT TO
HUNT BIG GAME

THE MAINE WOODS: Well stocked with white-tailed deer.

NEW BRUNSWICK: Well stocked with moose; a few caribou, deer and black bear.

WHITE MOUNTAINS OF NEW HAMPSHIRE AND VERMONT: For deer.

THE ADIRONDACKS, NEW YORK: Well stocked with white-tailed deer, only.

PENNSYLVANIA MOUNTAINS: Contain many deer and black bears, and soon will contain more.

NORTHERN MINNESOTA: Deer and moose.

NORTHERN MICHIGAN AND WISCONSIN: White-tailed deer.

NORTHWESTERN WYOMING: Thousands of elk in fall and winter; a few deer, grizzly and black bears, but no sheep that it would be right to kill.

WESTERN AND SOUTHWESTERN MONTANA: Elk in season, mule and white-tail deer; no sheep that it would be right to kill.

NORTHWESTERN MONTANA: Mule and white-tailed deer, only. No sheep, bear, moose, elk or antelope *to kill!*

WYOMING, EAST OF YELLOWSTONE PARK: A few elk, by migration from the Park; a few deer, and bear of two species.

NORTHERN WOODS OF ONTARIO AND QUEBEC: Moose; deer.

SOUTHERN BRITISH COLUMBIA: Goat, a few sheep and deer; grizzly bear. Moose, caribou and elk should not be killed.

NORTHERN BRITISH COLUMBIA: Six fine species of big game.

NORTHWESTERN ALBERTA: Grizzly bear, big-horn and mountain goat.

Under existing conditions I regard the above-named hunting grounds as *nearly all* in which it is right or fair for big-game hunting now to be permitted, even on a strict basis. Nearly all others should immediately be closed, for large game, for ten years.

Of course such a proceeding, if carried into effect, would provoke loud protests from sportsmen, gunners, game-hogs, pot-hunters and others; but I only wish to high heaven that we had the power to carry such a program as that into effect! *Then we would see some game in ten years;* and our grand-children would thank us for some real big-game protection at a critical period.

Except in the few localities above-mentioned, I regard the big-game situation in the United States and southern Canada as particularly desperate. Unless there is an immediate and complete revolution in this country from an era of slaughter to an era of preservation, as sure as the sun rises on the morrow, outside of the hard and fast game preserves, and places like Maine and the Adirondacks, this generation of Americans and near-Americans will live to see our country *swept clean of big game!*

Two years ago, I did not believe this; but I do now. It is impossible to exaggerate the wide extent or the seriousness of this situation. In a country where any and every individual can rise and bluster, "I'm-just-as-good-as-*you*-are," and bellow for his "rights" as a "tax-payer," there is no stopping the millions who kill whenever there is an open season. And to many Americans, no right is dearer than the right to kill the game which by even the commonest law of equity belongs, not to the shooter exclusively, but partly to two thousand other persons who don't shoot at all!

Unless we come to an "About, face!" in quick time, all our big game outside the preserves is doomed to sure and quick extermination. This is not an individual opinion, merely: it is a *fact;* and a hundred thousand men know it to be such.

Last winter (1911-12), because the deer of Montana were driven by cold and hunger out of the mountains and far down into the ranchmen's valleys, eleven thousand of them were ruthlessly slaughtered. State Game Warden Avare says that often heads of families took out as many licenses as there were persons in the family, and the whole quota was killed. Such people deserve to go deerless into the future; but we can not allow them to rob innocent people.

OUR SPECIES OF BIG GAME

THE PRONG-HORNED ANTELOPE, unique and wonderful, will be one of *the first species of North American big game to become totally extinct.* We may see this come to pass within twenty years. They can not be bred in protection, *save in very large fenced ranges.* They are delicate, capricious, and easily upset. They die literally "at the drop of a hat." They are quite subject to actinomycosis (lumpy-jaw), which in wild animals is incurable.

Already all the states that possess wild antelope, except Nevada, have passed laws giving that species long close seasons; which is highly creditable to the states that have done their duty. Nevada must get in line at the next session of her legislature!

In 1908, Dr. T. S. Palmer published in his annual report of "Progress in Game Protection" the following in regard to the prong-horned antelope:

"Antelope are still found in diminished numbers in fourteen western states. A considerable number were killed during the year in Montana, where the species seems to have suffered more than elsewhere since the season was opened in 1907.

"A striking illustration of the decrease of the antelope is afforded by Colorado. In 1898 the State Warden estimated that there were 25,000 in the state, whereas in 1908 the Game Commissioner places the number at only 2,000. The total number of antelope now in the United States probably does not exceed 17,000, distributed approximately as follows:

Colorado	2,000	Yellowstone Park	2,000
Idaho	200	Other States	2,000
Montana	4,000		
New Mexico	1,300	Saskatchewan	2,000
Oregon	1,500		
Wyoming	4,000		19,000

To-day (1912), Dr. Palmer says the total number of antelope is less than it was in 1908, and in spite of protection the number is steadily diminishing. This is indeed serious news. The existing bands, already small, are steadily growing smaller. The antelope are killed lawlessly, and the crimes of such slaughter are, in nearly every instance, successfully concealed.

Previously, we have based strong hopes for the preservation of the antelope species on the herd in the Yellowstone Park, but those animals are vanishing fearfully fast. In 1906, Dr. Palmer reported that "About fifteen hundred antelope came down to the feeding grounds near the haystacks in the vicinity of Gardiner." In 1908 the Yellowstone Park

PRONG-HORNED ANTELOPE

was credited with two thousand head.   *To-day, the number alive, by actual count, is only five hundred head*; and this after twenty-five years of protection!   Where have the others gone?   This shows, alas! that perpetual close seasons can not *always* bring back the vanished thousands of game!

Here is a reliable report (June 29, 1912) regarding the prong-horned antelope in Lower California, from E. W. Nelson: "Antelope formerly ranged over nearly the entire length of Lower California, but are now gone from a large part of their ancient range, and their steadily decreasing numbers indicate their early extinction throughout the peninsula."

In captivity the antelope is exasperatingly delicate and short-lived. It has about as much stamina as a pet monkey. As an exhibition animal in zoological gardens and parks it is a failure; for it always looks faded, spiritless and dead, like a stuffed animal ready to be thrown into the discard.   Zoologists can not save the prong-horn species save at long range, in preserves so huge that the sensitive little beast will not even suspect that it is confined.

Two serious attempts have been made to transplant and acclimatize the antelope—in the Wichita National Bison Range, in Oklahoma. and in the Montana Bison Range, at Ravalli. In 1911 the Boone and Crockett Club provided a fund which defrayed the expenses of shipping from the Yellowstone Park a small nucleus herd to each of those ranges. Eight were sent to the Wichita Range, of which five arrived alive. Of the seven sent to the Montana Range, four arrived alive and were duly set free. While it seems a pity to take specimens from the Yellowstone Park herd, the disagreeable fact is that there is no other source on which to draw for breeding stock.

The Provinces of Alberta and Saskatchewan, in Canada, still permit the hunting and killing of antelope; which is wholly and entirely wrong.

THE BIG-HORN SHEEP.—Of North American big game, the big-horn of the Rockies will be, after the antelope, the next species to become extinct outside of protected areas. In the United States that event is fast approaching. It is far nearer than even the big-game sportsmen realize. There are to-day only two localities in the four states that still *think* they have killable sheep, in which it is worth while to go sheep-hunting. One is in Montana, and the other is in Wyoming. In the United States a really big, creditable ram may now be regarded as an impossibility. There are now perhaps half a dozen guides who can find killable sheep in our country, but the game is nearly always young rams, under five years of age.

That Wyoming, Montana, Idaho and Washington still continue to permit sheep slaughter is outrageous. Their answer is that "The sportsmen won't stand for stopping it altogether." I will add:—and the great mass of peeople are too criminally indifferent to take a hand in the matter, and *do their duty* regardless of the men of blood.

The seed stock of big-horn sheep now alive in the United States aggregates a pitifully small number. After twenty-five years of unbroken protection in Colorado, Dillon Wallace estimates, after an investigation on the ground, that the state possesses perhaps thirty-five hundred head. He credits Montana and Wyoming with five hundred each—which I think is far too liberal a number. I do not believe that either of those states contains more than one hundred unprotected sheep, at the very utmost limit. If there are more, where are they?

In the Yellowstone Park there are 210 head, safe and sound, and slowly increasing. I can not understand why they have not increased more rapidly than they have. In Glacier Park, now under permanent protection, three guides on Lake McDonald, in 1910, estimated the number of sheep at seven hundred. Idaho has in her rugged Bitter Root and Clearwater Mountains and elsewhere, a remnant of possibly two hundred sheep, and Washington has only what chemists call "a trace." It has recently been discovered that California still contains "a few sheep, and in southwestern Nevada there are a few more.

In Utah, the big-horn species is probably quite extinct. In Arizona, there are a few very small bands, very widely scattered. They are in the Santa Catalina Mountains, the Grand Canyon country, the Gila Range, and the Quitovaquita Mountains, near Sonoyta. But who

can protect from slaughter those Arizona sheep?   Absolutely no one!
They are too few and too widely scattered for the game wardens to keep
in touch with them.   The "prospectors" have them entirely at their
mercy, and the world well knows what prospectors' "mercy" to edible
big game looks like on the ground.   It leads straight to the frying-pan,
the coyotes and the vultures.

The Lower California peninsula contains about five hundred mountain sheep, without the slightest protection save low, desert mountains,
heat and thirst.   But that is no real protection whatever.   Those sheep
are too fine to be butchered the way they have been, and now are being,
butchered.   In 1908 I strongly called the attention of the Mexican Government to the situation; and the Departmento de Fomento secured the
issue of an executive order forbidding the hunting of any big game in
Lower California without the written authority of the government.   I
am sure, however, that owing to the political and military upheaval
it never stopped the slaughter of sheep.   In such easy mountains as those
of Lower California, it is a simple matter to exterminate quickly all the
mountain sheep that they possess.   The time for President Madero
and his cabinet to inaugurate serious protective measures has fully
arrived.

Both British Columbia and Alberta have even yet fine herds of big-
horn, and we can count three large game preserves in which they are
protected.   They are Goat Mountain Park (East Kootenay district, between the Elk and Bull Rivers); the Rocky Mountains Park, near
Banff, and Waterton Lakes Park, in the southwestern corner of Alberta.

In view of the number of men who desire to hunt them, the bag limit
on big-horn rams in British Columbia and Alberta still is too liberal, by
half.   One ram per year for one man is *quite enough;* quite as much so
as one moose is the limit everywhere.   To-day "a big, old ram" is
regarded by sportsmen as a much more desirable and creditable trophy
than a moose; because moose-killing is easy, and the bagging of an old
mountain ram in real mountains requires five times as much effort and
skill.

The splendid high and rugged mountains of British Columbia and
Alberta form an ideal home for the big-horn (and mountain goat), and it
would be an international calamity for that region to be denuded of its
splendid big game.   With resolute intent and judicial treatment that
region can remain a rich and valuable hunting ground for five hundred
years to come.   Under falsely "liberal" laws, it can be shot into a state
of complete desolation within ten years, or even less.

Other Mountain Sheep.—In northern British Columbia, north of
Iskoot Lake, there lies a tremendous region, extending to the Arctic
Ocean, and comprehending the whole area between the Rocky Mountain
continental divide and the waters of the Pacific.   Over the southern end
of this great wilderness ranges the black mountain sheep, and throughout
the remainder, with many sheepless intervals, is scattered the white
mountain sheep.

Owing to the immensity of this wilderness, the well-nigh total lack of railroads and also of navigable waters, excepting the Yukon, it will not be thoroughly "opened up" for a quarter of a century. The few resolute and pneumonia-proof sportsmen who can wade into the country, pulling boats through icy-cold mountain streams, are not going to devastate those millions of mountains of their big game. The few head of game which sportsmen can and will take out of the great northwestern wilderness during the next twenty-five years will hardly be missed from the grand total, even though a few easily-accessible localities are shot out. It is the deadly resident trappers, hunters and prospectors who must be feared! And again,—*who* can control them? Can any wilderness government on earth make it possible? Therefore, *in time, even the great wilderness will be denuded of big game.* This is absolutely fixed and certain; for within much less than another century, every square rod of it will have been gone over by prospectors, lumbermen, trappers and skin-hunters, and raked again and again with fine-toothed combs. A railway line to Dawson, the Copper River and Cook Inlet is to-day merely the next thing to expect, after Canada's present railway program has been wrought out.

Yes, indeed! In time the wilderness will be opened up, and the big game will *all* be shot out, save from the protected areas.

THE MOUNTAIN GOAT.—Even yet, this species is not wholly extinct in the United States. It survives in Glacier Park, Montana, and the number estimated in that region by three guide friends is too astoundingly large to mention.

This animal is much more easily killed than the big-horn. Its white coat renders it fatally conspicuous at long range during the best hunting season; it is almost devoid of fear, and it takes altogether too many chances on man. Thanks to the rage for sheep horns, the average sportsman's view-point regarding wild life ranks a goat head about six contours below "old ram" heads, in desirability. Furthermore, most guides regard the flesh of the goat as almost unfit for use as food, and far inferior to that of the big-horn. These reasons, taken together, render the goats much less persecuted by the sportsmen, ranchmen and prospectors who enter the home of the two species. It was because of this indifference toward goats that in 1905 Mr. John M. Phillips and his party saw 243 goats in thirty days in Goat Mountain Park, and only fourteen sheep.

Unless the preferences of western sportsmen and gunners change very considerably, the coast mountains of the great northwestern wilderness will remain stocked with wild mountain goats until long after the last big-horn has been shot to death. Fortunately, the skin of the mountain goat has no commercial value. I think it was in 1887 that I purchased, in Denver, 150 nicely tanned skins of our wild white goat *at fifty cents each!* They were wanted for the first exhibit ever made to illustrate the extermination of American large mammals, and they were shown at the Louisville Exposition. It must have cost the price of those skins to tan them; and I was pleased to know that some one lost money on the venture.

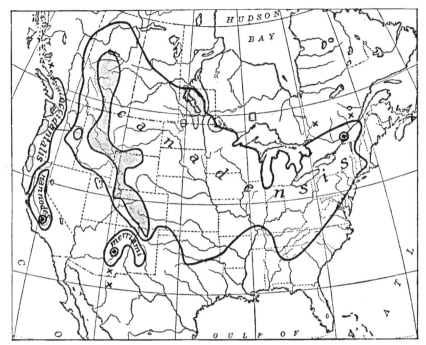

MAP OF THE FORMER AND EXISTING RANGES OF THE AMERICAN ELK

From "Life History of Northern Animals," Copyright 1909 by E. T. Seton

At present the mountain goat extends from north-western Montana to the head of Cook Inlet, but it is not found in the interior or in the Yukon valley. Whenever man decides that the species has lived long enough, he can quickly and easily exterminate it. It is one of the most picturesque and interesting wild animals on this continent, and there is not the slightest excuse for shooting it, save as a specimen of natural history Like the antelope, it is so unique as a natural curiosity that it deserves to be taken out of the ranks of animals that are regularly pursued as game.

THE ELK.—The story of the progressive extermination of the Ameri can elk, or wapiti, covers practically the same territory as the tragedy of the American bison—one-third of the mainland of North America. The former range of the elk covered absolutely the garden ground of our continent, omitting the arid region. Its boundary extended from central Massachusetts to northern Georgia, southern Illinois, northern Texas and central New Mexico, central Arizona, the whole Rocky Mountain region up to the Peace River, and Manitoba. It skipped the arid country west of the Rockies, but it embraced practically the whole Pacific slope from central California to the north end of Vancouver Island. Mr. Seton roughly calculated the former range of *canadensis* at two and a half million square miles, and adds: "We are safe, therefore, in believing that in those days there may have been ten million head."

The range of the elk covered a magnificent domain. The map prepared by Mr. Ernest T. Seton, after twenty years of research, is the last word on the subject. It appears on page 43, Vol. I, of his great work, "Life Histories of Northern Animals," and I have the permission of author and publisher to reproduce it here, as an object lesson in wild-animal extermination. Mr. Seton recognizes (for convenience, only?) four forms of American elk, two of which, *C. nannodes* and *occidentalis*, still exist on the Pacific Coast. The fourth, *Cervus merriami*, was undoubtedly a·valid species. It lived in Arizona and New Mexico, but became totally extinct near the beginning of the present century.

In 1909 Mr. Seton published in the work referred to above a remarkably close estimate of the number of elk then alive in North America. Recently, a rough count—the first ever made—of the elk in and around the Yellowstone Park, revealed the real number of that largest contingent. By taking those results, and Mr. Seton's figures for elk outside the United States, we obtain the following very close approximation of the wild elk alive in North America in 1912:

LOCALITY	NUMBER	AUTHORITY
Yellowstone Park and vicinity........	47,000	U. S. Biological Survey.
Idaho (permanently),................	600	
Washington........................	1,200	Game Warden Chris. Morgenroth.
Oregon............................	500	
California.........................	400	
New York, Adirondacks.............	400	State Conservation Commission.
Minnesota........................	50	E. T. Seton.
Vancouver Island.....	2,000	E. T. Seton.
British Columbia (S.-E.)............	200	E. T. Seton.
Alberta...........................	1,000	E. T. Seton.
Saskatchewan.....................	500	E. T. Seton
In various Parks and Zoos..........	1,000	E. T. Seton.
Total, for all America.	54,850	

In 1905, a herd of twenty of the so-called dwarf elk of the San Joaquin Valley, California, were taken to the Sequoia National Park, and placed in a fenced range that had been established for it on the Kaweah River.

The extermination of the wapiti began with the settlement of the American colonies. Naturally, the largest animals were the ones most eagerly sought by the meat-hungry pioneers, and the elk and bison were the first game species to disappear. The colonists believed in the survival of the fittest, and we are glad that they did. The one thing that a hungry pioneer cannot withstand is—temptation—in a form that embraces five hundred pounds of succulent flesh. And let it not be supposed that in the eastern states there were only a few elk. The Pennsylvania salt licks were crowded with them, and the early writers describe them as existing in "immense bands" and "great numbers."

Of course it is impossible for wild animals of great size to exist in countries that are covered with farms, villages and people. Under such conditions the wild and the tame cannot harmonize. It is a fact, however, that elk could exist and thrive in every national forest and national park in our country, and also on uncountable hundreds of thousands of rough, wild, timbered hills and mountains such as exist in probably twenty-five different states. There is no reason, except man's short-sighted greed and foolishness, why there are not to-day one hundred thousand elk living in the Allegheny Mountains, furnishing each year fifty thousand three-year-old males as free food for the people.

The trouble is,—the greedy habitants *could not* be induced to kill only the three-year-old-males, in the fall, and let the cows, calves and breeding bulls alone! By sensible management the Rocky Mountains, the Sierra Nevadas and the Coast Range would support enough wild elk to feed a million people. But we Americans seem utterly incapable of maintaining anywhere from decade to decade a large and really valuable supply of wild game. Outside the Yellowstone Park and northwestern Wyoming, the American elk exists only in small bands—mere remnants and samples of the millions we could and should have.

If they could be protected, and the surplus presently killed according to some rational, working system, then *every national forest in the United States should be stocked with elk!* In view of the awful cost of beef (to-day 10½ cents per pound in Chicago *on the hoof!*), it is high time that we should consider the raising of game on the public domain on such lines that it would form a valuable food supply without diminishing the value of the forests.

Just now (1912) the American people are sorely puzzled by a remarkable elk problem that each winter is presented for solution in the Jackson Hole country, Wyoming. Driven southward by the deep snows of winter, the elk thousands that in summer graze and grow fat in the Yellowstone Park march down into Jackson Hole, to find in those valleys less snow and more food. Now, it happens that the best and most of the former winter grazing grounds of the elk are covered by fenced ranches! As a result, the elk that strive to winter there, about fifteen thousand head, are each winter threatened with starvation; and during three or four winters of recent date, an aggregate of several thousand calves, weak yearlings and weakened cows perished of hunger. The winters of 1908, 1909 and 1910 were progressively more and more severe; and 1911 saw about 2500 deaths, (S. N. Leek).

In 1909-10, the State of Wyoming spent $7,000 for hay, and fed it to the starving elk. In 1911, Wyoming spent $5,000 more, and appealed to Congress for help. Thanks to the efforts of Senator Lodge and others, Congress instantly responded with a splendid emergency appropriation of $20,000, partly for the purpose of feeding the elk, and also to meet the cost of transporting elsewhere as many of the elk as it might seem best to move. The starving of the elk ceased with 1911.

Outdoor Life magazine (Denver, Colo.) for August, 1912, contains an excel`ent article by Dr. W. B. Shore, entitled, "Trapping and Shipping Elk." I wish I could reprint it entire, for the solid information that it contains. It gives a clear and comprehensive account of last spring's operations by the Government and by the state of Montana in capturing and shipping elk from the Yellowstone Park herd, for the double purpose of diminishing the elk surplus in the Park and stocking vacant ranges elsewhere.

The operations were conducted on the same basis as the shipping of cattle—the corral, the chute, the open car, and the car-load in bulk. Dr. Shore states that the undertaking was really no more difficult than the shipping of range cattle; but the presence of a considerable proportion of young and tender calves, such as are never handled with beef cattle, led to 8.8 per cent of deaths in transit. The deaths and the percentage are nothing at which to be surprised, when it is remembered that the animals had just come through a hard winter, and their natural vitality was at the lowest point of the year.

The following is a condensed summary of the results of the work:

Destination		Number of Elk	Hours on Road	Killed or Died in Car	Died After Unloading
1 Car.	Startup, Washington.	60: calves, yearlings and two-year olds	94	11	-
1 "	Hamilton, Montana	43: cows & calves	30	4	1
1 "	Thompson Falls, Montana	40		2	0
1 "	Stephensville, Montana	36		1	1
1 "	Deer Lodge, Montana	40	24	2	0
1 "	Hamilton, Montana.	40		0	0
1 "	Mt. Vernon, Washington	46	4 days; unloaded & fed twice	7	0
		305		27	9

The total deaths in transit and after, of 36 elk out of 305, amounted to 11.4 per cent. All those shipped to Montana points were shipped by the state of Montana.

In order to provide adequate winter grazing grounds for the Yellowstone-Wyoming elk, it seems imperative that the national government should expend between $30,000 and $40,000 in buying back from ranchmen certain areas in the Jackson valley, particularly a tract known as "the swamp," and others on the surrounding foothills where the herds annually go to graze in winter. A measure to render this possible was presented to Congress in the winter of 1912, and without opposition an appropriation of $45,000 was made.

The splendid photographs of the elk herds that recently have been made by S. N. Leek, of Jackson Hole, clearly reveal the fact that the

HUNGRY ELK IN JACKSON HOLE. WYOMING
Part of a Herd of About 2,500 Head, being fed on hay, in the Winter of 1910-11
Note the Absence of Adult Bulls.   Copyright, 1911, by S. N. Leek

herds now consist chiefly of cows, calves, yearlings and young bulls with small antlers. In one photograph showing about twenty-five hundred elk, there are not visible even half a dozen pairs of antlers that belong to adult bulls. There should be a hundred! This condition means that the best bulls, with the finest heads, are constantly being selected and killed by sportsmen and others who want their heads; and the young, immature bulls are left to do the breeding that alone will sustain the species.

It is a well-known principle in stock-breeding that sires should be fully adult, of maximum strength, and in the prime of life. No stock-breeder in his senses ever thinks of breeding from a youthful, immature sire. The result would be weak offspring not up to the standard.

This inexorable law of inheritance and transmission is just as much a law for the elk, moose and deer of North America as it is for domestic cattle and horses. If the present conditions in the Wyoming elk herds continue to prevail for several generations, as sure as time goes on we shall see a marked deterioration in the size and antlers of the elk.

If the foundation principles of stock-breeding are correct, then it is im possible to maintain any large-mammal species at its zenith of size, strength and virility by continuous breeding of the young and imma ture males.   By some sportsmen it is believed that through long-con tinued killing of the finest and largest males, the red deer of Europe have been growing smaller; but on that point I am not prepared to offer evidence.

In regard to the in-breeding of the elk herds in large open parks and preserves throughout North America, there are positively *no ill effects to fear*. Wild animals that are *closely* confined generation after generation are bound to deteriorate physically; but with healthy wild animals living in large open ranges, feeding and breeding naturally, the in-breeding that occurs produces no deterioration.

In the twin certainties of over-population, and deterioration from excessive killing of the good sires, we have to face two new problems of very decided importance. Nothing short of very radical measures will provide a remedy. For the immediate future, I can offer a solution. While it seems almost impossible deliberately to kill females, I think that the present is a very exceptional case, and one that compels us to apply the painful remedy that I now propose.

Premises: 1.—There are at present *too many* breeding cows in the Yellowstone herds.

2.—There are far too few good breeding bulls.

Conclusion:—For five years, entirely prohibit the killing of adult male elk, and kill only females, and young males. This would gradually diminish the number of calves born each year, by about 2,500, and by the end of five years it would reduce the number, *and the annual birth*, of females to a figure sufficiently limited that the herds could be maintained on existing ranges.

Corollary.—At the end of five years, stop killing females, and kill only *young* males. This plan would permit a large number of bull elk to mature; and then the largest and strongest animals would do the breeding,—just as Nature always intends shall be done.

SOUTH AMERICA

Of all the big-game regions of the earth, South America is the poorest. Of hoofed game she possesses only a dozen species that are worth the attention of sportsmen; and like all other animal life in that land of little game, they are desperately hard to find. In South America you must work your heart out in order to get either game or specimens that will be worth showing.

At present, we need not worry about the marsh deer, the pampas deer, the guemal, or the venado, nor the tapir, jaguar, ocelot and bears. All these species are abundantly able to take care of themselves; and to find and kill any one of them is a man's task. In Patagonia the natives do wastefully slaughter the guanacos; and there are times also when great numbers of guanacos come down in winter to certain mountain lakes, presumably in search of food, and perish by hundreds through starvation. (H. Hesketh Prichard.)

MEXICO

About ten years more will see the extinction of the mountain sheep of Lower California,—in the wake of the recently exterminated Mexican sheep of the Santa Maria Lakes region. In 1908, I solemnly warned the government of President Diaz, and at that time the Mexican government expressed much concern.

It is a great pity that just now political conditions are completely estopping wild-life protection in Mexico; but it is true. If the code of proposed laws that I drew up (by request) in 1908 and submitted to Minister Molina were adopted, it would have a good effect on the fauna of Mexico.

In Mexico there is little hoofed game to kill,—deer of the white-tail groups, seven or eight species; the desert mule deer; the brocket; the prong-horned antelope, the mountain sheep and the peccary. The deer will not so easily be exterminated, but the antelope and sheep will be utterly destroyed. They will be the first to go; and I think they can not by any possibility last longer than ten years. Is it not too bad that Mexico should permit her finest species of hoofed and horned game to be obliterated before she awakens to the desirability of conservation! The Mexicans could protect their small stock of big game if they would; but in Lower California they are leasing huge tracts of land to cattle companies, and they permit the lessees to kill all the wild game they please on their leased lands, even with the aid of ·dogs. This is a vicious and fatal system, and contrary to all the laws of nations.

CHAPTER XVII

PRESENT AND FUTURE OF NORTH AMERICAN BIG GAME
(Concluded)

THE WHITE-TAILED DEER.—Five hundred years hence, when the greed and rapacity of "civilized" man has completed the loot and ruin of the continent of North America, the white-tailed deer will be the last species of our big game to be exterminated. Its mental traits, its size, its color and its habits all combine to render it the most persistent of our large animals, and the best fitted to survive. It neither bawls nor bugles to attract its enemies, it can not be called to a sportsman, like the moose, and it sticks to its timber with rare and commendable closeness. When it sees a strange living thing walking erect, it does not stop to stare and catch soft-nosed bullets, but dashes away in quest of solitude.

The worst shooting that I ever did or saw done at game was at running white-tailed deer, in the Montana river bottoms.

For the reasons given, the white-tail exists and persists in a hundred United States localities from which all other big game save the black bear have been exterminated. For example, in our Adirondacks the moose were exterminated years and years ago, but the beloved wilderness called the "North Woods" still is populated by about 20,000 deer, and about 8,000 are killed annually. The deer of Maine are sufficiently numerous that in 1909 a total of 15,879 were killed. With some assistance from the thin sprinkling of moose and caribou, the deer of Maine annually draw into that state, for permanent dedication, a huge sum of money, variously estimated at from $1,000,000 to $2,000,000. In spite of heavy slaughter, and vigorous attempts at extermination by over-shooting, the deer of northern Michigan obstinately refuse to be wiped out.

There is, however, a large group of states in which this species has been exterminated. The states comprising it are Ohio, Indiana, Illinois, Iowa, and adjacent portions of seven other states.

As if to shame the people of Iowa, a curious deer episode is recorded. In 1885, W. B. Cuppy, of Avoca, Iowa, purchased five deer, and placed them in a paddock on his 600-acre farm. By 1900 they had increased to 32 head; and then one night some one kindly opened the gate of their enclosure, and gave them the freedom of the city. Mr. Cuppy made no effort to capture them, possibly because they decided to annex his farm as their habitat. When a neighbor led them with a bait of corn to their owner's door, he declined to impound them, on the ground that it was unnecessary.

By 1912, those deer had increased to 400, and the portion of this story that no one will believe is this: they spread all through the suburbs and hinterland farms of Avoca, and *the people not only failed to assassinate all of them and eat them, but they actually killed only a few, protected the rest, and made pets of many!* Queer people, those men and boys of Avoca. Nearly everywhere else in the world that I know, that history would have been ended differently. Here in the East, 90 per cent of our people are like the Avocans, but the other 10 per cent think only of slaying and eating, sans mercy, sans decency, sans law. Now the State of Iowa has taken hold, to capture some of those deer, and set them free in other portions of the state.

Elsewhere I shall note the quick and thorough success with which the white-tailed deer has been brought back in Vermont, Massachusetts, Connecticut, and southern New York.

No state having waste lands covered with brush or timber need be without the ubiquitous white-tailed deer. Give them a semblance of a fair show, and they will live and breed with surprising fecundity and persistence. If you start a park herd with ten does, soon you will have more deer than you will know how to dispose of, unless you market them under a Bayne law, duly tagged by the state. In close confinement this species fares rather poorly. In large preserves it does well, but during the rutting season the bucks are to be dreaded; and those that develop aggressive traits should be shot and marketed. This is the only way in which the deer parks of England are kept safe for unarmed people.

Dr. T. S. Palmer has taken much pains to ascertain the number of deer killed in the eastern United States. His records, as published in May, 1910, are as follows:

STATE	1908	1909	1910	STATE	1908	1909	1910
Maine..........	15,000	15,879	15,000	Virginia........	207	210	224
New Hampshire.	(a)	(a)	(a)	North Carolina.	(a)	(a)	(a)
Vermont........	2,700	4,736	3,649	South Carolina.	1,000	(a)	(a)
New York.......	6,000	9,000	9,000	Georgia........	(a)	367	369
New Jersey......	. . . .	(a)	120	Florida.........	2,209	2,021	1,526
Pennsylvania....	500	500	800	Alabama.......	152	148	132
Michigan.......	9,076	6,641	13,347	Mississippi.....	411	458	500
Wisconsin......	11,000	6,000	6,000	Louisiana......	5,500	5,470	5,000
Minnesota......	6,000	6,000	3,147	Massachusetts..	. . . .	. . . .	1,281
West Virginia....	107	51	49				
Maryland.......	16	13	6	Total....	59,878	57,494	60,150

(a) *No* statistics available.

At this date deer hunting is not permitted at any time in Indiana, Illinois, Iowa, Nebraska and Kansas,—where there are no wild deer; nor in Rhode Island, Connecticut, Delaware, Tennessee or Kentucky. The long close seasons in Massachusetts, Connecticut and southern New York have caused a great migration of deer into those once-depopulated regions,—in fact, right down to tide-water.

THE MULE DEER.—This will be the first member of the Deer Family to become extinct in North America outside of the protected portions of its haunts. Its fatal preference for open ground and its habit of pausing to stare at the hunter have been, and to the end will be, its undoing. Possibly there are now two of these deer in the United States and British Columbia for every 98 that existed forty years ago, but no more. It is a deer of the bad lands and foothills, and its curiosity is fatal.

The number of sportsmen who have hunted and killed this fine animal in its own wild and picturesque bad-lands is indeed quite small. It has been four-fifths exterminated by the resident hunter and ranchman, and to-day is found in the Rocky Mountain region most sparingly. Ten years ago it seemed right to hunt the so-called Rocky Mountain "black-tail" in northwestern Montana, because so many deer were there it did not seem to spell extermination. Now, conditions have changed. Since last winter's great slaughter in northwestern Montana, of 11,000 hungry deer, the species has been so reduced that it is no longer right to kill mule deer anywhere in our country, and a universal close season for five years is the duty of every state which contains that species.

THE REAL BLACK-TAILED DEER, of the Pacific coast, (*Odocoileus columbianus*) is, to most sportsmen of the Rocky Mountains and the East actually less known than the okapi! Not one out of every hundred of them can recognize a mounted head of it at sight. It is a small, delicately-formed, delicately-antlered understudy of the big mule deer, and now painfully limited in its distribution. It is *the* deer of California and western Oregon, and it has been so ruthlessly slaughtered that to-day it is going fast. As conditions stand to-day, and without a radical change on the part of the people of the Pacific coast, this very interesting species is bound to disappear. It will not be persistent, like the white-tailed deer, but in the heavy forests, it will last much longer than the mule deer.

My information regarding this deer is like the stock of specimens of it in museum collections,—meager and unsatisfactory. We need to know in detail how that species is faring to-day, and what its prospects are for the immediate future. In 1900, I saw great piles of skins from it in the fur houses of Seattle, and the sight gave me much concern.

THE CARIBOU, GENERALLY.—I think it is not very difficult to forecast the future of the Genus *Rangifer* in North America, from the logic of the conditions of to-day. Thanks to the splendid mass of information that has been accumulated regarding this group, we are able to draw certain conclusions. I think that the caribou of the Canadian Barren Grounds and northeastern Alaska will survive in great numbers for at least another century; that the caribou herds of Newfoundland will last nearly as long, and that in fifty years or less all the caribou of the great northwestern wilderness will be swept away.

The reasons for these conclusions are by no means obscure, or far-fetched.

In the first place, the barren-ground caribou are to-day enormously numerous,—undoubtedly running up into millions. It can not be possible that they are being killed faster than they are breeding; and so they must be increasing. Their food supply is unlimited. They are protected by two redoubtable champions,—Jack Frost and the Mosquito. Their country never will contain a great human population. The natives are so few in number, and so lazy, that even though they should become supplied with modern firearms, it is unlikely that they ever will make a serious impression on the caribou millions. The only thing to fear for the barren-ground caribou throngs is disease,—a factor that is beyond human prediction.

It is reasonably certain that the Barren Grounds never will be netted by railways,—unless gold is discovered over a wide area. The fierce cold and hunger, and the billions of mosquitoes of the Barren Grounds will protect the caribou from the wholesale slaughter that "civilized" man joyously would inflict—if he had the chance.

The caribou thousands of Newfoundland are fairly accessible to sportsmen and pot-hunters, but at the same time the colonial government can protect them from extermination if it will. Already much has been done to check the reckless and wicked slaughter that once prevailed. A bag limit of three bull caribou per annum has been fixed, which is enforced as to non-residents and sportsmen, but in a way that is much too "American" it is often ignored by residents in touch with the game. For instance, the guide of a New York gentleman whom I know admitted to my friend that each year he killed "about 25" caribou for himself and his family of four other persons. He explained thus: "When the inspector comes around, I show him two caribou hanging in my wood-shed, but back in the woods I have a little shack where I keep the others until I want them."

The real sportsmen of the world never will make the slightest perceptible impression on the caribou of Newfoundland. For one thing, the hunting is much too tame to be interesting. If the caribou of that Island ever are exterminated, it will be strictly by the people of Newfoundland, themselves. If the government will tighten its grip on the herds, they need never be exterminated.

The caribou of New Brunswick, Quebec and Ontario are few and widely scattered. Unless carefully conserved, they are not likely to last long; for their country is annually penetrated in every direction by armed men, white and red. There is no means by which it can be proven, but from the number of armed men in those regions I feel sure that the typical woodland caribou species is being shot faster than it is breeding. The sportsmen and naturalists of Canada and New Brunswick would render good service by making a close and careful investigation of that question.

The caribou of the northwestern wilderness are in a situation peculiarly their own. They inhabit a region of naked mountains and *thin* forests, wherein they are conspicuous, easily stalked and easily killed. Nowhere do they exist in large herds of thousands, or even of many hundreds. They live in small bands of from ten to twenty head, and even those are far apart. The region in which they live is certain to be thoroughly opened up by railways, and exploited. Fifty years from now we will find every portion of the now-wild Northwest fairly accessible by rail. The building of the railways will be to the caribou—and to other big game —the day of doom. In that wild, rough region, no power on earth,— save that which might be able to deprive *all* the inhabitants and all visitors of firearms,—can possibly save the game outside of a few preserves that are diligently patroled.

The big game of the northwest region, in which I include the interior of Alaska, *will go*! It is only a question of time. Already the building of the city of Fairbanks, and the exploitation of the mining districts surrounding it, have led to such harrassment and slaughter of the migrating caribou that the great herd which formerly traversed the Tanana country once a year has completely changed its migration route, and now keeps much farther north. The "crossing" of the Yukon near Eagle City has been abandoned. A hundred years hence, the northwestern wilderness will be dotted with towns and criss-crossed with railways; but the big game of it will be gone, except in the preserves that are yet to be made. This will particularly involve the caribou, moose, and mountain sheep of all species, which will be the first to go. The mountain goat and the forest bears will hold out longer than their more exposed neighbors of the treeless mountains.

THE MOOSE.—In the United States the moose is found in five states,— Maine, Minnesota, Montana, Wyoming and Idaho. There are 550 in the Yellowstone Park. In Maine and Minnesota only may moose be hunted and killed. In the season of 1909, 184 moose were killed in Maine, —a large number, considering the small moose population of that state. In northern Minnesota, we now possess a great national moose preserve of 909,743 acres; and in 1908 Mr. Fullerton, after a personal inspection in which he saw 189 moose in nine days, estimated the total moose population of the present day at 10,000 head. This is a moose preserve worth while.

Outside of protected areas, the moose is the animal that is most easily exterminated. Its trail is easily followed, and its habits are thoroughly known, down to three decimal places. As a hunter's reward it is Great. Strange to say, New Brunswick has found that the moose is an animal that it is possible, and even easy, to protect. The death of a moose is an event that is not easily concealed! Wherever it is thoroughly understood that the moose law will be enforced, the would-be poacher pauses to consider the net results to him of a jail sentence.

In New Brunswick we have seen two strange things happen, during our own times. We have seen the moose migrate into, and permanently occupy, an extensive area that previously was destitute of that species. At the same time, we have seen a reasonable number of bull moose killed by sportsmen without disturbing in the least the general equanimity of the general moose population! And at this moment, the moose population of New Brunswick is almost incredible. Every moose hunter who goes there sees from 20 to 40 moose, and two of my friends last year saw, "in round numbers, about 100!" Up to date the size of adult antlers seem to be maintaining a high standard.

In summer, the photographing of moose in the rivers, lakes and ponds of Maine and New Brunswick amounts to an industry. I am uneasy about the constant picking off of the largest and best breeding bulls of the Mirimachi country, lest it finally reduce the size and antlers of the moose of that region; but only the future can tell us just how that prospect stands to-day.

In Alaska, our ever thoughtful and forehanded Biological Survey of the Department of Agriculture has by legal proclamation at one stroke converted the whole of the Kenai Peninsula into a magnificent moose preserve. This will save *Alces gigas*, the giant moose of Alaska, from extermination; and New Brunswick and the Minnesota preserve will save *Alces americanus*. But in the northwest, we can positively depend upon it that eventually, wherever the moose may legally be hunted and killed by any Tom, Dick or Harry who can afford a twenty-dollar rifle and a license, the moose surely will disappear.

The moose laws of Alaska are strict—toward sportsmen, only! The miners, "prospectors" and Indians may kill as many as they please, "for food purposes." This opens the door to a great amount of unfair slaughter, Any coffee-cooler can put a pan and pick into his hunting outfit, go out after moose, and call himself a "prospector."

I grant that the *real* prospector, who is looking for ores and minerals with an intelligent eye, and knows what he is doing, should have special privileges on game, to keep him from starving. The settled miner, however, is in a different class. No miner should ask the privilege of living on wild game, any more than should the farmer, the steamboat man, the railway laborer, or the soldier in an army post. The Indian should have no game advantages whatever over a white man. He does not own the game of a region, any more than he owns its minerals or its water-power. He should obey the general game laws, just the same as white men. In Africa, as far as possible, the white population wisely prohibits the natives from owning or using firearms, and a good idea it is, too. I am glad there is one continent on which the "I'm-just-as-good-as-you-are" nightmare does not curse the whole land.

THE MUSK-OX.—Now that the north pole has been safely discovered, and the south pole has become the storm-center of polar exploration, the harried musk-ox herds of the farthest north are having a rest. I think that most American sportsmen have learned that as a sporting proposition there is about as much fun and glory in harrying a musk-ox herd with dogs, and picking off the members of it at "parade rest," as there is in shooting range cattle in a round-up. The habits of the animal positively eliminate the real essence of sport,—difficulty and danger. When a musk-ox band is chased by dogs, or by wolves, the full-grown members of it, bulls and cows alike, instantly form a close circle around the calves, facing outward shoulder to shoulder, and stand at bay. Without the aid of a gunner and a rifle, such a formation is invincible! Mr. Paul Rainey's moving pictures tell a wonderful story of animal intelligence, bravery and devotion to the parental instinct.

For some reason, the musk-ox herds do not seem to have perceptibly increased since man first encountered them. The number alive to-day appears to be no greater than it was fifty years ago; and this leads to the conclusion that the present delicate balance could easily be disturbed the wrong way. Fortunately, it seems reasonably certain that the Indians of the Canadian Barren Grounds, the Eskimo of the far north, and the stray explorers all live outside the haunts of the species, and come in touch only with the edge of the musk-ox population as a whole. This leads us to hope and believe that, through the difficulties involved in reaching them, the main bodies of musk-ox of both species are safe from extermination.

At the same time, the time has come for Canada, the United States and Denmark to join in formulating a stiff law for the prevention of wholesale slaughter of musk-ox for sport. It should be rendered impossible for another sportsman to kill twenty-three head in one day, as once occurred. Give the sportsman a bag of three bulls, and no more. To this, no true sportsman will object, and the objections of game-hogs only serve to confirm the justice of the thing they oppose.

THE GRIZZLY BEAR.—To many persons it may seem strange that anyone should feel disposed to accord protection to such fierce predatory animals as grizzly bears, lions and tigers. But the spirit of fair play springs eternal in some human breasts. The sportsmen of the world do not stick at using long-range, high-power repeating rifles on big game, but they draw the line this side of traps, poisons and extermination. The sportsmen of India once thought,—for about a year and a day,— that it was permissible to kill troublesome and expensive tigers by poison. Mr. G. P. Sanderson tried it, and when his strychnine operations promptly developed three bloated and disgusting tiger carcasses, even his native followers revolted at the principle. That was the alpha and omega of Sanderson's poisoning activities.

I am quite sure that if the extermination of the tiger from the whole of India were possible, and the to-be or not-to-be were put to a vote of the sportsmen of India, the answer would be a thundering "*No!*" Says Major J. Stevenson-Hamilton in his "Animal Life in Africa:" "It is impossible to contemplate the use against the lion of any other weapon than the rifle."

The real sportsmen and naturalists of America are decidedly opposed to the extermination of the grizzly bear. They feel that the wilds of North America are wide enough for the accommodation of many grizzlies, without crowding the proletariat. A Rocky Mountain without a grizzly upon it, or at least a bear of some kind, is only half a mountain,—commonplace and tame. Put one two-year-old grizzly cub upon it, and presto! every cubic yard of its local atmosphere reeks with romantic uncertainty and fearsome thrills.

A few persons have done considerable talking and writing about the damage to stock inflicted by bears, but I think there is little justification for such charges. Certainly, there is not one-tenth enough real damage done by bears to justify their extermination. At the present time, we hear that the farmers (!) of Kadiak Island, Alaska, are being seriously harassed and damaged by the big Kadiak bear,—an animal so rare and shy that it is very difficult for a sportsman to kill one! I think the charges against the bears,—if the Kadiak Islanders ever really have made any,— need to be proven, by the production of real evidence.

In the United States, outside of our game preserves, I know of not one locality in which grizzly bears are sufficiently numerous to justify a sportsman in going out to hunt them. The California grizzly, once represented by "Monarch" in Golden Gate Park, is almost, if not wholly, extinct. In Montana, outside of Glacier Park it is useless to apply for wild grizzlies. In the Bitter Root Mountains and Clearwater Mountains of Idaho, there are grizzlies, but they hide so effectually under the snow-bent willows on the "slides" that it is almost imposssible to get a shot. Northwestern Wyoming still contains a few grizzlies, but there are so many square miles of mountains around each animal it is now almost useless to go hunting for them. British Columbia, western Alberta and the coast mountains at least as far as Skaguay, and Yukon Territory generally, all contain grizzlies, and the sportsman who goes out for sheep, caribou and moose is reasonably certain to see half a dozen bears and kill at least one or two. In those countries, the grizzly species will hold forth long after all killable grizzlies have vanished from the United States

I think that it is now time for California, Montana, Washington, Oregon, Idaho and Wyoming to give grizzly bears protection of some sort. Possibly the situation in those states calls for a five-year close season. Even British Columbia should now place a bag limit on this species. This has seemed clear to me ever since two of my friends killed (in the spring of 1912) *six* grizzlies in one week! But Provincial Game Warden A. Bryan Williams says that at present it would be impossible to impose a bag limit of one per year on the grizzlies of British Columbia; and Mr. Williams is a sincere game-protector.

THE BROWN BEARS OF ALASKA.—These magnificent monsters present a perplexing problem, which I am inclined to believe can be satisfactorily solved by the Biological Survey only in short periods, say of three or four years each. Naturally, the skin hunters of Alaska ardently desire the skins of those bears, for the money they represent. That side of the bear problem does not in the least appeal to the ninety odd millions of people who live this side of Alaska. The skins of the Alaskan brown bears have little value save as curiosities, nailed upon the wall, where they can not be stepped upon and injured. The *hunting* of those bears, however, is a business for men; and it is partly for that reason they

THE WICHITA NATIONAL BISON HERD
Presented by the New York Zoological Society

should be preserved. A bear-hunt on the Alaska Peninsula, Admiralty or Montagu Islands, is an event of a lifetime, and with a bag limit of *one* brown bear, the species would be quite safe from extermination.

In Alaska there is some dissatisfaction over the protection accorded the big brown bears; but those rules are right *as far as they go!* A governor of Alaska once said to me: "The preservation of the game of Alaska should be left to the *people* of Alaska. It is their game; and they will preserve it all right!"

The answer? *Not by a long shot!*

Only three things were wrong with the ex-governor's view:

1.—The game of Alaska does *not* belong to the people who live in Alaska—with the intent to get out to-morrow! It belongs to the 93,000,000 people of the Nation.

2.—The preservation of the Alaskan fauna on the public domain should not be left unreservedly to the people of Alaska, because

3.—As sure as shooting, they will *not* preserve it!

Congress is right in appropriating $15,000 for game protection in Alaska. It is very necessary that the regulations for conserving the wild life should be fixed by the Secretary of Agriculture, with the advice of the Biological Survey.

THE BLACK BEAR is an interesting citizen. He harms nobody nor anything; he affords good sport; he objects to being exterminated, and wherever in North America he is threatened with extermination, he should at once be given protection! A black bear *in the wilds* is harmless. In captivity, posed as a household "pet," he is decidedly dangerous, and had best be given the middle of the road. In big forests he is a grand stayer, and will not be exterminated from the fauna of the United States until Washington is wrecked by anarchists.

THE AMERICAN BISON.—I regard the American bison species as now reasonably secure against extermination. This is due to the fact that it breeds persistently and successfully in captivity, and to the great efforts that have been put forth by the United States Government, the Canadian Government, the American Bison Society, the New York Zoological Society, and several private individuals.

The species reached its lowest ebb in 1889, when there were only 256 head in captivity and 835 running wild. The increase has been as follows:

```
1888—W. T. Hornaday's census.........................  1,300
1902—S. P. Langley's census..........................  1,394
1905—Frank Baker's census............................  1,697
1908—W. T. Hornaday's census.........................  2,047
1910—W. P. Wharton's census (in North America).        2,108
1912—W. P. Wharton's census (in North America).......  2,907
```

To-day, nearly one-half of the living bison are in very large governmental parks perpetually established and breeding rapidly, as follows:

IN THE UNITED STATES.

```
Yellowstone Park fenced herd, founded by Congress..........................  125
Montana National Bison Range, founded by The American Bison Society........   69
Wichita Bison Range, founded by The New York Zoological Society............   39
Wind Cave Bison Range, S. Dakota, founded by Am. Bison Society....To be stocked
Niobrara (Neb.) National Bison Range, now in process of creation......To be stocked
```

IN CANADA.

```
Buffalo Park, Wainwright, Alberta.........................  1,052
Elk Island Park, Alberta..................................     53
Rocky Mountains Park, Banff, Alberta......................     27
                                                          _____
   Total National and Provincial Preserves................  1,365
```

Of wild bison there are only three groups: 49 head in the Yellowstone National Park, about 75 Pablo "outlaws" around the Montana Bison Range, and between 300 and 400 head in northern Athabasca, southwest of Fort Resolution, existing in small and widely scattered bands.

The efforts of man to atone for the great bison slaughter by preserving the species from extinction have been crowned with success. Two governments and two thousand individuals have shared this task,—solely for sentimental reasons. In these facts we find reason to hope and believe that other efforts now being made to save other species from annihilation will be equally successful.

CHAPTER XVIII

THE PRESENT AND FUTURE OF AFRICAN GAME

Thanks to the diligence with which sportsmen and field naturalists have recorded their observations in the haunts of big game, it is not at all difficult to forecast the immediate future of the big game of the world. We may safely assume that all lands well suited to agriculture, mining and grazing will become populated by rifle-bearing men, with the usual result to the wild mammals and birds. At the same time, the game of the open mountains everywhere is thinly distributed and easily exterminated. On the other hand, the unconquerable forest jungles of certain portions of the tropics will hold their own, and shelter their four-footed inhabitants for centuries to come.

On the open mountains of the world and on the grazing lands most big game is now being killed much faster than it breeds. This is due to the attacks of five times too many hunters, open seasons that are too long, and bag limits that are far too liberal. As an example, consider Africa. Viewed in any way it may be taken, the bag limit in British East Africa is appallingly high. Notice this astounding array of wild creatures that *each hunter* may kill under a license costing *only $250!*

2	Buffalo	
2	Rhinoceros	
2	Hippopotamus	
1	Eland	
2	Grevy Zebra	
20	Common Zebra	
2	Fringe-eared Oryx	
4	Beisa Antelope	
4	Waterbuck	
1	Sable Antelope	
1	Roan Antelope	
1	Greater Kudu	
4	Lesser Kudu	
10	Topi	
20	Coke Hartebeest	
2	Neumann Hartebeest	
4	Jackson Hartebeest	
6	Hunter's Antelope	
4	Thomas Kob	
2	Bongo	
4	Pallah	
2	Sitatunga	

3	Gnu
12	Grant Gazelle
4	Waller's Gazelle
10	Harvey's Duiker
10	Isaac's Duiker
10	Blue Duiker
10	Kirk's Dik-dik
10	Guenther's Dik-dik
10	Hinde's Dik-dik
10	Cavendish Dik-dik
10	Abyssinian Oribi
10	Haggard's Oribi
10	Kenya Oribi
10	Suni
10	Klipspringer
10	Ward's Reedbuck
10	Chanler's Reedbuck
10	Thompson Gazelle
10	Peters Gazelle
10	Soemmerring Gazelle
10	Bushbuck
10	Haywood Bushbuck

The grand total is a possible 300 large hoofed and horned animals representing *44 species!* Add to this all the lions, leopards, cheetahs, cape hunting dogs and hyænas that the hunter can kill, and it will be enough to stock a zoological garden!

Quite a number of these species, like the sable antelope, kudu, Hunter's antelope, bongo and sitatunga are already rare, and therefore they are all the more eagerly sought.

Into the fine grass-lands of British East Africa, suitable for crops and stock grazing, settlers are steadily going. Each one is armed, and at once becomes a killer of big game. And all the time the visiting sportsmen are increasing in number, going farther from the Uganda Railway, and persistently seeking out the rarest and finest of the game. The buffalo has recovered from the slaughter by rinderpest only in time to meet the onset of oversea sportsmen.

Mr. Arthur Jordan has seen much of the big game of British East Africa, and its killing. Him I asked to tell me how long, in his opinion, the big game of that territory will last outside of the game preserves, as it is now being killed. He said, "Oh, it will last a long time. I think it will last fifteen years!"

Fifteen years! And this for the richest big-game fauna of any one spot in the whole world, which Nature has been *several million years in developing and placing there!*

At present the marvelous herds of big game of British East Africa and Uganda constitute the grandest zoological spectacle that the world ever has seen in historic times. For such an area, the number of species is incredible, and until they are seen, the thronging masses of individuals are beyond conception. It is easy to say "a herd of 3,000 zebras;" but no mere words can give an adequate impression of the actual army of stripes and bars, and hoofs thundering in review over a grassy plain.

But the settlers say, "The zebras must go! They break through our best wire fences, ruin our crops, despoil us of the fruits of long and toilsome efforts, and much expenditure. We simply can not live in a country inhabited by herds of wild zebras." And really, their contention is well founded. When it is necessary to choose between wild animals and peaceful agriculture for millions of men, the animals must give way.

In those portions of the great East African plateau region that are suited to modern agriculture, stretching from Buluwayo to northern Uganda, the wild herds are doomed to be crowded out by the farmer and the fruit-grower. This is the inevitable result of civilization and progress in wild lands. Marauding battalions of zebras, bellicose rhinoceroses and murderous buffaloes do not fit in with ranches and crops, and children going to school. Except in the great game preserves, the swamps and the dense jungles it is certain that the big game of the whole of eastern Africa is foredoomed to disappear,—the largest and most valuable species first.

Five hundred years from now, when North America is worn out, and wasted to a skeleton of what it now is, the great plateau region of East Africa between Cape Town and Lake Rudolph will be a mighty empire,

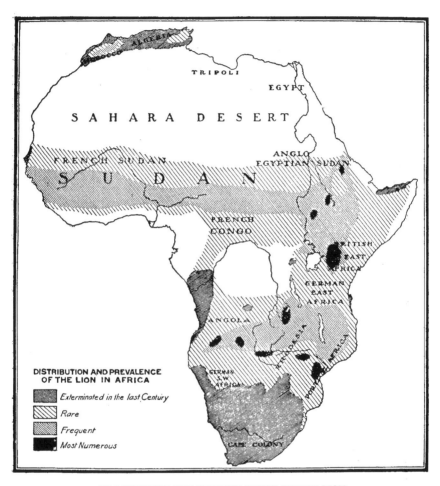

DISTRIBUTION AND PREVALENCE
OF THE LION IN AFRICA

Exterminated in the last Century

Rare

Frequent

Most Numerous

MAP SHOWING THE DISAPPEARANCE OF THE LION

Incidentally, it is also an Index of the Disappearance of African Big Game Generally.
From an Article in the Review of Reviews, for August, 1912, by Cyrus C. Adams, and
Based Largely upon the Exhaustive Studies of Dr. C. M. Engel, of Copenhagen.

teeming with white population. Giraffes and rhinoceroses now are
trampling over the sites of the cities and universities of the future. Then
the herds of grand game that now make Africa a sportsman's wonderland
will exist only in closed territory, in books, and in memory.

From what has befallen in South Africa, we can easily and correctly
forecast the future of the big game of British East Africa and Uganda.
Less than fifty years ago, Cape Colony, Natal, Zululand, and every

country up to the Zambesi was teeming with herds of big wild animals, just as the northern provinces now are. As late as 1890, when Rhodesia was taken over by the Chartered Company, and the capital city of Salisbury was staked out, an American boy in the Pioneer Corps, now Honorable William Harvey Brown, of Salisbury, wrote thus of the Gwibi Flats, near Salisbury:

"That evening I beheld on those flats a sight which probably will never again be seen there to the end of the world. The variety deploying before me was almost incredible! There, within the range of my vision were groups of roan, sable and tsessebi antelopes, Burchell zebras, [now totally extinct!] elands, reedbucks, steinbucks and ostriches. It was like Africa in the days of Livingstone. As I sat on my horse, viewing with amazement this wonderful panorama of wild life, I was startled by a herd that came galloping around a small hill just behind me."—(*"On the South African Frontier,"* p. 114.)

That was in 1890. And how is it to-day?

Salisbury is a modern city, endorsed by two lines of railway. The Gwibi Flats are farms. There is some big game yet, in Rhodesia south of the Zambesi, but to find it you must go at least a week's journey from the capital, to the remote corners that have not yet been converted into farms or mining settlements. North of the Zambesi, Rhodesia yet contains plenty of big game. The Victoria Falls station is a popular starting point for hunting expeditions headed northeast and northwest. In the northwest the game is yet quite in a state of nature. Unfortunately the Barotse natives of that region can procure from the Portuguese traders all the firearms and ammunition that they can pay for, and by treaty they retain their hunting rights. The final result will be—extermination of the game.

Elsewhere throughout Rhodesia the natives are not permitted to have guns and gunpowder,—a very wise regulation. In Alaska our Indians are privileged to kill game all the year round, and they have modern firearms with which to do it.

And how is it with the game of that day?

The true Burchell's zebra is now regarded as *extinct!* In Cape Colony and Natal, that once teemed with big game in the old-fashioned African way, they are *counting the individual wild animals that remain!* Also, they are making game preserves, literally everywhere.

Now that the best remaining game districts of Africa are rapidly coming under British control, it is a satisfaction to observe that the governing bodies and executive officers are alive to the necessity of preserving the big game from actual extinction. Excepting German East Africa, from Uganda to Cape Colony the game preserves form an almost continuous chain. It is quite impossible to enumerate all of them; but the two in British East Africa are of enormous size, and are well stocked with game. South Africa contains a great many smaller preserves and a few specimen herds of big game, but that is about all. Except in a few localities the hunting of big game in that region is done forever.

The Western Districts Game and Trout Protective Association of South Africa recently, (1911), has made careful counts and estimates of the number of individual game animals remaining in Cape Colony, with the following result:

Big Game in the Cape Province

From information kindly placed at the disposal of the Association by the Government, it was found that the following varieties of big game are still found in the Province. The numbers, however, are only approximate:

Blesbok: About 400 in Steynsburg, and 35 in Queen's Town divisions.

Bontebok: About 30 in Bredasdorp and 45 in Swellendam divisions.

Buffalo: About 340 in Uitenhage, 120 in Alexandria, and 75 in Bathurst divisions.

Elephants: About 130 in Alexandria, 160 in Uitenhage, 40 in Bathurst, and 20 in Knysna divisions.

Gemsbok: About 2,450 in Namaqualand, 4,500 in Vryburg, 4,000 in Gordonia, and 670 in the Kenhardt, Mafeking and Barkly West divisions.

Koodoo: About 10,000, found chiefly in the divisions of Albany, Barkly West, Fort Beaufort, Hay, Herbert, Jansenville, Kuruman, Ladismith, Mafeking, Mossel Bay, Oudtshoorn, Riversdale, Steytlerville, Uitenhage, Victoria East and Vryburg.

Oribi: About 120, in the divisions of Albany and Alexandria.

Rietbok: About 170, in the Komgha division.

Zebra: About 560, most of which are to be found in the divisions of Cradock, George and Oudtshoorn. A few are to be found in the divisions of Uniondale and Uitenhage.

Springbok: Being migratory, it is difficult to estimate their number. In some years they are compelled by drought to invade the Province in large numbers. They are then seen as far south as Calvinia and Fraserburg. Large numbers are, however, fenced in on private estates in various parts of the Province.

Klipspringers: About 11,200, in the following divisions, viz.: Namaqualand, 6,559; Kuruman, 2,100; Steytlerville, 1,530; Oudtshoorn, 275; Hay, 250; Ladismith, 220; Graaff-Reinet, 119; Kenhardt, 66; and Cradock, 56.

Hartebeest: About 9,700, principally in the divisions of Vryburg, Gordonia, Kuruman, Mafeking, Kimberley, Hay and Beaufort West.

Wildebeest: About 3,450 in Vryburg, 80 each in Gordonia and Kuruman, 65 in Mafeking, 20 in Queen's Town, and a few in the Bredasdorp divisions.

Eland: About 12 in the Graaff-Reinet division, privately bred.

The above showing of the pitifully small numbers of the specimens that constitute the remnant of the big-game of the Cape suggest just one thing:—a universal close season throughout Cape Colony, and no hunting whatever for ten years. And yet, what do we see?

The Report from which the above census was taken contains half a column of solid matter, in small type, giving a list of the *open seasons* all over Cape Colony, during which killing may be done! So it seems that the spirit of slaughter is the same in Africa that it is in America,—*kill*, as long as there is *anything* alive to kill!

This list is of startling interest, because it shows how closely the small remnants of big game are now marked down in South Africa.

In view of the success with which Englishmen protect their game when once they have made up their minds to do so, it is fair to expect that the herds now under protection, as listed above, will save their respective species from extinction. It is alarming, however, to note the wide territory covered by the deadly "open seasons," and to wonder when the bars really will be put up.

To-day, Mashonaland is a very-much-settled colony. The Cape to Cairo railway and trains de luxe long ago attained the Falls of the Zambesi, and now the Curator of the Salisbury Museum will have to search diligently in far off Nyassaland, and beyond the Zambesi River, to find enough specimens to fill his cases with representatives of the vanished Rhodesian fauna. Once (1892) the white rhinoceros was found in northern Rhodesia; but never again. In Salisbury, elands and zebras are nearly as great a curiosity as they are in St. Louis.

But for the discovery of white rhinoceroses in the Lado district, on the western bank of the Nile below Gondokoro, we would now be saying that *Rhinoceros simus* is within about ten specimens of total extinction.

From South Africa, as far up as Salisbury, in central Rhodesia, at least 99 per cent of the big game has disappeared before the white man's rifle. Let him who doubts this scan the census of wild animals still living in Cape Colony.

From all the other regions of Africa that are easily accessible to gunners, the animal life is vigorously being shot out, and no man in his senses will now say that the big game is breeding faster than it is being killed. The reverse is painfully true. Mr. Carl Akeley, in his quest for a really large male elephant for the American Museum found and looked over *a thousand* males without finding one that was really fine and typical. All the photographs of elephant herds that were taken by Kermit Roosevelt and Akeley show a striking absence of adult males and of females with long tusks. There are only young males, and young females with small, short tusks. The answer is—the white ivory hunters have killed nearly all the elephants bearing good ivory.

The slaughter of big game is going on furiously in British East Africa, because the Uganda Railway opens up the entire territory to hunters. Anyone, man or woman, who can raise $5,000 in cash can go there and make a huge "bag" of big game. With a license costing only $250 he can kill enough big game to sink a ship.

The bag limit in British East Africa is ruinously extravagant. If the government desires the extermination of the game, such a bag limit surely will promote that end. It is awful to think that for a petty sum any man may buy the right to kill *300 head* of hoofed and horned animals, of 44 species, not counting the carnivorous animals that also may be killed. That bag limit should *immediately* be reduced *75 per cent!*

As matters stand to-day in British East Africa, the big game of the country, outside the three preserves, is absolutely certain to disappear, in about one-fourth of the time that it took South Africa to accomplish the same result. The reasons are obvious:—superior accessibility, more deadly rifles, expert professional guides, and a widespread craze for killing big game. With care and economy, British East Africa should furnish good hunting for two centuries, but as things are going on to-day, twenty years will see a tremendous change for the worse, and a disappearance of game that will literally astonish the natives.

German East Africa and Uganda will not exterminate their quotas of big game quite so soon. The absence of railways is a great factor in game-existence. The Congo Free State contains game and sporting possibilities—on the unexplored uplands *between the rivers*,—that are as yet totally unknown to sportsmen at large. We are accustomed to thinking of the whole basin of the Congo as a vast, gloomy and impenetrable forest.

There is to-day in Africa a vast reserve supply of grand game. It inhabits regions that are either unknown, or most difficult to penetrate. As a species in point, consider the okapi. Only the boldest and most persistent explorers ever have set foot in its tangled and miasmatic haunts. It may be twenty years before a living specimen can be brought out. The gorilla and the chimpanzee are so well protected by the density of their jungles that they never can be exterminated—until the natives are permitted to have all the firearms that they desire! When that day arrives, it is "good-night" to all the wild life that is large enough to eat or to wear.

The quagga and the blaubok became *extinct* before the world learned that their existence was threatened! The giant eland, the sable antelope, the greater kudu, the bontebok, blessbok, the mountain and Burchell zebras, all the giraffes save that of Nigeria, the big waterbucks, the nyala, the sitatunga, the bongo, and the gerenuk—all will go in the same way, everywhere outside the game preserves. The buffalo, zebra and rhinoceros are especially marked for destruction, as annoyances to colonists. You who read of the killing of these species to-day will read of their total disappearance to-morrow. So long as the hunting of them is permitted, their ultimate disappearance is fixed and certain. It is not the way of rifle-shooting English colonists to permit herds of big game to run about merely to be looked at.

Naturally, the open plains of Africa, and the thin forests of the plateau regions, will be the first to lose their big game. In the gloomy fastnesses of the great equatorial forests, and other really dense forests wherever found, the elephants, the Derby eland, the bongo, the okapi, the buffaloes (of three species), the bush-pigs, the bushbucks and the forest-loving antelopes generally will live, for possibly one hundred years, —*or until the natives secure plenty of modern firearms and ammunition.* Whenever and wherever savages become supplied with rifles, then it is time to measure each big-game animal for its coffin.

The elephants of the great equatorial forest westward of the lake region will survive long after the last eastern elephant has bitten the dust. The pygmy elephant of the lower Congo region (*Elephas pumilio*) will be the last African elephant species to disappear—because it inhabits dense miasmatic jungles, its tusks are of the smallest size, and it has the least commercial value.

CHAPTER XIX

THE PRESENT AND FUTURE OF THE GAME OF ASIA

After a successful survival of man's influence through two thousand years, at last the big game of India has made a good start on the road to vanishment. Up to 1870 it had held its own with a tenacity that was astonishing. In 1877, I found the Ganges—Jumna dooab, the Animallai Hills, the Wynaad Forest and Ceylon literally teeming with herds of game. The Animallais in particular were a hunter's paradise. In each day of hunting, large game of some kind was a certainty. The Nilgiri Hills had been quite well shot out, but in view of the very small area and open, golf-links character of the whole top of that wonderful sky plateau, that was no cause for wonderment.

In those days no native shikaree owned and operated a gun,—or at the most very, very few of them did. If a rogue elephant, a man-eating tiger or a nasty leopard became a public nuisance, it was a case for a sahib to come and doctor it with a .577 double-barreled express rifle, worth $150 or more; and the sahibs had shooting galore.

I think that no such great wild-life sights as those of the plateau regions of Africa ever were seen in southern Asia. Conditions there are different, and usually the game is widely scattered. The sambar deer and muntjac of the dense forests, the axis of the bamboo glades, the thameng deer of the Burmese jungles, the sladang, or gaur, of the awful Malay tangle, and the big cats and canines will last long and well. The ibexes, markhors, tahr and all the wild sheep eventually will be shot out by sportsmen who are "sheep crazy." The sheep and goats of Asia will disappear soon after the plains animals of Africa, because no big game that lives in the open can much longer endure the modern, inexpensive long-range rifles of deadly accuracy and limitless repetition of fire.

Eventually, I fear that by some unlucky turn of Fortune's wheel all the native hunters of Asia will obtain rifles; and when they do, we soon will see the end of the big game.

Even to-day we find that the primitive conditions of 1877 have been greatly changed. In the first place, about every native shikaree (hunter) owns a rifle, at a cost of about $25; and many other natives possess guns, and assume to hunt with them. The logical conclusion of this is more hunting and less game. The development of the country has reduced the cover for game. New roads and railways have made the game districts easily accessible, and real sportsmen are now three or four times as numerous as they were in 1877.

At Toonacadavoo, in the Animallai Hills where thirty-five years ago there modestly nestled on the ridge beside the river only Forest Ranger Theobold's bungalow, built of mud and covered with grass thatch and bamboo rats, there is now a regular hill station lighted by electricity, a modern sanatorium high up on the bluff, a *club*, golf links, and other modern improvements. In my day there were exactly four guns on the Animallais. Now there are probably one hundred; and it is easy to guess how much big game remains on the Delectable Mountains in comparison with the golden days of 1877. I should say that there is now only one game animal for every twenty-five that were there in my day.

I am told that it is like that all over India. Beyond question, the gun-sellers and gun-users have been busy there, as everywhere else. The game of India is on the toboggan slide, and the old days of abundance have gone forever.

The first fact that strikes us in the face is the impending fate of the great Indian rhinoceros, an animal as wonderful as the Titanothere or the Megatherium. It is like a gift handed down to us straight out of the Pleistocene age, a million years back. The British paleontologists to-day marvel at *Elephas ganesa*, and by great labor dig his bones out of the Sewalik rocks, but what one of them all has yet made a move to save *Rhinoceros indicus* from the quick extermination that soon will be his portion unless he is accorded perpetual and real protection from the assaults of man?

Let the mammalogists of the world face this fact. The available cover of the Indian rhinoceros is *alarmingly* decreasing, throughout Assam and Bengal where the behemoth of the jungle has a right to live. It is believed that the few remaining rhinos are being shot much faster then they are breeding; and what will be the effect of this upon an animal that requires fourteen years to reach full maturity? To-day, the most wonderful hoofed mammal of all Asia is booked for extermination, and unless very radical measures for its preservation are at once carried into effect, it is probable that twenty years more will see the last Indian rhino go down to rise no more. One remedy would be a good, ample rhinoceros preserve; and another, the most absolute and permanent protection for the species, all along the line. Half-way measures will not suffice. It is time to ring in a general alarm.

During the past eighteen years, only three specimens of that species have come out of India for the zoological gardens and parks of the world, and I think there are only five in captivity, all told.

We are told that in India now the natives are permitted to have about all the firearms they can pay for. Naturally, in a country containing over 300,000,000 people this is a deadly thing. Of course there are shooting regulations, many of them; but their enforcement is so imperfect that it is said that the natives are attacking the big game on all sides, with deadly effect. I fear it is utterly impossible for the Indian government to put enough wardens into the field to watch the doings of the grand army of native poachers.

Fortunately, the Indian native,—unlike the western frontiersman,—does not contend that *he owns* the big game, or that "all men are born free and equal." At the same time, he means to have his full share of it, to eat, and to sell in various forms for cash. Even in India, the sale-of-game dragon has reared its head, and is to-day in need of being scotched with an iron hand.

When I received direct from a friend in the native state of Kashmir a long printed circular setting forth the hunting laws and game-protective measures of that very interesting principality, it gave me a shock. It was disquieting to be thus assured that the big game of Kashmir has disappeared to such an extent that strong protective measures are necessary. It was as if the Chief Eskimo of Etah had issued a strong proclamation for the saving of the musk-ox.

In Kashmir, the destruction of game has become so serious that a Game Preservation Department has been created, with the official staff that such an organization requires. The game laws are printed annually, and any variations from them may be made only by the authority of the Maharajah himself. Up to date, *eight* game preserves have been created, having a total area of about thee hundred square miles. In addition to these, there are twelve small preserves, each having an area of from twenty-five to fifty square miles. By their locations, these seem to provide for all the species of big game that are found in Kashmir,—the ibex, two forms of markhor, the tahr, Himalayan bighorn sheep, burrhel and goral.

In our country we have several states that are very large, very diversified in surface, and still inhabited by large game. Has any one of those states created a series of game preserves even half way comparable with those of Kashmir? I think not. Montana has made a beginning with two preserves,—Snow Creek and the Pryor Mountains,—but beside the splendid series of Kashmir they are not worthy of serious mention.

And then following closely in the wake of that document came a lengthy article in the "Proceedings of the Zoological Society of London," by E. C. Stebbing, in which a correspondent of the Indian *Field* clearly sets forth the fact that the big game of the Himalayas now is menaced by a peril new to our consideration, but of a most deadly character. Hear him:

"In this inventory (of game destroyers in India), the Gurkha soldier does not find a place, for he belongs to a class which he amply fills by himself with his small but very important personality. He deserves separate notice. From the banks of the Sarda on the frontier of Nepal, to the banks of the Indus, the battalions of these gallant little men are scattered in cantonments all along the outer spurs of the Himalayan range. In seven or eight of these locations there are at least 14,000 of these disciplined warriors, who, in the absence of opportunities for spilling human blood legitimately, are given a free hand for slaughtering wild animals, along five-hundred miles of the best hunting grounds of Upper India."

Now, since those facts must be true as reported, do they not in themselves constitute a severe arraignment of the Indian government? Why should that state of game slaughter endure, when a single executive order to the C. O. of each post would effectually stop it?

In the making of game preserves, or "sanctuaries" as they are called out there, the Government of India has shown rare and commendable diligence. The total number is too great for enumeration here. The native state of Mysore has seven, and the Nilgiri Hills have sanctuaries aggregating about 100,000 acres in area. In the Wynaad Forest, my old hunting-grounds at Mudumallay have been closed to bison shooting, because of the alarming decrease of bison (gaur) through shooting and disease. The Kundah Forest Reserve has been made a partial game preserve, but the door might as well have been left wide open as so widely ajar.

In eastern Bengal and Assam, several game preserves have been created. On the whole, by the diligence and thoroughness with which sanctuaries, as they are termed, have been created quite generally throughout India, it is quite evident that the government and the sportsmen of India have become thoroughly alarmed by the great decrease of the game, and the danger of the extermination of species. In the past India has been the finest and best-stocked hunting-ground of all Asia, quite beyond compare, and the destruction of her once-splendid fauna of big game would be a zoological calamity.

Tibet.—As yet, Tibet offers free hunting, without legal let or hindrance, to every sportsman who can climb up to her lofty, wind-swept and whizzing-cold plateau. The man who hunts the *Ovis poli*, superb creature though it be, pays in full for his trophies. The ibex of the south help out the compensatory damages, but even with that, the list of species available in southern Tibet is painfully small. The Mitchell takin can be reached from China, via Chungking, after a long, hard journey, over Consul Mason Mitchell's trail; but the takin is about the only large hoofed game available.

The Altai Mountains, of western China, contain the magnificent Siberian argali, the grandfather of all sheep species, whose horns must be seen to be believed. Through a quest for that species the Russian military authorities played upon Mr. George L. Harrison and his comrade a very grim and unsportsmanlike joke. At the frontier military post, on the Russo-Chinese border, the two Americans were courteously halted, hospitably entertained, and *prevented* from going into the argali-infested mountains that loomed up before them only a few miles away! The Russian officers said:

"Sheep? Why, if you really want sheep, we will send out some of our brave soldiers to shoot some for you; but there is no need for *you* to take the trouble to go after them!"

After Mr. Harrison and his comrade had spent $5,000, and traveled half way around the world for those sheep, that is in brief the story of how the cup of Tantalus was given them by the Russians, actually *at their goal!* As spoil-sports, those Russian officers were the champions of the world.

Seven hundred miles southeastward of the Altai Mountains of western China, guarded by the dangerous hostility of savage native tribes, there exists and awaits the scientific explorer, according to report, an undiscovered wild horse. The Bicolored Wild Horse is black and white, and joy awaits the zoologist or sportsman who sees it first. Evidently it will not soon be exterminated by modern rifles.

The Impenetrable Forests.—Although the mountains of central Asia will in time be cleared of their big game,—when by hook and by crook the natives secure plenty of modern firearms, — there are places in the Far East that we know will contain big game forever and a day. Take the Malay Peninsula, Borneo and Sumatra as examples.

Mr. C. William Beebe, who recently has visited the Far East, has described how the state of Selangor, between Malacca and Penang, has taken on many airs of improvement since 1878, and sections of Sarawak Territory are being cut down and burned for the growing of rubber. Despite this I am trying to think that those developments menace the total volume of the wild life of those regions but little. I wonder if those tangled, illimitable, ever-renewing jungles yet know that their faces have been scratched. White men never will exterminate the big game of the really dense jungles of the eastern tropics; but with enough axes, snares, guns and cartridges *the natives* may be able to accomplish it!

In Malayana there are some jungles so dense, so tangled with lianas and so thorny with Livistonias and rattan that nothing larger than a cat can make way through them. There are thousands of square miles so boggy, so swampy, so dark, gloomy and mosquito-ridden that all men fear them and avoid them, and in them rubber culture must be impossible. In those silent places the gaur, the rhino, the Malay sambar, the clouded leopard and the orang-utan surely are measurably safe from the game-bags and market gunners of the shooting world. It is good to think that there is an equatorial belt of jungle clear around the world, in Central and South America as well as in the old World, in which there will be little extermination in our day, except of birds for the feather market. But the open plains, open mountains, and open forests of Asia and Australasia are in different case. Eventually they will be "shot out."

China, all save Yunnan and western Mongolia, is now horribly barren of wild life. Can it ever be brought back? We think it can not. The millions of population are too many; and except in the great forest tracts, the spread of modern firearms will make an end of the game. Already the pheasants are being swept out of China for the London market, and extinction is staring several species in the face. On the whole, the pheasants of the Old World are being hit hard by the rubber-planting craze. Mr. Beebe declares that owing to the inrush of aggressive capital, the haunts of many species of pheasants are being denuded of all their natural cover, and some mountain species that are limited to small areas are practically certain to be exterminated at an early date.

DESTRUCTION OF ANIMALS FOR FUR.—In the far North, only the interior of Kamchatka seems to be safe from the iron heel of the skin-hunter. A glance at the list of furs sold in London last year reveals one or two things that are disquieting. The total catch of furs for the year 1911 is enormous,—considering the great scarcity óf wild life on two continents. Incidentally it must be remembered that every trapper carries a gun, and in studying the fur list one needs no help in trying to imagine the havoc wrought with firearms on the edible wild life of the regions that contributed all that fur. I have been told by trappers that as a class, trappers are great killers of game.

In order that the reader may know by means of definite figures the extent to which the world is being raked and combed for fur-bearing animals, we append below a statement copied from the *Fur News Magazine* for November, 1912, of the sales of the largest London fur house during the past two years.

With varying emotions we call attention to the wombat of Australia, 3,841; grebe, 51,261, and house cat, 92,407. Very nearly all the totals of Lampson & Co. for each species are much lower for the sales of 1912 than for those of 1911. Is this fact significant of a steady decline?

FURS SOLD BY C. M. LAMPSON & CO., LONDON

	Totals for 1911, Skins	Totals for 1912, Skins
Raccoon	354,057	215,626
Musquash (Muskrat)	3,382,401	2,937,150
Musquash, Black	78,363	60,000
Skunk	1,310,185	979,612
Cat, Civet	329,180	229,155
Opossum, American	1,011,824	948,189
Mink	183,574	100,951
Marten	29,881	26,895
Fox, Red	58,900	40,300
Fox, Cross	1,294	1,569
Fox, Silver	761	590
Fox, Grey	43,909	32,471
Fox, Kit	30,278	35,222
Fox, White	16,709	13,341
Fox, Blue	3,137	1,778
Otter	17,399	13,899
Sea Otter	328	202
Cat, Wild, etc.	38,870	29,740
Cat, House	92,407	65,641
Lynx	2,424	5,144
Fisher	1,918	656
Badger	16,338	15,325
Beaver	21,137	17,036
Bear	16,851	13,377
Wolf	65,893	74,535
Wolverine	1,530	1,172
Hair Seal, Dry	6,455	5,378
Grebe	51,261	19,571
Fur Seal, Dry	897	1,453
Sable, Russian	10,285	8,972

Furs Sold By C. M. Lampson & Co., London
(Continued)

	Totals for 1911, Skins	Totals for 1912, Skins
Kolinsky	138,921	120,933
Marten, Baum	1,853	1,481
Marten, Stone	7,504	6,331
Fitch	26,731	20,400
Ermine	328,840	248,295
Squirrel	976,395	707,710
Saca, etc	40,982	13,599
Chinchilla, Real	6,282	11,457
Chinchilla, Bastard	7,533	8,145
Marten, Japanese	26,005	3,294
Sable, Japanese	1,429	52
Fox, Japanese	60,831	13,725
Badger, Japanese	183	2,949
Opossum, Australian	1,613,799	1,782,364
Wallaby, Australian	1,003,820	540,608
Kangaroo, Australian	21,648	16,193
Wombat, Australian	3,841	1,703
Fox, Red, Australian	60,435	40,724

CHAPTER XX

THE DESTRUCTION OF BIRDS IN THE FAR EAST*

By C. William Beebe
Curator of Birds, New York Zoological Park

In chapter XIII, treating of the "Extermination of Birds for Women's Hats," Dr. Hornaday has dealt fully with the feather and plumage traffic after it enters the brokers' hands, and has proved conclusively that the plumes of egrets are gathered from the freshly killed birds. We may trace the course of the plumes and feathers backward through the tightly-packed bales and boxes in the holds of the vessels to the ports of the savage lands whence they were shipped; then to the skilful, dark hands of Mexican peon, Venezuelan Indian, African negro or Asiatic Chinaman or Malay, who stripped the skin from the flesh; and finally to the jungle or mountain side or terai where the bird gave up its life to blowpipe, cross-bow, blunderbuss or carefully set snare.

In various trips to Mexico, Venezuela and other countries in the tropics of the New World I have seen many such scenes, but not until I had completed a seventeen months' expedition in search of pheasants, through some twenty wild countries of Asia and the East Indies, did I realize the havoc which is being wrought week by week everywhere on the globe. While we were absent even these few months from the great centers of civilization, tremendous advances had been made in air-ships and the thousand and one other modern phases of human development, but evolution in the world of Nature as we observed it was only destructive—a world-wide katabolism—a retrogression often discernible from month to month. We could scarcely repeat the trip and make the same observations upon pheasants, so rapidly is this group of birds approaching extinction.

The causes of this destruction of wild life are many and diverse, and resemble one another only in that they all emanate from mankind. To the casual traveller the shooting and trapping of birds for millinery purposes at first seems to hold an insignificant place among the causes. But this is only because in many of the larger ports, the protective laws are more or less operative and the occupation of the plume hunter is

*The observations which furnished this valuable chapter were made by Mr. Beebe in 1911 while conducting an expedition in southern Asia, Borneo and Java for the purpose of studying in life and nature all the members of the Pheasant Family inhabiting that region. The results of these studies and collections will shortly appear in a very complete monograph of the Phasianidae.—W. T. H.

carried on in secret ways. But it is as far-reaching and insidious as any; and when we add to the actual number of birds slain, the compound interest of eggs grown cold, of young birds perishing slowly from hunger, of the thousands upon thousands of birds which fall wounded or dead among the thick tropical jungle foliage and are lost, the total is one of ghastly proportions.

Not to weaken my argument with too many general statements, let me take at once some concrete cases. First, that of the Himalayan pheasants and game-birds. In a recent interesting article by E. P. Stebbing* the past, present and hoped-for future of game birds and animals in India is reviewed. Unfortunately, however, most of the finest creatures in Asia live beyond the border of the British sphere of influence, and though within sight, are absolutely beyond reach of civilized law. The heart of the Himalayas,—the haunts of some of the most beautiful birds in the world, the tragopans, the blood and impeyan pheasants— lies within the limits of Nepal, a little country which time and time again has bade defiance to British attacks, and still maintains its independence. From its northern border Mt. Everest looks down from its most exalted of all earthly summits and sees valley after valley depleted of first one bird and then another. I have seen and lived with Nepalese shepherds who have nothing to do month after month but watch their flocks. In the lofty solitudes time hangs heavy on their hands, and with true oriental patience they weave loop after loop of yak-hair snares, and then set them, not in dozens or scores, but in hundreds and thousands up and down the valleys.

In one locality seven great valleys had been completely cleared of pheasants, only a single pair of tragopans remaining; and from one of these little brown men I took two hundred nooses which had been prepared for these lone survivors. In these cases, the birds were either cooked and eaten at once, or sold to some passing shepherd or lama for a few annas. But in other parts of this unknown land systematic collecting of skins goes on, for bale after bale of impeyan and red argus (tragopan) pheasant skins goes down to the Calcutta wharves, where its infamous contents, though known, are safe from seizure under the Nepal Raja's seal! Thus it is that the London feather sales still list these among the most splendid of all living birds. And shame upon shame, when we read of 80 impeyan skins "dull," or "slightly defective," we know that these are female birds. Then, if ever, we realize that the time of the bird and the beast is passing, the acme of evolution for these wonderful beings is reached, and at most we can preserve only a small fragment of them.

To the millinery hunter, what the egret is to America, and the bird of paradise to New Guinea, the impeyan pheasant is to India—the most coveted of all plumages. There is a great tendency to blame the native hunter for the decrease of this and other pheasants, and from what I have personally seen in many parts of the Himalayas there is no question that

*"Game Sanctuaries and Game Protection in India," Proc. Zool. Soc., London, 1912. pp. 23–35.

PHEASANT SNARES
Made of Yak Hair, Taken from a Shepherd in Nepal by Mr. Beebe

the Garwhalese and Nepalese hill-men have wrought havoc among the birds. But these men are by no means the sole cause. As long ago as 1879 we read that "The great demand for the brilliant skins of the moonal that has existed for many years has led to their almost total extermination in some parts of the hills, as the native shikaris shoot and snare for the pot as well as for skins, and kill as many females as males. On the other hand, though for nearly thirty years my friend Mr. Wilson has yearly sent home from 1,000 to 1,500 skins of this species and the tragopan, there are still in the woods whence they were obtained as many as, if not more than, when he first entered them, simply because he has rigidly preserved females and nests, and (as amongst English pheasants) one cock suffices for several hens."

Ignoring the uncertainty of the last statement, it is rather absurd to think of a single man "preserving" females and nests in the Himalayas from 1850 to 1880, when the British Government, despite most efficient laws and worthy efforts is unable to protect the birds of these wild regions to-day. The statement that after thirty to forty-five thousand cock impeyans were shot or snared, as many or more than the original quota remained, could only emanate from the mind of a professional feather-hunter, and Hume should not be blamed for more than the mere repetition of such figures. Let it be said to the credit of Wilson, the slaughterer of something near forty-five thousand impeyans, that he was a careful observer of the birds' habits, and has given us an excellent account, somewhat coloured by natives, but on the whole, the best we have had in the past. But it is not pleasant to read of his waiting until "twenty or thirty have got up and alighted in the surrounding trees, and have then walked up to the different trees and fired at those I wished to procure without alarming the rest, only those very close to the one fired at being disturbed at each report."

Hume's opinion that in 1879 there were scores of places where one might secure from ten to eighteen birds in a day, is certainly not true to-day. Indeed, as early as 1858 we read that "This splendid bird, once so abundant on the Western Himalayas is now far from beng so, in consequence of the numbers killed by sportsmen on account of its beauty. Whole tracts of mountain forest once frequented by the moonal are now

SILVER PHEASANT SKINS SEIZED AT RANGOON, BRITISH BURMA

About 600 Skins out of Several Thousand Confiscated in the Custom House, on their way to the
London Feather Market.   Photographed by Mr. Beebe

almost without a single specimen." The same author goes on naively
to tell the reader that "Among the most pleasant reminiscences of by-
gone days is a period of eleven days, spent by the author and a friend
on the Choor Mountain near Simla, when among other trophies were
numbered sixty-eight moonal pheasants, etc."

For some unaccountable reason there is, or was for many years, a
very prevalent idea that the enormous number of skins which have poured
into the London market were from birds bred in the vicinity of Calcutta.
When we remember the intense heat of that low-lying city, and learn
from the records of the Calcutta Zoological Garden that impeyans and
tragopans are even shorter-lived than in Europe, the absurdity of the
idea is apparent. In spite of numberless inquiries throughout India, I
failed to learn of a single captive young bird ever hatched and reared
even in the high, cool, hill-stations. The commercial value of an impeyan
skin has varied from five dollars to twenty dollars, according to the number received annually. In 1876 an estimate placed the monthly average
of impeyans received in London at from two to eight hundred.

In such a case as Nepal, direct protective laws are of no avail. All
humane arguments are useless, but if the markets at the other end *can
be closed*, the slaughter will cease instantly and automatically.

DEADFALL TRAPS IN BURMA

A Long Series set Across a Valley, by the Kachins of the Burma-Chinese Border. A Wholesale
Method of Wild-life Slaughter, Photographed by C. William Beebe, 1910

As a contrast to the millinery hunter of fifty years ago it is refreshing to find that at last sincere efforts are being made in British possessions to stop this traffic. I happened to be at Rangoon when six large bales of pheasant skins were seized by the Custom officials. A Chinaman had brought them from Yunnan via Bhamo, and was preparing to ship them as ducks' feathers. Two of the bales were opened for my inspection. The first contained about five hundred Lady Amherst pheasant skins, falling to pieces and lacking heads and legs. The second held over four hundred silver pheasants, in almost perfect condition. The chief collector had put the absolutely prohibitive fine of £200 on them, and was waiting for the expiration of the legal number of days before burning the entire lot. They must have represented years of work in decimating the pheasant fauna of western China.

Far up in the wilderness of northern Burma, and over the Yunnan border, we often came upon some of the most ingenious examples of native trapping, a system which we found repeated in the Malay States, Borneo, China and other parts of the Far East. A low bamboo fence is built directly across a steep valley or series of valleys, about half way from the summit to the lower end, and about every fifteen feet a narrow opening is left, over which a heavy log is suspended. Any creature attempting to make its way through, treads upon several small sticks and by so doing springs the trap and the dead-fall claims a victim.

When a country is systematically strung with traps such as these, sooner or later all but a pitiful remnant of the smaller mammals, birds and reptiles are certain to be wiped out. Morning after morning I have visited such a runway and found dead along its path, what must have been all the walking, running or crawling creatures which the night before had sought the water at the bottom; pheasants, cobras, mouse-deer, rodents, civets, and members of many other groups. In some countries nooses instead of dead-falls guard the openings, but the result is equally deadly.

I have described this method of trapping because of its future importance in the destruction of wild life in the Far East. The Chinaman in all his many millions is undergoing a remarkably swift and radical evolution both of character and dress. In many ways, if only from the viewpoint of the patient, thrifty store-keeper he is a most powerful factor in the East, and is becoming more so. In many cases he imitates the white nations by cutting off his queue and altering his dress. In some mysterious correlated way his diet seems simultaneously affected, and while for untold generations rice and fish has satisfied all his gastronomic desires, a new craving, that for meat, has come to him. The result is apparent in many parts of the East. The Chinaman is willing and able to pay for meat, and the native finds a new market for the creatures about him. Again and again when I wished a few specimens of some certain pheasant I had but to hail passing canoes and bid a few annas or "cash" or "ringits" higher than the prospective Chinese purchaser would give, and the pheasants were mine.

In the catalogues of the brokers' sales of feathers we read of many thousands of the wonderful ocellated wing feathers of the argus pheasant, but no less horrible is the sight of a canoe crammed with the bedraggled bodies of these magnificent birds on their way to some Chinese hamlet where they will be sold for a pittance, the flesh eaten to the last tendon and the feathers given to the children and puppies to play with. The newly-aroused appetite of the Mongolian will soon be an important factor in the extermination of animals and birds, few species being exempt, for the Chinaman lives up to his reputation and is not squeamish as to the nature of his meat.

Before we leave the subject of Chinamen let us consider another recent factor in the destruction of wild life which is at present widely operative in China itself. This is the cold storage warehouse, of which six or eight enormous ones have gone up in different parts of the East. To speak in detail only of the one at Hankow, six hundred miles up the Yangtze, we found it to be the largest structure in the city. Surrounded by a high wall, with each entrance and exit guarded by armed Sikhs, it seemed like the feudal castle of some medieval baron. Why such secrecy is necessary I could not learn, as there are no laws against its business. But so carefully guarded is its premises that until a short time ago even the British consul-general of Hankow had not been allowed to enter. He, however, at last refused to sign the papers for any more outgoing shipments until he should be allowed to see what was going on within the warehouse. I hoped to be able to look over some of the frozen pheasants for interesting scientific material, but of course was not allowed to do so.

Although here in the heart of China, outside changes are not felt so strongly and the newly-acquired meat diet of the border and emigrant Chinese is hardly apparent, these warehouses have opened up a new source of revenue, which has met with instant response. Thousands and tens of thousands of wild shot or trapped pheasants and other birds are now brought to these establishments by the natives from far and near. The birds are frozen, and twice a year shipped on specially refrigerated P. and O. steamships to England and the continent of Europe where they seem to find a ready sale. Pigs and chickens also figure in the shipments. Now the pheasants have for centuries existed in enormous numbers in the endless ricefields of China, without doing any damage to the crops. In fact they could not be present in such numbers without being an important factor in keeping down insect and other enemies of the grain. When their numbers are decimated as they are being at present, there must eventually result a serious upsetting of the balance of nature. Let us hope that in some way this may be avoided, and that the present famine deaths of thirty thousand or more in some provinces will not be increased many fold.

When I started on this search for pheasants I was repeatedly told by old explorers in the east that my task would be very different from theirs of thirty years ago; that I would find steamers, railroads and automobiles where formerly were only canoes and jungle. I indeed found this as reported, but while my task was different it was made no easier. Formerly, to be sure, one had from the start to paddle slowly or push along the trails made by natives or game animals. But then the wild life was encountered at once, while I found it always far from the end of the steamer's route or the railroad's terminal, and still to be reached only by the most primitive modes of travel.

I cite this to give point to my next great cause of destruction; the burning and clearing of vast stretches of country for the planting of rubber trees. The East seems rubber mad, and whether the enormous output which will result from the millions of trees set out month after month will be profitable, I cannot say. I can think only of the vanishing of the *entire fauna* and *flora* of many districts which I have seen as a direct result of this commercial activity. One leaves Port Swettenham on the west coast of Selangor, and for the hour's run to Kuala Lumpur sees hardly anything but vast radiating lines of spindling rubber trees, all underbrush cleared, all native growths vanished. From Kuala Lumpur to Kuala Kubu at the very foot of the mountain backbone of the Malay Peninsula, the same holds true. And where some area appears not under cultivation, the climbing fern and a coarse, useless "lalang" grass covers every inch of ground. One can hardly imagine a more complete blotting out of the native fauna and flora of any one limited region. And ever-extending roads for the increasing motor cars are widening the cleared zone, mile after mile to the north and south.

In this region, as we pushed on over the mountains into the wilderness of Pahang, we saw little of the actual destruction of the primeval native growth, but elsewhere it became a common sight. Once, for many days we studied the wonderful life of a jungle which stretched up to our very camp. Troops of rollicking wa-was or gibbons frequented the forest; squirrels, tupaias, birds and insects in myriads were everywhere during the day. Great fruit-bats, flying lemurs, owls and other nocturnal creatures made the evenings and nights full of interest.

And then, one day without warning came the sound of an ax, and another and another. From that moment the songs, cries, chirps and roars of the jungle were seldom heard from our camp. Every day saw new phalanxes of splendid primeval trees fallen, or half suspended in their rigging of lianas. The leaves withered, the flower petals fell and we heard no more the crackling of bamboos in the wind. Then the pitiful survivors of the destruction were brought to us; now a baby flying lemur, flung from its hole by the falling of some tree; young tupaias, nestling birds; a few out of the thousands of creatures from insects to mammals which were slain so that a Chinaman or Malay might eke a few dollars, four or five years hence, from a grove of rubber trees. I do not say it is wrong. Man has won out, and might is right, as since the dawn of creation; but to the onlooker, to the lover of nature and the animal world it is a terrible, a hopeless thing.

One cannot at present leave the tourist line of travel in the East without at once encountering evidence of the wholesale direct slaughter of wild life, or its no less certain extermination by the elimination of the haunts and the food plants of the various beasts and birds.

CHAPTER XXI

THE SAVAGE VIEW-POINT OF THE GUNNER

The mental attitude of the men who shoot constitutes a deadly factor in the destruction of wild life and the extermination of species. Fully ninety-five per cent of the sportsmen, gunners and other men and boys who kill game, all over the world and in all nations, regard game birds and mammals only as things to be killed *and eaten*, and not as creatures worth preserving for their beauty or their interest to mankind. This is precisely the viewpoint of the cave-man and the savage, and it has come down from the Man-with-a-Club to the Man-with-a-Gun absolutely unchanged save for one thing: the latter sometimes is prompted to save to-day in order to slaughter to-morrow.

The above statement of an existing fact may seem harsh; and some persons may be startled by it; but it is based on an acquaintance with thousands of men who shoot all kinds of game, all over the world. My critics surely will admit that my opportunities to meet the sportsmen and gunners of the world are, and for thirty-five years have been, rather favorable. As a matter of fact, I think the efforts of the hunters of my personal acquaintance have covered about seven-tenths of the hunting grounds of the world. If the estimate that I have formed of the average hunter's viewpoint is wrong, or even partially so, I will be glad to have it proven in order that I may reform my judgment and apologize.

In working with large bodies of bird-shooting sportsmen I have steadily—and also painfully—been impressed by their intentness on killing, and by the fact that *they seek to preserve game only to kill it!* Who ever saw a bird-shooter rise in a convention and advocate the preservation of any species of game bird on account of its beauty or its esthetic interest *alive?* I never did; and I have sat in many conventions of sportsmen. All the talk is of open seasons, bag limits and killing rights. The man who has the hardihood to stand up and propose a five-year close season has "a hard row to hoe." Men rise and say: "It's all nonsense! There's plenty of quail shooting on Long Island yet."

Throughout the length and breadth of America, the ruling passion is to kill as long as anything killable remains. The man who will openly advocate the stopping of quail-shooting because the quails are of such great value to the farmers, or because they are so *beautiful* and companionable to man, receives no sympathy from ninety per cent of the bird-killing sportsmen. The remaining ten per cent think seriously about the matter, and favor long close seasons. It is my impression that of the men who shoot, it is only among the big-game hunters that we find much genuine admiration for game animals, or any feeling remotely resembling regard for it.

The moment that a majority of American gunners concede the fact that game birds are worth preserving for their beauty, and their value as living neighbors to man, from that moment there is hope for the saving of the Remnant. That will indeed be the beginning of a new era, of a millennium in fact, in the preservation of wild life. It will then be easy to enact laws for ten-year close seasons on whole groups of species. Think what it would mean for such a close season to be enacted for all the grouse of the United States, all the shore-birds of the United States, or the wild turkey wherever found!

To-day, the great—indeed, the *only*—opponents of long close seasons on game birds are the gunners. Whenever and wherever you introduce a bill to provide such a season, you will find that this is true. The gun clubs and the Downtrodden Hunters' and Anglers' Protective Associations will be quick to go after their representatives, and oppose the bill. And state senators and assemblymen will think very hard and with strong courage before they deliberately resolve to do their duty regardless of the opposition of "a large body of sportsmen,"—men who have votes, and who know how to take revenge on lawmakers who deprive them of their "right" to kill. The greatest speech ever made in the Mexican Congress was uttered by the member who solemnly said: "I rise to sacrifice ambition to honor!"

Unfortunately, the men who shoot have become possessed of the idea that they have certain inherent, God-given "rights" to kill game! Now, as a matter of fact, a sportsman with a one-hundred-dollar Fox gun in his hands, a two-hundred-dollar dog at his heels and five one-hundred-dollar bills in his pocket has no more "right" to kill a covey of quail on Long Island than my milkman has to elect that it shall be let alone for the pleasure of his children! The time has come when the people who don't shoot must do one of two things:

1. They must demonstrate the fact that they have rights in the wild creatures, and demand their recognition, or

2. See the killable game all swept off the continent by the Army of Destruction.

Really, it is to me very strange that gunners never care to save game birds on account of their beauty. One living bob white on a fence is better than a score in a bloody game-bag. A live squirrel in a tree is poetry in motion; but on the table a squirrel is a rodent that tastes as a rat smells. Beside the ocean a flock of sandpipers is needed to complete the beautiful picture; but on the table a sandpiper is beneath contempt. A live deer trotting over a green meadow, waving a triangular white flag, is a sight to thrill any human ganglion; but a deer lying dead,—unless it has an exceptionally fine head,—is only so much butcher's meat.

One of the finest sights I ever saw in Montana was a big flock of sage grouse slowly stalking over a grassy flat thinly sprinkled with sage-brush. It was far more inspiring than any pile of dead birds that I ever saw.

ONE M

Anothe L ne of Extermination Appar

I remember scores of beautiful game birds that I have seen and not killed; but of all the game birds that I have eaten or tried to eat in New York, I remember with sincere pleasure only *one*. Some of the ancient cold-storage candidates I remember "for cause," as the lawyers say.

Sportsmen and gunners, for God's sake elevate your viewpoint of the game of the world. Get out of the groove in which man has run ever since the days of Adam! There is something in a game bird over and above its pound of flesh. You don't "need" the meat any longer; for you don't know what hunger is, save by reading of it. Try the field-glass and the camera, instead of the everlasting gun. Any fool can take a five-dollar gun and kill a bird; but it takes a genius to photograph one wild bird and get "a good one." As hunters, the camera men have the best of it. One good live-bird photograph is more of a trophy and a triumph than a bushel of dead birds. The birds and mammals now are literally dying for *your* help in the making of long close seasons, and in the real stoppage of slaughter. Can you not hear the call of the wild remnant?

It is time for the people who don't shoot to call a halt on those who do; "and if this be treason, then let my enemies make the most of it!"

Since the above was written, I have read in the *Outdoor World* for April, 1912, the views of a veteran sportsman and writer, Mr. Emerson Hough, on the wild-life situation as it seems to him to-day. It is a strong utterance, even though it reaches a pessimistic and gloomy conclusion which I do not share. Altogether, however, its breadth of view, its general accuracy, and its incisiveness, entitle it to a full hearing. The following is only an extract from a lengthy article entitled, "God's Acre·"

EMERSON HOUGH'S VIEW OF THE SITUATION

The truth is none the less the truth because it is unpleasant to face. There is no well posted sportsman in America, no manufacturer of sporting goods in America, no man well versed in American outdoor matters, who does not know that we are at the evening of the day of open sport in America. Our old ways have failed, all of them have failed. The declining fortunes of the best sportsman's journals of America would prove that, if proof were asked. Our sportsmanship has failed. Our game laws have failed, and we know they have failed. Our game is almost gone, and we know it is almost gone. America has changed and we know that it has changed, although we have not changed with it. The old America is done and it is gone, and we know that to be the truth. The old order passeth, and we know that the new order must come soon if it is to work any salvation for our wild game and our life in the open in pursuit of it.

There are many reasons for this fact, these facts. Perhaps the greatest lies in the steady advance of civilization into the wilderness, the usurpation for agricultural or industrial use of many of the ancient breeding and feeding places of the wild game. All over the West and now all over Canada, the plow advances, that one engine which cannot be gainsaid, which never turns a backward furrow.

Another great agency is the rapid perfection of transportation all over the world. Take the late influx of East African literature. If there really were not access to that country we would not have this literature, would not have so many pictures from that country. And if even Africa will soon be overrun, if even Africa soon will be shot out, what hope is there for the game of the wholly accessible North American continent?

It is all too easy now for the slaughterer to get to his work. all too easy for him to transport the fruits of the slaughter. At the hands of the ignorant, the unscrupulous and the unsparing, our game has steadily disappeared until it is almost gone. We have handled it in a wholly greedy, unscrupulous and selfish fashion. This has been our policy as a nation. If there is to be success for any plan to remedy this, it must come from a few large-minded men, able to think and plan, and able to do more than that— to follow their plans with deeds.

I have seen the whole story of modern American sportsmanship, so called. It has been class legislation and organized selfishness—that is what it has been, and nothing else. I do not blame country legislators, game dealers, farmers, for calling the sports-men of America selfish and thoughtless. I do not blame them for saying that the so-called protective measures advanced by sportsmen have been selfish measures, and looking to destruction rather than to protection. At least that has been their actual result. I have no more reverence for a sportsman than for anyone else, and no reverence for him at all because he is or calls himself a sportsman. He has got to be a man. He has got to be a citizen.

I have seen millions of acres of breeding and feeding grounds pass under the drain and under the plow in my own time, so that the passing whisper of the wild fowl's wing has been forgotten there now for many years. I have seen a half dozen species of fine game birds become extinct in my own time and lost forever to the American people.

And you and I have seen one protective society after another, languidly organized, paying in a languid dollar or so per capita each year, and so swiftly passing, also to be forgotten. We have seen one code and the other of conflicting and wholly selfish game laws passed, and seen them mocked at and forgotten, seen them all fail, as we all know.

We have seen even the nation's power—under that Ark of the Covenant known as the Interstate Commerce Act—fail to stop wholly the lessening of our wild game, so rapidly disappearing for so many reasons.

We have seen both selfish and unselfish sportsmen's journals attempt to solve this problem and fail to do so. Some of them were great and broad-minded journals. Their record has not been one of disgrace, although it has been one of defeat; for some of them really desired success more than they desired dividends. These, all of them, bore their share of a great experiment, an experiment in a new land, under a new theory of government, a theory which says a man should be able to restrain himself, and to govern himself. Only by following their theory through to the end of that experiment could they know that it was to fail in one of its most vitally interesting and vitally important phases.

But now, as we know, all of these agencies, selfish or unselfish, have failed to effect the salvation of American wild game. Not by any scheme, device, or theory, not by any panacea can the old days of America be brought back to us.

Mr. Hough's views are entitled to respectful consideration; but on one vital point I do not follow him.

I believe most sincerely—in fact, *I know*,—that it is *possible* to make a few new laws which, in addition to the many, many good protective laws we already have, will bring back the game, just as fast and as far as man's settlements, towns, railroads, mines and schemes in general ever can permit it to come back.

If the American People as a whole elect that our wild life shall be saved, and to a reasonable extent brought back, then by the Eternal it will be saved and brought back! The road lies straight before us, and the going is easy—*if* the Mass makes up its mind to act. But on one vital point Mr. Hough is right. The sportsman alone never will save the game! The people who do not kill must act, independently.

PART II.—PRESERVATION

CHAPTER XXII

OUR ANNUAL LOSSES BY INSECTS

"You take my life when you do take the means whereby I live."

"In no country in the world," says Mr. C. L. Marlatt, of the U. S. Department of Agriculture, "do insects impose a heavier tax on farm products than in the United States." These attacks are based upon an enormous and varied annual output of cereals and fruits, and a great variety and number of trees. For every vegetable-eating insect, native and foreign, we seem to have crops, trees and plant food galore; and their ravages rob the market-basket and the dinner-pail. In 1912 there were riots in the streets of New York over the high cost of food.

In 1903, this state of fact was made the subject of a special inquiry by the Department of Agriculture, and in the "Yearbook" for 1904, the reader will find, on page 461, an article entitled, "The Annual Loss Occasioned by Destructive Insects in the United States." The article is not of the sensational type, it was not written in an alarmist spirit, but from beginning to end it is a calm, cold-blooded analysis of existing facts, and the conclusions that fairly may be drawn from them. The opinions of several experts have been considered and quoted, and often their independent figures are stated.

With the disappearance of our birds generally, and especially the slaughter of song and other insect-eating birds both in the South and North, the destruction of the national wealth by insects forges to the front as a subject of vital importance. The logic of the situation is so simple a child can see it. Short crops mean higher prices. If ten per cent of our vegetable food supply is destroyed by insects, as certain as fate we will feel it *in the increased cost of living.*

I would like to place Mr. Marlatt's report in the hands of every man, boy and school-teacher in America; but I have not at my disposal the means to accomplish such a task. I cannot even print it here in full, but the vital facts can be stated, briefly and in plain figures.

CROPS AND INSECTS.

CORN.—The principal insect enemies of corn are the chinch bug, corn-root worm (*Diabrotica longicornis*), bill bug, wire worm, boll-worm

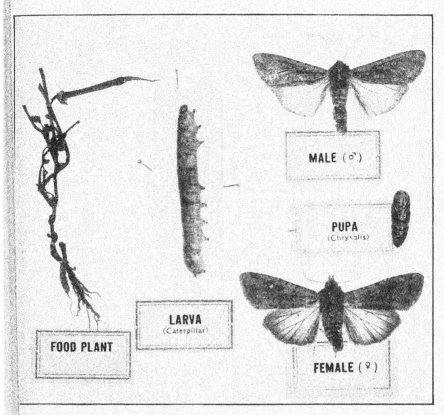

MALE (♂)

PUPA
(Chrysalis)

LARVA
(Caterpillar)

FOOD PLANT

FEMALE (♀)

THE CUT-WORM, *(Peridroma sancia)*
Very Destructive to Crops

or ear-worm, cut-worm, army worm, stalk worm, grasshopper, and plant ice, in all a total of about fifty important species! Several of these pests work secretly. At husking time the wretched ear-worm that ruins the erminal quarter or fifth of an immense number of ears, is painfully in vidence. The root-worms work insidiously, and the moles and shrews re supposed to attack them and destroy them. The corn-root worm is harged with causing an annual loss of two per cent of the corn crop, or 20,000,000; the chinch bug another two per cent; the boll or ear-worm wo per cent more. The remaining insect pests are charged with two er cent, which makes eight per cent in all, or a total of $80,000,000 ost each year to the American farmer through the ravages of insects. This is not evenly distributed, but some areas suffer more than others.

WHEAT.—Of all our cereal crops, wheat is the one that suffers most om insects. There are three insects that cause to the wheat industry an annual loss of about ten per cent. The *chinch bug* is the worst, and it is charged with five per cent ($20,000,000) of the total loss. The *Hessian fly* comes next in order, and occasionally rolls up enormous losses. In the year 1900, that insect caused to Indiana and Ohio alone the loss of 2,577,000 *acres* of wheat, and the total cost to us of that insect in that year "undoubtedly approached $100,000,000." Did that affect the price of wheat or not? If not, then there is no such thing as a "law of supply and demand."

Wheat plant-lice form collectively the third insect pest destructive to wheat, of which it is reported that "the annual loss occasioned by wheat plant-lice probably does not fall short of two or three per cent of the crop."

HAY AND FORAGE CROPS.—These are attacked by locusts, grasshoppers, army worms, cut-worms, web worms, small grass worms and leaf hoppers. Some of these pests are so small and work so insidiously that even the farmer is prone to overlook their existence. "A ten per cent shrinkage from these and other pests in grasses and forage plants is a minimum estimate."

COTTON.—The great enemies of the cotton-planter are the cotton boll weevil, the bollworm and the leaf worm; but other insects inflict serious damage. In 1904 the loss occasioned by the boll weevil, chiefly in Texas, was conservatively estimated by an expert, Mr. W. D. Hunter, at $20,000,000. The boll worm of the southwestern cotton states has sometimes caused an annual loss of $12,000,000, or four per cent of the crops in the states affected. Before the use of arsenical poisons, the leaf worm caused an annual loss of from twenty to thirty million dollars; but of late years that total has been greatly reduced.

FRUITS.—The insects that reduce our annual fruit crop attack every portion of the tree and its product. The woolly aphis attacks the roots of the fruit tree, the trunk and limbs are preyed upon by millions of scale insects and borers, the leaves are devastated by the all-devouring leaf worms, canker worms and tent caterpillars, while the fruit itself is attacked by the codling moth, curculio and apple maggot. To destroy fruit is to take money out of the farmer's pocket, and to attack and injure the tree is like undermining his house itself. By an annual expenditure of about $8,250,000 in cash for spraying apple trees, the destructiveness of the codling moth and curculio have been greatly reduced, but that money is itself a cash loss. Add to this the $12,000,000 of actual shrinkage in the apple crop, and the total annual loss to our apple-growers due to the codling moth and curculio is about $20,000,000. In the high price of apples, a part of this loss falls upon the consumer.

In 1889 Professor Forbes calculated that the annual loss to the fruit growers of Illinois from insect ravages was $2,375,000. In 1892, insects caused to Nebraska apple-growers a loss computed at $2,000,000 and, in 1897, New York farmers lost $2,500,000 from that cause. "In many sections of the Pacific Northwest the loss was from fifty to seventy-five per cent." (Yearbook, page 470.)

FORESTS.—"The annual losses occasioned by insect pests to forest

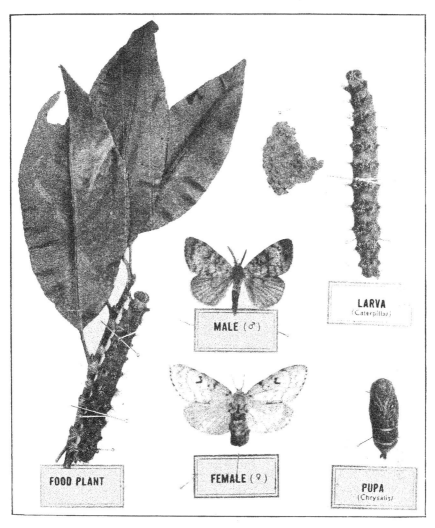

THE GYPSY MOTH, (*Portheria dispar*)
Very Destructive to the Finest Shade Trees

and forest products (in the United States) have been estimated by Dr. A. D. Hopkins, special agent in charge of forest insect investigations, at not less than $100,000,000. * * * It covers both the loss from insect damages to standing timber, and to the crude and manufactured forest products.   The annual loss to growing timber is conservatively placed at $70,000,000.''

There are other insect damages that we will not pause to enumerate here. They relate to cattle, horses, sheep and stored grain products of many kinds. Even cured tobacco has its pest, a minute insect known as the cigarette beetle, now widespread in America and "frequently the cause of very heavy losses."

The millions of the insect world are upon us. Their cost to us has been summed up by Mr. Marlatt in the table that appears below.

ANNUAL VALUES OF FARM PRODUCTS, AND LOSSES CHARGEABLE
TO INSECT PESTS.

Official Report in the Yearbook of the Department of Agriculture, 1904.

PRODUCT	VALUE	PERCENTAGE OF LOSS	AMOUNT OF LOSS
Cereals............	$2,000,000,000	10	$200,000,000
Hay..................................	530,000,000	10	53,000,000
Cotton...............................	600,000,000	10	60,000,000
Tobacco..............................	53,000,000	10	5,300,000
Truck Crops..........................	265,000,000	20	53,000,000
Sugars...............................	50,000,000	10	5,000,000
Fruits...............................	135,000,000	20	27,000,000
Farm Forests.........................	110,000,000	10	11,000,000
Miscellaneous Crops..................	58,000,000	10	5,800,000
Total........................	$3,801,000,000		$420,100,000
Animal Products......................	1,750,000,000	10	175,000,000
Natural Forests and Forest Products.....	....	..	100,000,000
Products in Storage..................	....	..	100,000,000
GRAND TOTAL..................	$5,551,000,000	..	$795,100,000

The millions of the insect world are upon us. The birds fight them for us, and when the birds are numerous and have nestlings to feed, the number of insects they consume is enormous. They require absolutely nothing at our hands save *the privilege of being let alone while they work for us!* In fighting the insects, our only allies in nature are the song-birds, woodpeckers, shore-birds, swallows and martins, certain hawks, moles, shrews, bats, and a few other living creatures. All these wage war at their own expense. The farmers might just as well lose $8,250,000 through a short apple crop as to pay out that sum in labor and materials in spraying operations. And yet, fools that we are, we go on slaughtering our friends, and allowing others to slaughter them, under the same brand of fatuous folly that leads the people of Italy to build anew on the smoking sides of Vesuvius, after a dozen generations have been swept away by fire and ashes.

In the next chapter we will consider the work of our friends, The Birds

CHAPTER XXIII.

THE ECONOMIC VALUE OF BIRDS

To-day, from Halifax to Los Angeles, and from Key West to Victoria, a deadly contest is being waged. The fruit-growers, farmers, forest owners and "park people" are engaged in a struggle with the insect hordes for the possession of the trees, shrubs and crops. Go out into the open, with your eyes open, and you will see it for yourself. Millions of dollars are being expended in it. Look at this exhibit of what is going on around me, at this very moment,—July 19, 1912:

The bag insects, in thousands, are devouring the leaves of locust and maple trees.

The elm beetles are trying to devour the elms; and spraying is in progress.

The hickory-bark borers are slaughtering the hickories; and even some park people are neglecting to take the measures necessary to stop it!

The tent caterpillars are being burned.

The aphis (scale insects) are devouring the tops of the *white potatoes* in the New York University school garden, just as the potato beetle does.

The codling moth larvae are already at work on the apples.

The leaves affected by the witch hazel gall fly are being cut off and burned.

These are merely the most conspicuous of the insect pests that I now see daily. I am not counting those of second or third-rate importance.

Some of these hordes are being fought with poisonous sprays, some are being killed by hand, and some are being ignored.

In view of the known value of the remaining trees of our country, each woodpecker in the United States is worth twenty dollars in cash. Each nuthatch, creeper and chickadee is worth from five to ten dollars, according to local circumstances. You might just as well cut down four twenty-inch trees and let them lie and decay, as to permit one woodpecker to be killed and eaten by an Italian in the North, or a negro in the South. The downy woodpecker is the relentless enemy of the codling moth, an insect that annually inflicts upon our apple crop damages estimated by the experts of the U. S. Department of Agriculture at twelve million dollars!

Now, is a federal strong-arm migratory bird law needed for such birds or not? Let the owners of orchards and forests make answer.

THE CASE OF THE CODLING MOTH AND CURCULIO.—The codling moth and curculio are twin terrors to apple-growers, partly because of

DOWNY WOODPECKER

their deadly destructiveness, and partly because man is so weak in resisting them. The annual cost of the fight made against them, in sprays and labor and apparatus, has been estimated at $8,250,000. And what do the birds do to the codling moth, — when there are any birds left alive to operate? The testimony comes from all over the United States, and it is worth while to cite it briefly as a fair sample of the work of the birds upon this particularly deadly pest. These facts and quotations are from the "Yearbook of the Department of Agriculture," for 1911.

The Downy Woodpecker is the champion tree-protector, and also one of the greatest enemies of the codling moth. When man is quite unable to find the hidden larvae, Downy locates it every time, and digs it out. It extracts worms from young apples so skillfully that often the fruit is not permanently injured. Mr. F. M. Webster reports that the labors of this bird "afford actual and immediate relief to the infected fruit." Testimony in favor of the downy woodpecker has come from New York, New Jersey, Texas and California, "and no fewer than twenty larvae have been taken from a single stomach."

Take the *Red-Shafted Flicker* vs. the codling moth. Mr. A. P. Martin, of Petaluma, Cal., states that during the early spring months (of 1890) they were seen by hundreds in his orchard, industriously examining the trunks and larger limbs of the fruit trees; and he also found great numbers of them around sheds where he stored his winter apples and pears. As the result of several hours' search, Mr. Martin found only one worm, and this one escaped only by accident, for several of the birds had been within a quarter of an inch of it. "So eager are woodpeckers in search of codling moths that they have often been known to riddle the shingle traps and paper bands which are placed to attract the larvae about to spin cocoons.

Behold the array of birds that devour the larvae of the codling moth to an important extent.

Birds that Devour the Codling Moth

Downy Woodpecker (*Dryobates pubescens*).
Hairy Woodpecker (*Dryobates villosus*).
Texan Woodpecker (*Dryobates scalaris bairdi*).
Red-Headed Woodpecker (*Melanerpes erythrocephalus*).
Red-Shafted Flicker (*Colaptes cafer collaris*).
Pileated Woodpecker (*Phloeotomus pileatus*).
Kingbird (*Tyrranus tyrranus*).
Western Yellow-Bellied Flycatcher (*Empidonax difficilis*).
Blue Jay (*Cyanocitta cristata*).
California Jay (*Aphelocoma californica*).
Magpie (*Pica pica hudsonia*).
Crow Blackbird (*Quiscalus quiscula*).
Brewer Blackbird (*Euphagus cyanocephalus*).
Bullock Oriole (*Icterus bullocki*).
English Sparrow (*Passer domesticus*).
Chipping Sparrow (*Spizella passerina*).
California Towhee (*Pipilo crissalis*).
Cardinal (*Cardinalis cardinalis*).
Black Headed Grosbeak (*Zamelodia melanocephala*).
Lazuli Bunting (*Passerina cyanea*).
Barn Swallow (*Hirundo erythrogastra*).
Western Warbling Vireo (*Vireosylva gilva swainsoni*).
Summer, or Yellow Warbler (*Dendroica aestiva*).
Lutescent Warbler (*Vermivora celata lutescens*)
Brown Creeper (*Certhia familiaris americana*).
White-Breasted Nuthatch (*Sitta carolinensis*).
Black-Capped Chickadee (*Penthestes atricapillus*).
Plain Titmouse (*Baeolophus inornatus*).
Carolina Chickadee (*Penthestes carolinensis*).
Mountain Chickadee (*Penthestes gambeli*).
California Bush Tit (*Psaltriparus minimus californicus*).
Ruby-Crowned Kinglet (*Regulus calendula*)
Robin (*Planesticus migratorius*).
Bluebird (*Sialia sialis*).

In all, says Mr. W. L. McAtee, thirty-six species of birds of thirteen families help man in his irrepressible conflict against his deadly enemy, the codling moth. "In some places they destroy from sixty-six to eighty-five per cent of the hibernating larvae."

Now, are the farmers of this country content to let the Italians of the North, and the negroes of the South, shoot those birds for food, and devour them? What is the great American farmer going to *do* about this matter? What he should do is to write and urge his members of Congress to work for and vote for the federal migratory bird bill.

THE COTTON BOLL WEEVIL.—Let us take one other concrete case. The cotton boll weevil invaded the United States from Mexico in 1894. Ten years later it was costing the cotton planters an annual loss estimated at fifteen million dollars per year. Later on that loss was estimated at twenty million dollars. The cotton boll weevil strikes at the heart of the industry by destroying the boll of the cotton plant. While the total loss never can be definitely ascertained, we know that it has amounted to many millions of dollars. The figure given above has been widely quoted, and so far as I am aware, never disputed.

Fortunately we have at hand a government publication on this subject which gives some pertinent facts regarding the bird enemies of the cotton boll weevil. It is Circular No. 57 of the Biological Survey, Department of Agriculture. Any one can obtain it by addressing that Department. I quote the most important portions of this valuable document:

BIRDS USEFUL IN THE WAR AGAINST THE COTTON BOLL WEEVIL.

By H. W. Henshaw, Chief of the Biological Survey.

The main purpose of this circular is to direct the attention of cotton growers and others in the cotton growing states to the importance of birds in the boll weevil war, to emphasize the need of protection for them, and to suggest means to increase the numbers and extend the range of certain of the more important kinds.

Investigations by the Biological Survey show that thirty-eight species of birds eat boll weevils. While some eat them only sparingly others eat them freely, and no fewer than forty-seven adult weevils have been found in the stomach of a single cliff swallow. Of the birds known at the present time to feed on the weevil, among the most important are the orioles, nighthawks, and, foremost of all, the swallows (including the purple martin).

ORIOLES.—Six kinds of orioles live in Texas, though but two inhabit the southern states generally. Orioles are among the few birds that evince a decided preference for weevils, and as they persistently hunt for the insects on the bolls, they fill a place occupied by no other birds. They are protected by law in nearly every state in the Union, but their bright plumage renders them among the most salable of birds for millinery purposes, and despite protective laws, considerable numbers are still killed for the hat trade. It is hardly necessary to point out that their importance as insect eaters everywhere demands their protection, but more especially in the cotton belt.

NIGHTHAWK.—The nighthawk, or bull-bat, also renders important service in the destruction of weevils, and catches them on the wing in considerable numbers, especially during its migration. Unfortunately, *the nighthawk is eaten for food in some sections of the South, and considerable numbers are shot for this purpose.* The bird's value for food, however, is infinitesimal as compared with the service it renders the cotton grower and other agriculturists, and every effort should be made to spread broadcast a knowledge of its usefulness as a weevil destroyer, with a view to its complete protection.

SWALLOWS.—Of all the birds now known to destroy weevils, swallows are the most important. Six species occur in Texas and the southern states. The martin, the barn swallow, the bank swallow, the roughwing, and the cliff swallow breed locally in Texas, and all of them, except the cliff swallow, breed in the other cotton states. The white-bellied, or tree swallow, nests only in the North, and by far the greater number of cliff swallows nest in the North and West.

As showing how a colony of martins thrives when provided with sufficient room to multiply, an experiment by Mr. J. Warren Jacobs, of Waynesburg, Pa., may be cited. The first year five pairs were induced to occupy the single box provided, and raised eleven young. The fourth year three large boxes, divided into ninety-nine rooms, contained fifty-three pairs, and they raised about 175 young. The colony was thus nearly three hundred strong at the close of the fourth season. The effect of this number of hungry martins on the insects infesting the neighborhood may be imagined.

From the "American Natural History"

THE BALTIMORE ORIOLE
The Deadly Enemy of the Cotton-Boll Weevil

From the standpoint of the farmer and the cotton grower, swallows are among the most useful birds. Especially designed by nature to capture insects in midair, their powers of flight and endurance are unexcelled, and in their own field they have no competitors. Their peculiar value to the cotton grower consists in the fact that, like the night-hawk, they capture boll weevils when flying over the fields, which no other birds do. Flycatchers snap up the weevils near trees and shrubbery. Wrens hunt them out when concealed under bark or rubbish. Blackbirds catch them on the ground, as do the killdeer, titlark, meadow lark, and others; while orioles hunt for them on the bolls. But it is the peculiar function of swallows to catch the weevils as they are making long flights, leaving the cotton fields in search of hiding places in which to winter or entering them to continue their work of devastation.

Means have been taken to inform residents of the northern states of the value of the swallow tribe to agriculturists generally, and particularly to cotton planters, in the belief that the number of swallows breeding in the North can be substantially increased. The cooperation of the northern states is important, since birds bred in the North migrate directly through the southern states in the fall on their way to the distant tropics, and also in the spring on their return.

Important as it is to increase the number of northern breeding swallows, it is still more important to increase the number nesting in the South and to induce

THE NIGHTHAWK

A Goatsucker, not a Song-bird; but it Feeds
Exclusively Upon Insects

the birds there to extend their range over as much of the cotton area as possible. Nesting birds spend much more time in the South than migrants, and during the weeks when the old birds are feeding young they are almost incessantly engaged in the pursuit of insects.

It is not, of course, claimed that birds alone can stay the ravages of the cotton boll weevil in Texas, but they materially aid in checking the advance of the pest into the other cotton states. Important auxiliaries in destroying these insects, birds aid in reducing their numbers within safe limits, and once within safe limits in keeping them there. Hence it is for the interests of the cotton states that special efforts be made to protect and care for the weevil-eating species, and to increase their numbers in every way possible.—(End of the circular.)

Condensed Notes on the Food Habits of Certain North American Birds.

Millions of Americans and near-Americans, both old and young, now need to be shown the actual figures that represent the value of our birds as destroyers of the insects, weeds and the small rodents that are swarming to overrun and devour our fields, orchards and forests. Will our people never learn that in fighting pests the birds are worth ten times more to men than all the poisons, sprays and traps that ever were invented or used?

We cannot spray our forests; and if the wild birds do not protect them from insects, *nothing will!* If you will watch a warbler collecting the insects out of the top of a seventy-foot forest oak, busy as a bee

THE PURPLE MARTIN

A Representative of the Swallow Family. A Great Insect-eater; one of the Most Valuable of all Birds to the Southern Cotton planter, and Northern farmer. Shot for "Food" in the South. Driven out of the North by the English Sparrow Pest.

hour after hour, it will convince you that the birds do for the forests that which man with all his resources cannot accomplish. You will then realize that to this country every woodpecker, chickadee, titmouse, creeper and warbler is easily worth its weight in gold. The killing of any member of those groups of birds should be punished by a fine of twenty-five dollars.

THE BOB-WHITE.—And take the *Bob White Quail*, for example, and the weeds of the farm. To kill weeds costs money—hard cash that the farmer earns by toil. Does the farmer put forth strenuous efforts to protect the bird of all birds that does most to help him keep down the weeds? Far from it! All that the *average* farmer thinks about the quail is of killing it, for a few ounces of meat on the table.

It is fairly beyond question that of all birds that influence the fortunes of the farmers and fruit-growers of North America, the common quail, or bob white, is one of the most valuable. It stays on the farm all the year round. When insects are most numerous and busy, Bob White devotes to them his entire time. He cheerfully fights them, from sixteen to eighteen hours per day. When the insects are gone, he turns his attention to the weeds that are striving to seed down the fields for another year. Occasionally he gets a few grains of wheat that have been left on the ground by the reapers; but he does *no damage*. In California, where the valley quail once were very numerous, they sometimes consumed altogether too much wheat for the good of the farmers; but outside of California I believe such occurrences are unknown.

Let us glance over the bob white's bill of fare:

Weed Seeds.—One hundred and twenty-nine different weeds have been found to contribute to the quail's bill of fare. Crops and stomachs have been found crowded with rag-weed seeds, to the number of one thousand, while others had eaten as many seeds of crab-grass. A bird shot at Pine Brook, N. J., in October, 1902, had eaten five thousand seeds of green fox-tail grass, and one killed on Christmas Day at Kinsale, Va., had taken about ten thousand seeds of the pig-weed. (Elizabeth A. Reed.)

In Bulletin No. 21, Biological Survey, it is calculated that if in Virginia and North Carolina there are four bob whites to every square mile, and each bird consumes one ounce of seed per day, the total destruction to weed seeds from September 1st to April 30th in those states alone will be 1,341 tons.

In 1910 Mrs. Margaret Morse Nice, of Clark University, Worcester, Mass., finished and contributed to the Journal of Economic Entomology (Vol. III., No. 3) a masterful investigation of "The Food of the Bob-White." It should be in every library in this land. Mrs. Nice publishes the entire list of 129 species of weed seeds consumed by the quail,—and it looks like a rogue's gallery. Here is an astounding record, which proves once more that truth is stranger than fiction:

NUMBER OF SEEDS EATEN BY A BOB-WHITE IN ONE DAY

Barnyard grass	2,500	Milkweed	770
Beggar ticks	1,400	Peppergrass	2,400
Black mustard	2,500	Pigweed	12,000
Burdock	600	Plantain	12,500
Crab grass	2,000	Rabbitsfoot clover	30,000
Curled dock	4,175	Round-headed bush clover	1,800
Dodder	1,560	Smartweed	2,250
Evening primrose	10,000	White vervain	18,750
Lamb's quarter	15,000	Water smartweed	2,000

NOTABLY BAD INSECTS EATEN BY THE BOB-WHITE

(Prof. Judd and Mrs. Nice.)

Colorado potato beetle	Clover leaf beetle
Cucumber beetle	Cotton boll weevil
Chinch bug	Cotton boll worm
Bean-leaf beetle	Striped garden caterpillar
Wireworm	Cutworms
May beetle	Grasshoppers
Corn billbug	Corn-louse ants
Imbricated-snout beetle	Rocky Mountain locust
Plant lice	Codling moth
Cabbage butterfly	Canker worm
Mosquito	Hessian fly
Squash beetle	Stable fly

SUMMARY OF THE QUAIL'S INSECT FOOD

Orthoptera—Grasshoppers and locusts	13	species.
Hemiptera—Bugs	24	"
Homoptera—Leaf hoppers and plant lice	6	"
Lepidoptera—Moths, caterpillars, cut-worms, etc	19	
Diptera—Flies	8	
Coleoptera—Beetles	61	
Hymenoptera—Ants, wasps, slugs	8	
Other insects	6	

Total 145

THE BOB-WHITE

For the Smaller Pests of the Farm, This Bird is the Most
Marvelous Engine of Destruction Ever put
Together of Flesh and Blood

A few sample meals of insects.—The following are records of single individual meals of the bob white:

Of grasshoppers, 84; chinch bugs, 100; squash bugs, 12; army worm, 12; cut-worm, 12; mosquitoes, 568 in three hours; cotton boll weevil, 47; flies, 1,350; rose slugs, 1,286. Miscellaneous insects consumed by a laying hen quail, 1,532, of which 1,000 were grasshoppers; total weigh of the lot, 24.6 grams.

"F. M. Howard, of Beeville, Texas, wrote to the U. S. Bureau of Entomology, that the bob whites shot in his vicinity had their crops filled with the weevils. Another farmer reported his cotton fields full of quail, and an entire absence of weevils." Texas and Georgia papers (please copy.)

And yet, because of its few pitiful ounces of flesh, two million gunners and ten thousand lawmakers think of the quail *only as a bird that can be shot and eaten!* Throughout a great portion of its former range, including New York and New Jersey, the species is surely and certainly on the verge of *total extinction.* And yet sportsmen gravely discuss the "bag limit," and "enforcement of the bag-limit law" as a means of bringing back this almost vanished species! Such folly in grown men is very trying.

To my friend, the Epicure:—The next time you regale a good appetite with blue points, terrapin stew, filet of sole and saddle of mutton, touched up here and there with the high lights of rare old sherry, rich claret and dry monopole, pause as the dead quail is laid before you, on a funeral pyre of toast, and consider this: "Here lies the charred remains of the Farmer's Ally and Friend, poor Bob White. In life he devoured 145 different kinds of bad insects, and the seeds of 129 anathema weeds. For the smaller pests of the farm, he was the most marvelous engine of destruction that God ever put together of flesh and blood. He was good, beautiful and true; and his small life was blameless. And here he lies, dead; snatched away from his field of labor, and destroyed, in order that I may be tempted to dine three minutes longer, after I have already eaten to satiety."

Then go on, and finish Bob White.

THE CASE OF THE ROBIN.—For a long time this bird has been slaughtered in the South for food, regardless of the agricultural interests of the North. No Southern gentleman ever shoots robins, or song birds of any kind, but the negroes and poor whites do it. The worst case of recent occurrence was the slaughter in the town of Pittsboro, North Carolina.

It was in January, 1912. The Mayor of the town, Hon. Bennet Nooe, was away from home; and during a heavy fall of snow "the robins came into the town in great numbers to feed upon the berries of the cedar trees. In order that the birds might be killed without restriction, the Board of Aldermen suspended the ordinance against the firing of guns in the town, and permitted the inhabitants to kill the robins."

A disgraceful carnival of slaughter immediately followed in which "about all the male population" participated. Regarding this, Mayor Nooe later on wrote to the editor of Bird Lore as follows:

"Hearing of this, on my return, I went to the Aldermen, *all of whom were guilty*, and told them that they and all others who were guilty would have to be fined. Three out of the five submitted and paid up, but they insisted that the ordinance be changed to read exactly as it is written here, with the exception that *all could shoot* robins in the town until the first of March; whereupon I resigned, as was stated."—(*Bird Lore*, XIV, 2. p 140.)

The Mayor was quite right. The robin butchers of Pittsboro were not worthy to be governed by him.

THE MEADOW LARK is one of the most valuable birds that frequent farming regions. Throughout the year insects make up 73 per cent of its food, weed-seeds 12 per cent, and grain only 5 per cent. During the insect season, insects constitute 90 per cent of its food.

THE BALTIMORE ORIOLE is as valuable to man as it is beautiful. Its nest is the most wonderful example of bird architecture in our land. In May insects constitute 90 per cent of this bird's food. For the entire year, insects and other animal food make 83.4 per cent and vegetable matter 16.6 per cent.

THE CROW BLACKBIRD feeds as follows, throughout the whole year: insects, 26.9 per cent; other animal food 3.4; corn 37.2; oats, 2.9; wheat, 4.8; other grain, 1.6; fruits, 5; weed seeds and mast 18.2! This report was based on the examination (by the Biological Survey) of 2,346 stomachs, and "the charge that the blackbird is an habitual robber of birds' nests was disproved by the examinations." (F. E. L. Beal.)

FLYCATCHERS.—The high-water mark in insect-destruction by our birds is reached by the flycatchers,—dull-colored, modest-mannered little creatures that do their work so quietly you hardly notice them. All you see in your tree-tops is a two-foot flit or glide, now here and now there, as the leaves and high branches are combed of their insect life.

Bulletin No. 44 of the Department of Agriculture gives the residuum of an exhausting examination of 3,398 warbler stomachs, from seventeen species of birds, and the result is: 94.99 per cent of insect food,—mostly bad insects, too,—and 5.01 per cent vegetable food. What more can any forester ask of a bird?

THE SPARROWS.—All our sparrows are great consumers of weed seeds. Professor Beal has calculated the total quantity consumed in Iowa in one year, —in the days when sparrows were normally numerous,—at 1,750,000 pounds.

THE ROSE-BREASTED GROSBEAK

"The Potato-bug Bird," Greatest Enemy of the Potato Beetles
From the "American Natural History"

THE AMERICAN GOLDFINCH as a weed destroyer has few equals. It makes a specialty of the seeds of the members of the Order Compositæ, and is especially fond of the seeds of ragweed, thistles, wild lettuce and wild sunflower. But, small and beautiful as this bird is, there are hundreds of thousands of grown men in America who would shoot it and eat it if they dared!

THE HAWKS AND OWLS.—Let no other state repeat the error that once was made in Pennsylvania when that state enacted in 1885, her now famous hawk-and-owl bounty law. In order to accomplish the wholesale destruction of her birds of prey, a law was passed providing for the payment of a bounty of fifty cents each for the scalps of hawks and owls. Immediately the slaughter began. In two years 180,000 scalps were brought in, and $90,000 were paid out for them. It was estimated that the saving to the farmers in poultry amounted to one dollar for each $1,205 paid out in bounties.

The awakening came even more swiftly than the ornithologists expected. By the end of two years from the passage of "the hawk law," the farmers found their fields and orchards thoroughly overrun by destructive rats, mice and insects, and they appealed to the legislature for the quick repeal of the law. With all possible haste this was brought about; but it was estimated by competent judges that in damages to their crops the hawk law cost the people of Pennsylvania nothing less than two million dollars.

Moral: Don't make any laws providing for the destruction of hawks and owls until you have exact knowledge, and know in advance what the results will be.

In the space at my disposal for this subject, it is impossible to treat our species of hawks and owls separately. The reader can find in the "American Natural History" fifteen pages of text, numerous illustrations and many figures elucidating this subject. Unfortunately Dr. Fisher's admirable work on "The Hawks and Owls" has long been out of print, and unobtainable. There are, however, a few observations that must be recorded here.

Each bird of prey is a balanced equation. Each one, I think without a single exception, does *some* damage, chiefly in the destruction of valuable wild birds. The value of the poultry destroyed by hawks and owls is very small in comparion with their killing of wild prey. *Many of the species do not touch domestic poultry!* At the same time, when a hawk of any kind, or an owl, sets to work deliberately and persistently to clean out a farmer's poultry yard, and is actually doing it, that farmer is justified in killing that bird. But, the *occasional* loss of a broiler is not to be regarded as justification for a war of extermination on *all* the hawks that fly! Individual wild-animal nuisances can occasionally become so exasperating as to justify the use of the gun,—when scarecrows fail; but in all such circumstances the greatest judgment, and much forbearance also, is desirable and necessary.

The value of hawks and owls rests upon their perpetual warfare on the millions of destructive rats, mice, moles, shrews, weasels, rabbits and English sparrows that constantly prey upon what the farmer produces. On this point a few illustrations must be given. One of the most famous comes via Dr. Fisher, from one of the towers of the Smithsonian buildings, and relates to

THE BARN OWL, (*Strix flammea*).—Two hundred pellets consisting of bones, hair and feathers from one nesting pair of these birds were collected, and found to contain 454 skulls, of which 225 were of meadow mice, 179 of house mice, 2 of pine mice, 20 were of rats, 6 of jumping mice, 20 were from shrews, 1 was of a mole and 1 a vesper sparrow. *One* bird, and 453 noxious mammals! Compare this with the record of any cat on earth. Anything that the barn owl wants from me, or from any farmer, should at once be offered to it, on a silver tray. This bird is often called the Monkey-Faced Owl, and it should be called the Farmer's-Friend Owl.

THE LONG-EARED OWL, (*Asio wilsonianus*) has practically the same kind of a record as the barn owl,—scores of mice, rats and shrews de-

THE BARN OWL

Wonderfully Destructive of Rats and Mice, and Almost Never Touches Birds

stroyed, and only an occasional small bird. Its nearest relative, the *Short-eared Owl* (*A. accipitrinus*) may be described in the same words.

THE GREAT HORNED OWL fills us with conflicting passions. For the long list of dead rats and mice, pocket gophers, skunks, and weasels to his credit, we think well of him, and wish his prosperity. For the song-birds, ruffed grouse, quail, other game birds, domestic poultry, squirrels, chipmunks and hares that he kills, we hate him, and would cheerfully wring his neck, wearing gauntlets. He does an unusual amount of good, and a terrible amount of harm. It is impossible to strike a balance for him, and determine with mathematical accuracy whether he should be shot or permitted to live. At all events, whenever *Bubo* comes up for trial, we must give the feathered devil his due.

The names "CHICKEN HAWK or HEN HAWK" as applied usually refer to the RED-SHOULDERED or RED-TAILED species. Neither of these is really very destructive to poultry, but both are very destructive to mice, rats and other pestiferous creatures. Both are large, showy birds, not so very swift in flight, and rather easy to approach. Neither of them should be destroyed,—not even though they do, once in a great while, take a chicken or wild bird. They pay for them, four times over, by rat-killing. Mr. J. Alden Loring states that he once knew a pair of red-shouldered hawks to nest within fifty rods of a poultry farm on which there were 800 young chickens and 400 ducks, not one of which was taken. (See the American Natural History, pages 229–30.)

HAWKS THAT SHOULD BE DESTROYED.—There are two small, fierce, daring, swift-winged hawks both of which are so very destructive that they deserve to be shot whenever possible. They are COOPER'S HAWK (*Accipiter cooperi*) and the SHARP-SHINNED HAWK (*A. velox*). They are closely related, and look much alike, but the former has a rounded tail and the latter a square one. In killing them, *please do not kill any other hawk by mistake;* and if you do not positively recognize the bird, don't shoot.

THE GOSHAWK is a bad one, and so is the PEREGRINE FALCON, or DUCK HAWK. Both deserve death, but they are so rare that we need not take them into account.

Some of the hawks and owls are very destructive to song-birds, and members of the grouse family. In 159 stomachs of sharp-shinned hawks, 99 contained song-birds and woodpeckers. In 133 stomachs of Cooper's hawks, 34 contained poultry or game birds, and 52 contained other birds. The game birds included 8 quail, 1 ruffed grouse and 5 pigeons.

THE WOODPECKERS.*—These birds are the natural guardians of the trees. If we had enough of them, our forests would be fairly safe from insect pests. Of the six or seven North American species that are of the most importance to our forests, the DOWNY WOODPECKER, (*Dryobates pubescens*) is accorded first rank. It is one of the smallest species. The contents of 140 stomachs consisted of 74 per cent insects, 25 per cent vegetable matter and 1 per cent sand. The insects were ants, beetles, bugs, flies, caterpillars, grasshoppers and a few spiders.

THE HAIRY WOODPECKER, (*Dryobates villosus*), a very close relation of the preceding species, is also small, and his food supply is as follows: insects, 68 per cent, vegetable matter 31, mineral 1.

THE GOLDEN-WINGED WOODPECKER, (*Colaptes auratus*), is the largest and handsomest of all the woodpeckers that we really see in evidence. The Pileated is one of the largest, but we never see it. This bird makes a specialty of ants, of which it devours immense numbers. Its food is 56 per cent animal matter (three-fourths of which is ants), 39 per cent is vegetable matter, and 5 per cent mineral matter.

THE RED-HEADED WOODPECKER is a serious fruit-eater, and many complaints have been lodged against him. Exactly one-half his food supply consists of vegetable matter, chiefly wild berries, acorns, beech-nuts, and the seeds of wild shrubs and weeds. We may infer that about one-tenth of his food, in summer and fall, consists of cultivated fruit and berries. His proportion of cultivated foods is entirely too small to justify any one in destroying this species.

In view of the prevalence of insect pests in the state of New York, I have spent hours in trying to devise a practical plan for making wood-peckers about ten times more numerous than they now are. Contributions to this problem will be thankfully received. Yes; we *do* put out pork fat and suet in winter, quantities of it; but I grieve to say that to-day in the Zoological Park there is not more than one woodpecker for every ten that were there twelve years ago. Where have they gone? Only one answer is possible. They have been shot and eaten, by the guerrillas of destruction.

*The reader is advised to consult Prof. F. E. L. Beale's admirable report on "The Food of Woodpeckers," Bulletin No. 7, U. S. Department of Agriculture.

GOLDEN-WINGED WOODPECKER

A Bird of Great Value to Orchards and Forests, now
Rapidly Disappearing, Undoubtedly
Through Slaughter as "Food"

Surely no man of intelligence needs to be told to protect woodpeckers to the utmost, and to *feed them in winter.* Nail up fat pork, or large chunks of suet, on the south sides of conspicuous trees, and encourage the woodpeckers, nuthatches, chickadees and titmice to remain in your woods through the long and dreary winter.

THE ENGLISH SPARROW is a nuisance and a pest, because it drives away from the house and the orchard the house wren, bluebird, phœbe, purple martin and swallow, any one of which is more valuable to man than a thousand English sparrows. I never yet have seen one of the pest sparrows catch an insect, but Chief Forester Merkel says that he has seen one catching and eating small moths.

There is one place in the country where English sparrows have not yet come; and whenever they do appear there, they will meet a hostile reception. I shall kill every one that comes,—for the sake of retaining the wrens. catbirds, phœbes and thrushes that now literally make home happy for my family. A good way to discourage sparrows is to shoot them en masse when they are feeding on road refuse, such as the white-throated, white-crowned and other sparrows never touch. Persistent destruction of their nests will check the nuisance.

THE SHORE BIRDS.—Who is there who thinks of the shore-birds as being directly beneficial to man by reason of their food habits? I warrant not more than one man in every ten thousand! We think of them only as possible "food." The amount of actual cash value benefit that the shore-birds confer upon man through the destruction of bad things is, in comparison with the number of birds, enormous.

The Department of Agriculture never publishes and circulates anything that has already been published, no matter how valuable to the public at large. Our rules are different. Because I know that many of the people of our country need the information, I am going to reprint here, as an object lesson and a warning, the whole of the Biological Survey's valuable and timely circular No. 79, issued April 11, 1911, and written by Prof. W. L. McAtee. It should open the eyes of the American people to two things: the economic value of these birds, and the fact that they are everywhere far on the road toward extermination!

Our Vanishing Shorebirds

By Prof. W. L. McAtee

The term shorebird is applied to a group of long-legged, slender-billed, and usually plainly colored birds belonging to the order Limicolæ. More than sixty species of them occur in North America. True to their name they frequent the shores of all bodies of water, large and small, but many of them are equally at home on plains and prairies.

Throughout the eastern United States shorebirds are fast vanishing. While formerly numerous species swarmed along the Atlantic coast and in the prairie regions, many of them have been so reduced that extermination seems imminent. The black-bellied plover or beetlehead, which occurred along the Atlantic seaboard in great numbers years ago, is now seen only as a straggler. The golden plover, once exceedingly abundant east of the Great Plains, is now rare. Vast hordes of long-billed dowitchers formerly wintered in Louisiana; now they occur only in infrequent flocks of a half dozen or less. The Eskimo curlew within the last decade has probably been exterminated and the other curlews greatly reduced. In fact, all the larger species of shorebirds have suffered severely.

So adverse to shorebirds are present conditions that the wonder is that any escape. In both fall and spring they are shot along the whole route of their migration north and south. Their habit of decoying readily and persistently, coming back in flocks to the decoys again and again, in spite of murderous volleys, greatly lessens their chances of escape.

The breeding grounds of some of the species in the United States and Canada have become greatly restricted by the extension of agriculture, and their winter ranges in South America have probably been restricted in the same way.

Unfortunately, shorebirds lay fewer eggs than any of the other species generally termed game birds. They deposit only three or four eggs, and hatch only one brood yearly. Nor are they in any wise immune from the great mortality known to prevail among the smaller birds. Their eggs and young are constantly preyed upon during the breeding season by crows, gulls, and jaegers, and the far northern country to which so many of them resort to nest is subject to sudden cold storms, which kill many of the young. In the more temperate climate of the United States small birds, in general, do not bring up more than one young bird for every two eggs laid. Sometimes the proportion of loss is much greater, actual count revealing a destruction of 70 to 80 per cent of nests and eggs. Shorebirds, with sets of three or four eggs, probably do not on the average rear more than two young for each breeding pair.

It is not surprising, therefore, that birds of this family, with their limited powers of reproduction, melt away under the relentless warfare waged upon them. Until recent years shorebirds have had almost no protection. Thus, the species most in need of stringent protection have really had the least. No useful birds which lay only three or four eggs should be retained on the list of game birds. The shorebirds should be relieved from persecution, and if we desire to save from extermination a majority of the species, action must be prompt.

The protection of shorebirds need not be based solely on esthetic or sentimental grounds, for few groups of birds more thoroughly deserve protection from an economic standpoint. Shorebirds perform an important service by their inroads upon mosquitoes, some of which play so conspicuous a part in the dissemination of diseases. Thus, nine species are known to feed upon mosquitoes, and hundreds of the larvæ or "wigglers" were found in several stomachs. Fifty-three per cent of the food of twenty-eight northern phalaropes from one locality consisted of mosquito larvæ. The insects eaten include the salt-marsh mosquito (*Aedes sollicitans*), for the suppression of which the State of New Jersey has gone to great expense. The nine species of shorebirds known to eat mosquitoes are:

Northern phalarope (*Lobipes lobatus*).
Wilson phalarope (*Steganopus tricolor*).
Stilt sandpiper (*Micropalama himantopus*).
Pectoral sandpiper (*Pisobia maculata*).
Baird sandpiper (*Pisobia bairdi*).
Least sandpiper (*Pisobia minutilla*).

Semipalmated sandpiper (*Ereunetes pusillus*).
Killdeer (*Oxyechus vociferus*).
Semipalmated plover (*Aegialitis semipalmata*).

Cattle and other live stock also are seriously molested by mosquitoes as well as by another set of pests, the horse-flies. Adults and larvæ of these flies have been found in the stomachs of the dowitcher, the pectoral sandpiper, the hudsonian godwit, and the killdeer. Two species of shore birds, the killdeer and upland plover, still further befriend cattle by de vouring the North American fever tick.

Among other fly larvæ consumed are those of the crane flies (leatherjackets) devoured by the following species:

Northern phalarope (*Lobipes lobatus*).
Wilson phalarope (*Steganopus tricolor*).
Woodcock (*Philohela minor*).
Jacksnipe (*Gallinago delicata*).

Pectoral sandpiper (*Pisobia maculata*).
Baird sandpiper (*Pisobia bairdi*).
Upland plover (*Bartramia longicauda*).
Killdeer (*Oxyechus vociferus*).

Crane-fly larvæ are frequently seriously destructive locally in grass and wheat fields. Among their numerous bird enemies, shorebirds rank high.

Another group of insects of which the shorebirds are very fond is grasshoppers. Severe local infestations of grasshoppers, frequently involving the destruction of many acres of corn, cotton, and other crops,

The Killdeer Plover   The Jacksnipe

TWO MEMBERS OF THE GROUP OF SHORE-BIRDS

These, with 28 other species, destroy enormous numbers of locusts, grasshoppers, crane-fly larvae, mosquito larvae, army-worms, cut-worms cotton-worms, boll-weevils, curculios, wire-worms and clover-leaf weevils. It is insane folly to shoot any birds that do such work! Many species of the shore-birds are rapidly being exterminated.

are by no means exceptional. Aughey found twenty-three species of shorebirds feeding on Rocky Mountain locusts in Nebraska, some of them consuming large numbers, as shown below.

>9 killdeer stomachs contained an average of 28 locusts each.
>11 semipalmated plover stomachs contained an average of 38 locusts each.
>16 mountain plover stomachs contained an average of 45 locusts each.
>11 jacksnipe stomachs contained an average of 37 locusts each.
>22 upland plover stomachs contained an average of 36 locusts each.
>10 long-billed curlew stomachs contained an average of 48 locusts each.

Even under ordinary conditions grasshoppers are a staple food of many members of the shorebird family, and the following species are known to feed on them:

Northern phalarope (*Lobipes lobatus*).
Avocet (*Recurvirostra americana*).
Black-necked stilt (*Himantopus mexicanus*).
Woodcock (*Philohela minor*).
Jacksnipe (*Gallinago delicata*).
Dowitcher (*Macrorhamphus griseus*).
Robin snipe (*Tringa canutus*).
White-rumped sandpiper (*Pisobia fuscicollis*).
Baird sandpiper (*Pisobia bairdi*).
Least sandpiper (*Pisobia minutilla*).

Buff-breasted sandpiper (*Tryngites subruficollis*).
Spotted sandpiper (*Actitis macularia*).
Long-billed curlew (*Numenius americanus*).
Black-bellied plover (*Squatarola squatarola*).
Golden plover (*Charadrius dominicus*).
Killdeer (*Oxyechus vociferus*).
Semipalmated plover (*Aegialitis semipalmata*).

Marbled godwit (*Limosa fedoa*). Ringed plover (*Aegialitis hiaticula*).
Yellowlegs (*Totanus flavipes*). Mountain plover (*Podasocys montanus*).
Solitary sandpiper (*Helodromas solitarius*). Turnstone (*Arenaria interpres*).
Upland plover (*Bartramia longicauda*).

Shorebirds are fond of other insect pests of forage and grain crops, including the army worm, which is known to be eaten by the killdeer and spotted sandpiper; also cutworms, among whose enemies are the avocet, woodcock, pectoral and Baird sandpipers, upland plover, and killdeer. Two caterpillar enemies of cotton, the cotton worm and the cotton cutworm, are eaten by the upland plover and killdeer. The latter bird feeds also on caterpillars of the genus *Phlegethontius*, which includes the tobacco and tomato worms.

The principal farm crops have many destructive beetle enemies also, and some of these are eagerly eaten by shorebirds. The boll weevil and clover-leaf weevil are eaten by the upland plover and killdeer, the rice weevil by the killdeer, the cowpea weevil by the upland plover, and the clover-root curculio by the following species of shorebirds:

Northern phalarope (*Lobipes lobatus*). White-rumped sandpiper (*Pisobia fuscicollis*)
Pectoral sandpiper (*Pisobia maculata*). Upland plover (*Bartramia longicauda*)
Baird sandpiper (*Pisobia bairdi*). Killdeer (*Oxyechus vociferus*)

The last two eat also other weevils which attack cotton, grapes and sugar beets. Bill-bugs, which often do considerable damage to corn, seem to be favorite food of some of the shorebirds. They are eaten by the Wilson phalarope, avocet, black-necked stilt, pectoral sandpiper, killdeer, and upland plover. They are an important element of the latter bird's diet, and no fewer than eight species of them have been found in its food.

Wireworms and their adult forms, click beetles, are devoured by the northern phalarope, woodcock, jacksnipe, pectoral sandpiper, killdeer, and upland plover. The last three feed also on the southern corn leaf-beetle and the last two upon the grapevine colaspis. Other shorebirds that eat leaf-beetles are the Wilson phalarope and dowitcher.

Crayfishes, which are a pest in rice and corn fields in the South and which injure levees, are favorite food of the black-necked stilt, and several other shorebirds feed upon them, notably the jacksnipe, robin snipe, spotted sandpiper, upland plover, and killdeer.

Thus it is evident that shorebirds render important aid by devouring the enemies of farm crops and in other ways, and their services are appreciated by those who have observed the birds in the field. Thus W. A. Clark, of Corpus Christi, Tex., reports that upland plovers are industrious in following the plow and in eating the grubs that destroy garden stuff, corn, and cotton crops. H. W. Tinkham, of Fall River, Mass., says of the spotted sandpiper: "Three pairs nested in a young orchard behind my house and adjacent to my garden. I did not see them once go to the shore for food (shore about 1,500 feet away), but I did see them many times make faithful search of my garden for cutworms, spotted squash bugs, and green flies. Cutworms and cabbage worms were their special prey. After the young could fly, they still kept at work in my garden, and showed no inclination to go to the shore until about August 15th. They and a flock of quails just over the wall helped me wonderfully.''

In the uncultivated parts of their range also, shorebirds search out and destroy many creatures that are detrimental to man's interest. Several species prey upon the predaceous diving beetles (*Dytiscidae*), which are a nuisance in fish hatcheries and which destroy many insects, the natural food of fishes. The birds now known to take these beetles are:

Northern phalarope (*Lobipes lobatus*).   Dowitcher (*Macrorhamphus griseus*).
Wilson phalarope (*Steganopus tricolor*).   Robin snipe (*Tringa canutus*).
Avocet (*Recurvirostra americana*).   Pectoral sandpiper (*Pisobia maculata*).
Black-necked stilt (*Himantopus mexicanus*).   Red-backed sandpiper (*Pelidna alpina sak-*
Jacksnipe (*Gallinago delicata*).   *halina*).
                                   Killdeer (*Oxyechus vociferus*).

Large numbers of marine worms of the genus *Nereis*, which prey upon oysters, are eaten by shorebirds. These worms are common on both the Atlantic and Gulf coasts and are eaten by shorebirds wherever they occur. It is not uncommon to find that from 100 to 250 of them have been eaten at one meal. The birds known to feed upon them are·

Northern phalarope (*Lobipes lobatus*)   White-rumped sandpiper (*Pisobia fuscicol-*
Dowitcher (*Macrorhamphus griseus*).   *lis*).
Stilt sandpiper (*Micropalama himantopus*).   Red-backed sandpiper (*Pelidna alpina sak-*
Robin snipe (*Tringa canutus*).   *halina*).
Purple sandpiper (*Arquatella maritima*).   Killdeer (*Oxyechus vociferus*).

The economic record of the shorebirds deserves nothing but praise. These birds injure no crop, but on the contrary feed upon many of the worst enemies of agriculture. It is worth recalling that their diet includes such pests as the Rocky Mountain locust and other injurious grasshoppers, the army worm, cutworms, cabbage worms, cotton worm, cotton cutworm, boll weevil, clover leaf weevil, clover root curculio, rice weevil, corn bill-bugs wireworms, corn leaf-beetles, cucumber beetles, white grubs, and such foes of stock as the Texas fever tick, horseflies, and mosquitoes. Their warfare on crayfishes must not be overlooked, nor must we forget the more personal debt of gratitude we owe them for preying upon mosquitoes. They are the most important bird enemies of these pests known to us.

Shorebirds have been hunted until only a remnant of their once vast numbers is left. Their limited powers of reproduction, coupled with the natural vicissitudes of the breeding period, make their increase slow, and peculiarly expose them to danger of extermination.

In the way of protection a beginning has been made, and a continuous close season until 1915 has been established for the following birds: The killdeer, in Massachusetts and Louisiana; the upland plover, in Massachusetts, and Vermont; and the piping plover in Massachusetts. But, considering the needs and value of these birds, this modicum of protection is small indeed.

The above-named species are not the only ones that should be exempt from persecution, for all the shorebirds of the United States are in great need of better protection. They should be protected, first, to save them from the danger of extermination, and, second, because of their economic importance. So great, indeed, is their economic value, that their retenion on the game list and their destruction by sportsmen is a serious loss to agriculture.—(End of the circular.)

*   *   *   *

The following appeared in the *Zoological Society Bulletin*, for January, 1909, from Richard Walter Tomalin, of Sydney, N. S. W.:

"In the subdistricts of Robertson and Kangaloon in the Illawarra district of New South Wales, what ten years ago was a waving mass of English cocksfoot and rye grass, which had been put in gradually as the dense vine scrub was felled and burnt off, is now a barren desert, and nine families out of every ten which were renting properties have been compelled to leave the district and take up other lands. This is through the grubs having eaten out the grass by the roots. Ploughing proved to be useless, as the grubs ate out the grass just the same. Whilst there recently I was informed that it took three years from the time the grubs were first seen until to-day, to accomplish this complete devastation; in other words, three years ago the grubs began work in the beautiful country of green mountains and running streams.

"The birds had all been ruthlessly shot and destroyed in that district, and I was amazed at the absence of bird life. The two sub-districts I have mentioned have an area of about thirty square miles, and form a table-land about 1200 feet above sea level."

The same kind of common sense that teaches men to go in when it rains, and keep out of fiery furnaces, teaches us that as a business proposition it is to man's interest to protect the birds. Make them plentiful and keep them so. When we strike the birds, we hurt ourselves. The protection of our insect-eating and seed-eating birds is a cash proposition,—protect or pay.

Were I a farmer, no gun ever should be fired on my premises at any bird save the English sparrow and the three bad hawks. Any man who would kill my friend Bob White I would treat as an enemy. The man who would shoot and eat any of the song-birds, woodpeckers, or shorebirds that worked for me, I would surely molest.

Every farmer should post every foot of his lands, cultivated and not cultivated. The farmer who does not do so is his own enemy; and he needs a guardian.

At this stage of wild life extermination, it is impossible to make our bird-protection laws too strict, or too far-reaching. The remnant of our birds should be protected, with clubs and guns if necessary. All our shore birds should be accorded a ten-year close season. Don't ask the gunners whether they will *agree* to it or not. *Of course they will not agree to it,—never!* But our duty is clear,—to go ahead and *do it!*

CHAPTER XXIV

GAME AND AGRICULTURE; AND DEER AS A FOOD SUPPLY

As a state and county asset, the white-tailed deer contains possibilities that as yet seem to be ignored by the American people as a whole. It is quite time to consider that persistent, prolific and toothsome animal.

The proposition that large herds of horned game can not becomingly roam at will over farms and vineyards worth one hundred dollars per acre, affords little room for argument. Generally speaking, there is but one country in the world that breaks this well-nigh universal rule; and that country is India. On the plains between and adjacent to the Ganges and the Jumna, for two thousand years herds of black-buck, or sasin antelope, have roamed over cultivated fields so thickly garnished with human beings that to-day the rifle-shooting sportsman stands in hourly peril of bagging a five-hundred-rupee native every time he fires at an antelope.

Wherever rich agricultural lands exist, the big game must give way,— *from those lands*. To-day the bison could not survive in Iowa, eastern Nebraska or eastern Kansas, any longer than a Shawnee Indian would last on the Bowery. It was foredoomed that the elk, deer, bear and wild turkey should vanish from the rich farming regions of the East and the middle West.

To-day in British East Africa lions are being hunted with dogs and shot wholesale, because they are a pest to the settlers and to the surviving herds of big game. At the same time, the settlers who are striving to wrest the fertile plains of B. E. A. from the domain of savagery declare that the African buffalo, the zebra, the kongoni and the elephant are public nuisances that must be suppressed by the rifle.

Even the most ardent friend of wild life must admit that when a settler has laboriously fenced his fields, and plowed and sowed, only to have his whole crop ruined in one night by a herd of fence-breaking zebras, the event is sufficient to abrade the nerves of the party most in interest. While I take no stock in stories of dozens of "rogue" elephants that require treatment with the rifle, and of grown men being imperiled by savage gazelles, we admit that there are times when wild animals can make nuisances of themselves. Let us consider that subject now.

WILD ANIMAL NUISANCES.—Complaints have come to me, at various times, of great destruction of lambs by eagles; of trout by blue herons; of crops (on Long Island) by deer; of pears destroyed by birds, and of valuable park trees by beavers that chop down trees not wisely but too well. I do not, however, include in this category any cherries eaten by robins, or orioles, or jays; for they are of too small importance to consider in this court.

A FOOD SUPPLY OF WHITE-TAILED DEER
The Killing of the Does was Wrong

To meet the legitimate demands for the abatement of unbearable wild-animal nuisances, I recommend the enactment of a law similar to Section 158 of the Game laws of New York, which provides for the safe and legitimate abatement of unbearable wild creatures as follows:

Section 158. *Power to Take Birds and Quadrupeds.* In the event that any species of birds protected by the provisions of section two hundred and nineteen of this article, or quadrupeds protected by law, shall at any time, in any locality, become destructive of private or public property, the commission shall have power in its discretion to direct any game protector, or issue a permit to any citizen of the state, to take such species of birds or quadrupeds and dispose of the same in such manner as the commission may provide. Such permit shall expire within four months after the date of issuance.

This measure should be adopted by every state that is troubled by too many, or too aggressive, wild mammals or birds.

But to return to the subject of big game and farming. We do not complain of the disappearance of the bison, elk, deer and bear from the farms of the United States and Canada. The passing of the big game from all such regions follows the advance of real civilization, just so surely and certainly as night follows day.

But this vast land of ours is not wholly composed of rich agricultural lands; not by any means. There are millions of acres of forest lands, good, bad and indifferent, worth from nothing per acre up to one hundred dollars or more. There are millions of acres of rocky, brush-covered mountains and hills, wholly unsuited to agriculture, or even horticulture. There are other millions of acres of arid plains and arboreal deserts, on which nothing but thirst-proof animals can live and thrive. The South contains vast pine forests and cypress swamps, millions of acres of them, of which the average northerner knows less than nothing.

We can not stop long enough to look it up, but from the green color on our national map that betokens the forest reserves, and from our own personal knowledge of the deserts, swamps, barrens and rocks that we have seen, we make the estimate that *fully one-third* of the total area of the United States is incapable of supporting the husbandman who depends for his existence upon tillage of the soil. People may talk and write about "dry farming" all they please, but I wish to observe that from Dry-Farming to Success is a long shot, with many limbs in the way. When it rains sufficiently, dry farming is a success; but otherwise it is not; and we heartily wish it were otherwise.

The logical conclusion of our land that is utterly unfit for agri ulture is a great area of land available for occupancy by valuable wild animals. Every year the people of the United States are wasting uncountable millions of pounds of venison, because we are neglecting our opportunities for producing it practically without cost. Imagine for a moment bestowing upon land owners the ability to stock with white-tailed and Indian sambar deer all the wild lands of the United States that are suitable for those species, and permitting only bucks over one year of age to be shot. With the does even reasonably protected, the numerical results in annual pounds of good edible flesh fairly challenges the imagination.

About six years ago, Mr. C. C. Worthington's deer, in his fenced park at Shawnee-on-Delaware, Pennsylvania, became so numerous and so burdensome that he opened his fences and permitted about one thousand head to go free.

We are losing each year a very large and valuable asset in the intangible form of a million hardy deer that we might have raised but did not! Our vast domains of wooded mountains, hills and valleys lie practically untenanted by big game, save in a few exceptional spots. We lose because we are lawless. We lose because we are too improvident to conserve large forms of wild life unless we are compelled to do so by the stern edict of the law! The law-breakers, the game-hogs, the conscienceless doe-and-fawn slayers are everywhere! Ten per cent of all the grown men now in the United States are to-day poachers, thieves and law-breakers, or else they are liable to become so to-morrow. If you doubt it, try risking your new umbrella unprotected in the next mixed company of one hundred men that you encounter, in such a situation that it will be easy to "get away" with it.

We could raise two million deer each year on our empty wild lands; but without fences it would take half a million real game-wardens, on duty from dawn until dark, to protect them from destructive slaughter.

At present our land of liberty contains only 9,354 game wardens.* The states that contain the greatest areas of wild lands naturally lack in population and in tax funds, and not one such state can afford to put into the field even half enough salaried game wardens to really protect her game from surreptitious slaughter. The surplus of "personal liberty" in this liberty-cursed land is a curse to the big game. The average frontiersman never will admit the divine right of kings, but he does ardently believe in the divine right of settlers,—to reach out and take any of the products of Nature that they happen to fancy

WILD MEAT AS A FOOD SUPPLY.—We hear much these days about the high cost of living, but thus far we have made no move to mend the situation. With coal going straight up to ten dollars per ton, beef going up to fifteen dollars per hundred on the hoof and wheat and hay going-up—heaven alone knows where, it is time for all Americans who are not rich to arouse and take thought for the morrow. *What are we going to do about it?* The tariff on the coarser necessities of life is now booked to come down; but what about the fresh meat supply?

I desire to point out that between Bangor and San Diego and from Key West to Bellingham, our country contains millions of acres of wild, practically uninhabited forests, rough foot-hills, bad-lands and mountains that could produce two million deer each year, without deducting $50,000 a year from the wealth of the country. I grant that in the total number of deer that would be necessary to produce two million deer per annum, the farms situated on the edges of forests, and actually within the forests, would suffer somewhat from the depredations of those deer. As I will presently show by documentary records, every one of those individual damages that exceeds two dollars in value could be compensated in cash, and afterward leave on the credit side of the deer account an enormous annual balance.

Stop for a moment, you enterprising and restless men and women who travel all over the United States, and think of the illimitable miles of unbroken forest that you have looked upon from your Pullman windows in the East, in the South, in the West and in southern Canada. Recall the wooded mountains of the Appalachian system, the White Mountain region, the pine forests of the Atlantic Coast and the Gulf States, the forests of Tennessee, Arkansas and southern Missouri; of northern Minnesota, and every state of the Rocky Mountain region. Then, think of the silent and untouched forests of the Pacific Coast and tell me whether you think five million deer scattered through all those forests would make any visible impression upon them. That would be only about twenty-five times as many as are there now! I think the forests would not be over populated; and they would produce *two million killable deer each year!*

Last year, 11,000 deer were forced down out of their hiding places in the Rocky Mountains, and were killed in Montana. Even the natives

* Of this force, there are only 1,200 salaried wardens. The most of those who serve without salaries naturally render but little continuous or regular service.

had not dreamed there were so many available; and they were slaughtered not wisely but too ill. It is not right that six members of one family should "hog" twelve deer in one season. At present no deer supply can stand such slaughter.

Assuming that the people of the United States *could* be educated into the idea of so conserving deer that they could draw two million head per year from the general stock, what would it be worth?

It is not very difficult to estimate the value of a deer, when the whole animal can be utilized. In various portions of the United States, deer vary in size, but I shall take all this into account, and try to strike a fair average. In some sections, where deer are large and heavy, a full-grown buck is easily worth twenty-five dollars. Let him who doubts it, try to replace those generous pounds of flesh with purchased beef and mutton and veal, and see how far twenty-five dollars will go toward it. Every man who is a householder knows full well how little meat one dollar will buy at this time.

I think that throughout the United States as a whole every full-grown deer, male or female contains on an average ten dollars worth of good meat. I know of one large preserve which annually sells its surplus of deer at that price, wholesale, to dealers; and in New York City (doubtless in many other cities, also) venison often has sold in the market at one dollar per pound!

Two million deer at $10 each mean $20,000,000. The licenses for the killing of two million deer should cost one million men one dollar each; and that would pay 1,666 new game wardens each fifty dollars per month, all the year round. The damages that would need to be paid to farmers, on account of crops injured by deer, would be so small that each county could take care of its own cases, from its own treasury, as is done in the State of Vermont.

There are certain essentials to the realization of a dream of two million deer per year that are absolutely required. They are neither obscure nor impossible.

Each state and each county proposing to stock its vacant woods with deer must resolutely educate its own people in the necessity of playing fair about the killing of deer, and giving every man and every deer a square deal. This is *not* impossible! Not as a general thing, even though it may be so in some specially lawless communities. If the *leading men* of the state and the county will take this matter seriously in hand, it can be done in two years' time. The American people are not insensible to appeals to reason, when those appeals are made by their own "home folks." The governors, senators, assemblymen, judges, mayors and justices of the peace could, *if they would*, make a campaign of education and appeal that would result in the creation of an immense volume of free wild food in every state that possesses wild lands.

When the shoe of Necessity pinches the People hard enough, remember the possibilities in deer.

From the "American Natural History"

WHITE-TAILED DEER

If Honestly and Intelligently Conserved, this Species could be made to Produce on our Wild Lands
Two Million Deer per annum, as a new Food Supply

The best wild animal to furnish a serious food supply is the white-tailed deer. This is because of its persistence and fertility. The elk is too large for general use. An elk carcass can not be carried on a horse; it is impossible to get a sled or a wagon to where it lies; and so, fully half of it usually is wasted! The mule deer is good for the Rocky Mountains, and can live where the white-tail can not; but it is *too easy to shoot!* The Columbian black-tail is the natural species for the forests of the Pacific states; but it is a trifle small in size.

THE EXAMPLE OF VERMONT.—In order to show that all the above is not based on empty theory,—regarding the stocking of forests with deer, their wonderful powers of increase, and the practical handling of the damage question,—let us take the experience and the fine example of Vermont.

In April, 1875, a few sportsmen of Rutland, of whom the late Henry W. Cheney was one, procured in the Adirondacks thirteen white-tailed deer, six bucks and seven does. These were liberated in a forest six miles from Rutland, and beyond being protected from slaughter, they were left to shift for themselves. They increased, slowly at first, then rapidly, and by 1897, they had become so numerous that it seemed right to have a short annual open season, and kill a few. From first to last, many of those deer have been killed contrary to law. In 1904–5, it was known that 294 head were destroyed in that way; and undoubtedly there were others that were not reported.

ACCOUNT OF DEER KILLED IN VERMONT, OF RECORD SINCE KILLING BEGAN, IN 1897

From John W. Titcomb, State Game Commissioner, Lyndonville, Vt., Aug. 23, 1912

Year	By Hunters, Legally	By Hunters, Illegally	By Dogs	Wounded Deer Killed	By Railroad Trains	By Various Accidents	Average Weight (lbs.)	Gross Weight (lbs.)
1897*	103	47						
1898	131	30	40					
1899	90							
1900	123							
1901	211							
1902	403	81	50	13	14		171	68,747
1903	753	199					190	142,829
1904	541							
1905	497	163	74	22	18	17	198	
1906	634						200	127,193
1907	991	287	208	62	31	21	196	134,353
1908	2,208						207	457,585
1909	4,597	381	168	69	24	72	155	716,358

* First open season after deer restored to state in 1875.

DAMAGES TO CROPS BY DEER.—For several years past, the various counties of Vermont have been paying farmers for damages inflicted upon their crops by deer. Clearly, it is more just that counties should settle these damages than that they should be paid from the state treasury, because the counties paying damages have large compensation in the value of the deer killed each year. The hunting appears to be open to all persons who hold licenses from the state.

In order that the public at large may know the cost of the Vermont system, I offer the following digest compiled from the last biennial report of the State Fish and Game Commissioner:

DAMAGES PAID FOR DEER DEPREDATIONS IN VERMONT DURING TWO YEARS

Total damages paid from June 8, 1908, to June 22, 1910	$4,865.98
Total number of claims paid	311
Total number of claims under $5	80
Number between $5 and $10, inclusive	102
Number over $25 and under $51	23
Number between $50 and $100	11
Number in excess of $100	4
Number in excess of $200	1
Largest claim paid	$326.50

VALUE OF WHITE-TAILED DEER.—Having noted the fact that in two years (1908-9), the people of Vermont paid out $4,865 in compensation for damages inflicted by deer, it is of interest to determine whether that money was wisely expended. In other words, did it pay?

We have seen that in the years 1908 and 9, the people of Vermont killed, legally and illegally, and converted to use, 7,186 deer. This does not include the deer killed by dogs and by accidents.

Regarding the value of a full-grown deer, it must be remembered that much depends upon the locality of the carcass. In New York or Pittsburg or Chicago, a whole deer is worth, at wholesale, at least twenty-five dollars. In Vermont, where deer are plentiful, they are worth a less sum. I think that fifteen dollars would be a fair figure,—at least low enough!

Even when computed at fifteen dollars per carcass, those deer were worth to the people of Vermont $107,790. It would seem, therefore, that the soundness of Vermont's policy leaves no room for argument; and we hope that other states, and also private individuals, will profit by Vermont's very successful experiment in bringing back the deer to her forests, and in increasing the food supply of her people.

KILLING FEMALE DEER.—To say one word on this subject which might by any possibility be construed as favoring it, is like juggling with a lighted torch over a barrel of gunpowder. Already, in Pennsylvania at least one gentleman has appeared anxious to represent me as favoring the killing of does, which in nine hundred and ninety-nine cases out of every thousand I distinctly and emphatically do not. The slaughter of female hoofed game animals is necessarily destructive and reprehensible, and not one man out of every ten thousand in this country ever will see the place and time wherein the opposite is true.

At present there are just two places in America, and I think only two, wherein there exists the slightest exception on this point. The state of Vermont is becoming overstocked with deer, and the females have in *some* counties (not in all), become so tame and destructive in orchards, gardens and farm crops as to constitute a great annoyance. For this reason, the experiment is being made of permitting does to be killed under license, until their number is somewhat reduced.

The first returns from this trial have now come in, from the county game wardens of Vermont to the state game warden, Mr. John W. Titcomb. I will quote the gist of the opinion of each. •

The State Commissioner says: "This law should remain in force at least until there is some indication of a decrease in the number of deer." Warden W. H. Taft (Addison County) says: "The killing of does I believe did away with a good many of these tame deer that cause most of the damage to farmers' crops." Harry Chase (Bennington County) says the doe-killing law is "a good law, and I sincerely trust it will not be repealed." Warden Hayward of Rutland County says: "The majority of the farmers in this county are in favor of repealing the doe law. . . A great many does and young deer (almost fawns) were killed in this county during the hunting season of 1909." R. W. Wheeler, of Rutland County says: "Have the doe law repealed! We don't need it!" H. J. Parcher of Washington County finds that the does did more damage to the crops than the bucks, and he thinks the doe law is "a just one." R. L. Frost, of Windham County, judicially concludes that "the law allowing does to be killed should remain in force one or two seasons more." C. S Parker, of Orleans County, says his county is not overstocked with deer, and he favors a special act for his county, to protect females.

A summary of the testimony of the wardens is easily made. When deer are too plentiful, and the over-tame does become a public nuisance too great to be endured, the number should be reduced by regular shooting in the open season; but,

As soon as the proper balance of deer life has been restored, protect the does once more.

The pursuit of this policy is safe and sane, provided it can be wrought out without the influence of selfishness, and reckless disregard for the rights of the next generation. On the whole, its handling is like playing with fire, and I think there are very, very few states on this earth wherein it would be wise or safe to try it. As a wise friend once remarked to me, "Give some men a hinch, and they'll always try to take a hell." In Vermont, however, the situation is kept so well in hand we may be sure that at the right moment the law providing for the decrease of the number of does will be repealed.

HIPPOPOTAMI AND ANTELOPES.—Last year a bill was introduced in the lower House of Congress proposing to provide funds for the introduction into certain southern states of various animals from Africa, especially hippopotami and African antelopes. The former were proposed partly for the purpose of ridding navigation of the water hyacinths that now are choking many of the streams of Louisiana and Mississippi. The antelopes were to be acclimatized as a food supply for the people at large.

This measure well illustrates the prevailing disposition of the American people to-day,—to ignore and destroy their own valuable natural stock of wild birds and mammals, and when they have completed their war of extermination, reach out to foreign countries for foreign species. Instead of preserving the deer of the South, the South reaches out for the utterly impossible antelopes of Africa, and the preposterous hippopotamus. The North joyously exterminates her quail and ruffed grouse, and goes to Europe for the Hungarian partridge. That partridge is a failure here, and I am *heartily glad of it*, on the ground that the exterminators of our native species do not deserve success in their efforts to displace our finest native species with others from abroad.

The hippo-antelope proposition is a climax of absurdity, in proposing the replacing of valuable native game with impossible foreign species.

CHAPTER XXV

LAW AND SENTIMENT AS FACTORS IN PRESERVATION

There is grave danger that through ignorance of the true character of about 80 per cent of the men and boys who shoot wild creatures, a great wrong will be done the latter. Let us not make a fatal mistake.

After more than thirty years of observation among all kinds of sportsmen, hunters and gunners, I am convinced that it is utterly futile and deadly dangerous to rely on humane, high-class sentiment to diminish the slaughter of wild things by game-hogs and pot-hunters.

In some respects, the term "game-hog" is a rude, rough word; but it is needed in the English language, and it has come to stay. It is a disagreeable term, but it was brought into use to apply to a class of very disagreeable persons.

A "game-hog" is a hunter of game who knows no such thing as sentiment or conscience in the killing of game, so long as he keeps within the limit of the law. Regardless of the scarcity of game, or of its hard struggle for existence, he will kill right up to the bag limit every day that he goes out, provided it is possible to do so. He uses the "law" as a salve for the spot where his conscience should be. He will shoot with any machine gun, or gun of big calibre, in every way that the law allows, and he knows no such thing as giving the game a square deal. He brags of his big bags of game, and he loves to be photographed with a wagon-load of dead birds as a background. He believes in automatic and pump guns, spring shooting, longer open seasons and "more game." He is quite content to shoot half tame ducks in a club preserve as they fly between coop and pond, whenever he secures an opportunity. He will gladly sell his game whenever he can do so without being found out, and sometimes when he is.

Often a true sportsman drifts without realizing it into some one way of the confirmed game-hog; but the moment he is made to realize his position, he changes his course and his standing. The game-hog is impervious to argument. You can shame a horse away from his oats more easily than you can shame him from doing "what the Law allows."

There are hundreds of thousands of gentlemen and gentlewomen who never once have come in touch with real cloven-footed game-hogs, who do not understand the species at all, and do not recognize its ear-marks. Thousands of such persons will tell you: "In my opinion, the best way to save the wild life is to *educate the people!*" I have heard that, many, many times.

For right-hearted people, a little law is quite sufficient; and the best people need none at all! But the game-hogs are different. For them, the strict letter of the law, backed up by a strong-arm squad, is the only controlling influence that they recognize. To them it is necessary to say: "You shall!" and "You shall not!"

Only yesterday the latest game-hog case was related to me by a game-protector from Kansas. Into a certain county of southern Kansas, from which the prairie-chicken had been totally gone for a dozen years or more, a pair of those birds entered, settled down and nested. Their coming was to many habitants a joyous event. "Now," said the People, "we will care for these birds, and they will multiply, and presently the county will be restocked."

But Ahab came! Two men from another county, calling themselves sportsmen but not entitled to that name, heard of those birds, and resolved to "get them." They waited until the young were just leaving the nest: and they went down and camped near by. On the first day they killed the two parent birds and half the flock of young birds, and the next day they got all the rest.

But there is a sequel to this story. One of those men was a dealer in guns and ammunition; and when his customers heard what he had done, "they simply put him out of business, by refusing to trade with him any more." He is now washing dirty dishes in a restaurant; but at heart he is a game-hog, just the same.

Near Bridgeport, Connecticut, a gentleman of my acquaintance owns a fine estate which is adorned with a trout stream and a superfine trout pond. Once he invited a business man of Bridgeport to be his guest, and fish for trout in his pond. On that guest, during a visit of three days all the finest forms of hospitality were bestowed.

Two weeks later, my friend's game-warden caught that guest, early on a Sunday morning, *poaching* on the trout-pond, and spoiled his carefully arranged get-away.

In his book "Saddle and Camp in the Rockies," Mr. Dillon Wallace tells a story of a man from New York who in the mountains of Colorado deliberately corrupted his guides with money or other influences, shot mountain sheep *in midsummer*, and "got away with it."

In northern Minnesota, George E. Wood has been having a hand-to-hand fight with the worst community of game-hogs and alien-born poachers of which I have heard. There appears to be no game law that they do not systematically violate. The killers seem determined to annihilate the last head of game, in spite of fines and imprisonments. The foreigners are absolutely uncontrollable. The latest feature of the war is the discovery of a tannery in the woods, where the hides of illegally-slaughtered deer and moose are dressed. Apparently the only kind of a law that will save the game of northern Minnesota is one that will totally disarm the entire population.

In Pennsylvania, there exists an association which was formed for the express purpose of fighting the State Game Commission, preventing the enactment of a hunter's license law and repealing the law against the killing of female deer and hornless fawns. The continued existence of that organization on that basis would be a standing disgrace to the fair name of Pennsylvania. I think, however, that that organization was founded on secret selfish purposes, and that ere long the general body of members will awaken to a realizing sense of their position, and range themselves in support of the excellent policies of the commission.

A POT-HUNTER is a man or boy who kills game as a business, for the money that can be derived from its sale, or other use. Such men have the same feelings as butchers. From their point of view, they can see no reason why all the game in the world should not be killed and marketed. Like the feather-dealers, they wish to get out of the wild life all the money there is in it; that is all. Left to themselves, with open markets they would soon exterminate the land fauna of the habitable portions of the globe.

No one can "educate" such people. For the gunners, game-hogs and pot-hunters, there is no check, save specific laws that sternly and amply safeguard the rights of the wild creatures that can not make laws for themselves.

Nor can anyone educate the heartless woman of fashion who is determined to wear aigrettes as long as her money can buy them. The best women of the world have *already been educated* on the bird-millinery subject, and they are already against the use of the gaudy badges of slaughter and extermination. But in the great cities of the world there are thousands of women who are at heart as cruel as Salome herself, and whose vicious tastes can be curbed only by the strong hand of the law. "Sentiment" for wild birds is not in them.

Because of the vicious and heartless elements among men and women, we say, Give us *far-reaching, iron-bound* LAWS for the protection of wild life, *and plenty of courageous men to enforce them.*

CHAPTER XXVI

THE ARMY OF THE DEFENSE

It now seems that the friends of wild life who themselves are not on the firing-line should be afforded some definite information regarding the Army of the Defense, and its strength and weakness. It is an interesting subject, but the limitations of space will not permit an extended treatment.

Over the world at large, I think the active Destroyers outnumber the active Defenders of wild life at least in the ratio of 500 to 1; and the money available to the Destroyers is to the funds of the Defenders as 500 is to 1. The *average* big-game sportsman cheerfully expends from $500 to $1,000 on a hunting trip, but resents the suggestion that he should subscribe from $50 to $100 for wild life preservation. If he puts down $10, he thinks he has done a Big Thing. Worse than this, I am forced to believe that at least 75 per cent of the big-game sportsmen of the world never have contributed one dollar in money, or one hour of effort, to that cause. But there are exceptions; and I can name at least fifty sportsmen who have subscribed $100 each to campaign funds, and some who have given as high as $1,000.

Once I sat down beside a financially rich slaughterer of game, and asked him to subscribe a sum of real money in behalf of a very important campaign. I needed funds very much; and I explained, exhorted and besought. I pointed out his duty—*to give back something* in return for all the game slaughter that he had *enjoyed*. For ten long minutes he stood fire without flinching, and without once opening his lips to speak. He made no answer no argument. no defense· and finally he never gave up one cent.

Wherever the English language is spoken, from Tasmania to Scotland, and from Porto Rico to the Philippines, the spirit of wild life protection exists. Elsewhere there is much more to be said on this point. To all cosmopolitan sportsmen, the British "Blue Book" on game protection, the annual reports of the two great protective societies of London, and the annual "Progress" report of the U. S. Department of Agriculture are reassuring and comforting. It is good to know that Uganda maintains a Department of Game Protection (A. L. Butler, Superintendent), that so good a man as Maj. J. Stevenson-Hamilton is in control of protection in the Transvaal, and that even the native State of Kashmir officially recognizes the need to protect the Remnant.

There are of course many parts of the world in which game laws and limits to slaughter are quite unknown: all of which is entirely wrong, and in need of quick correction. No state or nation can be accounted wholly civilized that fails to recognize the necessity to protect wild life. I am tempted to make a list of the states and nations that were at latest advices destitute of game laws and game protectors, but I fear to do injustice through lack of the latest information. However, the time has come to search out delinquents, and hold up to each one a mirror that will reflect its shortcomings.

Naturally, we are most interested in our own contingent of the Army of the Defense.

THE UNITED STATES GOVERNMENT.—To-day the feeling in Congress toward the conservation of wild life and forests is admirable. Both houses are fully awake to the necessity of saving while there is yet something to be saved. The people of the United States may be assured that the national government is active and sympathetic in the prosecution of such conservation measures as it might justly be expected to promote. For example, during the past five years we have seen Congress take favorable action on the following important causes, nearly every one of which cost money:

The saving of the American bison, in four National ranges.

The creation of fifty-eight bird refuges.

The creation of five great game preserves.

The saving of the elk in Jackson Hole.

The protection of the fur seal.

The protection of the wild life of Alaska.

There are many active friends of wild life who confidently expect to see this fine list gloriously rounded out by the passage in 1913 of an ideal bill for the federal protection of all migratory birds. To name the friends of wild life in Congress would require the printing of a list of at least two hundred names, and a history of the rise and progress of wild life conservation by the national government would fill a volume. Such a volume would be highly desirable.

When the story of the national government's part in wild-life protection is finally written, it will be found that while he was president, THEODORE ROOSEVELT made a record in that field that is indeed enough to make a reign illustrious. He aided every wild-life cause that lay within the bounds of possibility, and he gave the vanishing birds and mammals the benefit of every doubt. He helped to establish three national bison herds, four national game preserves, fifty-three federal bird refuges, and to enact the Alaska game laws of 1902 and 1907.

It was in 1904 that the national government elected to accept its share of the white man's burden and enter actively into the practical business of wild life protection. This special work, originally undertaken and down to the present vigorously carried on by Dr. Theodore S. Palmer, has considerably changed the working policy of the Biological Survey of the Department of Agriculture, and greatly influenced game protection throughout the states. The game protection work of that bureau is alone worth to the people of this country at least twenty times more per

| MADISON GRANT
Secretary and Chairman Executive Committee,
New York Zoological Society | HENRY FAIRFIELD OSBORN
President, New York Zoological
Society |

| JOHN F. LACEY
Ex-Member of Congress; Author of the
"Lacey Bird Law" | WILLIAM DUTCHER
Founder and President, National Association
of Audubon Societies |

NOTABLE PROTECTORS OF WILD LIFE (1)

annum than the entire annual cost of the Bureau. Next to the splendid services of Dr. Palmer, all over the United States, one great value of the Bureau is found in the fact-and-figure ammunition that it prepares and distributes for general use in assaults on the citadels of Ignorance and Greed. The publications of the Bureau are of great practical value to the people of the United States.

Dr. Palmer is a man of incalculable value to the cause of protection. No call for advice is too small to receive his immediate attention, no fight is too hot and no danger-point too remote to keep him from the fray. Wherever the Army of Destruction is making a particularly dangerous fight to repeal good laws and turn back the wheels of progress, there will he be found. As the warfare grows more intense, Congress may find it necessary to enlarge the fighting force of the Biological Survey.

The work that has been done by the Bureau in determining the economic value or lack of value of our most important species of insectivorous birds, has been worth millions to the agricultural interests of the United States. Through it we know where we stand. The reasons why we need to strive for protection can be expressed in figures and percentages; and it seems to me that they leave the American people no option but to *protect!*

STATE GAME COMMISSIONS.—Each of our states, and each province of Canada, maintains either a State Game Commission of several persons, one Commissioner, or a State Game Warden. All such officers are officially charged with the duty of looking after the general welfare of the game and other wild life of their respective states. Theoretically one of the chief duties of a State Game Commission is to initiate new legislative bills that are necessary, and advocate their translation into law. The official standing of most game commissioners is such that they can successfully do this. In 1909 Governor Hughes of New York went so far as to let it be known that he would sign no new game bill that did not meet the approval of State Game Commissioner James S. Whipple. As a general working principle, and quite aside from Mr. Whipple, that was wrong; because even a State game commissioner is not necessarily infallible, or always on the right side of every wild-life question.

As a rule, state commissioners and state wardens are keenly alive to the needs of their states in new game protective legislation, and a large percentage of the best existing laws are due to their initiative. Often, however, their usefulness is limited by the trammels of public office, and there are times when such officers can not be too aggressive without the risk of arousing hostile influences, and handicapping their own departmental work. For this reason, it is often advisable that bills which propose great and drastic reforms, and which are likely to become storm-centers, should originate outside the Commissioner's office, and be pushed by men who are perfectly free to abide the fortunes of open warfare. It should be distinctly understood, however, that lobbying in behalf of wild-life measures is *an important part of the legitimate duty of every state game commissioner*, and is a most honorable calling.

| EDWARD HOWE FORBUSH
Massachusetts State
Ornithologist | T. GILBERT PEARSON
Secretary, National Association of
Audubon Societies |

| JOHN B. BURNHAM
President, American Game Protective and
Propagation Association | ERNEST NAPIER
President, Fish and Game Commission
of New Jersey |

NOTABLE PROTECTORS OF WILD LIFE. (II)

Of the many strong and aggressive state game commissions that I would like to mention in detail, space permits the naming of only a very few, by way of illustration.

NEW YORK.—Thanks to the great conservation Governor of this state, John A. Dix, the year 1911 saw our forest, fish and game business established on an ideal business basis. Realizing the folly of requiring a single man to manage those three great interests, and render to each the attention that it deserves and requires, by a well-studied legislative act a State Conservation Commission was created, consisting of three commissioners, one for each of the three great natural departments. These are salaried officers, who devote their entire time to their work, and are properly equipped with assistants. The state force of game wardens now consists of 125 picked men, each on a salary of $900 per year, and through a rigid system of daily reports (inaugurated by John B. Burnham) the activities and results of each warden promptly become known in detail at headquarters.

Fortunately, New York contains a very large number of true sportsmen, who are ever ready to come forward in support of every great measure for wild-life protection. The spirit of real protection runs throughout the state, and in time I predict that it will result in a great recovery of the native game of the commonwealth. That will be after we have stopped all shooting of upland game birds and shore birds for about eight years. Even the pinnated grouse could be successfully introduced over one-third of the state, if the people would have it so. It was our great body of conscientious sportsmen who made possible the Bayne-Blauvelt law, and the new codification of the game laws of the state.

TENNESSEE.—Clearly, Honorable Mention belongs to the unsalaried State Commissioner of Tennessee, Col. J. H. Acklen, "than whom," says Dr. Palmer, "there is no more active and enthusiastic game protectionist in this country. Whatever has been accomplished in that state is due to his activity and public spirit. Col. Acklen, who is now president of the National Association of Game Commissioners, is a prominent lawyer, and enjoys the distinction of being the only commissioner in the country who not only serves without pay, but also defrays a large part of the expenses of game protection out of his own pocket."

Surely the Commonwealth of Tennessee will not long permit this unsupported condition of such a game commissioner to endure. That state has a wild fauna worth preserving for her sons and grandsons, and it is inconceivable that the funds vitally necessary to this public service can not be found.

ALABAMA.—I cite the case of Alabama because, in view of its position in a group of states that until recently have cared little about game protection, it may be regarded as an unusual case. Commissioner John H. Wallace, Jr., has evolved order out of chaos,—and something approaching a reign of law out of the absence of law. To-day the State of Alabama stands as an example of what can be accomplished by and through one clear-headed, determined man who is right, and knows that he is right.

NEW JERSEY.—Alabama reminds one of New Jersey, and of State Game Commissioner Ernest Napier. I have seen him on the firing-line, and I know that his strong devotion to the interests of the wild life of his state, his determination to protect it at all costs, and his resistless confidence in asking for what is right, have made him a power for good. The state legislature believes in him, and enacts the laws that he says are right and necessary. He serves without salary, and gives to the state time, labor and money. It is a pleasure to work with such a man. In 1912 Commissioner Napier won a pitched battle with the makers of automatic and pump guns, both shotguns and rifles, and debarred all those weapons from use *in hunting* in New Jersey unless satisfactorily reduced to two shots.

MASSACHUSETTS.—The state of Massachusetts is fortunate in the possession of a very fine corps of ornithologists, nature lovers, sportsmen and leading citizens who on all questions affecting wild life occupy high ground and are not afraid to maintain it. It would be a pleasure to write an entire chapter on this subject. The record of the Massachusetts Army of the Defense is both an example and an inspiraion to the people of other states. Not only is the cause of protection championed by the State Game Commission but it also receives constant and powerful support from the State Board of Agriculture, which maintains on its staff Mr. E. H. Forbush as State Ornithologist. The bird-protection publications of the Board are of great economic value, and they are also an everlasting credit to the state. The very latest is a truly great wild-life-protection volume of 607 pages, by Mr. Forbush, entitled *"Game Birds, Wild-Fowl and Shore Birds."* It is a publication most damaging to the cause of the Army of Destruction, and I heartily wish a million copies might be printed and placed in the hands of lawmakers and protectors.

The fight last winter and spring for a no-sale-of-game law was the Gettysburg for Massachusetts. The voice of the People was heard in no uncertain tones, and the Destroyers were routed all along the line. The leaders in that struggle on the protection side were E. H. Forbush, William P. Wharton, Dr. George W. Field, Edward N. Goding, Lyman E. Hurd, Ralph Holman, Rev. Wm. R. Lord and Salem D. Charles. With such leaders and such supporters, any wild-life cause can be won, anywhere!

PENNSYLVANIA.—The case of Pennsylvania is rather peculiar. As yet there is no large and resistless organized body of real sportsmen to rally to the support of the State Game Commission in great causes, as is the case in New York. As a result, with a paltry fund of only $20,000 for annual maintenance, and much opposition from hunters and farmers, the situation is far from satisfactory. Fortunately Dr. Joseph Kalbfus, Secretary of the Commission and chief executive officer, is a man of indomitable courage and determination. But for this state of mind he would ere this have given up the fight for the hunter's license law (of one dollar per year), which has been bitterly opposed by a very aggressive and noisy group of gunners who do not seem to know that they are grievously misled.

Fortunately, Commissioner John M. Phillips, of Pittsburgh is the ardent supporter of Dr. Kalbfus and a vigorous fighter for justice to wild life. He devotes to the cause a great amount of time and effort, and in addition to serving without salary he pays all his campaign expenses out of his own pocket. His only recompense for all this is the sincere admiration of his friends, and the consciousness of having done his full duty toward the wild life and the people of his native state.

THE STATE AUDUBON SOCIETIES.—It is impossible to estimate the full value of the influence and work of the State Audubon Societies of the United States. Thus far these societies exist in thirty-nine states. From the beginning, their efforts have tended especially toward the preservation of the non-game birds, and it is well that the song and other insectivorous birds have thus been specially championed. Unfortunately, however, if that policy is pursued exclusively, it leaves 154 very important species of game birds practically at the mercy of the Army of Destruction! It would seem that the time has come when all Audubon Societies should take up, as a part of their work, active co-operation in helping to save the game birds from extermination.

THE NATIONAL ORGANIZATIONS OF NEW YORK CITY

On January 1, 1895, the United States of America contained, so far as I am aware, not one organization of national scope which was devoting any large amount of its resources and activities to the protection of wild life. At that time the former activities of the A.O.U. Committee on Bird Protection had lapsed. To-day the city of New York contains six national organizations, and it is now a great center of nation-wide activities in behalf of preservation. Furthermore, these activities are steadily growing, and securing practical results.

THE NEW YORK ZOOLOGICAL SOCIETY.—In 1895 there was born into the world a scientific organization having for its second declared object "the preservation of our native animals." It was the first scientific society or corporation ever formed, so far as I am aware, having a specifically declared object of that kind. It owes its existence and its presence in the field of wild-life conservation to the initiative and persistence of Mr. Madison Grant and Prof. Henry Fairfield Osborn. For sixteen years these two officers have worked together virtually as one man. It is not strange to find a sportsman like Mr. Grant promoting the wild-life cause, but it is a fact well worthy of note that of all the zoologists of the world, Professor Osborn is the only one of real renown who has actively and vigorously engaged in this cause, and taken a place in the front rank of the Defenders.

Mr. Grant's influence on the protection cause has been strong and far-reaching,—far more so than the majority of his own friends are aware. He has promoted important protectionist causes from Alaska to Louisiana and Newfoundland, and helped to win many important victories.

THE BOONE AND CROCKETT CLUB.—This organization of big game

| JOSEPH KALBFUS
Chief Game Protector and Secretary, Pennsylvania Board of Game Commissioners | JOHN M. PHILLIPS
Member, Pennsylvania Board of Game Commissioners |

| EDWARD A. McILHENNY
Founder of Wild-Fowl Preserves in Louisiana | CHARLES WILLIS WARD
Founder of Wild-Fowl Preserves in Louisiana |

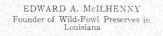

sportsmen was founded in 1885, and is the oldest of its kind in the United States. Its members always have supported the cause of protection, by law and by the making of game preserves. In all this work Mr. George Bird Grinnell, for twenty-five years editor of *Forest and Stream*, has been an important factor. As stated elsewhere, the club's written and unwritten code of ethics in big-game hunting is very strict. In course of time a Committee on Game Protection was formed, and it actively entered that field.

THE NATIONAL ASSOCIATION OF AUDUBON SOCIETIES.—This organization was founded by William Dutcher, in 1902, and in 1906 it was endowed to the extent of $322,000 by the bequest of Albert Wilcox. Subsequent endowments, together with the annual contributions of members and friends, now give the Association an annual income of $60,000. It maintains eight widely-separated field agents and lecturers and forty special game wardens of bird refuges. It maintains Secretary T. Gilbert Pearson and a number of other good men constantly on the firing-line; and these forces have achieved many valuable results. After years of stress and struggle, it now seems almost certain that this organization will save the two white egrets,—producers of "the white badge of cruelty,"—to the bird fauna of the United States, as in a similar manner it has saved the gulls, terns and other sea birds of our lakes and coast line.

This splendid organization is one of the monuments to William Dutcher. More than two years ago he was stricken with paralysis, and now sits in an invalid's chair at his home in Plainfield, New Jersey. His mind is clear and his interest in wild-life protection is keen, but he is unable to speak or to write. While he was active, he was one of the most resourceful and fearless champions of the cause of the vanishing birds. To him the farmers of America owe ten times more than they ever will know, and a thousand times more than they ever will repay, either to him or to his cause.

THE CAMP-FIRE CLUB OF AMERICA.—Although founded in 1897, this organization did not, as an organization, actively enter the field of protection until 1909. Since that time its work has covered a wide field, and enlisted the activities of many of its members. In order to provide a permanent fund for its work, each year the club members pay special annual dues that are devoted solely to the wild-life cause. The Committee on Game Protective Legislation and Preserves is a strong, hard-working body, and it has rendered good service in the lines of activity named in its title.

THE AMERICAN GAME PROTECTIVE AND PROPAGATION ASSOCIATION. —This is the youngest protective organization of national scope, having been organized in 1911. Its activities are directed by John B. Burnham, for five years Chief Game Protector of the State of New York, and a man thoroughly conversant with the business of protection. The organization is financed chiefly by means of a large annual fund contributed by several of the largest companies engaged in manufacturing firearms and ammunition, whose directors feel that the time has come;

when it is both wise and necessary to take practical measures to preserve the remnant of American game. Already the activities of this organization cover a wide range, and it has been particularly active in enlisting support for the Weeks bill for the federal protection of migratory birds.

THE WILD LIFE PROTECTIVE ASSOCIATION came into existence in 1910, rather suddenly, for the purpose of promoting the cause of the Bayne no-sale-of-game bill, and other measures. It raised the fund that met the chief expenses of that campaign. Since that time it has taken an important part in three other hotly contested campaigns in other states, two of which were successful.

At the present moment, and throughout the future, these New York organizations need *large sums of money* with which to meet the legitimate expenses of active campaigns for great measures. They need *some* money from outside the state of New York! *Too much of the burden of national campaigning has been and is being left to be borne by the people of New York City.* This policy is growing monotonous. There is every reason why Chicago, St. Louis, Cincinnati, Pittsburgh, Cleveland, Philadelphia, Baltimore and Boston should each year turn $100,000 into the hands of these well-equipped and well managed national organizations whose officers know *how to get results*, all over our country

Such organizations as these do not exist in other cities; and this is very unfortunate. New Orleans should be a center of protectionist activity for the South, San Francisco for the Pacific slope, and Chicago for the Middle West. Will they not become so?

TWO INDEPENDENT WORKERS.—At the western edge of the delta of the Mississippi there have arisen two men who loom up into promi nence at an outpost of the Army of Defense which they themselves have established. For what they already have done in the creation of wild-fowl preserves in Louisiana, Edward A. McIlhenny and Charles Willis Ward deserve the thanks of the American People-at-large. An account of their splendid activities, and the practical results already secured, will be found in Chapter XXXVIII, on "Private Game Preserves," and in the story of Marsh Island. Already the home of these gentlemen, Avery Island, Louisiana, has become an important center of activity in wild-life protection.

CHAPTER XXVII

HOW TO MAKE A NEW GAME LAW

THE LINE OF ACTION.—In the face of a calamity, the saving of life and property and the check of fire and flood depends upon good judgment and quick action at the critical moment. In emergencies, the slow and academic method will not serve. It is the run, the jump, the short cut and the violent method that saves life. If a woman is drowning, the sensible man does not wait for an introduction to her; nor does he run to an acquaintance to borrow his boat, or stop to put on a collar and necktie. He seizes the first boat that he can find, and breaks its lock and chain if necessary; or, failing that, he plunges in without one. When he reaches the imperiled party, he doesn't say, "Will you kindly let me save you?" He seizes her by the hair, and tries to keep her head above water, without ceremony.

That is to-day the condition and the treatment necessary regarding our remnant of wild life. We are compelled to act quickly, directly, and even violently at times, if we save anything worth while.

There is *no time* to depend upon the academic "education" of the public by the seductive illustrated lecture on birds, or the article about the habits of mammals. Those methods are all well enough in their places, but we must not depend upon them in emergencies like the present, for they do not pass laws or arrest lawbreakers. Give the public all of that material that you can supply, and the more the better, but for heaven's sake *do not* depend upon the spread of bird-lore "education" to stop the work of the game-hogs! If you do, all the wild life will be destroyed while the educational work is going on.

Often you can educate a gunner, and make him a protectionist; but you never can do it by showing him pictures of birds. He needs strong reasoning and exhortation, not bird-lore. To-day it is necessary to employ the most direct, forceful and at times even rude methods. Where slaughtering cannot be stopped by moral suasion, it must be stopped with a hickory club. The thing to do is to *get results, and get them quickly, before it is too late!*

If the business section of a town is burning down, no one goes into the suburbs to lecture on architecture, or exhibit pictures of fire apparatus. The rush is for water, fire-engines, red-blooded men and dynamite. When the birds all around you are being shot to death by poachers who fear not God nor regard man, and you need help to stop it on the instant, run to your neighbor's house, and ring his bell. If he fails to hear the bell, pound on his door until you jar the whole house.

When he comes down half-dressed, blinking and rubbing his eyes, shout at him:

"Come out! Your birds are all being shot to pieces!"

"Are they?" he will say. "But what can *I* do about it? I can't help it! I'm no game warden."

"Put on your clothes, get your shot-gun and come out and drive off the killing gang."

"But what good will that do? They will come back again."

"Not if we do our duty. We must have them arrested, and appear against them in court."

"But," says the sleepy citizen, "That won't do much good. The laws are not strict enough; and besides, they are not well enforced, even as they are!"

"Then let's make it our business to see that the present laws are enforced, and go to our members of the legislature, and have them pass some stronger laws."

And this brings me to a very important subject:

How to Pass a New Law

We venture to say that the average citizen little realizes how possible it is to secure the passage of a law that is clearly necessary for the better protection of wild life and forests. Because of this, and of the necessity for exact knowledge, I shall here set down specific instructions on this subject.

THE PERSONAL EQUATION.—One determined man can secure the passage of a good law, provided he is reasonably intelligent and sufficiently determined. The man who starts a movement must make up his mind to follow it up, direct its fortunes, stay with it when the storms of opposition beat upon it, and never give up until it is signed by the governor. He must be willing to sacrifice his personal convenience, many of his pleasures, and work when his friends are asleep or pleasuring.

In working for the protection of wild life there is one mighty and unfailing source of consolation. It is this:

Your cause always gains in strength, and the cause of the destroyers always loses strength!

THE CHOICE OF A CAUSE.—Be broad-minded. Do not rush to the legislature with a demand for a law to permit the taking of bull-heads with June-bugs in the creeks of your township, or to give your county a specially early open season on quail in order that your boy may try his new gun before he goes back to college. *Don't propose any "local" legislation;* for in progressive states, local game legislation is coming strongly into disfavor,—just as it should! Legislate for your whole state, and nothing less.

Do not bother your legislature with a trivial bill. Choose a cause that is worth while to grown men, and it shall be well with you It takes no more time to pass a large bill than a small one; and big men prefer to be identified with big measures.

Before you have a bill drawn, advise with men whose opinions are worth having. If the end you have in mind is a great and good one, *go ahead*, whether you secure support in advance or not. If the needs of the hour clearly demand the measure, *go ahead*, even though you start absolutely alone. A good measure never goes far without attracting company.

DRAFTING A BILL.—As a rule, the members of a legislative body do not have time to draft bills on subjects that are new or strange to them. A short bill is easily prepared by your own representative; but a lengthy bill, covering a serious reform. is a different matter. Hire a lawyer to draft the bill for you. A really good lawyer will not charge much for drafting a bill that is to benefit the public, and grind no private axe; but if the bill is long, and requires long study, even the good citizen must charge something.

Your bill must fully recognize existing laws. It must be either prohibitory or permissive; which means that it can say what shall not be done, or else that which may be done according to law, all other acts being forbidden. Your lawyer must decide which form is best. For my part, I greatly prefer the prohibitive form, as being the stronger and more impressive of the two. I think it is the province of the law to forbid the destruction of wild life and forests, under penalties.

PENALTIES.—Every law should provide a penalty for its infringement; but the penalty should not be out of all proportion to the offense. It is just as unwise to impose a fine of one dollar for killing song-birds for food as it is to provide for a fine of three hundred dollars. A fine that is too small fails to impress the prisoner, and it begets contempt for the law and the courts! A fine that is altogether too high is apt to be set aside by the court as "excessive." In my opinion, the best fines for wild life slaughter would be as follows:

Shooting, netting or trapping song-birds, and other non-game birds, each bird	$5 to	$25
Killing game birds out of season, each bird	10 to	50
Selling game contrary to law, each offense	100 to	200
Dynamiting fish	100 to	200
Seining or netting game fishes	50 to	200
Shooting birds with unfair weapons	10 to	100
Killing an egret, Carolina parakeet or whooping crane	100 to	200
Killing a mountain sheep or antelope anywhere in the U. S.		500
Killing an elk contrary to law		50
Killing a female deer, or fawn without horns, each offense		50
Trapping a grizzly bear for its skin		100

For killing a man "by mistake," the fine should be $500, payable in five annual instalments, to the court, for the family of the victim.

Whenever fines are not paid, the convicted party should be sentenced to imprisonment at hard labor at the rate of one-half day for each dollar of the fine imposed; and a sentence at hard labor should be the *first option of the court!* Many a rich and reckless poacher snaps his fingers at fines; but a sentence to hard labor would strike terror to the heart of the most brazen of them. To all such men, "labor" is the twin terror to "death."

THE INTRODUCTION OF A BILL.—Much wisdom is called for in the selection of legislative champions for wild-life bills. It is possible to state here only the leading principles involved.

Of course it is best to look for an introducer within the political party that is in the majority. A man who has many important bills on his hands is bound to give his best attention to his own pet measures; and it is best to choose a man who is not already overloaded. If a man has a host of enemies, pass him by. By all means choose a man whose high character and good name will be a tower of strength to your cause; and if necessary, *wait for him to make up his mind.* Mr. Lawrence W. Trowbridge waited three long and anxious weeks in the hope that Hon. George A. Blauvelt would finally consent to champion the Bayne bill in the New York Assembly. At last Mr. Blauvelt consented to take it up; and the time spent in waiting for his decision was a grand investment! He was the Man of all men to pilot that bill through the Assembly.

Very often the "quiet man" of a legislative body is a good man to champion a new and drastic measure. The quiet man who makes up his mind to take hold of "a hard bill to pass" often astonishes the natives by his ability to get results. Representative John F. Lacey, of Iowa, made his name a household word all over the United States by the quiet, steady, tireless and finally resistless energy with which for three long years in Congress he worked for "the Lacey bird bill." For years his colleagues laughed at him, and cheerfully voted down his bill. But he persisted. His cause steadily gained in strength; and his final triumph laid the axe at the root of a thousand crimes against wild life, throughout the length and breadth of this land. He rendered the people of America a service that entitles him to our everlasting gratitude and remembrance.

AFTER THE INTRODUCTION OF A BILL.—As soon as a bill is introduced it is referred to a committee, to be examined and reported upon. If there is opposition,—and to every bill that really does something worth while there always is opposition,—then there is a "hearing." The committee appoints a day, when the friends and foes of the bill assemble, and express their views.

The week preceding a hearing is your busy week. You must plan your campaign, down to the smallest details. Pick the men whom you wish to have speak (for ten minutes each) on the various parts of your bill, and divide the topics and the time between them. Call upon the friends of the bill in various portions of the state to attend and "say something." Go up with a strong body of fine men. *Have as many organizations represented as you possibly can!* The "organizations" represent the great mass of people, and the voters also.

When you reach the hearing, hand to your bill's champion, who will be floor manager for your side, a clear and concise list of your speakers, carefully arranged and stating who's who. That being done, you have only to fill your own ten minutes and afterward enjoy the occasion.

THE VALUE OF ACCURACY.—It is unnecessary to say, in working for a bill,—*always be sure of your facts.* Never let your opponents catch you tripping in accuracy of statement. If you make one serious error, your enemies will turn it against you to the utmost. Better understate facts than overstate them. This shrewd old world quickly recognizes the careful, conservative man whose testimony is so true and so rock-founded that no assaults can shake it. Legislators are quick to rely on the words and opinions of the man who can safely be trusted. If your enemies try to overwhelm you with extravagant statements, that are unfair to your cause, the chances are that the men who judge between you will recognize them by their ear-marks, and discount them accordingly.

WORK WITH MEMBERS.—Sometimes a subject that is put before a legislative body is so new, and the thing proposed is so drastic, it becomes necessary to take measures to place a great many facts before each member of the body. Under such circumstances the member naturally desires to be "shown." The cleanest and finest campaigning for a reform measure is that in which both sides deal with facts, rather than with personal importunities. With a good cause in hand, it is a pleasure to prepare concise statements of facts and conditions from which a legislator may draw logical conclusions. Whenever a bill can be won through in that way, game protection work becomes a delight.

In all important new measures affecting the rights and the property of the whole people of a state, the conscientious legislator wishes to know how the people feel about it. When you tell him that "The wild life belongs to the whole people of the state; and this bill is in their interest," he needs to know for certain that your proposition is true. Sometimes there is only one way in which he can be fully convinced; and that is by the people of his district.

Then it becomes necessary to send out a general alarm, and call upon the People to write to their representatives and express *their* views. Give them, in printed matter, the *latest facts* in the case, forecast the future as you think it should be forecast, then demand that the men and women who are interested do write to their senators and assemblyman, and express *their* views, in *their own way!* Let there be no "machine letters" sent out, all ready for signature; for such letters are a waste of effort, and belong in the waste baskets to which they are quickly consigned. The members of legislative bodies hate them, and rightly, too. They want to hear from men who can think for themselves, give reasons of their own, and express their desires in their own way.

THE PRESS AND THE NEWSPAPERS.—It is impossible to overestimate the influence of the newspapers and the periodical press in general, in the protection of wild life. But for their sympathy, their support and their independent assaults upon the Army of Destruction, our game species would nearly all of them have been annihilated, long ago. Editors are sympathetic and responsive good-citizens, as keenly sensitive regarding their duties as any of the rest of us are, and from the earliest times of protection they have been on the firing line, helping to beat back the destroyers. It is indeed a rare sight to see an editor giving aid, comfort or advice to the enemy. I can not recall more than a score of articles that I have seen or heard of during thirty years in this field that opposed the cause of wild life protection.* At this moment, for instance, I bear in particularly grateful remembrance the active campaign work of the following newspapers:

The New York Times
The New York Tribune
The New York Herald
The New York Globe
The New York Mail and Express
The New York World
The New York Sun
The Springfield (Mass.) Republican
The Chicago Inter-Ocean
The San Francisco Call
The Rochester Union and Advertiser

The Victoria Colonist
The Brooklyn Standard-Union
The New York Evening Post
The New York Press
The Buffalo News
The Minneapolis Journal
The Pittsburgh Index-Appeal
The St. Louis Globe-Democrat
The Philadelphia North American
The Utica Observer
The Washington Star.

These magazines have done good service in the cause; and some of them have spent many years on the firing line:

Forest and Stream
The American Field
Field and Stream
Recreation (old and new)
Rod and Gun in Canada
In the Open

Sports Afield
Western Field
Outdoor Life
Shield's Magazine
Sportsman's Review
Outing

Collier's Weekly
The Independent
Country Life
Outdoor World
Bird Lore

In campaigning, always appeal for the help of the newspapers. If there are no private axes to grind, they help generously. The weekly journals are of value, but the monthlies are printed so long in advance of their dates of issue that they seldom move fast enough to keep abreast of the procession. Their mechanical limitations are many and serious.

Every newspaper likes "exclusive" news, letters and articles. On that basis they will print about all the live matter that you can furnish. But at the same time, the important news of the campaign *must* be sent to the press broadcast, in the form of printed slips all ready for the foreman. Many of these are never used, but the others are; and it pays. The news in every slip must be vouched for by the sender, or it will not be used. Often it will appear as a letter signed by the sender; which is all right, only the news is most effective when printed without a signature. Do not count on the Associated Press; because its peculiar demands render it almost impossible for it to be utilized in game protection work.

How to Meet Opposition.—There is no rule for the handling of opposition that is fair and open. For opposition that is unfair and under-

* Just one hour after the above paragraph was written, a long telegram from San Francisco advised me that the *Examiner* of that city had begun an active and aggressive campaign for the sale of all kinds of game.

handed, there is one powerful weapon,—Publicity. The American people love fair play, and there is nothing so fatal to an unfair fighter as a searchlight, turned full on him without fear and without mercy. If it is reliably and persistently reported that some citizen who ought to be on the right side has for some dark reason become active on the wrong side, print the reports in a large newspaper, and ask him publicly if they are true. If the reports are false, he can quickly come out in a letter and say so, and end the matter. If they are true, the public will soon know it, and act accordingly.

ETERNAL VIGILANCE.—The progress of a bill must be watched by some competent person from day to day, and finally from hour to hour. I know one bill that was saved from defeat only because its promoter dragged it, almost by force, out of the hands of a tardy clerk, and accompanied it in person to the senate, where it was passed in the last hour of a session.

A bill should not be left to a long slumber in the drawer of a committee. Such delays nearly always are dangerous.

SIGNING THE BILL.—The promoter of a great measure always seeks the sympathy of the Chief Executive early in the day; but he should not make the diplomatic error of trying to exact promises or pledges in advance. Good judges do not give away their decisions in advance.

Because a Chief Executive remarks after a bill has been sent to him for signing that he "cannot approve it," it is no reason to give up in despair. Many an executive approval has been snatched at the last moment, as a brand from the burning. *Ask for a hearing before the bill is acted upon.* At the hearing, and before it and after, the People who wish the bill to become a law must express themselves,—by letter, by telegram, and by appeal in person. If the governor becomes convinced that an *overwhelming majority* of his people desire him to sign the bill, *he will sign it,* even though personally he is opposed to it! The hall mark of a good governor is a spirit of obedience to the will of the great majority.

Not until your bill has been signed by the governor are you ready to go home with a quiet mind, take off your armor, and put your ear to the telephone while you hear some one say as your only reward,—"Well done, good and faithful servant."

AS TO "CREDIT."—Do not count upon receiving any credit for what you do in the cause of game protection, outside the narrow circle of your own family and your nearest friends. This is a busy world; and the human mind flits like a restless bird from one subject to another. The men who win campaigns are forgotten by the general public, in a few hours! There is nothing more fickle or more fleeting than the bubble called "popular applause." Judging by the experiences of great men, I should say that it has no substance, whatever. The most valuable reward of the man who fights in a great cause, and helps to win victories, is the profound satisfaction that comes to every good citizen who bravely does his whole duty, and leaves the world better than he found it, without the slightest thought of gallery applause.

CHAPTER XXVIII

NEW LAWS NEEDED: A ROLL-CALL OF THE STATES

The principles of wild-life protection and encouragement are now so firmly established as to leave little room for argument regarding their value. When they are set forth before the people of any given state, the only question is of willingness to do the right thing; of duty or a defiance of duty; of good citizenship or the reign of selfishness. Men who do not wish to do their duty purposely befog great issues by noisy talk and tiresome academic discussions of trivial details; and such men are the curse and scourge of reform movements.

There are a very few persons who foolishly assert that "there are too many game laws!" It is entirely wrong for any person to make such a statement, for it tends to promote harmful error. The fact that our laws are *too lenient*, or are not fully enforced, is no excuse for denouncing their purposes. We have all along been too timid, too self indulgent, and too much afraid of hurting the feelings of the game-hogs.

Give me the power to make the game laws of any state or province and I will guarantee to save the *non-migratory* wild life of that region I will not only make adequate laws, but I will also provide means, men and penalties by which *they will be enforced!* It is easy and simple, for men who are not afraid.

I have been at considerable pains to analyze the game laws of each state, ascertain their shortcomings, and give a list of the faults that need correction by new legislation. It has required no profound wisdom to do this, because the principles involved are so plain that any intelligent schoolboy fifteen years old can master them in one hour. I have performed this task hopefully, in the belief that in many states the real issues have not been plainly put before the people. Hereafter no state shall destroy its wild life through ignorance of the laws that would preserve it.

Let no man say that "it is too late to save the wild life"; for excepting the dead-and-gone species, that is not true. Let no man say that "we can not save the wild life by law"; for that is not true, either. As long as laws are lax, even law-abiding people will take advantage of them.

There are millions of men who think it is *right to kill all the game that the law allows!* There are thousands of women who think it is right to wear aigrettes as long as the law permits their sale! And yet, if we are resolute and diligent there is plenty of hope for the future. During the past three years, to go no farther back, we have seen the whole state of New York swept clean of the traffic in native wild game by the Bayne law, and of the traffic in wild birds' plumage on women's hats through the Dutcher law. To-day, in this state, we find ninty-nine women out of every one hundred wearing flowers, and laces, and plush and satin on their hats, instead of the heads, bodies and feathers of wild birds that were the regular thing until three years ago. The change has been a powerful commentary on the value of good laws for the protection of wild life. The Dutcher law has caused the plumage of wild birds *almost wholly to disappear from the State of New York!*

We shall here point out the plain duty of each state; and then it will be up to them, individually, to decide whether they can stand the blood-test or not.

A state or a nation can be ungentlemanly, unfair or mean, just the same as an individual. No state has a right to maintain shambles for the slaughter of migratory game or song birds that belong in part to sister states. *Every state holds its migratory bird life in trust, for the benefit of the people of the nation at large.* A state is just as responsible for its treatment of wild life as any individual; and it is time to open books of account.

It is robbery, as well as murder, for any southern state to slaughter the robins of the northern states, where no robins may be killed. *No southern gentleman can permit such doings, after the crime has been pointed out to him!* In the North, the men who are caught shooting robins are instantly haled to court, and fined or imprisoned. If we of the North should kill for food the mockingbirds that visit us, the people of the South instantly would brand us as monsters of greed and meanness; and they would be perfectly justified in so doing.

Let us at least be honest in "agreeing upon a state of fact," as the lawyers say, whether we act sensibly and mercifully or not. Just so long as there remains in this land of ours a fauna of game birds, and the gunners of one-half the states are allowed to dictate the laws for the slaughter of it, just so long will our present protection remain utterly absurd and criminally inadequate. Look at these absurdities:

New York, New Jersey and many other northern states rigidly prohibit the late winter and spring shooting of waterfowl and shore birds, and limit the bag; North Carolina, South Carolina, Florida, and other southern states not only slaughter wild fowl and shore birds all winter and spring, without limit, but several of them kill certain non-game birds besides!

All the northern states protect the robin, for the good that it does; but in North Carolina, Tennessee, Mississippi, Louisiana and some other southern states, thousands of robins are shot for food. Minnesota has stopped spring shooting; but her sister state on the south, Iowa, obstinately refuses to do so.

THE UNITED STATES AT LARGE.—There are two great measures that should be carried into effect by the governing body of the United States. One is the enactment of a law providing federal protection for all migratory birds; and Canada and Mexico should be induced to join with the United States *in an international treaty to that effect.*

The other necessary measure is the passage of a joint resolution of Congress *declaring every national 'forest and 'forest reserve also a game preserve and general sanctuary for wild life,* in which there shall be no hunting or killing of wild creatures of any kind save predatory animals.

The tendency of the times,—and the universal slaughter of wild life on this continent,—point straight as an arrow flies in that direction. Soon or late, we have GOT to come to it! If Congress does not take the initiatory steps, *the People will!* Such a consummation is necessary; it is justified by common sense and the inexorable logic of the situation, and when done it will be right.

The time was when the friends of wild life did not dare speak of this subject in Washington save in whispers. That was in the days when the Appalachian Park bill could not be passed, and when there were angry mutterings and even curses leveled against Gifford Pinchot and the Forestry Bureau because so many national forests were being set aside. That was in the days when a few western sheep-men thought that they owned the whole Rocky Mountains without having bought them. To-day, the American people have grown accustomed to the idea of having the resources of the public domain saved and conserved for the benefit of the millions rather than lavished upon a favored few. To-day it is perfectly safe to talk about making every national forest a first class wild-life sanctuary, and it is up to the People to request Congress to take that action, at once.

The Weeks bill, the Anthony bill, and the McLean bill now before Congress to provide federal protection for migratory birds are practically identical. All three are good bills; and it matters not which one finally becomes a law. Whichever is put forward finally for passage should provide federal protection for *all* migratory birds that ever enter the United States, Alaska, or Porto Rico. Why favor the duck and leave the robin to its fate, or vice versa? It will be just as easy to do this task by wholes as by halves. The time to hesitate, to feel timid, or to be afraid of the other fellow has gone by. To-day the millions of honest and serious-minded Americans are ready to back the most thorough and most drastic policy, because that has become the most necessary and the best policy. Furthermore, it is the only policy worthy of serious consideration.

Some of our states have done rather well in wild-life protection,— considering the absurdity of our national policy as a whole; others have done indifferently, and some have been and still are very remiss. Here is where we intend to hew to the line, and without fear or favor set forth the standing of each state according to its merits or its lack of merits. In a life-or-death matter such as now confronts us regarding the wild life of our country, it is time to speak plainly.

In the following call of the States, the glaring deficiencies in state game laws will be set forth in detail, in order that the sore spots may be exposed to the view of the doctors. Conditions will be represented *as they exist at the end of the summer of 1912*, and it is to be hoped that these faults soon may be corrected.

A ROLL-CALL OF THE STATES

ALABAMA:

It is a satisfaction to be able to open this list with the name of a state that is entitled to a medal of honor for game protection. In this particular field of progress and enlightenment, the state of Alabama is the pioneer state of the South. New York now occupies a similar position in the North; but New York is an older state, and stronger in her general love of nature. The attainment of advanced protection in any southern state is a very different matter from what it is in the North.

Five years ago Alabama set her house in order. The slaughter of song and insectivorous birds has been so far stopped as any Southern state can stop it unaided by the federal government, and those birds are recognized and treated as the farmers' best friends. The absurd system of attempted protection through county laws has been abandoned. The sale of game has been stopped, and since that stoppage, quail have increased. The trapping and export of game have ceased, and wild turkeys and woodcock are now increasing. It is unlawful to kill or capture non-game birds. Bag limits have been imposed, but *the bag limit laws are all too liberal, and should be reduced*. A hunter's license law is in force, and the department of game and fish is self-supporting. Night hunting is prohibited, and female deer may not be killed. A comprehensive warden system has been provided. As yet, however, Alabama

Permits the shooting of waterfowl to March 15, which is too late, by one and one-half months.

The use of automatic and pump guns in hunting should be suppressed.

There should be a limit of two deer per year, and killing should be restricted to deer with horns not less than three inches long.

The story of game protection in Alabama began in 1907. Prior to that time, the slaughter of wild life was very great. It is known that enormous numbers of quail were annually killed by negro farm hands, who hunted at least three days each week, regardless of work to be done. The slaughter of quail, wild ducks woodcock, doves, robins and snipe was described as "nauseating."

The change that has been wrought since 1907 is chiefly due to the efforts of one man. Alabama owes her standing to-day to the admirable qualities of John H. Wallace, Jr., her Game and Fish Commissioner, author of the State's policy in wild-life conservation. His broad-mindedness, his judgment and his success make him a living object lesson of the power of one determined man in the conservation of wild life.

Commissioner Wallace is an ardent supporter of the Weeks and Anthony bills for federal protection, and as a lawyer of the South, he believes there is "no constitutional inhibition against federal legislation for the protection of birds of passage."

ALASKA·

The sale of game must be absolutely prohibited, forever.

The slaughter of big game by Indians, miners and prospectors should now be limited, and strictly regulated by law, on rational lines.

The slaughter of walrus for ivory and hides, both in the Alaskan and Russian waters of Bering Sea, should be totally prohibited for ten years.

The game-warden service should be quadrupled in number of wardens, and in general effectiveness.

The game-warden service should be supplied with two sea-going vessels, independent for patrol work.

The bag limit on hoofed game is 50% too large.

To accomplish these ends, Congress should annually appropriate $50,000 for the protection of wild life in Alaska. The present amount, $15,000, is very inadequate, and the great wild-life interests at stake amply justify the larger amount.

It is now time for Alaska to make substantial advances in the protection of her wild life. It is no longer right nor just for Indians, miners and prospectors to be permitted by law to kill all the big game they please, whenever they please. The indolent and often extortionate Indians of Alaska,—who now demand "big money" for every service they perform,—are not so valuable as citizens that they should be permitted to feed riotously upon *moose, and cow moose at that*, until that species is exterminated. Miners and prospectors are valuable citizens, but that is no reason why they should forever be allowed to live upon wild game, any more than that hungry prospectors in our Rocky Mountains should be allowed to kill cattle.

Alaska and its resources do not belong to the very few people from "the States" who have gone there to make their fortunes and get out again as quickly as possible. The quicker the public mind north of Wrangel is disabused of that idea, the better. Its game belongs to the people of this nation of ninety-odd millions, and it is a safe prediction that the ninety millions will not continue to be willing that the miners, prospectors and Indians shall continue to live on moose meat and caribou tongues in order to save bacon and beef.

Mr. Frank E. Kleinschmidt said to me that at Sand Point, Alaska, he saw eighty-two caribou tongues brought in by an Indian, and sold at fifty cents each, while (according to all accounts) most of the bodies of the slaughtered animals became a loss.

Governor Clark has recommended in his annual report for 1911 that the protection now enjoyed by the giant brown bear (*Ursus middendorffi*) on Kadiak Island be removed, for the benefit of settlers *and their stock!* It goes without saying that no one proposes that predatory wild animals shall be permitted to retard the development of any wild country that is required by civilized man. All we ask in this matter is that, as in the case of the once-proposed slaughter of sea-lions on the Pacific Coast, *the necessity of the proposed slaughter shall be fully and adequately proven before the killing begins!* It is fair to insist that the sea-lion episode shall not be repeated on Kadiak Island.

The big game of Alaska can not long endure against a "limit" of two moose, three mountain sheep, three caribou and six deer per year, per man. At that rate the moose and sheep soon will disappear. The limit should be one moose, two sheep, two caribou and four deer,—unless we are willing to dedicate the Alaskan big game to Commercialism. No sportsman needs a larger bag than the revised schedule; and commercialists should not be allowed to kill big game anywhere, at any time.

Let us bear in mind the fact that Alaska is being throughly "opened up" to the Man with a Gun. Here is the latest evidence, from the new circular of an outfitter:

"I will have plenty of good horses, and good, competent and courteous guides; also other camp attendants if desired. My intention is to establish permanently at that point, as I believe it is the gateway to the finest *and about the last* of the great game countries of North America."

The road is open; the pack-train is ready; the guides are waiting. Go on and slay the Remnant!

ARIZONA:

The band-tailed pigeons and all non-game birds should immediately be given pro‑ tection; and a salaried warden system should be established under a Commissioner whose term is not less than four years.

The use of automatic and pump guns, in hunting, should be prohibited.

Spring shooting should be prohibited.

Arizona has good reason to be proud of her up-to-date position in the ranks of the best game-protecting states. No other state or territory of her age ever has made so good a showing of protective laws. The enactment of laws to cover the points mentioned above would leave little to be desired in Arizona. That state has a bird fauna well worth protecting, and game wardens are extremely necessary.

ARKANSAS:

The enforcement of game laws should be placed in charge of a salaried commissioner.

Spring shooting of wildfowl should be stopped at once.

A reasonable close season should be provided for water fowl, and swans should be protected throughout the year.

A bag-limit law should be enacted.

A force of game wardens, salaried and unsalaried, should at once be created.

The killing of female deer and the hounding of deer, should be stopped.

No buck deer should be shot, unless horns three inches long are seen before firing.

A hunter's license law is necessary; and the fees should go to the support of the game protection department.

The local exemptions in favor of market hunters in Mississippi county should be repealed.

It appears that in Arkansas the laws for the protection and increase of wild life are by no means up to the mark. At this moment, Arkansas is next to Florida, the rearmost of all our states in wild-life protection. Awake, Arkansas! Consider the peril that threatens your fauna. The

Sunk Lands, in your northeastern corner along the St. Francis River, are the greatest wild-fowl refuge anywhere in the Mississippi Valley between the Gulf Coast of Louisiana and the breeding-grounds of Minnesota. A duty to the nation devolves upon you, to protect the migratory water-fowl that visit your great bird refuge from the automatic and pump guns of the pothunters who shoot for northern markets, and kill all that they can kill. *Protect those Sunken Lands!* Confer a boon on all the people of the Mississippi Valley by making that region a bird refuge in fact as well as in name.

Heretofore, you have permitted hired market gunners from outside your borders to slaughter the wild-fowl of your Sunk Lands literally by millions, and ship them to northern markets, with very little benefit to your people. It is time for that slaughter to cease. Don't maintain a duck and goose shambles in Mississippi County, year after year, as North Carolina does! Do unto other states as you would have other states do unto you. *Do not* be afraid to pass nine good laws in one act. Clear your record in the Family of States, and save your fauna before it is too late. It is not fair for you to permit the slaughter of the insectivorous birds that are like the blood of life to the farmer and fruit grower.

CALIFORNIA:

The sale of all wild game should be forever prohibited. .

The use of automatic and pump shotguns, in hunting, should be prohibited.

The killing of pigeons and doves as "game" and "food" should be stopped.

The sage grouse and every other species of bird threatened with extinction should be given ten year close seasons.

The mule deer (if any remain) and the Columbian black-tailed deer in the southern counties should be accorded a ten-year close season.

A large state game preserve should be created immediately, on or near Mount Shasta and abundantly stocked with nucleus herds of antelope, black-tailed deer, bison and elk.

A suitable preserve in the southern part of the state should be set aside for the dwarf elk.

As game laws are generally regarded, California has on her books a series that look rather good to the eye, but which are capable of considerable improvement. All along the line, the birds and quadrupeds of the Golden State are vanishing! Under that heading, a vigorous chapter could be written; but space forbids its development here. Just fancy laws that permit gunning and hunting with dogs, from August until January—one-half the entire year! Think of the nesting birds that are disturbed or killed by dogs and gunners after other birds!

California's wild ducks and geese have been slaughtered to an extent almost beyond belief. The splendid sage grouse and the sharp-tailed grouse are greatly reduced in numbers. Of her hundreds of thousands of antelope, once the cheapest game in the market, scarcely "a trace" remains. Her mountain sheep and mule deer are almost extinct. Her grizzly bears are gone!

The most terrible slaughter ever recorded for automatic guns occurred in Glenn County, Cal., on Feb. 5, 1906, when two men (whose story was published in *Outdoor Life*, xvii, p. 371, April, 1906), killed 450 geese in one day, and actually bagged 218 of them in *one hour!*

Every person who has paid attention to game protection on the Pacific coast well knows that during the past eight years or more, the work of game protection in California has been in a state of frequent turmoil. At times the lack of harmony between the State Fish and Game Commission and the sportsmen of the state has been damaging to the interests of wild life, and deplorable. In the case of Warden Welch, in Santa Cruz County, pernicious politics came near robbing the state of a splendid warden, but the courts finally overthrew the overthrowers of Mr. Welch, and reinstated him.

The fish and game commissioners of any state should be broad-minded, non-partisan, strictly honest and sincere. So long as they possess these qualities, they deserve and should have the earnest and aggressive support of all sportsmen and all lovers of wild life. The remnant of wild life is entitled to a square deal, and harmony in the camp of its friends. Fortunately California has an excellent force of salaried game wardens (82 in all) and 577 volunteer wardens serving without salary.

COLORADO

The State of Colorado should instantly stop the sale of native wild game to be used as food.

It should stop all late winter and spring shooting of native wild birds.

It should give the sage grouse, pinnated grouse and all shore birds a ten year close season, remove the dove from the list of game birds, and give it a permanent close season.

It should remove the crane and the swan from the list of game birds.

In twenty-five short years we have seen in Colorado a waste of wild life and the destruction of a living inheritance that has few parallels in history. Possibly the people of Colorado are satisfied with the residuum; but some outsiders regard all Rocky Mountain shambles with a feeling of horror.

A brief quarter-century ago, Colorado was a zoological park of grand scenery and big game. The scenery remains, but of the great wild herds, only samples are left, and of some species not even that.

The last bison of Colorado were exterminated in Lost Park by scoundrels calling themselves "taxidermists," in 1897. Of the 200,000 mule deer that inhabited Routt County and other portions of Colorado, not enough now remain to make deer hunting interesting. A perpetual close season was put on mountain sheep just in time to save a dozen small flocks as seed stock. Those flocks have been permitted to live, and they have bred until now there are perhaps 3,500 sheep in the state. Of elk, only a remnant is left, now protected for fifteen years.

The grizzly bear is so thoroughly gone that one is seen only by a rare accident; but black bears and pumas are sufficiently numerous to afford fair sport, provided the hunter has a fine outfit of dogs, horses and guides. Of prong-horned antelope, several bands remain, but it is reported that they are steadily diminishing. The herds and herders of domestic sheep are blamed for the decrease, and I have no doubt they deserve it. The sheep and their champions are the implacable enemies of all wild game, and before them the game vanishes, everywhere.

The lawmakers of Colorado have tried hard to provide adequate statutes for the protection of the wild life of the state. In fact, I think that no state has put forth greater or more elaborate efforts in that direction. For example, in 1899, under the leadership of Judge D. C. Beaman of Denver, Colorado initiated the "more game movement," by enacting a very elaborate law providing for the establishment of private game preserves and farms for the breeding of game under state license, and the tagging and sale of preserve-bred game under state supervision.

The history of game destruction in Colorado is a

BAND-TAILED PIGEON

Often Mistaken for the Passenger Pigeon. The rapid Slaughter of this Species has Alarmed the Ornithologists of California, who now fear its Extinction

repetition of the old, old story,—plenty of laws, but a hundred times too many hunters, killing the game both according to law and contrary to it, and doing it five times as fast as the game could breed. That combination can safely be warranted to wipe out the wild life of any country in the world, and accomplish it right swiftly.

As a big-game country, Colorado is distinctly out of the running. Her people are too lawless, and her frontiersmen are, in the main, far too selfish to look upon plenteous game without going after it. Some of these days, a new call of the wild will arise in Colorado, demanding an open season on mountain sheep. Those who demand it will say, "What harm will it do to kill a few surplus bucks? It will improve the breed. and make the herds increase faster!"

By all means, have an "open season" on the Colorado big-horn and the British Columbia elk. It will "do them good." The excitement of ram slaughter will be good for the females, will it not? Of course, they will breed faster after that,—with all the big rams dead. Any "surplus" wild life is a public nuisance, and should promptly be shot to pieces.

In Colorado there is some desire that Estes Park should be acquired as a national park, and maintained by the government; but the strong reasons for this have not yet appeared. As yet we have not heard any reason why the State of Colorado should not herself take it and make of it a state park and game preserve. If done, it could be offered as a partial atonement for her wastefulness in throwing away her inheritance of grand game.

Colorado has work to do in the preservation of her remnant of bird life. In several respects she is behind the times. The present is no time to hesitate, or to ask the gunners what *they* wish to have done about new laws for the saving of the remnant of game. The dictates of common sense are plain, and inexorable. Let the lawmakers do their whole duty by the remnant of wild life, whether the game killers like it or not.

The Curse of Domestic Sheep Upon Game and Cattle.—Much has been said in print and out of print regarding the extent to which domestic sheep have destroyed the cattle ranges and incidentally many game ranges of the West; but the half hath not been told. The American people as a whole do not realize that the domestic sheep has driven the domestic steer from the free grass of the wild West, with the same speed and thoroughness with which the buffalo-hunters of the 70's and 80's swept away the bison. I have seen hundreds of thousands of acres of what once were beautiful and fertile cattle-grazing lands in Montana, that has been left by grazing sheep herds looking precisely as if the ground had been shaven with razors and then sandpapered. The sheep have driven out the cattle, and the price of beef has gone up accordingly. Neither cattle, horses nor wild game can find food on ground that has been grazed over by sheep.

The following is the testimony of a reliable eye witness, Mr. Dillon Wallace, and the full text appears in his book, "*Saddle and Camp in the Rockies,*" (page 169):—

Domestic sheep and sheep herders are the greatest enemies of the antelope, as well as of other game animals and birds in the regions where herders take their flocks. The ranges over which domestic sheep pasture are denuded of forage and stripped of all growth, and antelope will not remain upon a range where sheep have been.

Thus the sheep, sweeping clean all before them and leaving the ranges over which they pass unproductive, for several succeeding seasons, of pasturage for either wild or domestic animals, together with the destructive shepherds, are the worst enemies at present of Utah's wild game, particularly of antelope, sage hens, and grouse.

In Iron county, which has already become an extensive sheep region, settlers tell us that before the advent of sheep, grass grew so luxuriantly that a yearling calf lying in it could not be seen. Not only has the grass here been eaten, but the roots tramped out and killed by the hoofs of thousands upon thousands of sheep, and now wide areas, where not long since grass was so plentiful, are as bare and desolate as sand-piles.

CHAPTER XXIX

NEW LAWS NEEDED IN THE STATES
(Continued)

CONNECTICUT:

> The sale of all native wild game, regardless of its source, should be prohibited at all times. Enact at once a five-year close season law on the remnant of ruffed grouse, quail, woodcock, snipe, and all shore birds.
>
> Even in the home of the newest and deadliest "autoloading" shotgun, those guns and pump guns should be prohibited in hunting.
>
> The enormous bag limits of 35 rail and 50 each per day of plover, snipe and shore birds is a crime! They should be replaced by a ten-year close season law for all of those species.
>
> The terms of the game commissioners should be not less than four years.

Like so many other states, Connecticut has recklessly wasted her wild-life inheritance. During the fifteen years preceding the year 1898, the bird life of that state had decreased 75 per cent. On March 6, 1912, Senator Geo. P. McLean, of Connecticut stated at the hearing held by his Committee on Forest Reservations and the Protection of Game this fact: "We have more cover than there was thirty or forty years ago, more brush probably, but there is not one partridge [ruffed grouse] to-day where there were twenty ten years ago!"

First of all, Connecticut needs a ten-year close season law to save her remnant of shore birds before it is completely annihilated. Then she needs a Bayne law, and needs it badly. Under such a law, and the tagging system that it provides, the state game wardens would have so strong a grip on the situation that the present unlawful sale of game would be completely stopped. Half-way measures in preventing the sale of game will not answer. Already Connecticut has wasted thousands of dollars in fruitless efforts to restock her desolated woodlands and farms with quail, and to introduce the Hungarian partridge; but even yet she *will not* protect her own native species!

Men of Connecticut, save the last remnants of your native game birds before they are all utterly exterminated within your borders! Don't ask the killers of game what *they* will agree to, but make the laws what *you know* they should be! If you want a gameless state, let the destruction go on as it now is going, with *16,000 licensed gunners* in the field each year, and you will surely have it, right soon.

DELAWARE:

> Stop all spring shooting, at once; stop killing shore birds for ten years, and protect swans indefinitely.

Enact bag-limit laws, in very small figures.
Stop the sale of all native wild game, regardless of its use, by enacting a Bayne law.
Enact a resident license law, and provide for a force of paid game wardens.
Stop the use of machine shot-guns in killing your birds.

The state of Delaware is nearly twenty years behind the times. Can it be possible that her Governor and her people are really satisfied with that position? We think not. I dare say they are afflicted with apathy, and game-hogs. The latter can easily back up General Apathy to an extent that spells "no game laws." In one act, and at one bold stroke, Delaware can step out of her position at the rear of the procession of states, and take a place in the front rank. Will she do it? We hope so, for her present status is unworthy of any right-minded, red-blooded state this side of the Philippines.

DISTRICT OF COLUMBIA.

The sale of all native wild game, regardless of its source, should be stopped immediately, by the enactment of a complete Bayne law.

If game-shooting within the District is continued, on the marshes of the Eastern Branch and on the Potomac River, common decency demands the enactment of bag-limit laws and long close-season laws of the most modern pattern.

Just why it is that gross abuses against wild life have so long been tolerated in the territorial center of the American nation, remains to be ascertained. But, whatever the reason the situation is absurd and intolerable, and Congress should terminate it immediately. As late as 1897, and I think for two or three years thereafter, thousands of *robins* were sold every year in the public markets of Washington as food! As a spectacle for gods and men, behold to-day the sale of quail, ruffed grouse, wild turkeys and other American game, half way between the Capitol and the White House! Look at Center Market as a national "fence" for the sale of game stolen by market gunners from Maryland, Virginia, the Carolinas and Pennsylvania.

It is time for Congress to bring the District of Columbia sharply into line; for Washington must be made to toe the mark beside New York. The reputation of the national capital demands it, whether the gods of the cafés will consent or not.

FLORIDA:

Shooting shore birds and waterfowl in late winter and spring should be stopped.
The sale of all native wild game should be prohibited.
A State Game Commissioner whose term of office should be not less than four years, and a force of salaried game wardens, should be appointed.
A general resident license should be required for hunting.
The killing of does and fawns should be stopped, and no deer should be killed save bucks with horns at least three inches long.
The bag limit of five deer per year should be two deer; of twenty quail, and two turkeys per day should be ten quail and one turkey.
The open season on all game birds should end on February 1, for domestic reasons.
Protection should be accorded doves, and robins should be removed from the game list.

In the destruction of wild life, I think the backwoods population of Florida is the most lawless and defiant that can be found anywhere in the United States. The "plume-hunters" have practically exterminated the plume-bearing egrets, wholly annihilated the roseate spoonbill, the flamingo, and also the Carolina parrakeet. On July 8, 1905, one of them killed an Audubon Association Warden, Guy M. Bradley, whose business it was to enforce the state laws protecting the egret rookeries. The people really to blame for the shooting of Guy Bradley, and the extermination of the egrets by lawless and dangerous men, are the vain and merciless women who wear the "white badges of cruelty" as long as they can be purchased! They have much to answer for!

Originally, Florida was alive with bird life. For number of species, abundance of individuals, and general dispersal throughout the whole state, I think no other state in America except possibly California ever possessed a bird fauna quite comparable with it. Once its bird life was one of the wonders of America. But the gunners began early to shoot, and shoot, and shoot. During the fifteen years preceding 1898, the general bird life of Florida decreased in volume 77 per cent. In 1900 it was at a very low point, and it has steadily continued to decrease. The rapidly-growing settlement and cultivation of the state has of course had much to do with the disappearance of wild life generally, and the draining and exploitation of the Everglades will about finish the birds of southern Florida.

The brown pelicans' breeding-place on Pelican Island, in Indian River, has been taken in hand by the national government as a bird refuge, and its marvelous spectacle of pelican life is now protected. Nine other islands on the coast of Florida have been taken as national bird refuges, and will render posterity good service.

The great private game and bird preserve of Dr. Ray V. Pierce, at Apalachicola, known as St. Vincent Island, containing twenty square miles of wonderful woods and waters, is performing an important function for the state and the nation.

The Forida bag limit on quail is entirely too liberal. I know one man who never once exceeded the limit of twenty birds per day, but in the season of 1908–9 he killed *865 quail!* Can the quail of any state long endure such drains as that?

From a zoological point of view, Florida is in bad shape. A great many of her people who shoot are desperately lawless and uncontrollable, and the state is not financially able to support a force of wardens sufficiently strong to enforce the laws, even as they are. It looks as if the slaughter would go on until nothing of bird life remains. At present I can see no hope whatever for saving even a good remnant of the wild life of the state.

The present status of wild-life protective laws in Florida was made the subject of an article in *Forest and Stream* of August 10, 1912, by John H. Wallace, Jr., Game Commissioner of the State of Alabama, in an article entitled "The Florida Situation." In view of his record, no one will question either the value or the honest sincerity of Mr. Wallace's opinions. The following paragraphs are from that article:

The enactment of a model and modern game law for the State of Florida is absolutely imperative in order to save many of the most valuable species of birds and game of that State from certain depletion and threatened extinction. The question of the protection of the birds and game in Florida is not a local one, but is national in its scope. Birds know no state lines, and while practically all the States lying to the north of Florida protect migratory birds and waterfowl, yet these are recklessly slaughtered in that state to such an extent as to be appalling to all sportsmen and bird lovers.

So alarming has become the decrease of the birds and game of Florida that unless a halt is called on the campaign of reckless annihilation that has been ceaselessly waged in that state, the sport and recreation enjoyed by primeval nimrods will linger only in history and tradition.

It is the sincerest hope of all lovers of wild life of the American continent that a strong and invincible sentiment, relative to the imperative necessity of real conservation legislation, be crystallized in the minds of the members elect of the Florida Legislature, to the end that the next Legislature will spread upon the statute books of the State of Florida a model and modern law for the preservation and protection of the birds and game of that State, which when put into practical operation will elicit the thanks of all good citizens, and likewise the gratitude of future generations.

GEORGIA:

Prohibit late winter and spring shooting, and provide rational seasons for wild fowl.
Reduce the limit on deer to two bucks a season, with horns not less than three inches long.
Protect the meadow lark and stop forever the killing of doves and wood-ducks.
Prohibit the use of automatic and pump shot-guns in hunting.
Extend the term of the game commissioner to four years.

We are glad to report that Georgia has already begun to take up the white man's burden. The protection of wild life is now a gentleman's proposition, and in it every real man with red blood in his veins has a duty to perform. The state of Georgia has recently awakened, and under the comprehensive law of 1911 has resolutely undertaken to do her whole duty in this matter.

IDAHO:

The imperative duties of Idaho are as follows:

Stop all hunting of mountain sheep, mountain goat and elk.
Give the sage grouse and sharp-tail ten-year close seasons, at once, to forestall their extermination.
Stop the killing of doves as "game."
Stop the killing of female deer, and of bucks with horns less than three inches long.
Enact the model law to protect non-game birds.
Prohibit the use of machine shot-guns in hunting.
Extend the State Warden's term to four years.

Like Montana, Wyoming and Colorado, the state of Idaho has wasted her stock of game, and it is to be feared that several species are now about to disappear from that state. I am told that the sage grouse is almost "gone"; and I think that the antelope, caribou, and mountain sheep are in the same condition of scarcity.

If the people of Idaho wish to save their wild fauna, they must be up and doing. The time to temporize, theorize, be conservative and easy-going has gone by. It is that fatal policy that causes men to slumber until it is too late to act; and we will watch with keen interest to see whether the real men of Idaho are big enough to do their whole duty in time to benefit their state.

In 1910, Dr. T. S. Palmer credited Idaho with the possession of about five hundred moose and two hundred antelope.

There is one feature of the Idaho game law that may well stand unchanged. The open season on "ibex," of which one per year may be killed, may as well be continued. One myth per year is not an extravagant bag for any intelligent hunter; and it seems that the "ibex" will not down. Being officially recognized by Idaho, its place in our fauna now seems assured.

ILLINOIS:

Enact a Bayne law, and stop the sale of all native wild game, regardless of source, and regardless of the gay revelers of Chicago.

In Illinois the bag limits on birds are nearly all at least 50 per cent too high. They should be as follows: *No* squirrels, doves or shore birds; six quail, five woodcock, ten coots, ten rail, ten ducks, three geese and three brant, with a total limit of ten waterfowl per day.

Doves should be removed from the game list.

All tree squirrels and chipmunks should be perpetually protected, as companions to man, unfit for food.

The sale of aigrettes should be stopped, and Chicago placed in the same class as Boston, New York, New Orleans and San Francisco.

The use of all machine shotguns in hunting should be prohibited.

The chief plague-spots for the grinding up of American game are Chicago, Philadelphia, Baltimore, New Orleans and San Francisco. St. Louis cleared her record in 1909. New York thoroughly cleaned her Augean stable in 1911, and Massachusetts won her Bayne law by a desperate battle in 1912. In 1913, Pennsylvania probably will enact a Bayne law.

Fancy a city in the center of the United States sending to Norway for 1,500 ptarmigan, to eat, as Chicago did in 1911; and that was only one order.

For forty years the marshes, prairies, farms and streams of the whole upper Mississippi Valley have been combed year after year by the guns of the market shooters. Often the migratory game was located by telegraphic reports. Game birds were slain by the wagon-load, boat-load, barrel, and car-load, "for the Chicago market." And the fool farmers of the Middle West stolidly plowed their fields and fed their hogs, and permitted the slaughter to go on. To-day the sons of those farmers go to the museums and zoological parks of the cities to see specimens of pinnated grouse, crane, woodcock, ducks and other species that the market shooters have "wiped out"; and their fathers wax eloquent in telling of the flocks of pigeons that "darkened the sky," and the big droves of prairie chickens that used to rise out of the corn-fields "with a roar like a coming storm."

To-day, Chicago stands half-way reformed. Her markets are open to only one-half the game killable in Illinois, but they are wide open to all "*legally*" killed game imported from other states, from Oct. 1 to Feb. 1." Through that hole in her game laws any game-dealer can drive a moving-van! Of course, any game offered in Chicago has been "legally killed in some other state!" Who can prove otherwise?

In addition to the imported game illegally killed in other states, the starving population of Chicago may also buy for cash, and consume with their champagne in November and December, all the Illinois doves that can be combed out by the market-gunners.

After the awful Iroquois Theatre fire in Chicago, in 1903, the game dealers reported a heavy falling off in the consumption of game! The tragedy caused the temporary closing of the theaters, and the falling off in after-theater suppers may be said to have taken away the appetites of thousands of erstwhile consumers of game. Incidentally it showed who consumes purchased game.

The people of Illinois should now enact a full-fledged Bayne law, without changing a single word, and bring Chicago up to the level of New York, St. Louis and Boston.

The present bag limits on Illinois game birds are fatally high. As they stand, with 190,000 licensed gunners in the field each year, what else do they mean than extermination? The men of Illinois have just two alternatives between which to choose: drastic and immediate preservation, or a gameless state. Which shall it be?

INDIANA:

Indiana should hasten to stop spring shooting.

She should enact a law, prohibiting the sale for millinery purposes of the plumage of all wild birds save ducks killed in their open season.

A Bayne law, absolutely prohibiting the sale of all native wild game, should be enacted at once.

The killing of squirrels should be prohibited; because they are not white men's game.

Ruffed grouse and quail should have five year close seasons.

The use of pump and autoloading guns in hunting should be prohibited.

In Indiana the white-tailed deer is extinct. This means very close hunting, and a bad outlook for all other game larger than the sparrow. On October 2, 1912, eleven heads of greater bird of paradise, with plumes attached, were offered for sale within one hundred feet of the headquarters of the Fourth National Conservation Congress. The prices ranged from $35 to $47.50; and while we looked, two ladies came up, one of whom pointed to a bird-of-paradise corpse and said: "There! I want one o' them, an' I'm a-goin' to *have* it, too!"

IOWA:

Spring shooting should be stopped, at once and forever.

The killing of all tree squirrels and chipmunks should cease.

All shore birds that visit Iowa deserve a five-year close season.

Especially is the shooting of plover, sandpiper, marsh and beach birds, rail, duck, geese and brant from September 1, to April 15, an outrage.

Iowa should prohibit the use of the machine guns, and it is to be hoped that she will awaken sufficiently to do so.

It is said that the Indian word "Iowa" means "the drowsy, or sleepy ones." Politically, and educationally, Iowa is all right, but in the protection of wild life she is ten years behind the times, in almost everything save the prohibition of the sale of game. *Iowa knows better than to pursue the course that she does!* She boasts about her corn and hogs, but she is deaf to the appeals of the states surrounding her on the subject of spring shooting. For years Minnesota has set her a good example; but nothing moves her to step up where she belongs in the phalanx of intelligent game-protecting states.

The foregoing may sound harsh, but in view of what other states have endured from Iowa's stubbornness regarding migratory game, the time for silent treatment of her case has gone by. She is to-day in the same class as North Carolina, South Carolina and Maryland,—at the tail end of the procession of states. She cares everything for corn and hogs, but little for wild life.

KANSAS:

Spring shooting should be stopped, at once; with apologies for not having done so long ago.

The continued shooting of prairie chickens when the species is near extermination is outrageous, and should be prohibited for ten years.

Doves should be removed permanently from the game list, partly as a measure of self respect.

Kansas should treat herself to a force of salaried game wardens rendering real service.

She should bar out the machine guns as unfit for use in a well-regulated State.

Kansas has calmly witnessed the extermination of her bison, elk, deer, antelope, wild turkeys, sage grouse, whooping cranes, and the beginning of the end of her pinnated grouse, without a pang. What is wild game in comparison with fat hogs and seventy-bushels-to-the-acre!

Draw a line around the hog-and-corn area of the United States, and within it you will find more spring shooting, more sale of game and more extermination of species than in any other area in the United States. I refer to Nebraska, Kansas, Iowa, Missouri, Illinois, Indiana, Ohio, Kentucky and Tennessee. In not one of these states except Missouri is there any big game hunting, and in the majority of them spring shooting is lawful!

In the Island of Mauritius, it was swine that exterminated the dodo. In the United States, hogs and game extermination still go hand in hand. Since the days of the dodo, however, a new species of swine has been developed. It is now widely known as the "game-hog," and it has been officially recognized by both bench and bar.

KENTUCKY

Nearly everything that a state should maintain in the line of wild life protection *Kentucky lacks!* It is easier to tell what she has than to recite what she should have. Kentucky *permits spring shooting;* she has *no bag limits,* and she has *long open seasons* on everything save introduced pheasants; She protects from sale only quail, grouse and wild turkey *killed within her own borders.* This means that her markets are practically wide open.

Until recently the people of Kentucky have been very indifferent to the value of her wild-life; but with the new law enacted this year providing for a game commission and a game protection fund, surely every member of the Army of the Defense will wish God-speed to her efforts in game conservation, and stand ready to lend a helping hand whenever help can be utilized.

Kentucky should at one grand coup *stop spring shooting and all sale of wild game, accord long close seasons to all species that are verging on extinction, protect doves, establish moderate bag limits and stop the use of machine guns.* If she takes up these measures at the rate of only one at each legislative session, by the time her laws are perfect *all her game will be gone!*

LOUISIANA:

On more counts than one, Louisiana is in the list of Great Delinquents; for behold the things that she needs to do:

Protect deer for five years.
Instantly take the robin, red-winged black-bird, dove, grosbeak, wood-duck and gull off the list of birds that may be killed as "game."
Stop all late winter and spring shooting.
Stop the sale of all native game, and the possession and transportation of game sold or intended for sale. In short,
Enact a Bayne law.
Re-establish a game warden system.

In legally permitting the slaughter of the robin, red-winged black bird, dove, grosbeak, wood-duck and gull the state of Louisiana is very culpable.

For good reasons, forty states of the American Union strictly prohibit the killing of song and insectivorous birds. The duty of every state to protect those birds is not a debatable proposition. I put this question to the people of Louisiana, Mississippi, North Carolina, Tennessee and other states where the robin is treated as a game bird: Is it fair of you to kill and eat robins when that species is carefully protected by forty other states of our country for grave economic reasons? What would you say of the people of the North if they slaughtered your mocking-bird *to eat!*

Remember this proportion:

The Robin : The North : : The Mockingbird : The South.

CHAPTER XXX

NEW LAWS NEEDED IN THE STATES

(Continued)

MAINE:

There are reasons for the belief that Maine is conserving her large game better than any other state or province in North America. One glance over her laws is sufficient to convince anyone that instead of studying the clamor of her shooting population, Maine has actually been studying the needs of her game, and providing for those needs. If all other states were doing equally well, the task of writing a book of admonition would have been unnecessary. The proof of Maine's alertness is to be found in the number of her extra short, or entirely closed, seasons on game. For example:

Cow and calf moose are permanently protected.

Only bull moose, with at least two 3-inch prongs on its horns, may be killed.

Caribou have had a close season since 1899.

On gray and black squirrels, doves and quail, there is no open season.

The open season for deer varies from ten weeks to four weeks, and in parts of three counties there is no open season at all.

Silencers are prohibited, and firearms in forests may be prohibited by the Governor during droughts.

Nearly all wild-fowl shooting ends January 1, but in two places, on December 1.

People who have not learned the facts habitually think of Maine as a vast killing-ground for deer; and it is well for it to be known that the hunting-grounds have been carefully designated, according to the abundance or scarcity of game.

Maine has wisely chosen to regard her hunting-grounds and her deer as a valuable asset, and she manages them accordingly. To be a guide in that state is to be a good citizen, and a protector of game from illegal slaughter. No non-resident may hunt without a licensed guide. The licenses for the thousands of deer killed in Maine each year, and the expenses of the visiting sportsmen who hunt them, annually bring into the state and leave there a huge sum of money, variously estimated at from $2,000,000 to $3,000,000. One can only guess at the amount from the number of non-resident licenses issued; but certainly the total can not be less than $1,000,000.

Although Mr. L. T. Carleton is no longer chairman of the Commission of Inland Fisheries and Game, the splendid services that he rendered the state of Maine during his thirteen years of service, especially in the creation of a good code of game laws, constitute an imperishable monument to his name and fame.

There is very little that Maine needs in the line of new legislation, or better protection to her game. With the enactment of a resident license law and a five-year close season for woodcock, plover, snipe and sandpipers, I think her laws for the protection of wild life would be sufficiently perfect for all practical purposes. The Pine-Tree State is to be congratulated upon its wise and efficient handling of the wild-life situation.

MARYLAND

How has it come to pass that Maryland *lacks* more good wild-life laws than any other state in the Union except North Carolina? Of the really fundamental protective laws, embracing the list that to every self-respecting state seems indispensable, Maryland has almost none save certain bag-limit laws! Otherwise, the state is wide open! It is indeed high time that she should abandon her present attitude of hostility to wild life, and become a good neighbor. She should do what is *fair* and *right* about the protection of the migratory game and bird life that annually passes twice through her territory!

At the last session of the Maryland legislature, the law preventing the use of power boats in wild-fowl shooting was repealed. That was a step ten years backward; and Maryland should be ashamed of it!

The list of things that Maryland must do in order to clear her record is a long one. Here it is:

Local regulations should be replaced by a uniform state law.

The sale of all native wild game should be stopped.

Spring and late winter shooting of game should be stopped.

All non-game birds not already included under the statutes should be protected.

The exportation of all game should be prohibited, unless accompanied by the man who shot it, bearing his license, and the law should be state-wide instead of depending upon a separate enactment for each county.

There should be a hunter's license law for all who hunt.

The use of machine shotguns in hunting should be stopped, at once.

Stop the use of power boats in wild-fowl shooting.

MASSACHUSETTS:

In 1912 the state of Massachusetts moved up into the foremost rank of states, where for one year New York had stood alone. She passed a counterpart of the New York law, absolutely prohibiting the sale of all wild American game in Massachusetts, but providing for the sale of game that has been reared in preserves and tagged by state officers. This victory was achieved only after three months of hard fighting. The coalition of sportsmen, zoologists and friends of wild life in general proved irresistible, just as a similar union of forces accomplished the Bayne law in New York in 1911. The victory is highly instructive, as great victories usually are. It proves once more that whenever the American people can be aroused from their normal apathy regarding wild life, *any good conservation legislation can be enacted!* The prime necessities to success are good measures, good management, a reasonable campaign fund, and tireless energy and persistence. Massachusetts is to be roundly congratulated on having so thoroughly cleaned up her sale-of-game situation.

Incidentally, five bills for the repeal of the Massachusetts law against spring shooting were introduced, and each one went down to the defeat that it deserved. *The repeal of a spring-shooting law, anywhere, is a step backward ten years!*

Massachusetts needs a bag-limit law more in keeping with her small remnant of wild life; and that she will have ere long. Very soon, also, her sportsmen will raise the standard of ethics in shotgun shooting, by barring out the automatic and pump shotguns so much beloved by the market shooters. As matters stand at this date (1912) the Old Bay State needs the following new laws·

> Low bag limits on all game.
> Five-year close seasons on all shore birds, snipe and woodcock.
> Expulsion of the automatic and pump shotguns, in hunting.

MICHIGAN:

On the whole, the game laws of Michigan are in excellent shape, and leave little to be desired in the line of betterment except to be simplified. All the game protected by the laws of the state is debarred from sale; squirrels, pinnated grouse, doves and wild turkeys enjoy long close seasons; the bag limits on deer and game birds are reasonably low; spring shooting still is possible on nine species of ducks; and this should be stopped without delay.

Only three or four suggestions are in order:

> All spring shooting should be prohibited.
> All shore birds should have a five-year close season.
> The use of the machine shotguns in hunting should be stopped.
> The laws should permit the sale, under tag, of all species of game that can successfully be reared in preserves on a commercial basis.
> Two or three state game preserves, for deer, each at least four miles square, should be established without delay.

MINNESOTA:

> This state should at once enact a bag-limit law that will do some good, instead of the statutory farce now on the books. Make it fifteen birds per day of waterfowl, all species combined, and no grouse or quail.
> There should be five-year close seasons enacted for quail, grouse, plover, woodcock, snipe, and all other shore birds.
> A law should be enacted prohibiting the use of firearms by unnaturalized aliens, and a $20 license for all naturalized aliens.
> Provision should be made for a large state game refuge in southern Minnesota.
> The state should prohibit the use of machine guns in hunting.

To-day, direct and reliable advices show that the game situation in Minnesota is far from encouraging. Several species are threatened with extinction at an early date.　In northern Minnesota it is reported that much game is surreptitiously trapped and slaughtered.　The bob white is reported as threatened with total extinction at an early date; but I think the prairie chicken will be the first bird species to go.　Moose will soon be extinct everywhere in Minnesota except in the game preserves.　Apparently there is now about one duck in Minnesota for every ten ducks that were there only ten years ago.

Now, what is Minnesota going to do about all this?　Is she willing through Apathy to become a gameless state?　Her people need to arouse themselves *now*, and pass several *strong* laws.　Her bag limit of forty-five birds *per day* of quail, grouse, woodcock and plover, and *fifty* per day of the waterbirds, is a joke, and nothing more; but it is no laughing matter. It spells extermination.

MISSISSIPPI:

> The legalized slaughter of robins, cedar birds, grosbeaks and doves should cease immediately, on the basis of economy of resources and a square deal to all the states lying northward of Mississippi.
>
> The shooting of all water-fowl should cease on January 1.
>
> A reasonable limit should be established on deer.
>
> A hunting license law should be passed at once, fixing the fee at $1 and devoting the revenue to the pay of a corps of non-political game wardens, selected on a basis of ability and fitness.
>
> The administration of the game laws should be placed in charge of a salaried game commissioner.

It is seriously to the discredit of Mississippi that her laws actually classify robins, cedar-birds, grosbeaks and doves as "game," and *make them killable as such from Sept. 1 to March 1!*　I should think that if no economic consideration carried weight in Mississippi, state pride alone would be sufficient to promote a correction of the evil.　If we of the North were to slaughter mockingbirds for food, when they come North to visit us, the men of the South would call us greedy barbarians; and they would be quite right.

MISSOURI:

> The Missouri bag limits that permit the killing or possession of fifty birds per day are absurd, and fatally liberal.　The utmost should be twenty-five; and even that is too high.
>
> Doves should be taken off the list of game birds, and protected throughout the year; and so should all tree squirrels.
>
> Spring shooting of shore birds and waterfowl should be prohibited without delay.
>
> A law against automatic and pump guns should be enacted at the next legislative session, as a public lesson on the raising of the standard of ethics in shooting.

The state of Missouri is really strong in her position as a game-protecting state.　She perpetually protects such vanishing species as the ruffed grouse, prairie chicken (pinnated grouse), woodcock, and all her shore birds save snipe and plover.　She prohibits the sale of native game and the killing of female deer; but she wisely permits the sale of preserve-bred elk and deer under the tags of the State Game Commission. For nearly all the wild game that is accessible, her markets are tightly closed.

We heartily congratulate Missouri on her advanced position on the sale of game, and we hope that the people of Iowa will even yet profit by her good example.

MONTANA:

Like Colorado and Wyoming, Montana is wasting a valuable heritage of wild game while she struggles to maintain the theory that she still is in the list of states that furnish big-game hunting. It is a fact that ten years ago most sportsmen began to regard Montana as a has-been for big game, and began to seek better hunting-grounds elsewhere. British Columbia, Alberta and Alaska have done much for the game of Montana by drawing sportsmen away from it. Mr. Henry Avare, the State Game Warden, is optimistic regarding even the big game, and believes that it is holding its own. This is partially true of white-tailed deer, or it was up to the time of great slaughter. It is said that in 1911, 11,000 deer were killed in Montana, all in the western part of the state, seventy per cent of which were white-tails. The deep snows and extreme cold of a long and unusually severe winter drove the hungry deer down out of the mountains into the settlements, where the ranchmen joyously slaughtered them. The destruction around Kalispell was described by Harry P. Stanford as "sickening."

Mr. Avare estimates the prong-horned antelope in Montana at three thousand head, of which about six hundred are under the quasi-protection of four ranches.

The antelope need three or four small ranges, such as the Snow Creek Antelope Range, where the bad lands are too rough for ranchmen, but quite right for antelopes and other big game.

All the grouse and ptarmigan of Montana need a five-year close season. The splendid sage grouse is now extinct in many parts of its previous range. Fifty-eight thousand licensed gunners are too many for them!

The few mountain sheep and mountain goats that survive should have a five-year close season, at once.

The killing of female hoofed animals should be prohibited by law.

Montana has not yet adopted the model law for the protection of non-game birds. Only seven states have failed in that respect.

The use of automatic and pump shotguns, and silencers, should immediately be prohibited.

Montana's bag-limits are not wholly bad; but the grizzly bear has almost been exterminated, save in the Yellowstone Park. Some of these days, if things go on as they are now going, the people of Montana will be rudely awakened to the fact that they have 50,000 licensed hunters but no longer any killable game! And then we will hear enthusiastic talk about "restocking."

NEBRASKA:

No other state has bestowed close seasons upon as many extinct species of game as Nebraska. Behold how she has resolutely locked the doors of her empty cage after all these species have flown: Elk, antelope, wild turkey, passenger pigeon, whooping crane, sage grouse, ptarmigan and curlew. In a short time the pinnated grouse can be added to the list of has-beens.

There is little to say regarding the future of the game of Nebraska; for its "future" is now history.

Provision should be made for one or more state game preserves.

Spring shooting of shore birds and waterfowl should be prohibited.

A larger and more effective warden service should be provided.

Doves should be removed from the game list.

NEVADA:

The sage grouse should be given a ten-year close season, for recuperation.

All non-game birds should have perpetual protection.

The cranes, now verging on extinction, and the pigeons and doves should at once be taken out of the list of game birds, and forever protected.

All the shore birds need five years of close protection.

A State Game Warden whose term of office is not less than four years should be provided for.

A corps of salaried game protectors should be chosen for active and aggressive game protection.

Nevada's bag limits are among the best of any state, the only serious flaw being "10 sage grouse" per day: which should be 0!

Nevada still has a few antelope; and *we beg her to protect them all from being hunted or killed!* It is my belief that if the antelope is really saved anywhere in the United States outside of national parks and preserves, it will be in the wild and remote regions of Nevada, where it is to be hoped that lumpy-jaw has not yet taken hold of the herds.

NEW HAMPSHIRE:

Speaking generally, the New Hampshire laws regulating the killing and shipment of game are defective for the reason that on birds, and in fact all game save deer, there appear to be no "bag" limits on the quantity that may be killed in a day or a season. The following bag limits are greatly needed, forthwith:

Gray Squirrel, none per day, or per year; duck (except wood-duck), ten per day, or thirty per season; ruffed grouse, four per day, twelve per season; hare and rabbit, four per day, or twelve per season.

Five-year close seasons should immediately be enacted for the following species: quail, woodcock, jacksnipe and all species of shore or "beach" birds.

The sale of all native wild game should be prohibited; and game-breeding in preserves, and the sale of such game under state supervision, should be provided for.

The use of automatic and pump guns in hunting should be barred,—through state pride, if for no other reason.

NEW JERSEY:

New Jersey enjoys the distinction of being the second state to break the strangle-hold of the gun-makers of Hartford and Ilion, and cast out the odious automatic and pump guns. It was a pitched battle,—that of 1912, inaugurated by Ernest Napier, President of the State Game and Fish Commission and his fellow commissioners. The longer the contest continued, the more did the press and the people of New Jersey awaken to the seriousness of the situation. Finally, the gun-suppression bill passed the two houses of the legislature with a total of only fourteen votes against it, and after a full hearing had been granted the attorneys of the gunmakers, was promptly signed by Governor Woodrow Wilson. *Governor Wilson could not be convinced that the act was "unconstitutional," or "confiscatory" or "class legislation."*

This contest aroused the whole state to the imperative necessity of providing more thorough protection for the remnant of New Jersey game, and it was chiefly responsible for the enactment of four other excellent new protective laws.

New Jersey always has been sincere in her desire to protect her wild life, and always has gone *as far as the killers of game would permit her to go!* But the People have made one great mistake,—common to nearly every state,—of permitting the game-killers to dictate the game laws! *Always and everywhere, this is a grievous mistake*, and fatal to the game. For example: In 1866 New Jersey enacted a five-year close-season law on the "prairie fowl" (pinnated grouse); but it was too late to save it. Now that species is as dead to New Jersey as is the mastodon. The moral is: Will the People apply this lesson to the ruffed grouse, quail and the shore birds generally before they, too, are too far gone to be brought back? If it is done, it must be done *against the will of the gunners;* for they prefer to shoot,—and shoot they will if they can dictate the laws, until the last game bird is dead.

In 1912, New Jersey is spending $30,000 in trying to restock her birdless covers with foreign game birds and quail. In brief, here are the imperative duties of New Jersey:

Provide eight-year close seasons for quail, ruffed grouse, woodcock, snipe, all shore birds and the wood-duck.

Prohibit the sale of all native wild game; but promote the sale of preserve-bred game.

Prevent the repeal of the automatic gun law, which surely will be attempted, each year.

Prohibit all bird-shooting after January 10, each year, until fall.

Prohibit the killing of squirrels as "game."

NEW MEXICO:

All things considered, the game laws of New Mexico are surprisingly up to date, and the state is to be congratulated on its advanced position. For example, there are long close seasons on antelope, elk (now extinct!), mountain sheep, bob white quail, pinnated grouse, wild pigeon and ptarmigan,—an admirable list, truly. It is clear that New Mexico is wide awake to the dangers of the wild-life situation. On two counts, her laws are not quite perfect. There is no law prohibiting spring shooting, and there is no "model law" protecting the non-game birds. The sale of game will not trouble New Mexico, because the present laws prevent the sale of all protected game except plover, curlew and snipe,—all of them species by no means common in the arid regions of the Southwest.

> A law prohibiting spring shooting of shore birds and waterfowl should be passed at the next session of the legislature.
>
> The enactment of the "model law" should be accomplished without delay to put New Mexico abreast of the neighboring states of Colorado, Oklahoma and Texas.
>
> The term of the State Warden should be extended to four years.

NEW YORK:

In the year of grace, 1912, I think we may justly regard New York as the banner state of all America in the protection of game and wild life in general. This proud position has been achieved partly through the influence of a great conservation Governor, John A. Dix, and the State Conservation Commission proposed and created by his efforts. In these days of game destruction, when our country from Nome to Key West is reeking with the blood of slaughtered wild creatures, it is a privilege and a pleasure to be a citizen of a state which has thoroughly cleaned house, and done well nigh the utmost that any state can do to clear her bad record, and give all her wild creatures a fair chance to survive. The people of the Empire State literally can point with pride to the list of things accomplished in the discharge of good-citizenship toward the remnant of wild life, and toward the future generations of New Yorkers. That we of to-day have borne our share of the burden of bringing about the conditions of 1912, will be a source of satisfaction, especially when the sword and shield hang useless upon the walls of Old Age.

New York began to protect her deer in 1705 and her heath hens in 1708. In 1912 she stopped the killing of female deer, and of bucks having horns less than three inches in length. Spring shooting was stopped in 1903. A comprehensive law protecting non-game birds was enacted in 1862. New York's first law against the sale of certain game during close seasons was enacted in 1837.

In 1911 New York enacted, with only one adverse vote, a law prohibiting the sale of all native wild game throughout the state, no matter where killed, and providing liberally for the encouragement of game-breeding, and the sale of preserve-bred game.

In 1912 a new codification of the state game laws went into effect, through the initiative of Governor Dix and Conservation Commissioners Van Kennen, Moore and Fleming, assisted (as special counsel) by Marshall McLean, George A. Lawyer and John B. Burnham. This code contains many important new provisions, one of the most valuable of which is a clause giving the Conservation Commission power, at its discretion, to shorten or to close any open season on any species of game in any locality wherein that species seems to be threatened with extermination. This very valuable principle should be enacted into law in every state!

In 1910 William Dutcher and T. Gilbert Pearson and the National Association of Audubon Societies won, after a struggle lasting five years, the passage of the "Shea plumage bill," prohibiting the sale of aigrettes or other plumage of wild birds belonging to the same families as the birds of New York (Chap. 256). This law *should be duplicated in every state.*

Two things remain to be done in the state of New York.

All the shore birds, quail and gray squirrels of the state should be given five-year close seasons, by the action of the State Conservation Commission.

For the good name of the state, and the ethical standing of its sportsmen, as an example to other states, and the last remaining duty toward our wild life, the odious automatic and pump shotguns should be barred from use in hunting, unless their capacity is reduced to two shots without reloading.

CHAPTER XXXI

NEW LAWS NEEDED IN THE STATES
(Concluded)

NORTH CAROLINA:

The game laws of North Carolina form a droll crazy-quilt of local and state measures, effective and ineffective. In 1909, a total of 77 local game laws were enacted, and only two of state-wide application. During the ten years ending in 1910, a total of 316 game laws were enacted! She sedulously endeavors to protect her quail, which do not migrate, but in Currituck County she persistently maintains the bloodiest slaughter-pen for waterfowl that exists anywhere on the Atlantic Coast. There is no bag limit on waterfowl, and unlimited spring shooting. So far as waterfowl are concerned, conditions could hardly be worse, except by the use of punt guns. Doves, *larks* and *robins* are shot and eaten as "game" from November 1 to March 1! Twenty-one counties have local restrictions on the sale of game, but the state at large has only one,—on quail.

The market gunners of Currituck Sound are a scourge and a pest to the wild-fowl life of the Atlantic Coast. For their own money profit, they slaughter by wholesale the birds that annually fly through twenty-two states. It is quite useless to suggest anything to North Carolina in modern game laws. As long as a killable bird remains, she will not stop the slaughter. Her standing reply is "It brings a lot of money into Currituck County; and the people want the money." Even the members of the sportsmen's clubs can shoot wild fowl in Currituck County, quite without limit; and I am told that the privilege often is abused. Quite recently I heard of a member of one of the clubs who shot 164 ducks and geese in two days!

Apparently any suggestions made to North Carolina would not be treated seriously, especially if they would tend really to elevate the sport of game shooting, or better protect the game. There is, however, a melancholy interest attached to the framing of good game laws, whether they ever are likely to be adopted or not. Here is the duty of North Carolina:

Stop the killing of robins, doves and larks for food, absolutely and forever. This measure is necessary to agriculture and to the good name of the state.

Stop the shooting of any game for sale, prohibit the possession of game for sale, and the sale of wild native game.

Establish bag limits on all waterfowl, and on all other game birds and mammals.

Prepare to protect, at an early date, the wild turkey and quail; for soon they will need it. Moreover, enact a law prohibiting the use of automatic and pump guns in hunting, covering the entire state.

Provide a resident-license system and thereby make the game department self-sustaining, and render it possible to employ a salaried State Game Commissioner.

It is quite wrong for the people of North Carolina to hold grudges against northern members of the ducking clubs of Currituck for the passage of the Bayne law. They had nothing whatever to do with it, and I can say this because I was in a position which enabled me to know.

NORTH DAKOTA:

In 1911, this sovereign state enacted a law *prohibiting the use of automobiles* in hunting wild-fowl; also rifles. North Dakota was the first state to recognize officially the fact that the use of automobiles in hunting is a serious menace to some forms of wild life. Beyond all question, the machines do indeed bring an extra number of birds within reach of the gun! They increase the annual slaughter; and it is right and necessary to prohibit by law their use in hunting game of any kind.

In Putman County, New York, I have seen them in action. A load of three or four gunners is whirled up to a likely mountain-side for ruffed grouse, and presently the banging begins. After an hour or so spent in combing out the birds, the hunters jump in, whirl away in a dust-cloud to another spot two miles away, and "bang-bang-bang" again. After that, a third locality; and so on, covering six or eight times the territory that a man in a buggy, or on foot, could possibly shoot over in the same time!

North Dakota has done well, in the passage of that act. On certain other matters, she is not so sound.

For instance:

The killing of pinnated grouse should be stopped for ten years; and it should be done immediately.

The killing of cranes as "game" should stop, instantly and forever. It is barbarous.

Fifty dead birds in possession at one time is fully thirty too many. The game cannot stand such slaughter!

All shore birds (*Order Limicolae*) should have at least a five-year close season, before they are exterminated.

The use of machine guns in hunting should be stopped, forever.

It is to the credit of the state that antelope are absolutely protected until 1920, and an unlimited close season has been accorded the quail, dove and swan.

OHIO:

I think that Ohio comes the nearest of all the states to being gameless. With but slight exceptions her laws are about as correct as those of most other states, but the desire to "kill" is so strong, and the majority of her gunners are so thoroughly selfish about their "rights" that the game has ruthlessly been swept away *according to law!* Ohio is a striking example of the deplorable results of *legalized* slaughter. The spirit of Ohio is like that of North Carolina. Her "sportsmen" will not have an automatic gun law! Oh, no! "Limit the bag, shorten the season, and the gun won't matter!"

To-day, the visible game supply of Ohio does not amount to anything; and when the last game bird of that state falls before the greediest shooter, we shall say, "A gameless state is just what you deserve!"

It is useless to make any suggestions to Ohio. Her shooting Shylocks want the last pound of flesh from wild life, and I think they will get it very soon. Ohio is in the area of barren states. The seed stock has been too thoroughly destroyed to be recuperated. I think that Ohio's last noteworthy exploit in lawmaking for the preservation (!) of her game was in 1904, when she put all her shore birds into the list of killable game, and bravely prohibited the shooting of doves *on the ground!* Great is Ohio in game conservation!

Oklahoma:

For a state so young, the wild-life laws of Oklahoma are in admirable shape; but it is reasonably certain that there, as elsewhere, the game is being killed much faster than it is breeding. The new commonwealth must arouse, and screw up the brakes much tighter.

Recently, an observing friend told me that on a trip of 250 miles westward from Lawton and back again, watching sharply for game all the way, he saw only five pinnated grouse! And this in a good season for "prairie chickens."

Oklahoma must stop all spring shooting.

The prairie chicken must have a ten-year close season, immediately.

Next time, her legislature will pass the automatic gun bill that failed last year only because the session closed too soon for its consideration.

Oklahoma is wise in giving long protection to her quail, and "wild pigeon," and such protection should be made equally effective in the case of the dove. She is wise in rigidly enforcing her law against the exportation of game.

The Wichita National Bison herd, near Cache, now contains forty head of bison, all in good condition. The nucleus herd consisted of fifteen head presented by the New York Zoological Society in 1907

Oregon:

The results of the efforts that have been made by Oregon to provide special laws for each individual shooter are painful to contemplate. Like North Carolina, Oregon has attempted the impossible task of pleasing everybody, and at the same time protecting her wild life. The two propositions can be blended together about as easily as asphalt and water.

The individual shooter desires laws that will permit him to shoot—*when* he pleases, *where* he pleases, and *what* he pleases! If you meet those conditions all over a great state, then it is time to bid farewell to the game; for it surely is doomed.

No, decidedly no! Do not attempt to pass game laws that will "please everybody." The more the game-hogs are *displeased*, the better for the game! The game-hogs form a very small and very insignificant minority of the whole People. Why please one man at the expense of ninty-nine others? The game of a state belongs to The People as a whole, not to the gunners alone. The great, patient,—and sometimes sleepy,— majority has vested rights in it, and it is for it to say how it shall and shall not be killed. Heretofore the gunning minority has been dictating the game laws of America, and the result is—progressive extermination.

First of all, Oregon should bury the pernicious idea of individual and local laws.

She should enact a concise, clearly cut, and thoroughly effective code of wild life laws, just as New York did last winter.

Her game seasons should be uniform in application, all over the state.

Every species of bird, mammal or fish that is threatened with extermination should be given a close season of from five to ten years.

It is now time to protect the white goose and brant. Squirrels, band-tailed pigeons and doves should be perpetually protected.

The State Game Commission should have power to close the shooting seasons on any species of game in any locality, whenever a species is threatened with extinction.

The sale of native wild game, from all sources, should be permanently stopped, by a Bayne law.

The use of automatic, "autoloading" and pump shot guns in hunting should be perpetually barred.

PENNSYLVANIA:

As a game protecting state, Pennsylvania is a close second to New York and Massachusetts. She protects all native game from sale; *she has the courage to prohibit aliens from owning guns; she bars out automatic shot-guns in hunting;* she makes refuges for deer, and feeds her quail in winter, and she permits the killing of no female deer, or fawns with horns less than three inches in length. Her splendid State Game Commission is fighting hard for a hunter's license law, and will win the fight for it at the next session of the legislature (1913).

But there are certain things that Pennsylvania should do·

She should stop all spring shooting. She must stop killing doves, blackbirds, wild turkeys, sandpipers, and all the squirrels save the red squirrel.

She should give all her shore birds a rest of at least five years, for recuperation.

She should enact a comprehensive Dutcher plumage law, stopping the sale of aigrettes.

She should provide a resident license to furnish her Game Commission with ade quate funds to carry on its work and exterminate game-killing vermin.

RHODE ISLAND:

Little Rhody needs some good, small bag limits; for now (1912) she has none!

She should enact a Bayne law, a Pennsylvania law against aliens, and a New Jersey law against the automatic and pump guns.

She should stop killing the beautiful wood-duck, and gray squirrel.

She should stop all spring shooting of waterfowl.

SOUTH CAROLINA

She should save her game while she still has some to save.

First of all, stop spring shooting; secondly, enact a Bayne law.

In the name of mystery, who is there in South Carolina who desires to kill grackles? And why?

And where is the gentleman sportsman who has come down to killing foolish and tame little doves for "sport?" Stop it at once, for the credit of the state.

Enact a dollar resident license law and thus provide adequate funds for game protection.

South Carolina bag limits are all 50 per cent too high; and they should be reduced.

It is strange to see one of the oldest of the states lagging in game protection, far behind such new states as New Mexico and Oklahoma; but South Carolina does lag. It is time for her to consider her position, and reform.

SOUTH DAKOTA:

South Dakota should stop all spring shooting.

Her game-bag limits are really no limits at all! They should be reduced about 66 per cent without a moment's unnecessary delay.

The two year term of the State Warden is too short for effective work. It should be extended to four years.

Unless South Dakota wishes to repeat the folly of such states as Indiana, Iowa, Illinois, Missouri and Ohio, she needs to be up and doing. If her people want a gameless state, except for migratory waterfowl, all they need do is to slumber on, and they surely will have it. Why wait until greedy sportsmen have killed the last game bird of the state before seriously taking the matter in hand? In one act, all the shortcomings of the present laws can be corrected.

South Dakota needs no Bayne law, because she prohibits at all times the sale or exportation of all wild game.

TENNESSEE:

In wild life protection, Tennessee has much to do. She made her start late in life, and what she needs to do is to draft with care and enact with cheerful alacrity certain necessary amendments.

We notice that there are open seasons for *blackbirds, robins, doves and squirrels!* It seems incredible; but it is true.

Behold the blackbird as a "game" bird, with a lawful open season from September 1 to January 1. Consider its stately carriage, its rapid flight on the wing, its running and hiding powers when attacked. As a test of marksmanship, as the real thing for the expert wing shot, is it not great? Will not any self-respecting dog be proud to point or retrieve them? And what flesh for the table!

Fancy an able-bodied sportsman going out in a fifty-dollar hunting suit, carrying a fifteen-dollar gun behind a seven-dollar dog, and returning with a glorious bag of twenty-five blackbirds! Or robins! Or doves! Proud indeed, would we be to belong (which we don't) to a club of "sportsmen" who go out shooting blackbirds, and robins, and foolish little doves, as "game!" "Game" indeed, are those birds,—for little lads of seven who do not know better; but not for boys of twelve who have in their veins any inheritance of sporting blood. (I am proud of the fact that at twelve years of age,—and ever so keen to "go hunting,"—I knew without being told that squirrels and doves were not *real* "game" for real boys.)

The killers of doves, squirrels, blackbirds and robins belong in the same class as the sparrow-and-linnet-killing Italians of Venice, Milan and Turin, and in that company we will leave them.

Tennessee needs:

A resident license system to provide funds for game protection.
A salaried warden force.
A law prohibiting spring shooting of shore birds and waterfowl.
A law protecting robins, doves and other non-game birds not covered by the present statute.

TEXAS:

I remember well when the great battle was fought in Texas by the gallant men and women of the State Audubon Society, to compel the people of Texas to learn the economic value to agriculture and cotton of the insectivorous birds. The name of the splendid Brigadier-General who led the Army of the Defense was Capt. M. B. Davis. That was in 1903.

Since that great fight was won, Texas has been a partly reformed state, at times quite jealous of her bird life; but still she tolerates spring shooting and has not made adequate close seasons for her waterfowl; which is wrong. To-day, the people of Texas do not need to be told that forty-three species of birds feed on the cotton boll weevil; for they know it.

On the whole, and for a southern state, the wild-life laws of Texas are in fairly good shape. On account of the absence of game-scourge markets, a Bayne law is not so imperatively necessary there as in certain other states. All the game of the state is protected from sale.

We do assert, however, that if robins are slaughtered as F. L. Crow, the former Atlantan asserts, all robin shooting should be forever stopped; that the pinnated grouse should be given a seven-year close season, and that doves should be taken off the list of game birds and perpetually protected, both for economic and sentimental reasons, and also because the too weak and confiding dove is not a "game" bird for red-blooded men.

Texas should enact without delay a law providing close seasons for ducks, geese and other waterfowl;
A law prohibiting spring shooting, and
A provision reducing the limit on deer to two bucks a season.

UTAH:

The laws of Utah are far from being up to the requirements of the present hour. One strange thing has happened in Utah.

When I spent a week in Salt Lake City in 1888, and devoted some time to inquiring into game conditions, the laws of the state were very bad. At the mouth of Bear River, ducks were being slaughtered for the markets by the tens of thousands. The cold-blooded, wide open and utterly shameless way in which it was being done, right at the doors of Salt Lake City, was appalling.

At the same time, the law permitted the slaughter of *spotted fawns.* I saw a huge drygoods box filled to the top with the flat skins of slaughtered innocents, *260 in number,* that a rascal had collected and was offering at fifty cents each. In reply to a question as to their use, he said: "I tink de sportsmen like 'em for to make vests oud of." He lived at Rawlins, Wyo.

After a long and somnolent period, during which hundreds of thousands of ducks, geese, brant and other birds had been slaughtered for market at the Bear River shambles and elsewhere, the state awoke sufficiently to abate a portion of the disgrace by passing a bag-limit law (1897).

And then came Nature's punishment upon Utah for that duck slaughter. The ducks of Great Salt Lake became afflicted with a terrible epidemic disease (intestinal coccidiosis) which swept off thousands, and stopped the use of Utah ducks as food! It was a "duck plague," no less. It has prevailed for three years, and has not yet by any means been stamped out. It seems to be due to the fact that countless thousands of ducks have been feeding on the exposed alluvial flats at the mouth of the creek that drains off the *sewage of Salt Lake City.* The conditions are said to be terrible.

To-day, Utah is so nearly destitute of big game that the subject is hardly worthy of mention. Of her upland game birds, only a fraction remains, and as her laws stand to-day, she is destined to become in the near future a gameless state. In a dry region like this, the wild life always hangs on by a slender thread, and it is easy to exterminate it!

Utah should instantly stop the sale of game that she now legally provides for, twenty-five shore birds and waterfowl per day to private parties!

Deer should be given a ten-year close season, at once. All bag limits should instantly be reduced one-half. The sage grouse, quail, swans, woodcock, dove, and all shore birds should be given a ten-year close season,—and rigidly protected,—before the stock is all gone.

The model law for the protection of non-game birds should be enacted at once.

The absolute protection of elk, antelope and sheep (until 1913) should be extended for twenty years.

Utah should create a big-game preserve, at once.

If Utah proposes to save even a remnant of her wild life for posterity, she must be up and doing.

VERMONT

In view of all conditions, it must be stated that the game laws of Vermont are, with but slight exceptions, in good condition. It is a pleasure to see that there is no spring shooting; that there is no "open" season of slaughter for the moose, caribou, wood-duck, swan, upland plover, dove or rail; that no buck deer with antlers less than three inches long may be killed; and that there is a law under which damages by deer to growing crops may be assessed and paid for by the county in which they occur. Moreover, if there is to be any killing of game, her bag limits are not extravagant. All the game protected by the state is immune from sale for food purposes, but preserve-reared game may legally be sold. We recommend the following new measures:

> Absolute close seasons of five-years' duration for ruffed grouse, quail, woodcock, snipe and all shore birds without a single exception.
> The gray squirrel should be perpetually protected,—because he is too beautiful, too companionable and too unfit for food to be killed. Even the hungry savages of the East Indies do not eat squirrels.
> Pass an automatic pump-gun law.
> Extend the term of the Fish and Game Commissioner to four years.

Vermont's great success in introducing and colonizing deer is both interesting and valuable. Fifty years ago, she had no wild deer, because the species had been practically exterminated. In 1875, thirteen deer were imported from the Adirondacks and set free in the mountains. The increase has been enormous. In 1909 the number of deer killed for the year was about 5,311, which was possible without adversely affecting the herds. It is a striking object-lesson in restoring the white-tailed deer to its own, and it will be found more fully described in chapter XXIV.

VIRGINIA:

Virginia is far below the position that she should occupy in wild-life conservation. To set her house in order, and come up to the level of the states that have been born during the past twenty years, she must bestir herself in these ways:

> She must provide for a resident hunting license, a State Game Commissioner and a force of salaried wardens.
> She must prohibit spring shooting.
> She must impose small bag limits on game-slaughter.
> She must resolutely stop the sale of all wild game.
> She must stop the killing of female deer, and of bucks with horns under three inches long.
> She must stop killing gray squirrels and doves as "game."
> She should not permit the beautiful wood-duck to be killed as "game."
> She should accord a five-year close season to grouse, and all shore birds.
> She should rule out the machine shot-guns which gentlemen can no longer use in hunting.

She should adopt at once a comprehensive code of game laws, and clean her house in one siege, instead of fiddling and fussing with all these matters one by one, through a series of ten long, weary years. The time for puttering with game protection has gone by. It is now time to make short cuts to comprehensive results, and save the game before it is too late

WASHINGTON:

The state of Washington still flatters herself that she has all kinds of big game to kill,—moose, antelope, goat, sheep, caribou and deer. Evidently this is on the theory that so long as a species is not extinct, it is "legal" and right to pursue it with rifles during a specified "open season."

The people of Washington need to be told that conditions have greatly changed, and it is now high time to put on the brakes. It is time for them to realize that if they wait any longer for the sportsmen to take the initiative in securing the enactment of really adequate preservation laws, all their big game will be dead before those laws are born! Every man shrinks from cutting off his own pet privilege.

Some of the game laws of Washington are up to date; and her big-game laws look all right to the unaided eye, but are not. Her bird laws are a chaotic jumble of local exceptions and special privileges. As a net result of all her shortcomings, the remnant of a once fine fauna of big game and feathered game is surely being *exterminated according to law.* A few local exceptions will not disprove the general truthfulness of this assertion.

Ten years ago a few men in Seattle resented the idea of outside cooperation in the protection of Washington game. They said they were abundantly able to take care of it; but the march of events has proven that they overestimated their capacity. To-day the wild-life laws of that state are only half baked. Come what may to me, I shall set down without malice the things that the great and admirable State of Washington should do to set her house in order. It is not good for the resourceful and progressive men of the Great Northwest to be clear behind the times in these matters.

Stop local game legislation, and enact a code of laws covering the entire state, uniformly. County legislation is twenty years behind the times!

For ten (10) full years, stop the killing of elk, mountain sheep, mountain goat, caribou, moose, and antelope. Regarding deer, I am in doubt.

Prohibit the sale of all wild game, no matter where killed, by the enactment of a Bayne law, complete, which will also

Promote the breeding, killing and sale of domestic game for food purposes.

Make a careful investigation of the present status of your sage grouse, every other grouse, quail, and all species of shore birds, then give a five-year close season, all over the state, to every species that is "becoming scarce." This will embrace certainly one-half of the whole number, if not two-thirds.

Provide two bird refuges in the eastern portion of the state, where they are very greatly needed to supplement the good effects of the State Game Preserve established on Puget Sound in 1911.

Bar the use in hunting of the odious automatic and pump shotguns that are now so generally in use all over the United States to the great detriment of the game and the people.

WEST VIRGINIA:

Considering the fact that West Virginia contains no plague-spot city for the consumption of commercial wild game, that the sale of all game is prohibited at all times, and the game of the state may not be exported for sale elsewhere, the wild life of West Virginia is reasonably secure from the market gunner,—if an adequate salaried warden force is provided. Without such a force her game must continue to be destroyed in the future as in the past to supply the markets of Pittsburgh, Philadelphia, Baltimore and Washington. The deer law is excellent, and the non-game birds, and the dove and wood-duck are perpetually protected.

One fly in the ointment is—spring shooting; which for ducks, geese and brant continues from September 1 to April 20. Unfortunately the law enacted in 1875 against spring shooting has been *repealed*, and so has the resident hunting license law (1911).

In view of the impossibility of imagining a good reason for the repeal of a good law, we recommend:

That the law against spring shooting be re-enacted.

That the resident hunter's license law be re-enacted, and the proceeds specifically devoted to the preservation and increase of game.

That a force of regular salaried wardens be provided to enforce the laws.

That the bag limit on quail should be 10 per day or 40 per season, instead of 12 and 96; and on ruffed grouse it should be 3 per day (as in New York) or 12 per season. One wild turkey per day, or three per season is quite enough for one man. The visible supply will not justify the existing limit of two and six.

WISCONSIN:

In spite of the fierce fight made in 1910–11 by the saloon-element game-shooters of Milwaukee for the control of the wild-life situation, and the repeal of the best protective laws of the state, the Army of Defense once more defeated the Allied Destroyers, and drove them off the field. Once more it was proven that when The People are aroused, they are abundantly able to send the steam roller over the enemies of wild life.

Alphabetically, Wisconsin may come near the end of the roll-call; but by downright merit in protection, she comes mighty close to the head of the list of states. Her slate of "Work to be done" is particularly clean; and she has our most distinguished admiration. Her force of game wardens is not a political-machine force. It amounts to something. The men who get within it undergo successfully a civil service examination that certainly separates the sheep from the goats. For particulars address Dr. T. S. Palmer, Department of Agriculture, Washington.

According to the standards that have been dragging along previous to this moment, Wisconsin has a good series of game laws. But the hour for a Reformation of ideas and principles has struck. We heard it first in April, 1911. The wild life of America must not be exterminated according to law, contrary to law, or in the absence of law! Wisconsin must take a fresh grip on her game situation, or it will get away from her, after all.

Not another prairie chicken or woodcock should be killed in Wisconsin between 1912 and 1922. When any small bird becomes so scarce that the bag limit needs to be cut down to five, as it now is for the above in Wisconsin, it is time to stop for ten years, before it is too late.

Wisconsin should immediately busy herself about the creation of bird and game preserves.

For goodness sake, Wisconsin, stop killing squirrels as "game!" You ought to know better—and you do! Leave that form of barbarism for the Benighted States.

And pass a law shutting out the machine guns. They are a disgrace to our country, and a scourge to our game. Continually are they leading good men astray.

Extend the term of your State Warden to four years.

WYOMING

The State of Wyoming once had a magnificent heritage of game. It embraced the Rocky Mountain species, and also those of the great plains. First and last, the state has worked hard to protect her wild life, and hold the killing of it down to a decent basis.

As far back as 1889, I met on the Shoshone River a very wide-awake warden, actually "on his job," who was maintained by a body of private citizens headed by Col. Pickett and known as the Northern Wyoming Game Protective Association. And even then we saw that the laws were too liberal for the game. In one man's cold-storage dug-out we saw enough sheep, deer and elk meat to subsist a company of hungry dragoons, all killed and possessed according to law.

In the protection of her mountain game, Wyoming has had a hard task. In the Yellowstone Park between 1889 and 1894, the poachers for the taxidermists of Livingston and elsewhere slaughtered 270 bison out of 300; and Howell was the only man caught. England can protect game in far-distant mountains and wildernesses; but America can not,—or at least *we don't!* With us, men living in remote places who find wild game about them say "To h— with the law!" They kill on the sly, in season and out of season, females and males; and the average local jury simply *will not* convict the average settler who is accused of such a trifling indiscretion as killing game out of season when he "needs the meat."

And so, with laws in full force protecting females, the volume of big game steadily disappears, *everywhere west of the Alleghanies where the law permits big-game hunting!* An interesting chapter might be written on game exterminated according to law.

The deadly defects in the protection of western big game are:

Structural weakness in the enforcement of the laws;

Collusion between offenders for the suppression of evidence;

Perjury on the witness stand;

Dishonesty and disloyalty on the part of local jurors when friends are on trial;

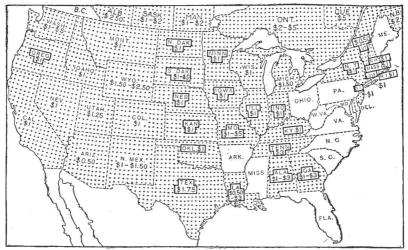

From Farmers' Bulletin No. 510, U. S. Dept. of Agriculture

STATES AND PROVINCES WHICH REQUIRE RESIDENTS TO OBTAIN HUNTING
LICENSES, 1912

In Connecticut, New Jersey, New York, Oklahoma and Rhode Island an additional fee of 10
to 20 cents is charged for issuing the license.

Inclosed names indicate States which permit residents to hunt on their own land without
license. Nova Scotia has a $5 resident license and exempts landowners.

Note that many of the States adopt the French method of exempting landowners, while some,
particularly in the West follow the English method of requiring everyone who hunts to obtain a
license.

Sympathy of judges for "the poor man" who wants to eat the
game to save his cattle and sheep.

Elsewhere there appears a statement regarding the elk of Jackson
Hole, and the efforts made and being made to save them. At this point
we are interested in the game of Wyoming as a whole.

First of all, the killing of mountain sheep should absolutely cease, for ten years.

A similar ten-year close season should be accorded moose and prong-horned antelope.

All grouse should now be classed with doves and swans (no open season), and kept
there for ten years.

Spring shooting is wrong in principle and vicious in practice; and it should be
stopped in Wyoming, as elsewhere.

The automatic and pump shotguns when used in hunting are a disgrace to Wyoming,
as they are to other states, and should be suppressed; and the silencer for use in hunting is in the black list.

CHAPTER XXXII

NEED FOR A FEDERAL MIGRATORY BIRD LAW, NO-SALE OF-GAME LAW, AND OTHERS

We are assuming that the American people sincerely desire the adequate protection and increase of bird life, for reasons that are both sentimental and commercial. Surely every good citizen dislikes to see millions of dollar's worth of national wealth foolishly wasted, and he dislikes to pay any unnecessary increased cost of living. There must be several millions of Americans who feel that way, and who are disposed to demand a complete revolution in bird protection.

There are four needs of wild bird life that are fundamental, and that can not be ignored, any more than a builder can ignore the four corner stones of his building. Listed in the order of their importance, they are as follows:

1.—*The federal protection of all migratory birds.*

2.—*The total suppression of the sale of native wild game.*

3.—*The total suppression of spring shooting and of shooting in the breeding season, and*

4.—*Long close seasons for all species that are about to be "shot out."*

If the gunners of America wish to have a gameless continent, all they need do to secure it is to oppose these principles, prevent their translation into law, and maintain the status quo. If they do this, then *all our best birds are doomed to swift destruction.* Let no man make a mistake on that point. The "open seasons" and "bag limits" of the United States to-day are just as deadly as the 5,000,000 sporting guns now in use, and the 700,000,000 annual cartridges. It is only the ignorant or the vicious who will seriously dispute this statement.

THE FEDERAL PROTECTION OF MIGRATORY BIRDS.—The bill now before Congress for the protection of all migratory birds by the national government is the most important measure ever placed before that body in behalf of wild life. A stranger to this proposition will need to pause for thought in order to grasp its full meaning, and appreciate the magnitude of its influence.

The urgent necessity for a law of this nature is due to the utter inadequacy of the laws that prevail throughout some portions of the United States concerning the slaughter and preservation of birds. Any law that is not enforced is a poor law. There is not one state in the

Union, nor a single province in Canada, in which the game birds, and other birds criminally shot as game, are not being killed far faster than they are breeding, and thereby being exterminated.

Several states are financially unable to employ a force of salaried game wardens; and wherever that is true, the door to universal slaughter is wide open. Let him who questions this take Virginia as a case in point. A loyal Virginian told me only this year that in his state the warden system is an ineffective farce, and the game is not protected, because the wardens can not afford to patrol the state for nothing.

This condition prevails in a number of states, north and south, especially south. It is my belief that throughout nine-tenths of the South, the negroes and poor whites are slaughtering birds exactly as they please. It is the *permanent residents* of the haunts of birds and game that are exterminating the wild life.

The value of the birds as destroyers of noxious insects, has been set forth in Chapter XXIII. Their total value is enormous—or it *would* be if the birds were alive and here in their normal numbers. To-day there are about one-tenth as many birds as were alive and working thirty years ago. During the past thirty years the destruction of our game birds has been enormous, and the insectivorous birds have greatly decreased.

The damages annually inflicted upon the farm, orchard and garden crops of this country are very great. When a city is destroyed by earthquake or fire, and $100,000,000 worth of property is swept away, we are racked with horror and pity; and the cities of America pour out money like water to relieve the resultant distress. We are shocked because we can *see* the flames, the smoke and the ruins.

And yet, we annually endure with perfect equanimity (*because we can not see it?*) a loss of nearly $400,000,000 worth of value that is destroyed by insects. The damage is inflicted silently, insidiously, without any scare heads or wooden type in the newspapers, and so we pay the price without protest. We know—when we stop to think of it—that not all this loss falls upon the producer. We know that every consumer of bread, cereals, vegetables and fruit *pays his share of this loss!* To-day, millions of people are groaning under the "increased cost of living." The bill for the federal protection of all migratory birds is directly intended to decrease the cost of living, by preventing outrageous waste; but of all the persons to whom the needs of that bill are presented, how many will take the time to promote its quick passage by direct appeals to their members of Congress? We shall see.

The good that would be accomplished, annually, by the enactment of a law for the federal protection of all migratory birds is beyond computation; but it is my belief that within a very few years the increase in bird life would prevent what is now an annual loss of $250,000,000. It is beyond the power of man to protect his crops and fruit and trees as the bird millions would protect them—if they were here as they were in 1870. The migratory bird bill is of vast importance because it would throw the strong arm of federal protection around 610 species of birds.

The power of Uncle Sam is respected and feared in many places where the power of the state is ignored.

The list of migratory birds includes most of the perching birds; all the shore birds (*great* destroyers of bad insects); all the swifts and swallows; the goat-suckers (whippoorwill and nighthawk); some of the woodpeckers; most of the rails; pigeons and doves; many of the hawks; some of the cranes and herons and all the geese, ducks and swans.

A movement for the federal protection of migratory game birds was proposed to Congress by George Shiras, 3rd, who as a member of the House in the 58th Congress introduced a bill to secure that end. An excellent brief on that subject by Mr. Shiras appeared in the printed hearing on the McLean bill, held on March 6, 1912, page 18. Omitting the bills introduced in the 59th, 60th and 61st sessions, mention need be made only of the measures under consideration in the present Congress. One of these is a bill introduced by Representative J. W. Weeks, of Massachusetts. and another is the bill of Representative D. R. Anthony, Jr., of Kansas, of the same purport.

Finally, on April 24, 1912, an adequate and entirely reasonable bill was introduced in the Senate by Senator George P. McLean, of Connecticut, as No. 6497 (Calendar No. 606). This bill provides federal protection for *all* migratory birds, and embraces all save a very few of the species that are specially destructive to noxious insects. The bill provides national protection to the farmer's and fruit-grower's best friends. It is entitled to the enthusiastic support of 90,000,000 of people, native and alien. Every producer of farm products and every consumer of them owes it to himself to write at once to his member of Congress and ask him (1) to urge the speedy consideration of the bill for the federal protection of all migratory birds, (2) to vote for it, and (3) to work for it until it is passed. It matters not which one of the three bills described finally becomes a law. Will the American people act rationally about this matter, and protect their own interests ?

SUPPRESS THE SALE OF ALL NATIVE WILD GAME.—The deadly effect of the commercial slaughter of game and its sale for food is now becoming well understood by the American people. One by one the various state legislatures have been putting up the bars against the exportation or sale of any "game protected by the state." The U. S. Department of Agriculture says, through Henry Oldys, that "free marketing of wild game leads swiftly to extermination;" and it is literally true.

Up to March, 1911, it appears that several states prohibited the sale of game, sixteen states permitted the sale of all unprotected game, and in eight more there was partial prohibition. Unfortunately, however, many of these states permitted the sale of *imported* game. Now, since it happened to be a fact that the vast majority of the states prohibit the *export* of their game, as well as the sale of it, a very large quantity of such game as quail, ruffed grouse, snipe, woodcock and shore birds was illegally shot for the market, exported in defiance both of state laws and

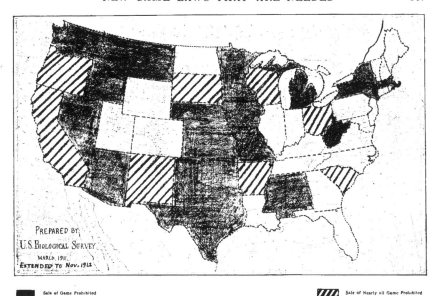

Sale of Game Prohibited   Sale of Nearly all Game Prohibited

EIGHTEEN STATES ENTIRELY PROHIBIT THE SALE OF GAME
WHY DO THE OTHERS LAG BEHIND?

the federal Lacey Act, and sold to the detriment of the states that produced it. In other words, in the laws of each state that merely sought
to protect *their own* game, regardless of the game of neighboring states,
there was not merely a loop-hole, but there was a gap wide enough to
drive through with a coach and four. The ruffed grouse of Massachusetts and Connecticut often were butchered to make Gotham holi-
days in joyous contempt of the laws at both ends of the line. As a
natural result the game of the Atlantic coast was disappearing at a
frightful rate.

In 1911, the no-sale-of-game law of New York was born out of sheer
desperation. The Army of Destruction went up to Albany well-organized,
well provided with money and attorneys, with three senators in the
Senate and two assemblymen in the lower house, to wage merciless warfare on the whole wild-life cause. The market gunners and game dealers
not only proposed to repeal the law against spring shooting but also to
defeat all legislation that might be attempted to restrict the sale of game,
or impose bag limits on wild fowl. The Milliners' Association proposed
to wipe off the books the Dutcher law against the use of the plumage of
wild birds in millinery, and an assemblyman was committed to that cause
as its special champion.

Then it was that all the friends of wild life in the Empire State resolved upon a death grapple with the Destroyers, and a fight to an abso-
ute finish. The Bayne bill, entirely prohibiting the sale of all native
wild game throughout the state of New York, was drafted and thrown

into the ring, and the struggle began. At first the no-sale-of-game bill looked like sheer madness, but no sooner was it fairly launched than supporters came flocking in from every side. All the organizations of sportsmen and friends of wild life combined in one mighty army, the strength of which was irresistible. The real sportsmen of the state quickly realized that the no-sale bill was *directly in the interest of legitimate sport.* The great mass of people who love wild life, and never kill, were quick to comprehend the far-reaching importance of the measure, and they supported it, with money and enthusiasm.

The members of the legislature received thousands of letters from their constituents, asking them to support the Bayne-Blauvelt bill. They did so. On its passage through the two houses, only *one* vote was recorded against it! Incidentally, every move attempted by the Army of Destruction was defeated and in the final summing up the defeat amounted to an utter rout.

In 1912, after a tremendous struggle, the legislature of Massachusetts passed a counterpart of the Bayne law, and took her place in the front rank of states. That was a great fight. The market-gunners of Cape Cod, the game dealers and other interests entered the struggle with men in the lower house of the legislature specially elected to look after their interests. Just as in New York in 1911, they proposed to repeal the existing laws against spring shooting and throw the markets wide open to the sale of game. From first to last, through three long and stormy months, the Destroyers fought with a degree of determination and persistence worthy of a better cause. They contested with the Defenders every inch of ground. In New York, the Destroyers were overwhelmed by the tidal wave of Defenders, but in Massachusetts it was a prolonged hand-to-hand fight on the ramparts. *Five times* was a bill to repeal the spring-shooting law introduced and defeated!

Even after the bill had passed both houses by good majorities, the Governor declared that he could not sign it. And then there poured into the Executive offices such a flood of callers, letters, telegrams and telephone calls that he became convinced that the People desired the law; so he signed the bill in deference to the wishes of the majority.

The principle that the sale of game is wrong, and fatal to the existence of a supply of game, is as fixed and unassailable as the Rocky Mountains. Its universal acceptance is only a question of intelligence and common honesty. The open states owe it to themselves and each other to enact both the spirit and the letter of the Bayne law, *and do it quickly,* before it is too late to profit by it! Let them remember the heath hen,—amply protected when entirely too late to save it from extinction!

It is fairly beyond question that the killing of wild game for the market, and its sale in the "open season" *and out of it,* is responsible for the disappearance of at least fifty per cent of our stock of American feathered game. It is the market-gunner, the game-hog who shoots "for sport" and sells his game, and the game dealer, who have swept away the wild ducks, the ruffed grouse, the quail and the prairie chickens that

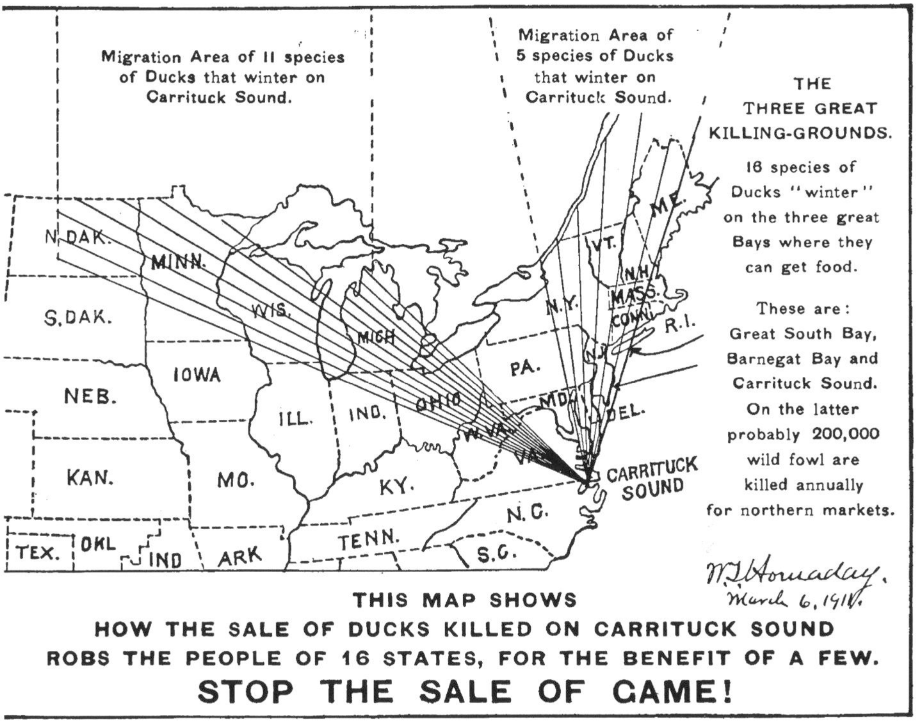

THIS MAP SHOWS
HOW THE SALE OF DUCKS KILLED ON CARRITUCK SOUND
ROBS THE PEOPLE OF 16 STATES, FOR THE BENEFIT OF A FEW.
STOP THE SALE OF GAME!

MAP USED IN THE CAMPAIGN FOR THE BAYNE LAW

thirty years ago were abundant on their natural ranges. The foolish farmers of the middle West permitted the market-hunters of Chicago and the East to slaughter their own legitimate game by the barrel and the car-load, and ship it "East," to market. To-day the waters of Currituck Sound are a wholesale slaughter-place for migratory wild fowl with which to supply the markets of Baltimore, Washington and Philadelphia. Furthermore, the market gunners of Currituck are robbing the people of 16 states of tens of thousands of wild-fowl that legitimately belong to them, during the annual autumn flight. The accompanying map shows how it is done.

To-day, the cash rewards of the market-hunter who can reach a large city with his product are dangerously great. Observe the following *wholesale* prices that prevailed in New York city in 1910, just prior to the passage of the Bayne law. They were compiled and published by Henry Oldys, of the Biological Survey.

```
Grouse, domestic....................per pair.....    $3.00
Grouse, foreign.....................  "    "  ....$1.25 to  1.75
Partridge, domestic.................  "    "  .....  3.50 "  4.00
```

Woodcock, domestic.................... " "	1.50 "	2.00
Golden plover.........................per dozen...	2.50 "	3.50
English snipe......................... " "	2.00 "	3.00
Canvasback duck.....................per pair.....	2.25 "	3.00
Redhead duck........................ " "	1.50 "	2.50
Mallard duck........................ " "		1.25
Bluewing teal........................	75 "	1.00
Greenwing teal.......................	75 "	.90
Broadbill duck....................... " "	.50 "	.75
Rail, No. 1...........................per dozen...		1.00
Rail, No.2........................... " " ...		.60
Venison, whole deer..................per pound...	.22 "	.25
Venison, saddle...................... " "	30 "	.35

All our feathered game is rapidly slipping away from us. *Are we going to save anything from the wreck?* Will we so weakly manage the game situation that later on there will be no legitimate bird-shooting for our younger sons, and our grandsons?

All laws that permit the killing of game for the market, and the sale of it afterward, are class legislation of the worst sort. They permit a hundred men selfishly to slaughter for their own pockets the game that rightfully belongs to a hundred thousand men and boys who shoot for the legitimate recreation that such field sports afford. Will any of the sportsmen of America "stand for" this until the game is *all* gone?

The people who pay big prices for game in the hotels and restaurants of our big cities are not men who *need* that game as food. Far from it. They can obtain scores of fine meat dishes without destroying the wild flocks. In civilized countries wild game is no longer necessary as "food," to satisfy hunger, and ward off starvation. In the United States the day of the hungry Indian-fighting pioneer has gone by and there is an abundance of food everywhere.

The time to temporize and feel timid over the game situation has gone by. The situation is desperate; and nothing but strong and vigorous measures will avail anything worth while. The sale of all wild game should be stopped, everywhere and at all seasons, throughout all North America, and throughout the world. To-day this particular curse is being felt even in India.

It is the duty of every true sportsman, every farmer who owns a gun, and every lover of wild life, to enter into the campaign for the passage of bills absolutely prohibiting all traffic in wild game no matter what its origin. Of course the market hunters, the game-hogs and the game dealers will bitterly oppose them, and hire a lobby to attempt to defeat them. But the fight for no-sale-of-game is now on, and it must not stop short of complete victory.

REASONS WHY THE SALE OF WILD GAME SHOULD CEASE EVERYWHERE

1.—Because fully 95 per cent of our legitimate stock of feathered game has already been destroyed.

2.—Because if market-gunning and the sale of game continue ten years longer, all our feathered game will be swept away.

3.—Because when the sale of game was permitted one dealer was able to sell 1,000,000 *game birds per year in New York City,* so he himself said.

4.—Because it is a fixed fact that every wild species of mammal, bird or reptile that is pursued for money-making purposes eventually is wiped out of existence. Even the whales of the sea are no exception.

5.—Because at least 50 per cent of the decrease in our feathered game is due to market-gunning, and the sale of game. Look at the prairie chicken of the Mississippi Valley, and the ruffed grouse of New England.

6.—Because the laws that permit the commercial slaughter of wild birds for the benefit of less than five per cent of the inhabitants of any state are directly against the interest of the 95 per cent of other people, to *whom that game partly belongs.*

7.—Because game killed "for sale" is not intended to satisfy "hunger." The people who eat game in large cities do not know what hunger is, save by hearsay. Purchased game is used chiefly in over-feeding; and as a rule it does far more harm than good.

8.—Because the greatest value to be derived from any game bird is in seeing it, and photographing it, and enjoying its living company in its native haunts. Who will love the forests when they become destitute of wild life, and desolate?

9.—Because stopping the sale of game *will help bring back the game birds to us, in a few years.*

10.—Because the pace that New York and Massachusetts have set in this matter will render it easier to procure the passage of Bayne laws in other states.

11.—Because those who legitimately desire game for their tables can be supplied from the game farms and preserves that now are coming into existence.

When New York's far-reaching Bayne bill became a law, the following dead birds lay in cold storage in New York City:

Wild duck	98,156
Plover	48,780
Quail	14,227
Grouse	21,202
Snipe	7,825
Woodcock	767
Rail	419
	191,376

They represented the last slaughterings of American game for New York. To-day the remaining plague-spots are Chicago, Philadelphia, San Francisco, Baltimore, Washington and New Orleans; but in New Orleans the brakes have at last (1912) been applied, and the market slaughter that formerly prevailed in that state has at least been checked.

As an instance of persistent market shooting on the greatest ducking waters of the eastern United States, I offer this report from a trustworthy agent sent to Currituck Sound, North Carolina, in March, 1911.

I beg to submit the following information relative to the number of wild ducks and geese shipped from this market and killed in the waters of Back Bay and the upper or north end of Currituck Sound, from October 20th to March 1st, inclusive.

Approximately there were killed and shipped in the territory above named, 130,000 to 135,000 wild ducks and between 1400 and 1500 wild geese. From Currituck Sound and its tributaries there were shipped approximately 200,000 wild ducks.

You will see from the above figures that each year the market shooter exacts a tremendous toll from the wild water fowl in these waters, and it is only a question of a short time when the wild duck will be exterminated, unless we can stop the ruthless slaughter. The last few years I have noted a great decrease in the number of wild ducks; some of the species are practically extinct. I have secured the above information from a most reliable source, and the figures given approximately cannot be questioned.

The effect of the passage of the Bayne law, closing the greatest American market against the sale of game was an immediate decrease of fully fifty per cent in the number of ducks and geese slaughtered on Currituck Sound. The dealers refused to buy the birds, and one-half the killers were compelled to hang up their guns and go to work. The duck-slaughterers felt very much enraged by the passage of the law, and at first were inclined to blame the northern members of Currituck ducking clubs for the passage of the measure; but as a matter of fact, not one of the persons blamed took any part whatever in the campaign for the new law.

THE UNFAIRNESS OF SPRING SHOOTING.—The shooting of game birds in late winter and spring is to be mentioned only to be condemned. It is grossly unfair to the birds, outrageous in principle, and most unsportsmanlike, no matter whether the law permits it or not. Why it is that any state like Iowa, for example, can go on killing game in spring is more than I can understand. I have endeavored to find a reason for it, in Iowa, but the only real reason is:—"The boys want the birds!"

I think we have at last reached the point where it may truthfully be said that now no gentleman shoots birds in spring. If the plea is made that "if we don't shoot ducks in the spring we can't shoot them at all!" then the answer is—if you can't shoot game like high-minded, red-blooded sportsman, *don't shoot it at all!* A gentleman can not afford to barter his standing and his own self-respect for a few ducks shot in the spring when the birds are going north to lay their eggs. And the man who insists on shooting in spring may just as well go right on and do various other things that are beyond the pale, such as shoot quail on the ground, shoot does and fawns, and fish for trout with gang hooks.

There are no longer two sides to what once was the spring shooting question. Even among savages, the breeding period of the wild creatures is under taboo. Then if ever may the beasts and birds cry "King's excuse!" It has been positively stated in print that high-class fox hounds have been known to refuse to chase a pregnant fox, even when in full view.

CHAPTER XXXIII

BRINGING BACK THE VANISHED BIRDS AND GAME

The most charming trait of wild-life character is the alacrity and confidence with which wild birds and mammals respond to the friendly advances of human friends. Those who are not very familiar with the mental traits of our wild neighbors may at first find it difficult to comprehend the marvelous celerity with which both birds and mammals recognize friendly overtures from man, and respond to them.

At the present juncture, this state of the wild-animal mind becomes a factor of great importance in determining what we can do to prevent the extermination of species, and to promote the increase and return of wild life.

I think that there is not a single wild mammal or bird species now living that can not, or does not, quickly recognize protection, *and take advantage of it.* The most conspicuous of all familiar examples are the wild animals of the Yellowstone Park. They embrace the elk, mountain sheep, antelope, mule deer, the black bear and even the grizzly. No one can say precisely how long those several species were in ascertaining that it was safe to trust themselves within easy rifle-shot of man; but I think it was about five years. Birds recognize protection far more quickly than mammals. In a comparatively short time the naturally wild and wary big game of the Yellowstone Park became about as tame as range cattle. It was at least fifteen years ago that the mule deer began to frequent the parade ground at the Mammoth Hot Springs military post, and receive there their rations of hay.

Whenever you see a beautiful photograph of a large band of big-horn sheep or mule deer taken at short range amid Rocky Mountain scenery, you are safe in labeling it as having come from the Yellowstone Park. The prong-horned antelope herd is so tame that it is difficult to keep it out of the streets of Gardiner, on the Montana side of the line.

But the bears! Who has not heard the story of the bears of the Yellowstone Park,—how black bears and grizzlies stalk out of the woods, every day, to the garbage dumping-ground; how black bears actually have come *into the hotels* for food, without breaking the truce, and how the grizzlies boldly raid the grub-wagons and cook-tents of campers, taking just what they please, because they *know* that no man dares to shoot them! Indeed, those raiding bears long ago became a public nuisance, and many of them have been caught in steel box-traps and shipped to zoological gardens, in order to get them out of the way. And yet, outside the Park boundaries, everywhere, the bears are as wary and wild as the wildest.

The arrogance of the bears that couldn't be shot once led to a droll and also exciting episode.

During the period when Mr. C. J. Jones ("Buffalo" Jones) was superintendent of the wild animals of the Park, the indignities inflicted upon tourist campers by certain grizzly bears quite abraded his nerves. He obtained from Major Pitcher authority to punish and reform a certain grizzly, and went about the matter in a thoroughly Buffalo-Jonesian manner. He procured a strong lariat and a bean-pole seven feet long and repaired to the camp that was troubled by too much grizzly

The particular offender was a full-grown male grizzly who had become a notorious raider. At the psychological moment Jones lassoed him in short order, getting a firm hold on the bear's left hind leg. Quickly the end of the rope was thrown over a limb of the nearest tree, and in a trice Ephraim found himself swinging head downward between the heavens and the earth. And then his punishment began.

Buffalo Jones thrashed him soundly with the bean-pole! The outraged bear swung to and fro, whirled round and round, clawing and snapping at the empty air, roaring and bawling with rage, scourged in flesh and insulted in spirit. As he swung, the bean-pole searched out the different parts of his anatomy with a wonderful degree of neatness and precision. Between rage and indignation the grizzly nearly exploded. A moving-picture camera was there, and since that day that truly moving scene has amazed and thrilled countless thousands of people.

When it was over, Mr. Jones boldly turned the bear loose! Although its rage was as boundless as the glories of the Yellowstone Park, it paused not to rend any of those present, but headed for the tall timber, and with many an indignant "Woof! Woof!" it plunged in and disappeared. It was two or three years before that locality was again troubled by impudent grizzly bears.

And what is the mental attitude of *every* Rocky Mountain black or grizzly bear *outside* of the Yellowstone Park? It is colossal suspicion of man, perpetual fear, and a clean pair of heels the moment man-scent or man-sight proclaims the proximity of the Arch Enemy of Wild Creatures. And yet there are one or two men who tell the American public that wild animals do not think, that they do not reason, and are governed only by "instinct"!

"A little knowledge is a dangerous thing!"

Taming Wild Birds.—As incontestable proof of the receptive faculties of birds, I will cite the taming of wild birds in the open, by friendly advances. There are hundreds, aye, thousands, of men, women, boys and girls who could give interesting and valuable personal testimony on this point.

My friend J. Alden Loring (one of the naturalists of the Roosevelt African Expedition), is an ardent lover of wild birds and mammals. The taming of wild creatures in the open is one of his pastimes, and his results serve well to illustrate the marvelous readiness of our wild neigh-

SIX WILD CHIPMUNKS DINE WITH MR. LORING

bors to become close friends with man *when protected*. I will quote from one of Mr. Loring's letters on this subject:

"Taming wild birds is a new field in nature study, and one never can tell what success he will have until he has experimented with different species. Some birds tame much more easily than others. On three or four occasions I have enticed a chickadee *to my hand* at the first attempt, while in other cases it has taken from fifteen minutes to a whole day.

"Chipping sparrows that frequent my doorway I have tamed in two days. A nuthatch required three hours before it would fly to my hand, although it took food from my stick the first time it was offered. When you find a bird on her nest, it is of course much easier to tame that individual that if you had to follow it about in the open, and wait for it to come within reach of a stick. By exercising extreme caution, and approaching inch by inch, I have climbed a tree to the nest of a yellow-throated vireo, and at the first attempt handed the bird a meal-worm with my fingers. At one time I had two house wrens, a yellow-throated vireo, a chipping sparrow and a flock of chickadees that would come to my hand."

It would be possible—and also delightful—to fill a volume with citations of evidence to illustrate the quick acceptance of man's protection by wild birds and mammals. Let me draw a few illustrations from my own wild neighbors.

On Lake Agassiz, in the N. Y. Zoological Park, within 500 feet of my office in the Administration Building, a pair of wild wood-ducks made their nest last spring, and have just finished rearing nine fine, healthy young birds. Whenever you see a wood-duck rise and fly in our Park, you may know that it is a wild bird. During the summer of 1912 a small flock of wild wood-ducks came every night to our Wild-Fowl Pond, and spent the night there.

A year ago, a covey of eleven quail appeared in the Park, and have persistently remained ever since. Last fall and winter they came at least twenty times to a spot within forty feet of the rear window of my office, in order to feed upon the wheat screenings that we placed there for them.

When we first occupied the Zoological Park grounds, in 1899, there was not one wild rabbit in the whole 264 acres. Presently the species appeared, and rabbits began to hop about confidently, all over the place. In 1906, we estimated that there were about eighty individuals. Then the 'marauding cats began to come in, and they killed off the rabbits until not one was to be seen. Thereupon, we addressed ourselves to those cats, in more serious earnest than ever before. Now the cats have disappeared; and one day last spring, as I left my office at six o'clock, everyone else having previously gone, I almost stepped upon two half-grown bunnies that had been visiting on the front door-mat.

When we were macadamizing the yards around the Elephant House, with a throng of workmen all about every day, a robin made its nest on the heavy channel-iron frame of one of the large elephant gates that swung to and fro nearly every day.

In 1900 we planted a young pine tree in front of our temporary office building, within six feet of a main walk; and at once a pair of robins nested in it and reared young there.

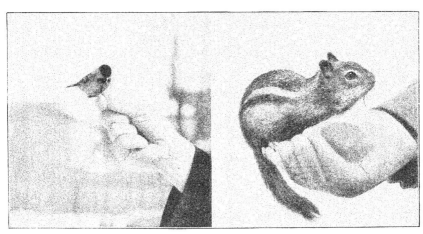

WILD CREATURES QUICKLY RESPOND TO FRIENDLY ADVANCES
Chickadee and Chipmunk Tamed by Mr. Loring

THE COLORADO OBJECT LESSON IN BRINGING BACK THE DUCKS

Up in Putnam County, where for five years deer have been protected, the exhibitions that are given each year of the supreme confidence of protected deer literally astonish the natives. They are almost unafraid of man and his vehicles, his cattle and his horses, but of course they are unwilling to be handled. Strangers are astonished; but people who know something about the mental attitude of wild animals under protection know that it is the natural and inevitable result of *real protection*.

At Mr. Frank Seaman's summer home in the Catskills, the phœbe birds nest on the beams under the roof of the porch. At my summer home in the Berkshires, no sooner was our garage completed than a phœbe built her nest on the edge of the lintel over the side door; and another built on a drain-pipe over the kitchen door.

Near Port Jervis, last year a wild ruffed grouse nested and reared a large brood in the garden of Mr. W. I. Mitchell, within *two feet* of the foundation of the house.

On the Bull River in the wilds of British Columbia two trappers of my acquaintance, Mack Norboe and Charlie Smith, once formed a friendship with a wild weasel. In a very few visits, the weasel found that it was among friends, and the trappers' log cabin became its home. I have a photograph of it, taken while it posed on the door-sill. The trappers said that often when returning at nightfall from their trap-lines, the weasel would meet them a hundred yards away on the trail, and follow them back to the cabin.

"Old Ben," the big sea-lion who often landed on the wharf at Avalon, Santa Catalina, to be fed on fish, was personally known to thousands of people.

An Object Lesson in Protection.—A remarkable object lesson in the recognition of protection by wild ducks came under my notice in the pages of "Recreation Magazine" in June, 1903, when that publication was edited by G. O. Shields. The article was entitled,—"A Haven of Refuge," and the place described well deserved the name. It is impossible for me to impress upon the readers of this volume with sufficient force and clearness the splendid success that is easily attainable in encouraging the return of the birds. The story of the Mosca "Haven of Refuge" was so well told by Mr. Charles C. Townsend in the publication referred to above, that I take pleasure in reproducing it entire.

One mile north of the little village of Mosca, Colorado, in San Luis valley, lives the family of J. C. Gray. On the Gray ranch there is an artesian well which empties into a small pond about 100 feet square. This pond is never entirely frozen over and the water emptying therein is warm even during the coldest winter.

Some five years ago, Mr. Gray secured a few wild-duck eggs, and hatched them under a hen. The little ducks were reared and fed on the little pond. The following spring they left the place, to return in the fall, bringing with them broods of young; also bringing other ducks to the home where protection was afforded them, and plenty of good feed was provided. Each year since, the ducks have scattered in the spring to mate and rear their families, returning again with greatly increased numbers in the fall, and again bringing strangers to the haven of refuge.

I drove out to the ranch November 24, 1902, and found the little pond almost black with the birds, and was fortunate enough to secure a picture of a part of the pond while the ducks were thickly gathered thereon. Ice had formed around the edges, and this ice was covered with ducks. The water was also alive with others, which paid not the least attention to the party of strangers on the shore.

From Mr. Gray I learned that there were some 600 ducks of various kinds on the pond at that time, though it was then early for them to seek winter quarters. Later in the year, he assured me, there would be between 2,000 and 3,000 teal, mallards, canvasbacks, redheads and other varieties, all perfectly at home and fearless of danger. The family have habitually approached the pond from the house, which stands on the south side, and should any person appear on the north side of the pond the ducks immediately take fright and flight. Wheat was strewn on the ground and in the water, and the ducks waddled around us within a few inches of our feet to feed, paying not the least attention to us, or to the old house-dog which walked near.

Six miles east of the ranch is San Luis lake, to which these ducks travel almost daily while the lake is open. When they are at the lake it is impossible to approach within gunshot of the then timid birds. Some unsympathetic boys and men have learned the habit of the birds, and place themselves in hiding along the course of flight to and from the lake. Many ducks are shot in this way, but woe to the person caught firing a gun on or near the home-pond. When away from home, the birds are as other wild-ducks and fail to recognize any members of the Gray family. While at home they follow the boys around the barn-yard, squawking for feed like so many tame ducks.

This is the greatest sight I have ever witnessed, and one that I could not believe existed until I had seen it. Certainly it is worth travelling many miles to see, and no one, after seeing it, would care to shoot birds that, when kindly treated, make such charming pets.

Since the above was published, the protected flocks of tame wild ducks have become one of the most interesting sights of Florida. At Palm Beach the tameness of the wild ducks when within their protected area, and their wildness outside of it, has been witnessed by thousands of visitors.

THE SAVING OF THE SNOWY EGRET IN THE UNITED STATES.—The time was when very many persons believed that the devastations of the plume-hunters of Florida and the Gulf Coast would be so long continued and so persistently followed up to the logical conclusion that both species of plume-furnishing egrets would disappear from the avifauna of the United States. This expectation gave rise to feelings of resentment, indignation and despair.

It happened, however, that almost at the last moment a solitary individual set on foot an enterprise calculated to preserve the snowy egret (which is the smaller of the two species involved), from final extermination. The splendid success that has attended the efforts of Mr. Edward A. McIlhenny, of Avery Island, Louisiana, is entitled not only to admiration and praise, but also to the higher tribute of practical imitation. Mr. McIlhenny is, first of all, a lover of birds, and a humanitarian. He has traveled widely throughout the continent of North America and elsewhere, and has seen much of wild life and man's influence upon it. To-day his highest ambition is to create for the benefit of the Present, and as a heritage to Posterity, a mid-continental chain of great bird refuges, in which migrating wild fowl and birds of all other species may find resting-places and refuges during their migrations, and protected feeding-grounds in winter. In this grand enterprise, the consummation of which is now in progress, Mr. McIlhenny is associated with Mr. Charles Willis Ward, joint donor of the splendid Ward-McIlhenny Bird Preserve of 13,000 acres, which recently was presented to the State of Louisiana by its former owners.

The egret and heron preserve, however, is Mr. McIlhenny's individual enterprise, and really furnished the motif of the larger movement. Of its inception and development, he has kindly furnished me the following account, accompanied by many beautiful photographs of egrets breeding in sanctuary, one of which appears on page 27.

In some recent publications I have seen statements to the effect that you believed the egrets were nearing extinction, owing to the persecution of plume hunters, so I know that you will be interested in the enclosed photographs, which were taken in my heron rookery, situated within 100 yards of my factory, where I am now sitting dictating this letter.

This rookery was started by me in 1896, because I saw at that time that the herons of Louisiana were being rapidly exterminated by plume hunters. My thought was that the way to preserve them would be to start an artificial rookery of them where they could be thoroughly protected. With this end in view I built a small pond, taking in a wet space that contained a few willows and other shrubs which grow in wet places.

In a large cage in this pond, I raised some snowy herons. After keeping the birds in confinement for something over six months I turned them loose, hoping that they would come back the next season, as they were perfectly tame and were used to seeing people. I was rewarded the next season by four of the birds returning, and nesting in the willows in the pond. This was the start of a rookery that now covers 35 acres, and contains more than twenty thousand pairs of nesting birds, embracing not only the egrets but all the species of herons found in Louisiana, besides many other water birds.

With a view to carrying on the preservation of our birds on a larger scale, Mr. Chas. W. Ward and I have recently donated to the State of Louisiana 13,000 acres of what I consider to be the finest wild fowl feeding ground on the Louisiana coast, as it contains the only gravel beach for 50 miles, and all of the geese within that space come daily to this beach for gravel. This territory also produces a great amount of natural food for geese and ducks.

SAVING THE GULLS AND TERNS.—But for the vigorous and long-continued efforts of the Audubon Societies, I think our coasts would by this time have been swept clean of the gulls and terns that now adorn it. Twenty years ago the milliners were determined to have them all. The fight for them was long, and hotly contested, but the Audubon Societies won. It was a great victory, and has yielded results of great value to the country at large. And yet, it was only a small number of persons who furnished the money and made the fight which inured to the benefit of the millions of American people. Hereafter, whenever you see an American gull or tern, remind yourself that it was saved to the nation by "the Audubon people."

In times of grave emergency, such as fire, war and scarcity of food, the wild creatures forget their fear of man, and many times actually surrender themselves to his mercy and protection. At such times, hard is the heart and low is the code of manly honor that does not respond in a manner becoming a superior species.

The most pathetic wild-animal situation ever seen in the United States on a large scale is that which for six winters in succession forced several thousand starving elk into the settlement of Jackson Hole, Wyoming, in quest of food at the hands of their natural enemies. The elk lost all fear, partly because they were not attacked, and they surrounded the log-enclosed haystacks, barns and houses, mutely begging for food. Previous to the winter of 1911, thousands of weak calves and cows perished around the haystacks. Mr. S. N. Leek's wonderful pictures tell a thrilling but very sad story.

To the everlasting honor of the people of Jackson Hole, be it recorded that they rose like Men to the occasion that confronted them. In 1909 they gave to the elk herds all the hay that their domestic stock could spare, not pausing to ascertain whether they ever would be reimbursed for it. They just handed it out! The famishing animals literally mobbed the hay-wagons. To-day the national government has the situation in hand.

In times of peace and plenty, the people of Jackson Hole take their toll of the elk herds, but their example during starvation periods is to be commended to all men.

A SLAUGHTER OF RESTORED GAME.—The case of the chamois in Switzerland teaches the world a valuable lesson in how *not* to slaughter game that has come back to its haunts through protected breeding.

A few years ago, one of the provinces of Switzerland took note of the fact that its once-abundant stock of chamois was almost extinct, and enacted a law by which the remnant was absolutely protected for a long period. During those years of protection, the animals bred and multiplied, until finally the original number was almost restored.

Then,—as always in such cases,—there arose a strong demand for an open season; and eventually the government yielded to the pressure of the hunters, and fixed a date whereon an open season should begin.

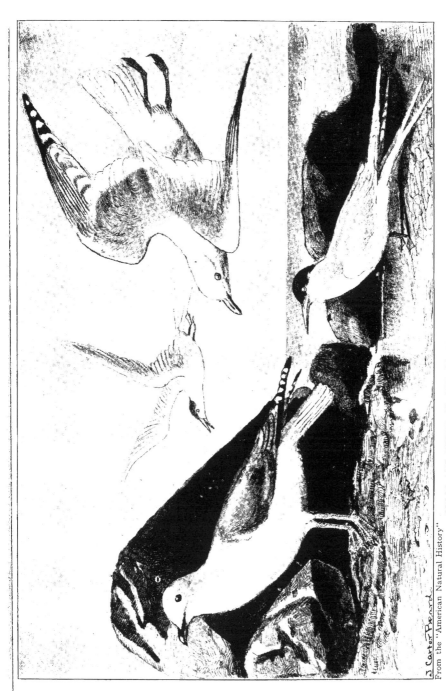

From the "American Natural History"

GULLS AND TERNS OF OUR COASTS, SAVED FROM DESTRUCTION

These Birds have been Saved and Brought back to us by the Splendid Efforts of the Audubon Societies, and other Bird-Lovers. But for the

During the period preceding that fatal date, the living chamois, grown half tame by years of immunity from the guns, were all carefully located and marked down by those who intended to hunt them. At daybreak on the fatal day, the onset began. Guns and hunters were everywhere, and the mountains resounded with the fusillade. Hundreds of chamois were slain, by hundreds of hunters; and by the close of that fatal "open season" the species was more nearly exterminated throughout that region than ever before. Once more those mountains were nice and barren of game.

Let that bloody and disgraceful episode serve as a warning to Americans who are tempted to demand an open season on game that has bred back from the verge of extinction. Particularly do we commend it to the notice of the people of Colorado who *even now* are demanding an open season on the preserved mountain sheep of that state. The granting of such an open season would be a brutal outrage. Those sheep are now so tame and unsuspicious that the killing of them would be *cold-blooded murder!*

THE LOGICAL CONCLUSION.—Within reasonable limits, any partly-destroyed wild species can be increased and brought back by giving absolute protection from harassment and slaughter. When a species is struggling to recuperate, it deserves to be left *entirely unmolested* until it is once more on safe ground.

Every breeding wild animal craves seclusion and entire immunity from excitement and all forms of molestation. Nature simply demands this as her unassailable right. It is my firm belief that any wild species will breed in captivity whenever its members are given a degree of seclusion that they deem satisfactory.

With species that have not been shot down to a point entirely too low, adequate protection generously long in duration will bring back their numbers. If the people of the United States so willed it, we could have wild white-tailed deer in every state and in every county (save city counties) between the Atlantic and the Rocky Mountains. We could easily have one thousand bob white quail for every one now living. We could have squirrels in every grove, and songbirds by the million,—merely by protecting them from slaughter and molestation. From Ohio to the great plains, the pinnated grouse could be made far more common than crows and blackbirds.

Inasmuch as all this is true,—and no one with information will dispute it for a moment,—is it not folly to seek to supplant our own splendid native species of game birds (*that we never yet have decently protected!*) with foreign species? Let the American people answer this question with "Yes" or "No."

The methods by which our non-game birds can be encouraged and brought back are very simple: Protect them, put up shelters for them, give them nest-boxes in abundance, protect them from cats, dogs, and all other forms of destruction, and feed those that need to be fed. I should think that every boy living in the country would find keen pleasure in making and erecting nest-boxes for martins, wrens, and squirrels; in putting up straw teepees in winter for the quail, in feeding the quail, and in nailing to the trees chunks of suet and fat pork every winter for the woodpeckers, nuthatches, and other winter residents.

Will any person now on this earth live long enough to see the present all-pervading and devilish spirit of slaughter so replaced by the love of wild creatures and the true spirit of conservation that it will be as rare as it now is common?

But let no one think for a moment that any vanishing species can at any time be brought back; for that would be a grave error. The point is always reached, by every such species, that the survivors are too few to cope with circumstances, and recovery is impossible. The heath hen could not be brought back, neither could the passenger pigeon. The whooping crane, the sage grouse, the trumpeter swan, the wild turkey, and the upland plover never will come back to us, and nothing that we can do ever will bring them back. Circumstances are against those species, —and I fear against many others also. Thanks to the fact that the American bison breeds well in captivity, we have saved that species from complete extinction, but our antelope seems to be doomed.

It is because of the alarming condition of our best wild life that quick action and strong action is vitally necessary. We are sleeping on our possibilities.

CHAPTER XXXIV

INTRODUCED SPECIES THAT HAVE BEEN BENEFICIAL

Man has made numerous experiments in the transplantation of wild species of mammals and birds from one country, or continent, to another. About one-half these efforts have been beneficial, and the other half have resulted disastrously.

The transplantation of any wild-animal species is a leap in the dark. On general principles it is dangerous to meddle with the laws of Nature, and attempt to improve upon the code of the wilderness. Our best wisdom in such matters may easily prove to be short-sighted folly. The trouble lies in the fact that concerning transplantation it is *impossible for us to know beforehand all the conditions that will affect it, or that it will effect, and how it will work out.* In its own home a species may *seem* not only harmless, but actually beneficial to man. We do not know, and *we can not know*, all the influences that keep it in check, and that mould its character. We do not know, and we can not know without a trial, how new environment will affect it, and what new traits of character it will develop under radically different conditions. The gentle dove of Europe may become the tyrant dove of Cathay. The Repressed Rabbit of the Old World becomes in Australia the Uncontrollable Rabbit, a devastator and a pest of pests.

No wild species should be transplanted and set free in a wild state to stock new regions without consulting men of wisdom, and following their advice. It is now against the laws of the United States to introduce and acclimatize in a wild state, anywhere in the United States, any wild-bird species without the approval of the Department of Agriculture. The law is a wise one. Furthermore, the same principle should apply to birds that it is proposed to transplant from one portion of the United States into another, especially when the two are widely separated.

On this point, I once learned a valuable lesson, which may well point my present moral. Incidentally, also, it was a narrow escape for me!

A gentlemen of my acquaintance, who admires the European magpie, and is well aware of its acceptable residence in various countries in Europe, once requested my cooperation in securing and acclimatizing at his country estate a number of birds of that species. As in duty bound, I laid the matter before our Department of Agriculture, and asked for an opinion. The Department replied, in effect, "Why import a foreign magpie when we have in the West a species of our own quite as handsome, and which could more easily be transplanted?"

The point seemed well taken. Now, I had seen much of the American magpie in its wild home,—the Rocky Mountains, and the western border of the Great Plains,—and I *thought* I was acquainted with it. I knew that a few complaints against it had been made, but they had seemed to me very trivial. To me our magpie seemed to have a generally unobjectionable record.

Fortunately for me, I wrote to Mr. Hershey, Assistant Curator of Ornithology in the Colorado State Museum, for assistance in procuring fifty birds, for transplanation to the State of New York. Mr. Hershey replied that if I really wished the birds for acclimatization, he would gladly procure them for me; but he said that in the *thickly-settled farming communities* of Colorado, the magpie is now regarded as a pest. It devours the eggs and nestlings of other wild birds, and not only that, it destroys so many eggs of domestic poultry that many farmers are compelled to keep their egg-laying hens shut up in wire enclosures!

Now, this condition happened to be entirely unknown to me, because I never had seen the American magpie in action *in a farming community!* Of course the proposed experiment was promptly abandoned, but it is embarrassing to think how near I came to making a mistake. Even if the magpies had been transplanted and had become a nuisance in this state, they could easily have been exterminated by shooting; but the memory of the error would have been humiliating to the party of the first part.

THE OLD WORLD PHEASANTS IN AMERICA.—In 1881 the first Chinese ring-necked pheasants were introduced into the United States, twelve miles below Portland, Oregon; twelve males and three females. The next year, Oregon gave pheasants a five-year close season. A little later, the golden and silver pheasants of China were introduced, and all three species throve mightily, on the Pacific Coast, in Oregon, Washington and western British Columbia. In 1900, the sportsmen of Portland and Vancouver were shooting cock golden pheasants according to law.

The success of Chinese and Japanese pheasants on the Pacific Coast soon led to experiments in the more progressive states, at state expense. State pheasant hatcheries have been established in Massachusetts, Connecticut, New York, New Jersey, Ohio, Illinois, Missouri, Iowa and California.

In many localities, the old-world pheasants have come to stay. The rise and progress of the ring-neck in western New York has already been noted. It came about merely through protection. That protection was protection in fact, not the false "protection" that shoots on the sly. It is the irony of fate that full protection should be accorded a foreign bird, in order that it may multiply and possess the land, while the same kind of protection is refused the native bob white, and it is now almost a dead species, so far as this state is concerned.

In looking about for grievances against the ring-necked and English pheasant, some persons have claimed that in winter these birds are "budders," which means that they harmfully strip trees and bushes of the buds that those bushes will surely need in their spring opening. On

that point Dr. Joseph Kalbfus, Secretary of the Pennsylvania Game
Commission, sent out a circular letter of inquiry, in response to which
he received many statements. With but one exception, all the testimony
received was to the effect that pheasants are *not* bud-eaters, and that
generally the charge is unfounded.

The introduction of old-world pheasants, and the attempted introduction of the Hungarian partridge, are efforts designed first of all to
furnish sportsmen something to shoot, and incidentally to provide a new
food supply for the table. The people of this country are not starving,
nor are they even very hungry for the meat of strange birds; but as a
food-producer, the pheasant is all right.

It disgusts me to the core, however, to see states that wantonly and
wickedly, through sheer apathy and lack of business enterprise, have
allowed the quail, the heath hen, the pinnated grouse and the ruffed
grouse to become almost exterminated by extravagant and foolish
shooters, now putting forth wonderfully diligent efforts and spending
money without end, in introducing *foreign* species! Many men actually
take the ground that our game "can't live" in its own country any
longer; but only the ignorant and the unthinking will say so! Give our
game birds decent, sensible, *actual* protection, stop their being slaughtered
far faster than they breed, and *they will live anywhere in their own native
haunts!* But where is there *one species* of upland game bird in America
that has been sensibly and adequately protected? From Portland,
Maine, to Portland, Oregon there is *not one,—not a single locality in which
protection from shooting has been sensible, or just, or adequate.*

We have universally given our American upland game birds an
unfair deal, and now we are adding insult to slaughter by bringing in
foreign game birds to replace them—because our birds "can't live"
before five million shot-guns!

Our American game birds CAN live, anywhere in the haunts where
nature placed them that are not to-day actually occupied by cities and
towns! Give me the making of the laws, and I will make the prairie
chicken and quail as numerous throughout the northern states east of
the Great Plains as domestic chickens are outside the regular poultry
farms. There is only one reason why there are not ten million quail
in the state of New York to-day,—one for each human inhabitant,—and
that reason is the infernal greed and selfishness of the men who have
almost exterminated our quail by over-shooting. Don't talk to me about
the "hard winters" killing off our quail! It is the hard cheek of the men
who shoot them when they ought to let them alone.

The State of Iowa could support 500,000 prairie chickens and never
miss the waste grain that they would glean in the fields; but now the
prairie chicken is practically extinct in Iowa, only a few scattered specimens remaining as "last survivors" in some of the northern counties.
The migration of those birds that unexpectedly came down from the
north last winter was like the fall of a meteor,—only the birds promptly
faded away again. Why should New York, New Jersey and Massachu-

setts exterminate the heath hen and coddle the ring-necked pheasant and the Hungarian partridge?

The introduction of the old-world pheasants interests me very little. Every one that I see is a painful reminder of our slaughtered quail and grouse,—the birds that never have had a square deal from the American people! Thus far the introduction of the Hungarian partridge has not been successful, anywhere. Connecticut, Missouri, New Jersey and I think other states have tried this, and failed. The failure of that species brings no sorrow to me. I prefer our own game birds; and if the American people will not conserve those properly and decently they deserve to have no game birds.

THE EUROPEAN RED DEER IN NEW ZEALAND.—Occasionally a game-less land makes a ten-strike by introducing a foreign game animal that does no harm, and becomes of great value. The greatest success ever made in the transplantation of game animals has been in New Zealand.

Originally, New Zealand possessed no large animals, and no "big-game." When Nature passed around the deer, antelopes, sheep, goats, wild cattle and bears, New Zealand failed to receive her share. For centuries her splendid forests, her grand mountains and picturesque valleys remained untenanted by big game.

In 1864, the Prince Consort of England caused seven head of European red deer to be taken from the royal park at Windsor, and sent to Christ-church, New Zealand. Only three of the animals survived the long voyage; a buck and two does. For several weeks the two were kept in a barn in Christchurch, where they served no good purpose, and were not likely to live long or be happy. Finally some one said, "Let's set them free in the mountains!"

The idea was adopted. The three animals were hauled an uncertain number of miles into the interior mountains and set free.

They promptly settled down in their new home. They began to breed, and now on the North Island there are probably five thousand European red deer, every one of which has descended directly from the famous three! And here is the strangest part of the story

The red deer of the North Island represent the greatest case of in-and-in breeding of wild animals on record. According to the experience of the world in the breeding of domestic cattle (*not horses*), we should expect physical deterioration, the development of diseases, and disaster. On the contrary, the usual evil results of in-breeding in domestic cattle have been totally absent. *The red deer of New Zealand are to-day physically larger and more robust animals, with longer and heavier antlers, and longer hair, than any of the red deer of Europe west of Germany!*

Red deer have been introduced practically all over New Zealand, and the total number now in the Islands must be somewhere near forty thousand. The sportsmen of that country have grand sport, and take many splendid trophies. That transplantation has been a very great success. Incidentally, the case of the in-bred deer of the North Island, taken along with other cases of which we know, establishes a new and important principle in evolution. It is this:

When healthy wild animals are established in a state of nature, either absolutely free, or confined in preserves so large that they roam at will, seek the food of nature and take care of themselves, in-and-in breeding produces no ill effects, and ceases to be a factor. The animals develop in physical perfection according to the climate and their food supply; and the introduction of new blood is not necessary.

THE FALLOW DEER ON THE ISLAND OF LAMBAY.—In the Irish Sea, a few miles from the southeast coast of Ireland, is the Island of Lambay, owned by Cecil Baring, Esq. The island is precisely one square mile in area, and some of its sea frontage terminates in perpendicular cliffs. In many ways the island is of unusual interest to zoologists, and its fauna has been well set forth by Mr. Baring.

In the year 1892 three fallow deer (*Dama vulgaris*) a buck and two does, were transplanted from a park on the Irish mainland to Lambay, and there set free. From that slender stock has sprung a large herd, which, but for the many deer that have been purposely shot, and the really considerable number that have been killed by going over the cliffs in stormy weather, the progeny of the original three would to-day number several hundred head. No new blood has been introduced, and *no deer have died of disease.* Even counting out the losses by the rifle and by accidental death, the herd to-day numbers more than one hundred head.

Mr. Baring declares that neither he nor his gamekeeper have ever been able to discover any deterioration in the deer of Lambay, either in size, weight, size of antlers, fertility or general physical stamina. The deterioration through disease, especially tuberculosis, that always is dreaded and often observed in closely in-bred domestic cattle, has been totally absent.

In looking about for wild species that have been transplanted, and that have thriven and become beneficial to man, there seems to be mighty little game in sight! The vast majority belong in the next chapter. We will venture to mention the bob white quail that were introduced into Utah in 1871, into Idaho in 1875, and the California valley quail in Washington in 1857. Wherever these efforts have succeeded, the results have been beneficial to man.

In 1879 a well-organized effort was made to introduce European quail into several of the New England and Middle States,—to take the place of the bob white, we may suppose,—the bird that "can't stand the winters!" About three thousand birds were distributed and set free,— and went down and out, just as might have been expected. During the past twenty years it is safe to say that not less than $500,000 have been expended in the northern states, and particularly in the northeastern states, in importing live quail from Kansas, the Indian Territory, Oklahoma, Texas, the Carolinas and other southern states, for restocking areas from which the northern bob white had been exterminated by foolish over-shooting! I think that fully nine-tenths of these efforts have ended in total failure. The quail could not survive in their strange environment. I cannot recall *a single instance* in which restocking northern covers with southern quail has been a success.

These is no royal road to the restoration of an exterminated bird species. Where the native seed still exists, by long labor and travail, thorough protection and a mighty long close season, it can be encouraged to *breed back and return;* but it is an evolution that can not be hurried in the least. Protect Nature, and leave the rest to her.

With mammals, the case is different. It is possible to restock depleted areas, provided Time is recognized as a dominant factor. I can cite two interesting cases by way of illustration, but this subject will form another chapter.

In the transplantation of fishes, conditions are widely different, and many notable successes have been achieved.

One of the greatest hits ever made by the United States Bureau of Fisheries in the planting of fish in new localities was the introduction of the striped bass or rock-fish (*Roccus lineatus*) of our Atlantic coast, into the coast waters of California. In 1879, 135 live fish were deposited in Karquines Strait, at Martinez, and in 1882, 300 more were planted in Suisun Bay, near the first locality chosen.

Twelve years after the first planting in San Francisco Bay, the markets of San Francisco handled 149,997 pounds of striped bass. At that time the average weight for a whole year was eleven pounds, and the average price was ten cents per pound. Fish weighing as high as forty-nine pounds have been taken, and there are reasons for the belief that eventually the fish of California will attain as great weight as those of the Atlantic and the Gulf.

The San Franisco markets now sell, annually, about one and one half million pounds of striped bass. This fish has taken its place among anglers as one of the game fishes of the California coast, and affords fine sport. Strange to say, however, it has not yet spread beyond the shores of California.

Regarding this species, the records of the United States Bureau of Fisheries are of interest. In 1897, the California markets handled 2,949,642 pounds, worth $225,527.— (American Natural History.)

Nowhere else in the world, we venture to say, were such extensive, costly and persistent efforts put forth in the transplantation of any wild foreign species as the old U. S. Fish Commission, under Prof. Spencer F. Baird, put forth in the introduction of the German carp into the fresh water ponds, lakes and rivers of the United States. It was held that because the carp could live and thrive in waters bottomed with mud, that species would be a boon to all inland regions where bodies of water, or streams, were scarce and dear. Although the carp is not the best fish in the world for the table, it seemed that the dwellers in the prairie and great plains regions would find it far better than bullheads, or no fish at all,—which are about the same thing.

By means of special fish cars, sent literally all over the United States, at a great total expense, live carp, hatched in the ponds near the Washington Monument were distributed to all applicants. The German carp spread far and wide; but to-day I think the fish has about as many enemies as friends. In some places, strong objections have been filed to the manner in which carp stir up the mud at the bottom of ponds and small lakes, greatly to the detriment of all the native fishes found therein.

CHAPTER XXXV

INTRODUCED SPECIES THAT HAVE BECOME PESTS

The man who successfully transplants or "introduces" into a new habitat any persistent species of living thing, assumes a very grave responsibility. Every introduced species is doubtful gravel until panned out. The enormous losses that have been inflicted upon the world through the perpetuation of follies with wild vertebrates and insects would, if added together, be enough to purchase a principality. The most aggravating feature of these follies in transplantation is that never yet have they been made severely punishable. We are just as careless and easygoing on this point as we were about the government of the Yellowstone Park in the days when Howell and other poachers destroyed our first national bison herd, and when caught red-handed—as Howell was, skinning seven Park bison cows,—*could not be punished for it, because there was no penalty prescribed by any law.*

To-day, there is a way in which any revengeful person could inflict enormous damage on the entire South, at no cost to himself, involve those states in enormous losses and the expenditure of vast sums of money, yet go absolutely unpunished!

THE GYPSY MOTH is a case in point. This winged calamity was imported at Malden, Massachusetts, near Boston, by a French entomologist, Mr. Leopold Trouvelot, in 1868 or '69. History records the fact that the man of science did not purposely set free the pest. He was endeavoring with live specimens to find a moth that would produce a cocoon of commercial value to America; and a sudden gust of wind blew out of his study, through an open window, his living and breeding specimens of the gypsy moth. The moth itself is not bad to look at, but its larvae is a great, overgrown brute, with an appetite like a hog. Immediately Mr. Trouvelot sought to recover his specimens, and when he failed to find them all, like a man of real honor, he notified the State authorities of the accident. Every effort was made to recover all the specimens, but enough escaped to produce progeny that soon became a scourge to the trees of Massachusetts. The method of the big, nasty-looking mottled-brown caterpillar was very simple. It devoured the entire foliage of every tree that grew in its sphere of influence.

The gypsy moth spread with alarming rapidity and persistence. In course of time the state authorities of Massachuestts were forced to begin a relentless war upon it, by poisonous sprays and by fire. It was awful! Up to this date (1912) the New England states and the United States Government service have expended in fighting this pest about $7,680,000!

The spread of this pest has been retarded, but the gypsy moth never will be wholly stamped out. To-day it exists in Rhode Island, Connecticut and New Hampshire, and it is due to reach New York at an early date. It is steadily spreading in three directions from Boston, its original point of departure, and when it strikes the State of New York, we, too, will begin to pay dearly for the Trouvelot experiment. It is said that General S. C. Lawrence, of Medford, Massachusetts, has spent $75,000 in trying to protect his trees from the ravages of this scourge.

THE RABBIT PLAGUE IN AUSTRALIA AND NEW ZEALAND.—The rabbit curse upon Australia and New Zealand is so well known as to require little comment. In this case the introduction was deliberate. In the days when the sheep industry was most prosperous, a patriotic gentleman conceived the idea that the introduction of the rabbit, and its establishment as a wild animal, would be a good thing. He reasoned that it would furnish a good food supply, that it would furnish sport, and being unable to harm any other creature of flesh and blood it was therefore harmless. Accordingly, three pairs of rabbits were imported and set free.

In a short time, the immense number of rabbits that began to overrun the country furnished food for reflection, as well as for the table. A very simple calculation brought out the startling information that, under perfectly favorable conditions, a single pair of rabbits could in three years' time produce progeny amounting to 13,718,000 individuals. Ever since that time, in discussing the rabbits of Australia it has been necessary to speak in millions.

"The inhabitants of the colony," says Dr. Richard Lydekker, "soon found that the rabbits were a plague, for they devoured the grass, which was needed for the sheep, the bark of trees, and every kind of fruit and vegetable, until the prospects of the colony became a very serious matter, and ruin seemed inevitable. In New South Wales upwards of 15,000,000 rabbits skins have been exported in a single year; while in thirteen years ending with 1889 no less than 39,000,000 were accounted for in Victoria alone.

"To prevent the increase of these rodents, the introduction of weasels, stoats, mongooses, etc., has been tried; but it has been found that those carnivores neglected the rabbits and took to feeding on poultry, and thus became as great a nuisance as the animals they were intended to destroy. The attempt to kill them off by the introduction of an epidemic disease has also failed. In order to protect such portions of the country as are still free from rabbits, fences of wire netting have been erected; one of these fences erected by the Government of Victoria extending for a distance of upwards of one hundred and fifty geographical miles. In New Zealand, where the rabbit has been introduced little more than twenty years, its increase has been so enormous, and the destruction it inflicts so great, that in some districts it has actually been a question whether the colonists should not vacate the country rather than attempt to fight against the plague. The average number of rabbit skins exported from New Zealand is now twelve millions."—(Royal Natural History.)

THE FOX PEST IN AUSTRALIA.—And now unfortunate Australia has a new pest, also acquired by importation of an alien species. It is the European fox (*Vulpes vulpes*).   The only redeeming feature about this fresh calamity is found in the fact that the species was not deliberately introduced into Australia for the benefit of the local fauna. Mr. O. W. Rosenhain, of Melbourne, informs me (1912) that about thirty years ago the Hunt Club brought to Australia about twenty foxes, for the promotion of the noble sport of fox hunting. In some untoward manner, the most of those animals escaped. They survived, multiplied, and have provided New South Wales, Victoria and South Australia with a fox pest of the first rank.

The destruction of wild bird life and poultry has become so serious that Australia now is making vigorous efforts to exterminate the pest. The government pays ten shillings bounty on fox scalps, besides which each prime fox skin is worth from four to five dollars. It is hoped that these combined values will eliminate the fox pest.

Regarding foxes in Australia, Mr. W. H. D. LeSouef has this to say in his extremely interesting and valuable book, "Wild Life in Australia," page 146:

"We found that foxes were unfortunately plentiful in this district, and in a hollow log that served to shelter some cubs were noticed the remains of ducks, fowls, rabbits, lambs, bandicoots and snakes; so they evidently vary their fare, snakes even not coming amiss. They also sneak on wild ducks that are nesting by the edge of the water among the rushes and tussocky grass, and catch quail also, especially sitting birds. *These animals are, and always will be, a great source of trouble in the thickly timbered country and stony ranges, and will gradually, like the rabbit, extend all over Australia.* They are evidently not contented with ground game only, as Mr. A. F. Kelly, of Barwonleigh, in Victoria, states: "When riding past a bull-oak tree about twenty-five feet high, with either a magpie's or crow's nest on top, I noticed the nest looked very bulky, and had something red in it. On going nearer I saw a large fox coiled up in it!"

THE MONGOOSE.—Circumstances alter cases, and a change of environment sometimes works marvelous changes in the character of an animal species.   Now, *why* should not the gray Indian mongoose (formerly called the ichneumon, (*Herpestes griseus*) destroy poultry in India, as it does elsewhere?   There is poultry in plenty to be destroyed, but "Rikki-Tikki-Tavi" elects to specialize on the killing of rats, and cobras, and other snakes.

In his own sphere of influence,—India and the orient,—the mongoose is a fairly decent citizen, and he fits into the time-worn economy of that region.   As a destroyer of the thrice-anathema domestic rat, he has no equal in the domain of flesh and blood.   His temper is so fierce that one "pet" mongoose has been known to kill a full grown male giant bustard, and put a greyhound to flight.

In an evil moment (1872) Mr. W. B. Espeut conceived the idea that it would be a good thing to introduce mongooses to the rats of Barbadoes and Jamaica that were pestering the cane-fields to an annoying extent. It was done. The mongooses attacked the rats, cleaned them out, multiplied, and then looked about for more worlds to conquer. Snakes and lizards were few; but they cheerfully killed and devoured all there were. Then, being continuously hungry, they attacked the wild birds and poultry, indiscriminately, and with their usual vigor. I have been told that in Barbadoes "they cleaned out every living thing that they could catch and kill, and then they attacked the sugar-cane." The last count in the indictment may seem hard to believe; but it is a fact that the Indian mongoose often resorts to fruit and vegetable food.

In Jamaica, at the end of the rat-killing period, the planters joyfully estimated that the labors of Herpestes had saved between £500,000 and £750,000 to the industries of that island. That was before the slaughter of wild birds and poultry began. I am told that up to date the damage done by the mongoose far exceeds the value of the benefit it once conferred, but the total has not been computed.

Up to this date, the mongoose has invaded and become a destructive pest in Barbadoes, Jamaica, Cuba, St. Vincent, St. Lucia, Trinidad, Nevis, Fiji and all the larger islands of the Hawaiian group. It would require many pages to contain a full account of each introduction, awakening, reckoning of damages and payment of bounties for destruction that the fiendish mongoose has wrought out wherever it has been introduced. The progress of the pest is everywhere the same,—sweeping destruction of rats, snakes, wild birds, small mammals, and finally poultry and vegetables.

Every country that now is without the mongoose will do well to shut and guard diligently all the doors by which it might be introduced.

Throughout its range in the western hemisphere, the mongoose is a pest; and the Biological Survey of the Department of Agriculture has done well in securing the enactment of a law peremptorily prohibiting the importation of any animals of that species into the United States or any of its colonies. The fierce temper, indomitable courage and vaulting appetite of the mongoose would make its actual introduction in any of the warm portions of the United States a horrible calamity. In the southern states, and all along the Pacific slope clear up to Seattle, it could live, thrive and multiply; and the slaughter that it could and would inflict upon our wild birds generally, especially all those that nest and live on the ground, saying nothing of the slaughter of poultry, would drive the American people crazy.

Fancy an animal with the murderous ferocity of a mink, the agility of a squirrel, the penetration of a ferret and the cunning of a rat, infesting the thickets and barnyards of this country. The mongoose can live wherever a rat can live, provided it can get a fair amount of animal food. Not for $1,000,000 could any one of the southern or Pacific states afford to have a pair of these little gray fiends imported and set free. If such a calamity ever occurs, all wheels should stop, and every habitant should turn out and hunt for the animals until they are found and pulverized. No matter if it should require a thousand men and $100,000, *find them!* If not found, the cost to the state will soon be a million a year, with no ending.

In spite of the vigilance of our custom house officers, every now and then a Hindoo from some foreign vessel sneaks into the country with a pet mongoose (and they do make great pets!) inside his shirt, or in the bottom of a bag of clothing. Of course, whenever the Department of Agriculture discovers any of these surreptitious animals, they are at once confiscated, and either killed or sent to a public zoological park for safe-keeping. In New York, the director of the Zoological Park is so genuinely concerned about the possibility of the escape of a female mongoose that he has issued two standing orders: All live mongooses offered to us shall at once be purchased, and every female animal shall immediately be chloroformed.

If *Herpestes griseus* ever breaks loose in the United States, the crime shall not justly be chargeable to us.

THE ENGLISH SPARROW.—In the United States, the English sparrow is a national sorrow, almost too great to be endured. It is a bird of plain plumage, low tastes, impudent disposition and persistent fertility. Continually does it crowd out its betters, or pugnaciously drive them away, and except on very rare occasions it eats neither insects nor weed seeds. It has no song, and in habits it is a bird of the street and the gutter. There is not one good reason why it should exist in this country. If it were out of the way, our native insect-eaters of song and beauty could return to our lawns and orchards. The English sparrow is a nuisance and a pest, and if it could be returned to the land of its nativity we would gain much.

CHAPTER XXXVI

NATIONAL AND STATE GAME PRESERVES, AND BIRD REFUGES

Out West, there is said to be a "feeling" that game and forest conservation has "gone far enough." In Montana, particularly, the National Wool-Growers' Association has for some time been firmly convinced that "the time has come to call a halt." Oh, yes! A halt on the conservation of game and forests; but not on the free grazing of sheep on the public domain. No, not even while those same sheep are busily growing wool that is so fearfully and wonderfully conserved by a sky-high tariff that the truly poor Americans are forced to wear garments made of shoddy because they cannot afford to buy clothing made of wool! (This is the testimony of a responsible clothing merchant, in 1912.)

We can readily understand the new hue and cry against conservation that the sheep men now are raising. Of course they are against all new game and forest reserves,—unless the woolly hordes are given the right to graze in them!

Many men of the Great West,—the West beyond the Great Plains,—are afflicted with a desire to do as they please with the natural resources of that region. That is the great curse that to-day rests upon our game. When the nearest game warden is 50 miles away, and big game is only 5 miles away, it is time for that game to take to the tall timber.

But in the West, and East and South, there are many men and women who believe in reasonable conservation, and deplore destruction. We have not by any means reached the point where we can think of stopping in the making of game preserves, or forest preserves. Of the former, we have scarcely begun to make. The majority of the states of our Union know of *state* game preserves only by hearsay. But the time is coming when the states will come forward, and perform the serious duty that they neglect to-day.

Let the statesmen of America be not afraid of making too many game preserves! For the next year, one per day would be none too many! Remember, that on one hand we have the Army of Destruction, and on the other the expectant millions of Posterity. No executor or trustee ever erred in safeguarding an estate too carefully. Fifty years hence, if your successors and mine find that too much land has been set aside for the good of the people, they can mighty easily restore any surplus to the public domain, and at a vastly increased valuation. Give Posterity at least *one* chance to debate the question: "Were our forefathers too liberal in the making of game and forest reserves?"

We can always carve up any useless surplus of the public domain, and restore it to commercial uses; but none of the men of to-day will live long enough to see so strange a proceeding carried into effect.

The game preserves of the United States government are so small (with the exception of the Yellowstone and Glacier Parks), that very few people ever hear of them, and fewer still know of them in detail. It seems to be quite time that they should be set forth categorically; and it is most earnestly to be hoped that this list soon will be doubled.

THE YELLOWSTONE NATIONAL PARK.—This was the first of the national parks and game preserves of the United States. Some of our game preserves are not exactly national parks, but this is both, by Act of Congress.

It is 62 miles long from north to south, 54 miles wide and contains a total area of 3,348 square miles, or 2,142,720 acres. Its western border lies in Idaho, and along its northern border a narrow strip lies in Montana. It is under the jurisdiction of the Secretary of the Interior, and it is guarded by a detachment of cavalry from the United States Army. The Superintendent is now a commissioned officer of the United States Army. The business of protecting the game is performed partly by four scouts, who are civilians specially engaged for that purpose, but the number has always been totally inadequate to the work to be performed.

At least one-half of the public interest attaching to the Yellowstone Park is based upon its wild animals. There, the average visitor sees, for the first time, wild mountain sheep, antelope, mule deer, elk, grizzly bears and white pelicans, roaming free. But for the tragedy of the Park bison herd,—slaughtered by poachers from 1890 to 1893, from 300 head down to 30—visitors would see wild bison also; but now the few wild bison remaining keep as far as possible from the routes of tourist travel. The bison were slaughtered through an inadequate protective force, and (then) utterly inadequate laws.

Lieut.-Col. L. M. Brett, U.S.A., Superintendent of the Yellowstone Park advises me (July 29, 1912) that the wild big game in the Yellowstone Park in the summer of 1912, is as shown below, based on actual counts and estimates of the Park scouts, and particularly Scout McBride. "The estimates of buffalo, elk, antelope, deer, sheep and bear are based on actual counts, or very close observations, and are pretty nearly correct." (Col. Brett).

Wild Buffalo	49
Moose	550
Elk (in summer)	35,000
Antelope	500
Mountain Sheep	210
Mule Deer	400
White-tailed Deer	100
Grizzly Bears	50
Black Bears	100

Pumas	100
Gray Wolves	none
Coyotes	400
Pelicans	1,000

The actual count of 49 wild bison in the Park, 10 of which are calves of 1912, will be to all friends of the bison a delightful surprise. Here tofore the little band had seemed to be stationary, which if true would soon mean a decline.

The history of the wild game of the Yellowstone Park is blackened by two occurrences, and one existing fact. The fact is: the town of Gardiner is situated on the northern boundary of the Park, in the State of Montana. In Gardiner there are a number of men, armed with rifles, who toward game have the gray-wolf quality of mercy.

The first stain is the massacre of the 270 wild bison for their heads and robes, already noted. The second blot is the equally savage slaughter in the early winter of 1911, by some of the people of Gardiner, reinforced by so-called sportsmen from other parts of the state, of all the park elk they could kill,—bulls, cows and calves,—because a large band wandered across the line into the shambles of Gardiner, on Buffalo Flats.

If the people of Gardiner can not refrain from slaughtering the game of the Park—the very animals annually seen by 20,000 visitors to the Park,—then it is time for the American people to summon the town of Gardiner before the bar of public opinion, to show cause why the town should not be wiped off the map.

The 35,000 elk that summer in the Park are compelled in winter to migrate to lower altitudes in order to find grass that is not under two feet of snow. In the winter of 1911–12, possibly 5,000 went south, into Jackson Hole, and 3,000 went northward into Montana. The sheep-grazing north of the Park, and the general settlement by ranchmen of Jackson Hole, have deprived the elk herds of those regions of their natural food. For several years past, up to and including the winter of 1910–11, some thousands of weak and immature elk have perished in the Jackson Hole country, from starvation and exposure. The ranchmen of that region have had terrible times,—in witnessing the sufferings of thousands of elk tamed by hunger, and begging in piteous dumb show for the small and all-too-few haystacks of the ranchmen.

The people of Jackson Hole, headed by S. N. Leek, the famous photographer and lecturer on those elk herds, have done all that they could do in the premises. The spirit manifested by them has been the exact reverse of that manifested in Gardiner. To their everlasting credit, they have kept domestic sheep out of the Jackson Valley,—by giving the owners of invading herds "hours" in which to get their sheep "all out, and over the western range."

In 1909, the State of Wyoming spent in feeding starving elk	$5,000
In 1911, the State of Wyoming spent in feeding starving elk	5,000

In 1911, the U. S. Government appropriated for feeding starving elk,
and exporting elk..$20,000
In 1912, the Camp-Fire Club of Detroit gave, for feeding hungry elk....   100
In 1910–11, about 3,000 elk perished in Jackson Hole
In 1911–12, Mr. Leek's photographs of the elk herds showed an alarming absence
of mature bulls, indicating that now the most of the breeding is done by
immature males. This means the sure deterioration of the species.

The prompt manner in which Congress responded in the late winter
of 1911 to a distress call in behalf of the starving elk, is beyond all ordinary
terms of praise. It was magnificent. In fear and trembling, Congress
was asked, through Senator Lodge, to appropriate $5,000. Congress and
Senator Lodge made it $20,000; and for the first time the legislature of
Wyoming appealed for national aid to save the joint-stock herds of Wyoming and the Yellowstone Park.

GLACIER PARK, MONTANA.—In the wild and picturesque mountains
of northwestern Montana, covering both sides of the great Continental
Divide, there is a region that has been splendidly furnished by the hand
of Nature. It is a bewildering maze of thundering peaks, plunging
valleys, evergreen forests, glistening glaciers, mirror lakes and roaring
mountain streams. Its leading citizens are white mountain goats,
mountain sheep, moose, mule deer and white-tailed deer, and among
those present are black and grizzly bears galore.

Commercially, the 1,400 square miles of Glacier Park, even with its
60 glaciers and 260 lakes, are worth exactly the price of its big trees,
and not a penny more. For mining, agriculture, horticulture and stock-
raising, it is a cipher. As a transcendant pleasure ground and recreation
wilderness for ninety millions of people, it is worth ninety millions of
dollars, and not a penny less. It is a pleasure park of which the greatest
of the nations of the earth,—whichever that may be,—might well be
overbearingly proud; and its accessibility is almost unbelievable until
seen.

This park is bounded on the south by the Great Northern Railway,
on the east by the Blackfoot Indian Reservation, on the north by Alberta
and British Columbia, and on the west by West Fork of the Flathead
River. Horizontally, it contains 1,400 square miles; but as the goat
climbs, its area is at least double that. Its valleys are filled and its lakes
are encircled by grand forests of Douglas fir, hemlock, spruce, white pine,
cedar and larch; and if ever they are destroyed by fire, it will be a national
calamity, a century long.

*So long as the American people keep out of the poorhouse, let there be no
lumber-cutting vandalism in that park, destroying the beauty of every acre
of forest that is touched by axe or saw. The greatest beauty of those forests
is the forest floor, which lumbering operations would utterly destroy.*

Never mind if there is "ripe timber" there! The American nation is
not suffering for the dollars that those lovely forest giants would fetch
by board measure. What if a tree does fall now and then from old age!
We can stand the expense. If Posterity a hundred years hence finds itself lumberless, and wishes to use those trees, then let Posterity pay the

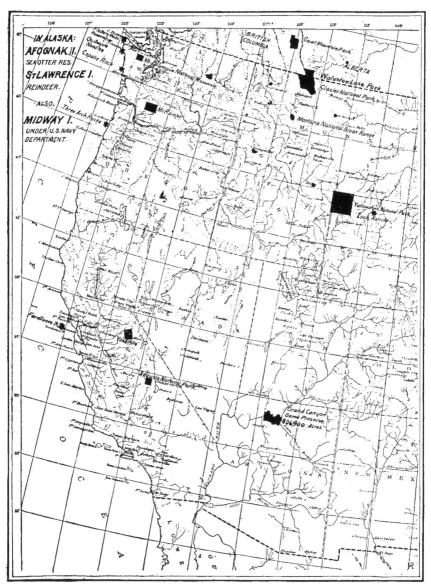

UNITED STATES NATIONAL GAME PRESERVES
and Five Pacific Bird Refuges

price, and take them. We are not suffering for them; and our duty is to save them inviolate, and hand them down as a heritage that we proudly transmit unimpaired.

The friends of wild life are particularly interested in Glacier Park as a national game reservoir, and refuge for wild life. On the north, in Alberta, it is soon to be extended by Waterton Lakes Park.

When I visited Glacier Park, in 1909, with Frederick H. Kennard and Charles H. Conrad, I procured from three intelligent guides their best estimates of the amount of big game then in the Park. The guides were Thomas H. Scott, Josiah Rogers and Walter S. Gibb.*

They compared notes, and finally agreed upon these figures:

Elk	200
Moose	2,500
Mountain Sheep	700
Mountain Goats	10,500
Grizzly Bears	1,000 to 1,500
Black Bears	2,500 to 3,000

As previously stated, one of the surprising features of this new wonder- land is its accessibility. The Great Northern lands you at Belton. A ride of three miles over a good road through a beautiful forest brings you to the foot of Lake McDonald, and in one hour more by boat you are at the hotels at the head of the lake. At that point you are within three hours' horse-back ride of Sperry Glacier and the marvelous panorama that unrolls before you from the top of Lincoln Peak. At the foot of that Peak we saw a big, wild white mountain goat: and another one watched us climb up to the Sperry Glacier.

Mt. Olympus National Monument.—For at least six years the advocates of the preservation of American wild life and forests vainly desired that the grand mountain territory around Mount Olympus, in northwestern Washington, should be established as a national forest and game preserve. In addition to the preservation of the forests, it was greatly desired that the remnant bands of Olympic wapiti (described as *Cervus roosevelti*) should be perpetuated. It now contains 1,975 speci- mens of that variety. In Congress, two determined efforts were made in behalf of the region referred to, but both were defeated by the enemies of forests and wild life.

In an auspicious moment, Dr. T. S. Palmer, Assistant Chief of the Biological Survey, Department of Agriculture, thought of a law under which it would be both proper and right to bring the desired preserve into existence. The law referred to expressly clothes the President of the United States with power to preserve any monumental feature of nature which it clearly is the duty of the state to preserve for all time from the hands of the spoilers.

With the enthusiastic approval and assistance of Representative William E. Humphrey, of Seattle, Dr. Palmer set in motion the machinery

*See *Recreation* Magazine, May, 1910, p. 213

necessary to the carrying of the matter before the President in proper form, and kept it going, with the result that on March 2, 1909, President Roosevelt affixed his signature to the document that closed the circuit.

Thus was created the Mount Olympus National Monument, preserving forever 608,640 acres of magnificent mountains, valleys, glaciers, streams and forests, and all the wild creatures living therein and thereon. The people of the state of Washington have good reason to rejoice in the fact that their most highly-prized scenic wonderland, and the last survivors of the wapiti in that state, are now preserved for all coming time. At the same time, we congratulate Dr. Palmer on the brilliant success of his initiative.

THE SUPERIOR NATIONAL GAME AND FOREST PRESERVE.—The people of Minnesota long desired that a certain great tract of wilderness in the extreme northern portion of that state, now well stocked with moose and deer, should be established as a game and forest preserve. Unfortunately, however, the national government could go no farther than to withdraw the lands (and waters) from entry, and declare it a forest reserve. At the right moment, some bright genius proposed that the national government should by executive order create a *"forest reserve,"* and then that the legislature of Minnesota should pass an act providing that every national forest of that state should also be regarded as a *state game preserve!*

Both those things were done,—almost as soon as said! Mr. Carlos Avery, the Executive Agent of the Board of Game and Fish Commissioners of Minnesota is entitled to great credit for the action of his state, and we have to thank Mr. Gifford Pinchot and President Roosevelt for the executive action that represented the first half of the effort.

The new Superior Preserve is valuable as a game and forest reserve, and nothing else. It is a wilderness of small lakes, marshes, creeks, hummocks of land, scrubby timber, and practically nothing of commercial value. But the wilderness contains many moose, and zoologically, it is for all practical purposes a moose preserve.

In it, in 1908 Mr. Avery saw fifty-one moose in three days, Mr. Fullerton saw 183 in nine days, and Mr. Fullerton estimated the total number of moose in Minnesota as a whole at 10,000 head.

In area it contains 1,420,000 acres, and the creation of this great preserve was accomplished on April 13, 1909.

THE WICHITA NATIONAL GAME PRESERVE.—In the Wichita Mountains, of southwestern Oklahoma, there is a National game preserve containing 57,120 acres. On this preserve is a fenced bison range and a herd of thirty-nine American bison which owe their existence to the initiative of the New York Zoological Society. On March 25, 1905, the Society proposed to the National Government the founding of a range and herd, on a basis that was entirely new. To the Society it seemed desirable that for the encouragement of Congress in the preservation of species that are threatened with extermination. the scientific corporations of America, and private individuals also, should do something more than to offer advice and exhortations to the government.

Accordingly, the Zoological Society offered to present to the Government, delivered on the ground in Oklahoma, a herd of fifteen pure-blood bison as the nucleus of a new national herd, provided Congress would furnish a satisfactory fenced range, and maintain the herd. The offer was at once accepted by Hon. James Wilson, Secretary of Agriculture, and the Society was invited to propose a site for a range. The Society sent a representative to the Wichita National Forest Reserve, who recommended a range, and made a report upon it, which the Society adopted.

By act of Congress the range was at once established and fenced. Its area is twelve square miles (9,760 acres). In October, 1908, the Zoological Society took from its herd in the Zoological Park nine female and six male bison, and delivered them at the bison range. There were many predictions that all those bison would die of Texas fever within one year; but the parties most interested persisted in trying conclusions with the famous tick of Texas.

Mr. Frank Rush was appointed Warden of the new National Bison Range, and his management has been so successful that only two of the bison died of the fever, the disease has been stamped out, and the herd now contains thirty-nine head. Within five years it should reach the one-hundred mark. Elk, deer and antelope have been placed in the range, and all save the antelope are doing well. The Wichita Bison Range is an unqualified success.

THE MONTANA NATIONAL BISON RANGE.—The opening of the Flathead Indian Reservation to settlement, in 1909, afforded a golden opportunity to locate in that region another national bison herd. Accordingly, in 1908, the American Bison Society formulated a plan by which the establishment of such a range and herd might be brought about. That plan was successfully carried into effect, in 1909 and '10.

The Bison Society proposed to the national government to donate a herd of at least twenty-five bison, provided Congress would purchase a range, fence it and maintain the herd. The offer was immediately accepted, and with commendable promptness Congress appropriated $40,000 with which to purchase the range, and fence it. The Bison Society examined various sites, and finally recommended what was regarded as an ideal location situated near Ravalli, Montana, north of the Jocko River and Northern Pacific Railway, and east of the Flathead River. The nearest stations are Ravalli and Dixon.

The area of the range is about twenty-nine square miles (18,521 acres) and for the purpose that it is to serve it is beautiful and perfect beyond compare. In it the bison herd requires no winter feeding whatever.

In 1910 the Bison Society raised by subscription a fund of $10,526, and with it purchased 37 very perfect pure-blood bison from the famous Conrad herd at Kalispell, 22 of which were females. One gift bison was added by Mr. and Mrs. Charles Goodnight, two were presented by the estate of Charles Conrad, and three were presented from the famous Corbin herd, at Newport, N. H., by the Blue Mountain Forest Association.

Starting with that nucleus (of 43 head) in 1910, the herd has already (1912) increased to 80 head. The herd came through the severe winter of 1911–1912 without having been fed any hay whatever, and the founders of it confidently expect to live to see it increase to one thousand head.

THE GRAND CANYON NATIONAL GAME PRESERVE of northern Arizona, embraces the entire Grand Canyon of the Colorado River, for a meandering distance of 101 miles, and adjacent territory to an extent of 2,333 square miles (1,492,928 acres). Owing to certain conditions, natural and otherwise, it is not the finest place in the world for the peaceful increase of wild game. The Canyon contains a few mountain sheep, and mule deer, but Buckskin Mountain, on the northwestern side, is reeking with mountain lions and gray wolves, and both those species should be shot out of the entire Grand Canyon National Forest. It was on Buckskin and the western wall of the Canyon itself that "Buffalo" Jones, Mr. Charles S. Bird, and their party caught nine live mountain lions, in 1909.

I regret to say that "Buffalo" Jones's catalo experiment on the Kaibab Plateau seems to have met an untimely and disappointing fate. For three years the bison and domestic cattle crossed, and produced a number of cataloes; but in 1911, practically the whole lot was wiped off the earth by cattle rustlers! Mr. Jones thinks that it was guerrillas from southern Utah who murdered his enterprise, partly for the reason that no other persons were within striking distance of the herd.

MOUNT RAINIER NATIONAL PARK.—This fine forest park is the great summer outing ground of the people of the state of Washington. Its area is 324 square miles, and as its name implies it embraces Mount Rainier. Easily accessible from Seattle and Tacoma, and fairly well—though not *adequately*—provided with roads, trails, tent camps, hotels and livery transportation, it is really the Yellowstone Park of the Northwest.

THE YOSEMITE NATIONAL PARK in California is so well known that no description of it is necessary. Its area is 1,124 square miles (719,622 acres). Its great value lies in its scenery, but along with that it is a sanctuary for such of the wild mammals and birds of California as will not wander beyond its borders to the certain death that awaits everything that may legally be killed in that state.

CRATER LAKE NATIONAL PARK.—Like all the National Parks of America generally, this one also is a game sanctuary. It is situated on the summit of the Cascade Mountains of Oregon. The wonderful Crater Lake itself is 62 miles from Klamath Falls, 83 miles from Ashland, and it is 6 miles long, 4 miles wide and 200 feet deep. This National Park was created by Act of Congress in 1902. Its area is 249 square miles (159,360 acres), and it contains Columbian black-tailed deer, black bear, the silver-gray squirrel, and many birds, chiefly members of the grouse family. Owing to its lofty elevation, there are few ducks.

THE SEQUOIA AND GENERAL GRANT NATIONAL PARKS were created for the special purpose of preserving the famous groves of "big trees," (*Sequoia gigantea*). The former is in Tulare County, the latter in Tulare and Fresno counties, California, on the western slope of the Sierra Nevadas. The area of Sequoia Park is 169,605 acres, and that of General Grant Park is 2,560 acres. They are under the control of the Interior Department. These Parks are important bird refuges, and Mr. Walter Fry, Forest Ranger, reports in them the presence of 261 species of birds, none of which may be hunted or shot. Into Sequoia Park 20 dwarf elk and 84 wild turkeys have been introduced, the former from the herd of Miller and Lux.

OTHER NATIONAL PARKS

SULLY HILLS NATIONAL PARK, at Devil's Lake (Fort Totten), North Dakota. Area 960 acres.

PLATT NATIONAL PARK, Sulphur Springs, Oklahoma; on account of many mineral springs. Area 848 acres.

MESA VERDE NATIONAL PARK, Southwestern Colorado; on account of cliff dwellings, and wonderful cliff and canyon scenery. Area, 66 square miles.

NATIONAL MONUMENTS

Under a special act of Congress, the President of the United States has the power forever to set aside from private ownership and occupation any important natural scenery, or curiosity, or wonderland, the preservation of which may fairly be regarded as of National importance, and a duty to the whole people of the United States. This is accomplished by presidential proclamation creating a "national monument."

Under the terms of this act, 28 national monuments have been created, up to 1912, of which 17 are under the jurisdiction of the Department of the Interior, and 11 are managed by the Department of Agriculture. The full list is as follows:

ALASKA:
 Sitka

ARIZONA:
 Montezuma Castle
 Petrified Forest
 Tonto
 Grand Canyon
 Tumacacori
 Navajo

CALIFORNIA:
 Lassen Peak
 Cinder Cove
 Muir Woods
 Pinnacles
 Devil's Postpile

COLORADO:
 Wheeler
 Colorado

MONTANA:
 Lewis & Clark Cavern
 Big Hole Battlefield

NEW MEXICO:
 El Morro
 Chaco Canyon
 Gila Cliff Dwellings
 Gran Quivira

OREGON:
 Oregon Caves

SOUTH DAKOTA:
 Jewel Cave

UTAH:
 Natural Bridges
 Mukuntuweap
 Rainbow Bridge

WASHINGTON:
 Mount Olympus

WYOMING:
 Devil's Tower
 Shoshone Cavern

THE NATIONAL BIRD REFUGES.—Says Dr. T. S. Palmer*: "National bird reservations have been established during the last ten years by Executive order for the purpose of affording protection to important breeding colonies of water birds, or to furnish refuges for migratory species on their northern or southern flights, or during winter. With few exceptions these reservations are either small rocky islets or tracts of marsh land of no agricultural value."

These reservations are of immense value to bird life, and their crea tion represents the highest possible wisdom in utilizing otherwise value less portions of the national domain. Dr. Palmer's alphabetical list of them is as follows, numbered in the order of their creation:

Belle Fourche, S. Dak..34	Green Bay, Wis.........56	Pelican Island, Fla...... 1
Bering Sea, Alaska.....44	Hawaiian Is., Hawaii....26	Pine Island, Fla........21
Bogoslof, Alaska... ..51	Hazy Islands, Alaska....54	Pribilof, Alaska.........50
Breton Island, La.. .. 2	Huron Islands, Mich.... 4	Quillayute N'dles, Alaska12
Bumping Lake, Wash...39	Indian Key, Fla........ 7	Rio Grande, N. Mex....32
Carlsbad, N. Mex......31	Island Bay, Fla........24	St. Lazaria, Alaska.....46
Chase Lake, N. Dak....20	Kachess, Wash........37	Salt River, Ariz. 27
Clealum, Wash... 38	Keechelus, Wash.......36	Shell Keys, La.. 9
Clear Lake, Cal... 52	Key West, Fla.........17	Shoshone, Wyo.. 42
Cold Springs, Oreg.....33	Klamath Lake, Oreg....18	Siskiwit, Mich... 5
Conconully, Wash...∴..40	Loch-Katrine, Wyo.....25	Strawberry Valley, Utah 35
Copalis Rock, Wash....13	Malheur Lake, Oreg....19	Stump Lake, N. Dak.... 3
Culebra, P. R.. 48	Matlacha Pass, Fla.....23	Tern Islands, La........ 8
Deer Flat, Idaho.. 29	Minidoka, Idaho. 43	Three Arch Rocks, Oreg.10
East Park, Cal. 28	Mosquito Inlet, Fla.....15	Tortugas Keys, Fla.....16
East Timbalier, La.....14	Niobrara, Nebr.........55	Tuxedni, Alaska........45
Farallon, Cal..........49	Palma Sola, Fla........22	Willow Creek, Mont....30
Flattery Rocks, Wash..11	Passage Key, Fla....... 6	Yukon Delta, Alaska....47
Forrester Island, Alaska.53	Pathfinder, Wyo........41	

In addition to the above, the following governmental reservations have been established for the protection of wild life: Yes Bay, Alaska, of 35,200 acres; Afognak Island, Alaska, 800 sq. miles; Midway Islands Naval Reservation, H. T.; Farallon Island, Point Reyes and Ano Nuevo Island, California; Destruction Island, Washington, and Hawaiian Islands Reservation (Laysan).

STATE GAME PRESERVES IN THE UNITED STATES

PENNSYLVANIA.—The proposition that every state, territory and province in North America and everywhere else, should establish a series of state forest and game preserves, is fairly incontestable. As a business proposition it is to-day no more a debatable question, or open to argu ment, than is the water supply or sewer system of a city. The only per feet way to conserve a water supply for a great human population is by acquiring title to water sheds, and either protecting the forests upon them, or planting forests in case none exist.

In one important matter the state of Pennsylvania has been wide awake, and in advance of the times. I will cite her system of forest

*National Reservations for the Protection of Wild Life, by T. S. Palmer, U. S. Dept. of Agriculture, Circular No. 87, Oct. 5, 1912.

reserves and game preserves as a model plan for other states to follow; and I sincerely hope that by the time the members of the present State Game Commission have passed from earth the people of Pennsylvania will have learned the value of the work they are now doing, and at least give them the appreciation that is deserved by public-spirited citizens who do large things for the People without hope of material reward. At this moment, Commissioner John M. Phillips and Dr. Joseph Kalbfus are putting their heart's blood into the business of preserving and increasing the game and other wild life of Pennsylvania; and the utter lack of appreciation that is now being shown *in some quarters* is really distressing. I refer particularly to the utterly misguided and mistaken body of hunters and anglers having headquarters at Harrisburg, whose members are grossly mislead into a wrong position by a man who seeks to secure a salaried state position through the hostile organization that he has built up, apparently for his own use. In the belief that those members generally are mislead and not mean-spirited, and that the organization contains a majority of conscientious sportsmen, I predict that ere long the evil genius of Pennsylvania game protection will be ordered to the rear, while the organization as a whole takes its place on the side of the Game Commission, where it belongs.

The game sanctuary scheme that Pennsylvania has developed is so new that as yet only a very small fraction of the people of that state either understand it, or appreciate its far-reaching importance.

To begin with, Pennsylvania has' acquired up to date about one million acres of forest lands, scattered through 26 of the 67 counties of the state. These great holdings are to be gradually increased. These wild lands, including many sterile mountain "farms" of no real value for agricultural purposes, have been acquired, first of all, for the purpose of conserving the water supply of the state; and they are called the State Forest Reserves.

Next in order, the State Game Commission has created, in favorable localities in the forest reserves, five great game preserves. The plan is decidedly novel and original, but is very simple withal. In the center of a great tract of forest reserve, a specially desirable tract has been chosen, and its boundaries marked out by the stringing of a single heavy fence wire, surrounding the entire selection. The area within that boundary wire is an absolute sanctuary for all wild creatures save those that prey upon game, and in it no man may hunt anything, nor fire a gun. The boundary wire is by no means a fence, for it keeps nothing out nor in.

Outside of the wire and the sanctuary, men may hunt in the open season, but at the wire every chase must end. If the hunted deer knows enough to flee to the sanctuary when attacked, so much the better for the deer. The tide of wild life ebbs and flows under the wire, and beyond a doubt the deer and grouse will quickly find that within it lies absolute safety. There the breeding and rearing of young may go on undisturbed.

In view of the fact that hunting may go on in the forest reserve areas surrounding these sanctuaries, no intelligent sportsman needs to be told that in a few years all such regions will be teeming with deer, grouse and other game. Where there is one deer to-day there will be twenty ten years hence,—because the law of Pennsylvania forbids the killing of does; and then there will be twenty times the legitimate hunting that there is to-day. For example, the Clinton County Game Preserve of 3,200 acres is surrounded by 128,000 acres of forest reserve, which form legitimate hunting grounds for the game bred in the sanctuary reservoir. In Clearfield County the game sanctuary is surrounded by 47,000 acres of Forest Reserve.

The *game* preserves created in Pennsylvania up to date are as follows:

In Clinton County	3,200 acres
In Clearfield County	3,200 acres.
In Franklin County	3,200 acres
In Perry County	3,200 acres
In Westmoreland County	2,500 acres

It is the deliberate intention of the Game Commission to increase these game preserves until there is at least one in each county.

It is the policy of the Commission to clear out of the game sanctuaries all the mammals and birds that destroy wild life, such as foxes, mink, weasels, skunks and destructive hawks and owls. This is accomplished partly by buying old horses, killing them in the preserves and poisoning them thoroughly with strychnine.

Each preserve now contains a nucleus herd of white-tailed deer, some of them imported from northern Michigan. Ruffed grouse are breeding rapidly, and in the Clearfield County Preserve there are said to be at least three thousand. The Game Commission considers it a patriotic duty to preserve the wild turkey, ruffed grouse and quail, rather than have those species replaced at great expense by species imported from the old world. In their work for the protection, preservation and increase of the game of Pennsylvania—partly for the purpose of providing legitimate hunting for the mechanic as well as the millionaire,—the State Game Commissioners are putting a great amount of thought and labor, and whenever their efforts are criticized, their motives impunged or their honesty questioned by men who are not worthy to unlace their shoes, it makes me tired and angry.

NEW YORK:

THE ADIRONDACK STATE PARK.—With wise and commendable fore thought, the state of New York has preserved in the Adirondack wilderness, familiarly known as "the North Woods," a magnificent forest domain forever dedicated to campers, outdoorsmen and hunters. At present (1912) it contains 2,031 square miles (1,300,000 acres) of forest-clad hills, valleys and mountains, adorned by countless lakes and streams. By some persons it has been believed that in the State's forests the cutting and sale of large trees would be justifiable business, and agreeable to the public; but it has been demonstrated that this is not the case. The people of the state firmly object to the havoc that is *unavoidably* wrought by logging operations in beautiful forests. The state does not yet need any of the money that could be derived from such operations. The chief anxiety of the public is that hereafter forest fires shall be prevented, no matter what fire protection may cost! The burning of coal on any railway operated through the Adirondacks should be made a penal offense.

MONTANA·

In 1911 Governor Norris, Senator Cone and the legislature of Montana, at the solicitation of W. R. Felton, L. A. Huffman and others, created the SNOW CREEK GAME PRESERVE, fronting for ten miles on the Missouri River, in the northern side of Dawson County. It is a magnificent tract of bad-lands, very deeply eroded and carved, and highly picturesque. The new state preserve contains 96 square miles, but there is so little grazing ground for antelope and bison it is absolutely imperative that a narrow strip of level grass land should be added along the southern border. This proposed addition is being fiercely resisted, by an organized movement of the sheep owners of Montana (the National Wool Growers' Association), who naturally want the public domain for the free grazing of their tariff-protected sheep-herds. It remains to be seen whether the *three* sheep men south of the preserve,—the only men who really are affected,—will be able to thwart a movement that has for its object the development of a very good game preserve for the benefit of the ninety millions of the general American public. The range is necessary to contain representatives of the big game of the plains that has been so ruthlessly swept away, and particularly the vanishing prong-horned antelope, once very numerous in that region.

In order to relieve the sheep men of all trouble on account of that preserve, the area should be enlarged to the right dimensions and made a national preserve. A bill for that purpose (Senate 5,286) is now before the Senate, in Senator McLean's Committee, and *help is needed* to overcome the active hostility of the sheep men, *who vow that it never shall be passed!* All persons who read this are invited to take this matter up with their Senators and Representatives, without a moment's delay.

WYOMING:

THE TETON STATE PRESERVE.—One of the largest and most important state game preserves thus far established by any of our states is that which was created by Wyoming, in 1904. It is situated along the south of, and fully adjoining, the Yellowstone Park, and its area is 900 square miles (576,000 acres). Its special purpose is to supplement for the elk herds and other big game the protection from killing that previously had been found in the Yellowstone Park alone. The State Preserve is an admirable half-way house for the migrating herds when they leave the National Park to seek their regular winter ranges in and around the Jackson Valley.

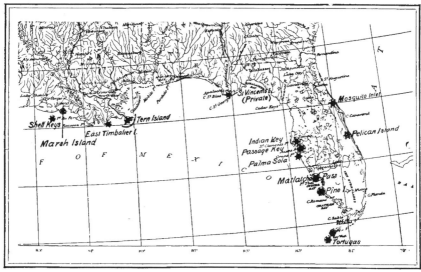

BIRD RESERVATIONS ON THE GULF COAST AND FLORIDA

In 1909, Wyoming established the Big Horn Game Preserve, in the mountain range of that name. Into it 25 elk were taken from Jackson Hole, and set free, in 1910, at the expense of the Sheridan County Sportsmen's Club.

LOUISIANA:

Great developments for the preservation of wild life have recently been witnessed in Louisiana, all due to the initiative and persistent activities of two men, Edward A. McIlhenny, of Avery Island, La., and Charles Willis Ward, of Michigan, lumberman and horticulturist.

THE LOUISIANA STATE WILD FOWL REFUGE on Vermillion Bay, has an area of 13,000 acres. It was presented to the state by Messrs. Ward and McIlhenny, and formally accepted and protected. It contains a great area of fresh-water ponds and marshy meadows, wherein grows an abundant supply of food for wild fowl. It contains several miles of gravel beach, which during the winter season is visited by thousands of wild geese in quest of their indispensable supply of gravel. The ponds within its borders furnish feeding-grounds for canvasback ducks, redhead, mallard, blackhead and various species of wild geese.

OTHER STATE GAME PRESERVES

	Acres
IDAHO.—Payette River Game Preserve	230,000
CALIFORNIA.—Pinnacles Game Preserve	2,080
WYOMING.—Big Horn Mountains Game Preserve.	
MONTANA.—Yellowstone Game Preserve.	
Pryor Mountain Game Preserve	

CHAPTER XXXVII

GAME PRESERVES AND GAME LAWS IN CANADA

As now set forth on the map of North America, Canada is a vast country. We must no longer think of Ontario and Quebec as "Canada West" and "Canada East," because the new assistant-nation owns and rules everything from Labrador to British Columbia, and all the northern mainland save Alaska.

Although the fauna of Canada is strictly boreal, it is sufficiently dispersed and diversified to demand wise legislation, and plenty of it. For a nation with an outfit of provinces so new, Canada already is well advanced in the matter of game laws and game preserves, and in some respects she has set the pace for her southern neighbors. For example, in New Brunswick we see the lordly moose successfully hunted for sport, not only without being exterminated but actually on a basis that permits it to increase in number. In Nova Scotia we see a law in force *which successfully prohibits the waste of moose meat*, a loss that characterizes moose hunting everywhere else throughout the range of that animal. All over southern Canada the use of automatic shotguns in hunting is strictly prohibited.

On the other hand, the laws of the Canadians are weak in not preventing .the sale of all wild game and the killing of antelope. In the matter of game-selling, there are far too many open doors, and a sweeping reform is very necessary.

Speaking generally, and with application from Labrador to British Columbia, the American process of game extermination according to law is vigorously and successfully being pursued by the people of Canada. The open seasons are too long, and the bag limits are too generous to the gunners. As it is elsewhere, the bag-limit laws on birds are a farce, because it is impossible to enforce them, save on every tenth man. For example, in his admirable "Final Report of the Ontario Game and Fisheries Commission" (1912), Commissioner Kelly Evans says:

"The prairie chicken, which formerly was comparatively plentiful throughout the greater portion of the Rainy River District, has now become practically extinct in that region. Various causes have been assigned for this, but it would seem, as usual, to have been mainly the fault of indiscriminate and excessive slaughter." (Page 226.)

Like the United States, the various portions of Canada have their various local troubles in wild-life protection. I think the greatest practical difficulties, and the most real opposition to adequate measures, is found in the Provinces of Quebec and Ontario. Is it because the French-descended population is impatient of real restraint, and objects to measures that are drastic, even though they are necessary? In Ontario, Commissioner Evans has been splendidly supported by the Government, and by all the real sportsmen of that province; but the gunners and guerrillas of destruction have successfully postponed several of the reforms that he has advocated, and which should have been carried into effect.

So far as *public* moral support for game protection is concerned I think that the prairie and mountain provinces have the best of it. In Manitoba, Saskatchewan, Alberta, Athabasca and British Columbia, the spirit of the people is mainly correct, and the chief thing that seems to be lacking is a Kelly Evans in each of those provinces to urge public sentiment into strong action. For example, why should Alberta still permit the hunting and killing of prong-horned antelope, when it is so well known that that species is vanishing like a mist before the morning sun? I think it is because no one seems to have risen up as G. O. Shields did in the United States, to make a big fuss about it, and demand a reform. At any rate, all the provinces of Canada that still possess antelope should *immediately pass laws giving that species absolute close seasons for ten years.* Why neglect it longer, when such neglect is now so very wrong? Whether this is done or not, I sincerely hope that hereafter no true American sportsman, will be guilty of killing one of the vanishing antelope of Canada, even though "the law doth give it."

The Game Preserves of Canada

In the creation of National parks and game preserves, some of the provinces of the Canadian nation have displayed a degree of foresight and enterprise that merits sincere admiration. While in different provinces the exact status of these establishments may vary somewhat, the main purpose of each is the same,—the preservation of the forests and the wild life. In all of them a regulated amount of fishing is permitted, and in some the taking of fur-bearing animals is permitted; but I believe in all the birds and furless mammals are strictly protected. In some parks the carrying of firearms still is permitted, but that privilege is quite out of harmony with the spirit and purposes of a game preserve, and should be abolished. If it is necessary to carry firearms through a preserve, as often happens in the Yellowstone Park, it can be done under seals that are affixed by duly appointed officers· and thus will temptation be kept out of the way of sinners.

Up to this date I never have seen a publication which set forth in one place even so much as an annotated list of the game preserves of the various provinces of Canada, and at present exact information regarding them is rather difficult to obtain. It seems that an adequate governmental publication on this subject is now due, and overdue.

ONTARIO.—"At the present time," says Commissioner Evans in his "Final Report," "the Algonquin National Park is the only actual game preserve in the Province, being in fact a game reserve and not a forest reserve; but in the past at least a measure of protection would seem to have been afforded the game in most of the [forest] reserves, owing to the fact that the carrying of firearms therein has been discouraged, and it would appear to require but the passing of an Order-in-Council to render the carrying of firearms in all reserves illegal. It is sincerely to be hoped that not only will such action be taken without delay, but also that all the forest reserves will be declared game reserves in the strictest sense."

To this sentiment all friends of wild life will join a fervent wish for its realization. As conditions are to-day, it is *impossible to have too many game reserves!* There is everything to gain and nothing to lose by making every national forest and forest reserve on the whole continent of North America a game preserve in the strictest sense, and we hope to live to see that end accomplished, both in the United States and Canada.

The Algonquin National Park is situated in the Parry Sound region, just above the Muskoka Lakes, and it has an area of 1,930 square miles. It is well stocked with moose, caribou, white-tailed deer, black bear and beaver. During the period of protection the beaver have increased so greatly that about 1,000 were trapped last year for the market, by officers of the government; and about 25 were sold to zoological gardens and parks, at $25 each.

The Quetico Forest Reserve, area 1,560 square miles, was created as the Canadian complement of the Minnesota National Forest and Game Preserve. The two join on the international boundary, and each helps to protect the other. Both are well stocked with moose, and will render valuable service in the preservation of a mid-continental contingent of that species.

ALBERTA.—In the making of game preserves the province of Alberta has been splendidly progressive and liberal. The total result is fairly beyond the reach of ordinary words of praise. It sets a pace that should result in wide-spread benefits to the wild life of North America. In it there is nothing faint-hearted. It should make some of our States think seriously regarding their own shortcomings in this particular field of endeavor.

ALBERTA'S NATIONAL PARKS

	Acres	Sq. miles
Rocky Mountains Park	2,764,800	4,320
Yoho Park	1,799,680	2,812
Glacier Park	1,474,560	2,304
Buffalo Park	384,000	600
Elk Island Park	40,000	62
Jasper Park	3,488,000	5,450
Waterton Lakes Park	34,560	54
	9,985,600	15,602

The Rocky Mountains Park is near Banff. The *Yoho* and *Glacier Parks* are near Field. The *Buffalo Park* is near Wainwright, on the plains, and it was created and fenced especially as a home for the herd of American bison that was purchased in Montana in 1909. It now contains 1,052 head of bison, 20 moose, 35 deer, 7 elk, and 6 antelope.

The Elk Island Park is near Fort Saskatchewan and Lamont, and at this date (1912) it contains 53 bison, 28 elk, 30 deer and 5 moose. The bison subsist entirely by grazing, and upon hay cut within the Park.

Jasper Park, established in 1908, is on the Athabasca River and the Grand Trunk Pacific Railway, near Strathcona. Sixty miles of the railway line lie within the Park. Scenically, Jasper Park is a rival of Rocky Mountains Park, and undoubtedly possesses great attractions for travellers who appreciate the beauties and grandeur of Nature as expressed in mountains, valleys, lakes and streams.

Waterton Lakes Park is situated in the extreme southwestern corner of Alberta, in the Rocky Mountains surrounding the Waterton Lakes. At present it is nine miles long from north to south and six miles wide, with its southern end resting on the international boundary, and adjoining our Glacier Park. It is the home of a few bands of mountain sheep that carry very large horns. Through the initiative of Frederick K. Vreeland, the Camp-Fire Club of America two years ago represented to the Government of Alberta the great desirability of enlarging this preserve, toward the north and west, the better to protect the mountain sheep and other big game of that region. The suggestion was received in a friendly spirit, and there is good reason to hope that at an early date the enlargement will be made.

BRITISH COLUMBIA.—This province has made an excellent beginning in the creation of game preserves. The first agitation on that subject was begun in 1906, by two sportsmen whose names in connection with it have long since been forgotten. On November 15, 1908, the Legislative Council of British Columbia issued a proclamation that created a very fine game preserve in the East Kootenai District, between the Elk and Bull Rivers and northwestward thereof to the White River country. By an unfortunate oversight, the new preserve never has been officially named, but we may designate it here as

The Elk River Game Preserve.—This preserve has a total area of about 450 square miles, and includes a fine tract of mountains, valleys, lakes and streams. It contained in 1908 about 1,000 mountain goats, 200 sheep, a few elk and deer, and about 50 grizzly bears. All these have notably increased during the period of absolute protection that they have enjoyed. It is probable that this preserve contains more white mountain goats than any other preserve that thus far has been made. It was in this region that Mr. John M. Phillips and Prof. Henry Fairfield Osborne made the first mountain goat photographs ever made at close range. It is to be hoped that the protection of this preserve, both as to its wild life and its timber, will be made perpetual.

Frazer River Preserve.—Next after the above there was created in British Columbia a game preserve covering a large portion of the mountain territory that rises between the North and South Forks of the Fraser River. It is about 75 miles long by 30 miles wide and contains

about 2,250 square miles. Concerning its character and wild-life population we have no details.

Yalakom Game Preserve.—On the north side of Bridge River (a
western tributary of the Fraser), about twenty miles above Lilloet,
there has been established a game preserve having an area of about
215 square miles.

MANITOBA.—In the making of game preserves, Manitoba has made
an excellent beginning. It is good to see from Duck Mountain in the
north to Turtle Mountain in the south a chain of four liberal preserves,
each one protected in unmistakable terms as follows: "Carrying firearms, hunting or trapping strictly prohibited within this area."

The lake regions of Manitoba, Saskatchewan and Alberta form what
is probably the most important wild-fowl breeding-ground in North
America. To a great extent it rests with those provinces to say
whether the central United States shall have any ducks and geese, or
not! *It is high time that an international treaty should be made between
the United States, Canada and Mexico for the 'federal protection of all
migratory birds.*

These preserves are of course intended to conserve wild-fowl, shorebirds, grouse and all other birds, as well as big game. Thanks to the
cooperation of Mr. J. M. Macoun, of the Canadian Geological Survey,
I am able to offer the following:

LIST OF MANITOBA'S GAME PRESERVES

DUCK MOUNTAIN PRESERVE............	324 sq. miles,	207,360 acres.
RIDING MOUNTAIN PRESERVE...........	360 "	" 230,000 "
SPRUCE WOODS PRESERVE..............	64 "	" 40,960 "
TURTLE MOUNTAIN PRESERVE..........	100 "	" 64,000 "
	848 "	" 542,320 "

Manitoba is to be congratulated on this record.

QUEBEC.—This province has created two huge game preserves, well
worthy of the fauna that they are intended to conserve when all hunt
ing in them is prohibited!

The Laurentides National Park is second in area of all the national
parks of Canada, being surpassed only by the Rocky Mountains Park of
British Columbia. Its area is 3565 square miles, or 2,281,600 acres.
It occupies the entire central portion of the great area surrounded by
Lake St. John, the Saguenay River, the wide portion of the St. Lawrence, and the St. Maurice River on the west. Its southern boundary
is in several places only 16 miles from the St. Lawrence, while its most
northern angle is within 13 miles of Lake St. John. Its greatest width
from east to west is 71 miles, and its greatest length from north to south
is 79 miles. It covers a huge watershed in which over a dozen large
rivers and many small ones have their sources. It is indeed a forest
primeval. The rivers are well stocked with fish, and the big game in-

eludes moose, woodland caribou, black bear, lynx, beaver, marten, fisher, mink, fox, and—sad to say—the gray wolf. The caribou live in rather small bands, from 10 up to 100.

Unfortunately, hunting under license is permitted in the Laurentian National Park, and therefore it is by no means a *real* game preserve! It is a near-preserve.

The Gaspesian Forest, Fish and Game Preserve, created in 1906, is in "the Gaspe country," and it has an area of 2500 square miles situated in the eastern Quebec counties of Gaspe and Matane.

The Connaught National Park, to be named in honor of H. R. H. the Duke of Connaught, has been proposed by Mr. J. M. Macoun, of the Canadian Geological Survey. The general location chosen is the mountains and forested territory north of Ottawa and the Ottawa River, within easy access from the Canadian capitol. On the map the location recommended lies between the Gatineau River on the east and Wolf Lake on the west. The proposal is meeting with much popular favor, and it is extremely probable that it will be carried into effect at an early date.

LABRADOR.—During the past two years Lieut.-Col. William Wood has strongly advocated the making of game preserves in Labrador, that will not only tend to preserve the scanty fauna of that region from extinction but will also aid in bringing it back. While Col. Wood's very energetic and praiseworthy campaign has not yet been crowned with success, undoubtedly it will be successful in the near future, because ultimately such causes always win their objects, provided they are prosecuted with the firm and unflagging persistence which has characterized this particular campaign. We congratulate Col. Wood on the success that he *will achieve* in the near future!

Game Laws of the Canadian Provinces

ALBERTA.—The worst feature of the Alberta laws is the annual open season on antelope, two of which may be killed under each license. This is *entirely wrong*, and a perpetual close season should at once be enacted. Duck shooting in August is wrong, and the season should not open until September. It is not right that duck-killing should be made so easy and so fearfully prolonged that extermination is certain. *All killing of cranes and shore birds should be absolutely stopped, for five years.* No wheat-producing province can afford the expense to the wheat crops of the slaughter of shore birds, *thirty species* of which are great crop-protectors.

The bag limit of two sheep is too high, by 50 per cent. It should immediately be cut down to one sheep, before sheep hunting in Alberta becomes a lost art. *Sheep hunting should not be encouraged*—quite the reverse! There are already too many sheep-crazy sportsmen. The bag limit on grouse and ptarmigan of 20 per day or 200 in a season is simply legalized slaughter, no more and no less, and if it is continued, a grouseless province will be the quick result. The birds are not sufficiently numerous to withstand the guns on that basis. Alberta should be wiser than the states below the international boundary that are annihilating their remnants of birds as fast as they can be found.

BRITISH COLUMBIA.—We note with much satisfaction that the Provincial Game Warden, Mr. A. Bryan Williams, has been allowed $37,000 for the pay of game wardens, and $28,000 for the destruction of wolves, coyotes, pumas and other game-destroying animals. During the past two years the following game-destroyers were killed, and bounties were paid upon them:

	1909–10	1910–11
Wolves	655	518
Coyotes	1,454	3,653
Cougars	382	277
Horned Owls	854	2,285
Golden Eagles	29	73
	3,374	6,806

"Now," says Warden Williams in his excellent annual report for 1911, "in these two years a total of 2,896 wolves and cougars and 5,141 coyotes were destroyed, as well as a number of others poisoned and not recovered for the bounty. Allowing fifty head for each wolf and cougar and ten for each coyote, by their bounties alone 196,210 head of game and domestic animals were saved. Is it any wonder that deer are increasing almost everywhere?"

The great horned owl has been and still is a great scourge to the upland game birds, partly because when game is abundant "they become fastidious, and eat only the brains of their prey." The destruction of 3,139 of them on the Lower Mainland during the last two years has made these owls sing very small, and says the warden, "Is it any wonder that grouse are again increasing?"

I have discussed with the Provincial Game Warden the advisability of putting a limit of one on the grizzly bear, but Mr. Williams advances good reasons for the opinion that it would be impracticable to do so at present. I am quite sure, however, that the time has already arrived when a limit of one is necessary. During the present year three of my friends who went hunting in British Columbia, *each killed 3 grizzly bears!* Hereafter I will "locate" no more bear hunters in that country until the bag limit is reduced to one grizzly per year. Since 1905 the trapping of bears south of the main line of the Canadian Pacific Railway has been stopped; and an excellent move too. A Rocky Mountain without a grizzly bear is like a tissue-paper rose.

The bag limit on the big game of British Columbia is at least twice too liberal,—five deer, two elk, two moose (one in Kootenay County), three caribou and three goats. There is no necessity for such wasteful liberality. Few sportsmen go to British Columbia for the sake of a large lot of animals. I know many men who have been there to hunt, and the great majority cared more for the scenery and the wild romance of camping out in ground mountains than for blood and trophies.

MANITOBA.—What are we to think of a "bag limit" of fifty ducks per day in October and November? A "limit" indeed! Evidently, Manitoba is tired of having ducks, ruffed grouse, pinnated and other grouse pestering her farmers and laborers. While assuming to fix bag limits that will be of some benefit to those species, the limit is distinctly off, and nothing short of a quick and drastic reform will save a remnant that will remain visible to the naked eye.

NEW BRUNSWICK.—This is the banner province in the protection of moose, caribou and deer, even while permitting them to be shot for sport. Of course, only males are killed, and I am assured by competent judges that thus far the killing of the finest and largest male moose has had no bad effect upon the stature or antlers of the species as a whole.

NOVA SCOTIA.—If there is anything wrong with the game laws of Nova Scotia, it lies in the wide-open sale of moose meat and all kinds of feathered game during the open season. If that province were more heavily populated, it would mean a great destruction of game. Even with conditions as they are, the sale permitted is entirely wrong, and against the best interests of 97 per cent of the people.

As previously mentioned, the law against the waste of moose meat is both novel and admirable. The saving of any considerable portion of the flesh of a full-grown bull moose, along with its head, is a large order; but it is right. The degree of accountability to which guides are held for the doings of the men whom they pilot into the woods is entirely commendable, and worthy of imitation. If a sportsman or gunner does the wrong thing, the guide loses his license.

SASKATCHEWAN.—This is another of the too-liberal provinces having no real surplus of big game with which to sustain for any length of time an excess of generosity. I am told that in this province there is now a great deal of open country around each wild animal. And yet, it cheerfully offers two moose, two elk, two caribou and two *antelope* per season to each licensed gunner or sportsman. The limit is too generous by half. Why throw away an extra $250 worth of game with each license? That is precisely what the people of Saskatchewan are doing to-day.

And that antelope-killing! It should be stopped at once, and for ten years.

YUKON.—This province permits the sale of all the finest and best wild game within its borders,—moose, elk, caribou, *bison*, musk-ox, sheep and goats! The flesh of all these may be sold during the open season, and for sixty days thereafter. Of the species named above, the barren ground caribou is the only one regarding which we need not worry; because that species still exists in millions. The Osborn caribou (*Rangifer osborni*), can be exterminated in our own times, because it is nowhere really numerous, and it inhabits exposed situations.

CHAPTER XXXVIII

PRIVATE GAME PRESERVES

Primarily, in the early days of the Man-on-Horseback, the self-elected and predatory lords of creation evolved the private game preserve as a scheme for preventing other fellows from shooting, and for keeping the game sacred to slaughter by themselves. The idea of conserving the game was a fourth-rate consideration, the first being the estoppel of the other man. The old-world owner of a game preserve delights in the annual killing of the surplus game, and we have even heard it whispered that in the Dark Ages there were kings who enjoyed the wholesale slaughter of deer, wild boar, pheasants and grouse. If we may accept as true the history of sport in Europe, there have been men who have loved slaughter with a genuine blood-lust that is quite foreign to the real nature-loving sportsman.

In America, the impulse is different. Here, there is raging a genuine fever for private game preserves. Some of those already existing are of fine proportions, and cost fortunes to create. Every true sportsman who is rich enough to own a private game preserve, sooner or later acquires one. You will find them scattered throughout the temperate zone of North America from the Bay of Fundy to San Diego. I have had invitations to visit preserves in an unbroken chain from the farthest corner of Quebec to the Pacific Coast, and from Grand Island, Lake Superior to the Gulf of Mexico. It was not necessarily to hunt, and kill something, but to *see* the game, and the beauties of nature.

The wealthy American and Canadian joyously buys a tract of wilderness, fences it, stocks it with game both great and small, and provides game keepers for all the year round. At first he has an idea that he will "hunt" therein, and that his guests will hunt also, and actually kill game. In a mild way, this fiction sometimes is maintained for years. The owner may each year shoot two or three head of his surplus big game, and his tenderfoot guests who don't know what real hunting is may also kill something, each year. But in most of the American preserves with which I am well acquainted, the gentlemanly "sport" of "hunting big game" is almost a joke. The trouble is, usually, the owner becomes so attached to his big game, and admires it so sincerely, he has not the heart to kill it himself; and he finds no joy whatever in seeing it shot down by others!

In this country the slaughter of game for the market is not considered a gentlemanly pastime, even though there is a surplus of preserve-bred game that must be reduced. To the average American, the slaughter of half-tame elk, deer and birds that have been bred in a preserve does not appeal in the least. He knows that in the protection of a preserve, the wild creatures lose much of their fear of man, and become easy marks; and shall a real sportsman go out with a gun and a bushel of cartridges, on a pony, and without warning betray the confidence of the wild in terms of fire and blood? Others may do it if they like; but as a rule that is not what an American calls "sport." One wide-awake and well-armed grizzly bear or mountain sheep outwitted on a mountain-side is worth more as a sporting proposition than a quarter of a mile of deer carcasses laid out side by side on a nice park lawn to be photographed as "one day's kill."

In America, the shooting of driven game is something of which we know little save by hearsay. In Europe, it is practiced on everything from Scotch grouse to Italian ibex. The German Crown Prince, in his fascinating little volume "From My Hunting Day-Book," very neatly fixes the value of such shooting, as a real sportsman's proposition, in the following sentence:

"The shooting of driven game is merely a question of marksmanship, and is after all more in the nature of a shooting exercise than sport."

I have seen some shooting in preserves that was too tame to be called sport; but on the other hand I can testify that in grouse shooting as it is done behind the dogs on Mr. Carnegie's moor at Skibo, it is sport in which the hunter earns every grouse that falls to his gun. At the same time, also, I believe that the shooting of madly running ibex, as it is done by the King of Italy in his three mountain preserves, is sufficiently difficult to put the best big-game hunter to the test. There are times when shooting driven game calls for far more dexterity with the rifle than is ordinarily demanded in the still-hunt.

In America, as in England and on the Continent of Europe, private game preserves are so numerous it is impossible to mention more than a very few of them, unless one devotes a volume to the subject. Probably there are more than five hundred, and no list of them is "up to date" for more than one day, because the number is constantly increasing. I make no pretense even of possessing a list of those in America, and I mention only a few of those with which I am best acquainted, by way of illustration.

One of the earliest and the most celebrated deer parks of the United States was that of Hon. John Dean Caton, of two hundred acres, located near Ottawa, Ill., established about 1859. It was the experiments and observations made in that park that yielded Judge Caton's justly famous book on "The Antelope and Deer of America."

The first game preserve established by an incorporated club was "Blooming Grove Park," of one thousand acres, in Pennsylvania, where great success has been attained in the breeding and rearing of white-tailed deer.

In the eastern United States the most widely-known game preserve is Blue Mountain Forest Park, near Newport, New Hampshire. It was founded in 1885, by the late Austin Corbin, and has been loyally and diligently maintained by Austin Corbin, Jr., George S. Edgell and the other members of the Corbin family. Ownership is vested in the Blue Mountain Forest Association. The area of the preserve is 27,000 acres, and besides embracing much fine forest on Croydon Mountain, it also contains many converted farms whose meadow lands afford good grazing.

This preserve contains a large herd of bison (86 head), elk, white-tailed deer, wild boar and much smaller game. The annual surplus of bison and other large game is regularly sold and distributed throughout the world for the stocking of other parks and zoological gardens. Each year a few surplus deer are quietly killed for the Boston market, but a far greater number are sold alive, at from $25 to $30 each in carload lots.

In the Adirondacks of northern New York, there are a great many private game preserves. Dr. T. S. Palmer, in his pamphlet on "Private Game Preserves" (Department of Agriculture) places the number at 60, and their total area at 791,208 acres. Some of them have caused much irritation among some of the hunting, fishing and trapping residents of the Adirondack region. They seem to resent the idea of the exclusive ownership of lands that are good hunting-grounds. This view of property rights has caused much trouble and some bloodshed, two persons having been killed for presuming to assert exclusive rights in large tracts of wilderness property.

"In the upland preserve under private ownership," says Dr. Palmer, "may be found one of the most important factors in the maintenance of the future supply of game and game birds. Nearly all such preserves are maintained for the propagation of deer, quail, grouse, or pheasants. They vary widely in area, character, and purpose, and embrace some of the largest game refuges in the country. Some of the preserves in North Carolina cover from 15,000 to 30,000 acres; several in South Carolina exceed 60,000 acres in extent." The Megantic Club's northern preserve, on the boundary between Quebec and Maine, embraces nearly 200 square miles, or upward of 125,000 acres.

Comparatively few of the larger preserves are enclosed, and on such grounds, hunting becomes sport quite as genuine as it is in regions open to free hunting. In some instances part of the tract is fenced, while large unenclosed areas are protected by being posted. The character of their tenure varies also. Some are owned in fee simple; others, particularly the larger ones, are leased, or else comprise merely the shooting rights on the land. In both size and tenure, the upland preserves of the United States are comparable with the grouse moors and large deer forests of Scotland.

Of the game preserves in the South, I know one that is quite ideal. It is St. Vincent Island, near Apalachicola, Florida, in the northern edge of the Gulf of Mexico. It was purchased in 1909 by Dr. Ray V. Pierce, and his guests kill perhaps one hundred ducks each year out of the thousands that flock to the ten big ponds that occupy the eastern third of the island. Into those ponds much good duck food has been intro-

MAP OF MARSH ISLAND AND ADJACENT WILD-FOWL PRESERVES

duced,—*Potamogeton pectinatus* and *perfoliatus.* The area of the island
is twenty square miles. Besides being a great winter resort for ducks,
its sandy, pine-covered ridges and jungles of palmeъto and live oak
afford fine haunts and feeding grounds for deer. Those jungles contain
two species of white-tailed deer (*Odocoileus louisiana* and *osceola*), and
Dr. Pierce has introduced the Indian sambar deer and Japanese sika deer
(*Cervus sika*), both of which are doing well. We are watching the progress of those big sambar deer with very keen interest, and it is to be
recorded that already that species has crossed with the Louisiana white-
tailed deer.

During the autumn of 1912, public attention in the United States
was for a time focused on the purchase of Marsh Island, Louisiana, by
Mrs. Russell Sage, and its permanent dedication to the cause of wild-
life protection. This delightful event has brought into notice the
Louisiana State Game Preserve of 13,000 acres near Marsh Island,
and its hinterland (and water) of 11,000 acres adjoining, which constitutes the Ward-McIlhenny Wild Fowl Preserve. These three great
preserves taken together as they lie form a wild-fowl sanctuary of great
size, and of great value to the whole Mississippi Valley. Now that all
duck-shooting therein has been stopped, it is safe to predict that they
shortly will be inhabited by a wild-fowl population that will really stagger
the imagination.

DUCK-SHOOTING "PRESERVES."—A ducking "preserve" is a large
tract of land and water owned by a few individuals, or a club, for the
purpose of preserving exclusively for themselves and their friends the
best possible opportunities for killing large numbers of ducks and

geese without interference. In no sense whatever are they intended to preserve or increase the supply of wild fowl. The real object of their existence is duck and goose slaughter. For example, the worst goose-slaughter story on record comes to us from the grounds of the Glenn County Club in California, whereon, as stated elsewhere, two men armed with automatic shotguns killed 218 geese in one hour, and bagged a total of 452 in one day.

I shall not attempt to give any list of the so-called ducking "pre-serves." The word "preserve," when applied to them, is a misnomer. Thirteen states have these incorporated slaughtering-grounds for ducks and geese, the greatest number being in California, Illinois, North Caro-lina and Virginia. California has carried the ducking-club idea to the limit where it is claimed that it constitutes an abuse. Dr. Palmer says that one or two of the club preserves on the western side of the San Joaquin Valley contain upward of *40 square miles, or 25,000 acres each!* With considerable asperity it is now publicly charged (in the columns of *The Examiner* of San Francisco) that for the unattached sportsmen there is no longer any duck-shooting to be had in California, because all the good ducking-grounds are owned and exclusively controlled by clubs. In many states the private game preserves are a source of great irritation, and many have been attacked in courts of law.*

But I am not sorrowing over the woes of the unattached duck-hunter, or in the least inclined to champion his cause against the ducking-club member. As slaughterers and exterminators of wild-fowl, rarely exer-cising mercy under ridiculous bag-limits, they have both been too heedless of the future, and one is just as bad for the game as the other. If either of them favored the game, I would be on his side; but I see no difference between them. They both kill right up to the bag-limit, as often as they can; and that is what is sweeping away all our feathered game.

Curiously enough, the angry unattached duck-hunters of California are to-day proposing to have revenge on the duck-clubbers by *removing all restrictions on the sale of game!* This is on the theory that the duckless sportsmen of the State of California would like to *buy* dead ducks and geese for their tables! It is a novel and original theory, but the sane people of California never will enact it into law. It would be a step just *twenty years backward!*

THE PUBLIC VS. THE PRIVATE GAME PRESERVE.—Both the executive and the judiciary branches of our state governments will in the future be called upon with increasing frequency to sit in judgment on this case. Conditions about us are rapidly changing. The precepts of yesterday may be out of date and worthless tomorrow. By way of introspection, let us see what principles of equity toward Man and Nature we would lay down as the basis of our action if we were called to the bench. Named in logical sequence they would be about as follows:

1. Any private game "preserve" that is maintained chiefly as a

"Private Game Preserves and their Future in the United States," by T. S. Palmer, United States Department of Agriculture, 1910.

EGRETS AND HERONS IN SANCTUARY ON MARSH ISLAND

slaughter-ground for wild game, either birds or mammals, may become detrimental to the interests of the people at large.

2. It is not necessarily the duty of any state to provide for the maintenance of private death-traps for the wholesale slaughter of *migratory* game.

3. An oppressive monopoly in the slaughter of migratory game is detrimental to the interests of the public at large, the same as any other monopoly.

4. Every de facto game preserve, maintained for the preservation of wild life rather than for its slaughter, is an institution beneficial to the public at large, and therefore entitled to legal rights and privileges above and beyond all which may rightly be accorded to the so-called "preserves" that are maintained as killing-grounds.

5. The law may justly discriminate between the actual game preserve and the mere killing-ground.

6. Whenever a killing-ground becomes a public burden, it may be abated, the same as any other public infliction.

In private game preserves the time has arrived when lawmakers and judges must begin to apply the blood-test, and separate the true from the false. And at every step, *the welfare of the wild life involved* must be given full consideration. No men, nor body of men, should be permitted to practice methods that spell extermination.

CHAPTER XXXIX

BRITISH GAME PRESERVES IN AFRICA AND AUSTRALIA

This brief chapter is offered as an object-lesson to the world at large.

In the early days of America, the founders of our states and territories gave little heed, or none at all, to the preservation of wild life. Even if they thought of that duty, undoubtedly they felt that the game would always last, and that they had no time for such sentimental side issues as the making of game preserves. They were coping with troubles and perplexities of many kinds, and it is not to be wondered at that up to forty years ago, real game protection in America went chiefly by default.

In South Africa, precisely the same conditions have prevailed until recent times. The early colonists were kept so busy shooting lions and making farms that not one game preserve was made. If any men can be excused from the work and worry of preserving game, and making preserves, it is those who spend their lives pioneering and state-building in countries like Africa. Men who continually have to contend with disease, bad food, rains, insect pests, dangerous wild beasts and native cussedness may well claim that they have troubles enough, without going far into campaigns to preserve wild animals in countries where animals are plentiful and cheap. It is for this reason that the people of Alaska can not be relied upon to preserve the Alaskan game. They are busy with other things that are of more importance to them.

In May, 1900, representatives of the great powers owning territory in Africa held a conference in the interests of the wild-animal life of that continent. As a result a Convention was signed by which those powers bound hemselves "to make provision for the prevention of further undue destruction of wild game." The principles laid down for universal observance were as follows:

1. Sparing of females and immature animals.
2. The establishment of close seasons and game sanctuaries.
3. Absolute protection of rare species.
4. Restrictions on export for trading purposes of skins, horns, tusks, etc.
5. Prohibition of the use of pits, snares and game traps.

The brave and hardy men who are making for the British people a grand empire in Africa probably are greater men than far-distant people realize. To them, the white man's burden of game preservation is accepted as all in the day's work. A mere handful of British civil officers, strongly aided by the Society for the Preservation of the Fauna of the British Empire, have carved out and set aside a great chain of game preserves reaching all the way from Swaziland and the Transvaal to Khartoum. Taken either collectively or separately, it represents grand work, characteristic of the greatest colonizers on earth. Those preserves are worthy stones in the foundation of what one day will be a great British empire in Africa. The names of the men who proposed them and wrought them out should, in some way, be imperishably connected with them as their founders, as the least reward that Posterity can bestow.

In Major J. Stevenson-Hamilton's fine work, "Animal Life in Africa,"* the author has been at much pains to publish an excellent series of maps showing the locations of the various British game preserves in Africa, and the map published herewith has been based chiefly on that work. It is indeed fortunate for the wild life of Africa that it has today so powerful a champion and exponent as this author, the warden of the Transvaal Game Preserves.

Events move so rapidly that up to this date no one, so far as I am aware, has paused long enough to make and publish an annotated list of the African game preserves. Herein I have attempted to *begin* that task myself, and I regret that at this distance it is impossible for me to set down under the several titles the names of the men who made these preserves possible, and actually founded them.

To thoughtful Americans I particularly commend this list as a showing of the work of men who have not waited until the game had been *practically exterminated* before creating sanctuaries in which to preserve it. In view of these results, how trivial and small of soul seems the mercenary efforts of the organized wool-growers of Montana to thwart our plan to secure a paltry fifteen square miles of grass lands for the rugged and arid Snow Creek Antelope Preserve that is intended to help save a valuable species from quick extermination.

At this point I must quote the views of a high authority on the status of wild life and game preserves in Africa. The following is from Major Stevenson-Hamilton's book.

"It is a remarkable phenomenon in human affairs how seldom the experience of others seems to turn the scale of action. There are, I take it, very few farmers, in the Cape Colony, the Orange Free State, or the Transvaal, who would not be glad to see an adequate supply of game upon their land. Indeed, the writer is constantly dealing with applications as to the possibility of reintroducing various species from the game reserves to private farms, and only the question of expense and the difficulty of transport have, up to the present, prevented this being done on a considerable scale. When, therefore, the relatively small populations of such protectorates as are still well stocked with game are heard airily discussing the advisability of getting rid of it as quickly as possible, one realizes how often vain are the teachings of history, and how well-nigh hopeless it is to quote the result of similar action elsewhere. It remains only to trust that things may be seen in truer perspective ere it is too late, and that those in whose temporary charge it is may not cast recklessly away one of nature's most splendid assets, one, moreover, which once lightly discarded, can never by any possibility, be regained."

*Published by Heinemann, London, 1912.

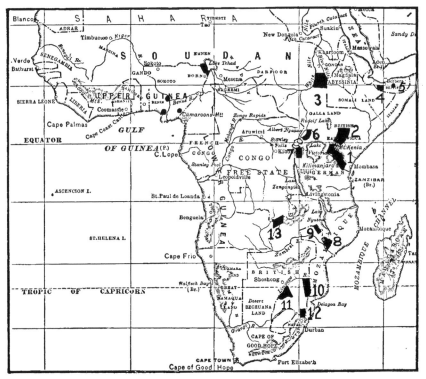

THE MOST IMPORTANT GAME PRESERVES OF AFRICA

The Numbers Refer to Corresponding Numbers in the Text

"It is idle to say that the advance of civilization must necessarily mean the total disappearance of all wild animals. This is one of those glib fallacies which flows only too readily from unthinking lips. Civilization in its full sense—not the advent of a few scattered pioneers—of course, implies their restriction, especially as regards purely grass-feeding species, within certain definite bounds, both as regards numbers and sanctuaries. But this is a very different thing from wholesale destruction, that a few more or less deserving individuals may receive some small pecuniary benefit, or gratify their taste for slaughter to the detriment of everyone else who may come after. *The fauna of an empire is the property of that empire as a whole, and not of the small portion of it where the animals may happen to exist; and while full justice and encouragement must be given to the farmer and pioneer, neither should be permitted to entirely demolish for his own advantage resources which, strictly speaking, are not his own.*"—("Animal Life in Africa," p. 24.)

African Game Preserves

British East Africa:

1.* *The Athi Plains Preserve.*—This is situated between the Uganda Railway and the boundary of German East Africa. Its northern boundary is one mile north of the railway track. It is about 215 miles long east and west by 105 miles from north to south, and its area is about 13,000 square miles. It is truly a great preserve, and worthy of the plains fauna that it is specially intended to perpetuate.

2. *The Jubaland Preserve.*—This preserve lies northwest of Mount Kenia. Its southwestern corner is near Lake Baringo, the Laikipia Escarpment is its western boundary up to Mt. Nyiro, and from that point its northern boundary runs 225 miles to Marsabit Lake. From that point the boundary runs south-by-west to the Guaso Nyiro River, which forms the eastern half of the southern boundary. Its total area appears to be about 13,000 square miles.

In addition to the two great preserves described above the government of British East Africa has established on the Uasin Gishu Plateau a centrally located sanctuary for elands, roan antelopes and hippopotamii. There is also a small special rhinoceros preserve about fifty miles southeastward of Nairobi, around Kiu station, on the railway.

Egyptian Sudan:

3. A great nameless sanctuary for wild life exists on the eastern bank of the Nile, comprising the whole territory between the main stream, the Blue Nile and Abyssinia. Its length (north and south) is 215 miles, and its width is about 125 miles; which means a total area of about 26,875 square miles. Natives and others living within this sanctuary may hunt therein—if they can procure licenses.

Somaliland:

4. *Hargeis Reserve*, about 1,800 square miles.

5. *Mirso Reserve*, about 300 square miles.

Uganda:

6. *Budonga Forest Reserve.*—This small reserve embraces the whole eastern shore and hinterland of Lake Albert Nyanza, and is shaped like a new moon.

7. *Toro Reserve.*—This small reserve lies between Lakes Albert Nyanza and Albert Edward Nyanza, touching both.

Nyasaland, or the British Central Africa Protectorate.—A small territory, but remarkably well stocked with game.

8. *Elephant Marsh Preserve.*—A small area in the extreme southern end of the Protectorate, on both sides of the Shire River, chiefly for buffalo.

9. *Angoniland Reserve.*—This was created especially to preserve about one thousand elephants. It is forty miles west of the southwestern arm of Lake Nyasa.

*These numbers refer to corresponding numbers on the map of Africa.

TRANSVAAL:

10. *Sabi-Singwitza-Pongola Preserve.*—This great preserve occupies the whole region between the Drakenberg Mountains and the Lebombo Hills. Its total area is about 10,500 square miles. It lies in a compact block about 210 miles long by 50 miles wide, along the Portuguese border.

11. *Rustenburg Reserve.*—This is situated at the head of the Limpopo River, and covers about 3,500 square miles.

SWAZILAND:

12. *The Swaziland Reserve* contains about 1,750 square miles, and occupies the southwestern corner of Swaziland.

RHODESIA:

13. *The Nweru Marsh Game Reserve* is in northwestern Rhodesia, bordering the Congo Free State. The description of its local boundaries is quite unintelligible outside of Rhodesia.

Luangwa Reserve.—The locality of this reserve cannot be determined from the official description, which gives no clue to its shape or size.

GAME PRESERVES IN AUSTRALASIA

NEW ZEALAND:

Little Barrier Island in the north, and *Resolution Island*, in the south; and concerning both, details are lacking.

AUSTRALIA:

Kangaroo Island, near Adelaide, South Australia, is 400 miles northwest of Melbourne. Of the total area of this rather large island of 300 square miles, 140 square miles have been set aside as a game preserve, chiefly for the preservation of the mallee bird (*Lipoa occelata*). It is believed that eventually the whole island will become a wild-life sanctuary, and it would seem that this can not be consummated a day too soon for the vanishing wild life.

Wilson's Promontory, Adelaide, is a peninsula well suited to the preservation of wild life, especially birds, and it is now a sanctuary.

Many private bird refuges have been created in Australia.

TASMANIA

Eleven Bird Refuges have been created, with a total area of 26,000 acres,—an excellent record for Tasmania!

Freycinet's Peninsula.—At present this wild-life sanctuary is not adequately protected from illicit hunting and trapping; but its full protection is now demanded, and no doubt this soon will be provided by the government. I am informed that this offers a golden opportunity to secure a fine wild-life sanctuary at ridiculously small cost to the public. The whole world is interested in the preservation of the remarkable fauna of Tasmania. The extermination of the thylacine would be a zoological calamity; but it is impending.

CHAPTER XL

BREEDING GAME AND FUR IN CAPTIVITY

GAME BREEDING.—The breeding of game in captivity for sale in the markets of the world is just as legitimate as the breeding of domestic species. This applies equally to mammals, birds, reptiles and fishes. It is the duty of the nation and the state to foster such industries and facilitate the marketing of their products without any unnecessary formalities, delays or losses to producers or to purchasers.

Already this principle has been established in several states. Without going into the records, it is safe to say that Colorado was the pioneer in the so-called "more-game" movement, about 1899; but there is one person who would like to have the world believe that it started in the state of New York, about 1909. The idea is not quite as "old as the hills," but the application of it in the United States dates back through a considerable vista of years.

The laws of Colorado providing for the creation of private game preserves and the marketing of their product under a tagging system, are very elaborate, and they show a sincere desire to foster an industry as yet but slightly developed in this country. The laws of New York are much more simple and easy to understand than those of Colorado.

There is one important principle now fully recognized in the New York laws for game breeding that other states will do well to adopt. It is the fact that certain kinds of wild game *can not be bred and reared in captivity on a commercial basis;* and this being true, it is clearly against public policy to provide for the sale of any such species. Why provide for the sale of preserve-bred grouse and ducks which we know can not be bred and reared in confinement in marketable numbers? For example, if we may judge by the numerous experiments that *thus far* have been made,—as we certainly have a right to do,—no man can successfully breed and rear in captivity, on a commercial basis, the canvasback duck, teal, pintail duck, ruffed grouse or quail. This being the case, no amount of clamor from game dealers and their allies ever should induce any state legislature to provide for the sale of any of those species *until it has been fully demonstrated* that they *have been* and *can be* bred in captivity in large numbers. The moment the markets of a state are thrown open to these impossible species, from that moment the state game wardens must make a continuous struggle to prevent the importation and sale of those birds contrary to law. This proposition is so simple that every honest man can see it.

All that any state legislature may rightfully be asked to do is to provide for the sale, under tags, of those species which *we know* can be bred in captivity in large numbers.

When the Bayne law was drafted, its authors considered with the utmost care the possibilities in the breeding of game in the United States on a commercial basis. It was found that as yet only two wild native species have been, and can be, reared in captivity on a large scale. These are the white-tailed deer and mallard duck. Of foreign species we can breed successfully for market the fallow deer, red deer of Europe and some of the pheasants of the old world. For the rearing, killing and marketing of all these, the Bayne law provides the simplest processes of state supervision that the best game protectors and game breeders of New York could devise. The tagging system is expeditious, cheap and effective. Practically the only real concession that is required of the game-breeder concerns the killing, which must be done in a systematic way, whereby a state game warden can visit the breeder's premises and affix the tags without any serious sacrifice of time or convenience on either side. The tags cost the breeder five cents each, and they pay the cost of the services rendered by the state.

By this admirable system, which is very plainly set forth in the New York Conservation Commission's book of game laws, all the *wild* game of New York, *and of every other state*, is absolutely protected at all times against illegal killing and illegal importation for the New York market. Now, is it not the duty of Connecticut, Maryland, Virginia, the Carolinas and every other state to return our compliment by passing similar laws? Massachusetts came up to public expectations at the next session of her legislature after the passage of our Bayne law. In 1913, California will try to secure a similar act; and we know full well that her ducks, geese, quail, grouse and band-tailed pigeon need it very much. If the California protectors of wild life succeed in arousing the great quiet mass of people in that state, their Bayne bill will be swept through their legislature on a tidal wave of popular sentiment.

Elk.—For people who own wild woodlands near large cities there are good profits to be made in rearing white-tailed deer for the market. I would also mention elk, but for the fact that every man who rears a fine herd of elk quickly becomes so proud of the animals, and so much attached to them, that he can not bear to have them shot and butchered for market! Elk are just as easy to breed and rear as domestic cattle, except that in the fall breeding season, the fighting of rival bulls demands careful and intelligent management. Concerning the possibilities of feeding elk on hay at $25 per ton and declaring an annual profit, I am not informed. If the elk require to be fed all the year round, the high price of hay and grain might easily render it impossible to produce marketable three-year-old animals at a profit.

White-tailed Deer.—Any one who owns from one hundred to one thousand acres of wild, brushy or forest-covered land can raise white-tailed (or Virginia) deer at a profit. With smaller areas of land, free range becomes impossible, and the prospects of commercial profits diminish and disappear. In any event, a fenced range is absolutely essential; and the best fence is the Page, 88 inches high, all horizontals of No. 9 wire, top and bottom wires of No. 7, and the perpendicular tie-wires of No. 12. This fence will hold deer, elk, bison and wild horses. In large enclosures, the white-tailed deer is hardy and prolific, and when fairly cooked its flesh is a great delicacy. In Vermont the average weights of the deer killed in that state in various years have been as follow:—in 1902, 171 lbs.; in 1903, 190 lbs.; in 1905, 198 lbs.; in 1906, 200 lbs.; in 1907, 196 lbs.; in 1908, 207 lbs.; and in 1909, 155 lbs. The reason for the great drop in 1909 is yet to be ascertained.

In 1910, in New York City the wholesale price of whole deer carcasses was from 22 to 25 cents per pound. Venison saddles were worth from 30 to 35 cents per pound. On the bill of fare of a first class hotel, a portion of venison costs from $1.50 to $2.50 according to the diner's location. It is probable that such prices as these will prevail only in the largest cities, and therefore they must not be regarded as general.

Live white-tailed deer can be purchased for breeding purposes at prices ranging from $25 to $35 each. A good eastern source of supply is Blue Mountain Forest, Mr. Austin Corbin, president (Broadway and Cortlandt St., New York). In the West, good stock can be procured from the Cleveland-Cliffs Iron Company, through C. V. R. Townsend, Negaunee, Mich, whose preserve occupies the whole of Grand Island, Lake Superior.

The Department of Agriculture has published for free distribution a pamphlet entitled "Raising Deer and Other Large Game Animals" in the United States, by David E. Lantz, which contains much valuable information, although it leaves much unsaid.

All breeders of deer are cautioned that during the fall and early winter months, all adult white-tailed bucks are dangerous to man, and should be treated accordingly. A measure of safety can be secured in a large park by compelling the deer always to keep at a respectful distance, and making no "pets," whatever. Whenever a buck finds his horns and loses his fear of man, climb the fence quickly. Bucks in the rutting season sometimes seem to go crazy, and often they attack men, wantonly and dangerously. The method of attack is to an unarmed man almost irresistible. The animal lowers his head, stiffens his neck and with terrible force drives straight forward for your stomach and bowels. Usually there are eight sharp spears of bone to impale you. The best defense of an unarmed man is to seize the left antler with the left hand, and with the right hand pull the deer's right front foot from under him. Merely holding to the horns makes great sport for the deer. He loves that unequal combat. The great desideratum is to put his fore legs out of commission, and get him down on his knees.

Does are sometimes dangerous, and inflict serious damage by rising on their hind feet and viciously striking with their sharp front hoofs. These tendencies in American deer are mentioned here as a duty to persons who may desire to breed deer for profit.

OUR VANISHING WILD LIFE

The Red Deer of Europe.—Anyone who has plenty of natural forest food for deer and a good market within fair range, may find the European red deer a desirable species. It is of size smaller, and more easily managed, than the wapiti; and is more easily marketed because of its smaller size. As a species it is hardy and prolific, and of course its venison is as good as that of any other deer. Live specimens for stocking purposes can be purchased of S. A. Stephan, Agent for Carl Hagenbeck, Cincinnati Zoological Gardens, or of Wenz & Mackensen, Yardley, Pa., at prices ranging from $60 to $100 each, according to size and age. At present the supply of specimens in this country on hand for sale is very small.

The Fallow Deer.—This species is the most universal park deer of Europe. It seems to be invulnerable to neglect and misuse, for it has persisted through countless generations of breeding in captivity, and the abuse of all nations. In size it is a trifle smaller than our white-tailed deer, with spots in summer, and horns that are widely flattened at the extremities in a very interesting way. It is very hardy and prolific, but of course it can not stand everything that could be put upon it. It needs a dry shed in winter, red clover hay and crushed oats for winter food; and no deer should be kept in mud. As a commercial proposition it is not so meaty as the white-tail, but it is *less troublesome to keep.* The adult males are not such vicious or dangerous fighters as white-tail bucks. Live specimens are worth from $50 to $75. The Essex County Park Commissioners (Orange, New Jersey) have had excellent success with this species. In 1906 they purchased twenty-five does and four bucks and placed them in an enclosure of 150 acres, on a wooded mountain-side. In 1912 they had 150 deer, and were obliged to take measures for a disposal of the surplus. Messrs. Wenz & Mackensen, keep an almost continuous supply of fallow deer on hand for sale.

The Indian Sambar Deer.—I have long advocated the introduction in the southern states, *wherever deer can be protected,* of this great, hulking, animated venison-factory. While I have not delved deeply into the subject of weight and growth, I feel sure from casual observations of the growth of about twenty-five animals that this species produces more venison during the first two years of its life than any other deer with which I am acquainted. I regard it as the greatest venison-producer of the whole Deer Family; and I know that is a large order. The size of a yearling is almost absurd, it is so great for an animal of tender years. When adult, the species is for its height very large and heavy. As a food-producing animal, located in the southern hill forests and taking care of itself, "there's millions in it!" But *it must be kept under fence;* for in no southern (or northern) state would any such mass of juicy wild meat long be permitted to roam at large unkilled. Through this species I believe that a million acres of southern timber lands, now useless except for timber growth, could be made very productive in choice venison. The price would be,—a good fence, and protection from poachers.

The Indian sambar deer looks like a short-legged big-bodied understudy of our American elk. It breeds well in captivity, and it is of quiet and tractable disposition. It can not live in a country where the temperature goes down to 25° F. and *remains there for long periods*. It would, I am firmly convinced, do well all along the Gulf coast, and if acclimatized along the Gulf, with the lapse of time and generations it would become more and more hardy, grow more hair, and push its way northward, until it reached the latitude of Tennessee. But then, in a wild state it could not be protected from poachers. As stated elsewhere, Dr. Ray V. Pierce has successfully acclimatized and bred this species in his St. Vincent Island game preserve, near Apalachicola, Florida. More than that, the species has crossed with the white-tailed deer of the Island.

Living specimen of the Indian Sambar deer are worth from $125 to $250, according to size and other conditions. Just at present it seems difficult for Americans to procure a sufficient number of *males!* We have had very bad luck with several males that we attempted to import for breeding purposes.

The Mallard Duck.—A great many persons have made persistent attempts to breed the canvasback, redhead, mallard, black duck, pintail, teal and other species, on a commercial basis. So far as I am aware the mallard is the only wild duck that has been bred in sufficient numbers to slaughter for the markets. The wood duck and mandarin can be bred in fair numbers, but only sufficient to supply the demand for *living* birds, for park purposes. One would naturally suppose that a species as closely allied to the mallard as the black duck is known to be, would breed like the mallard; but the black duck is so timid and nervous about nesting as to be almost worthless in captivity. All the species named above, except the mallard, must at present, and in general, be regarded as failures in breeding for the market.

Of all American ducks the common mallard is the most persistent and successful breeder. It quickly becomes accustomed to captivity, it enjoys park life, and when given even half a chance it will breed and rear its young.

Unquestionably, the mallard duck can be reared in captivity in numbers limited only by the extent of breeder's facilities. The amount of net profit that can be realized depends wholly upon the business acumen and judgment displayed in the management of the flock. The total amount of knowledge necessary to success is not so very great, but at the same time, the exercise of a fair amount of intelligence, and also careful diligence, is absolutely necessary. Naturally the care and food of the flock must not cost extravagantly, or the profits will inevitably disappear.

As a contribution to the cause of game-breeding for the market, and the creation of a new industry of value, Mr. L. S. Crandall and the author wrote for the New York State Conservation Commission a pamphlet on "Breeding Mallard Ducks for Market." Copies of it can be procured of our State Conservation Commission at Albany, by enclosing ten cents in stamps.

Breeding Fur-Bearing Animals

When hundreds of persons wrote to me asking for literature on the breeding of fur-bearing animals for profit, for ten years I was compelled to tell them that there was no such literature. During the past three years a few offerings have been made, and I lose not a moment in listing them here.

"*Life Histories of Northern Anmials,* by Ernest T. Seton (Charles Scribner's Sons, 2 volumes, $18), contains carefully written and valuable chapters on fox farming, skunk farming, marten farming, and mink farming, and other valuable life histories of the fur-bearing animals of North America.

Rod and Gun in Canada, a magazine for sportsmen published by W. J. Taylor, Woodstock, Ontario, contained in 1912 a series of articles on "The Culture of Black and Silver Foxes," by R. B. and L. V. Croft. *Country Life in America* has published a number of illustrated articles on fox and skunk farming.

With its usual enterprise and forethought, the Biological Survey of the Department of Agriculture has published a valuable pamphlet of 22 pages on "Silver Fox Farming," by Wilfred H. Osgood, copies of which can be procured by addressing the Secretary of Agriculture. In consulting that contribution, however, it must be borne in mind that just now, in fox farming, history is being made more rapidly than heretofore.

I do not mean to say that the above are the only sources of information on fur-farming for profit, but they are the ones that have most impressed me. The files of all the journals and magazines for sportsmen contain numerous articles on this subject, and they should be carefully consulted.

Black-Fox Farming.—The ridiculous prices now being paid in London for the skins of black or "silver" foxes has created in this country a small furore over the breeding of that color-phase of the red fox. The prices that actually have been obtained, both for skins and for live animals for breeding purposes, have a strong tendency to make people crazy. Fancy paying $12,000 in real money for one pair of live black foxes! That has been done, on Prince Edward Island, and $10,000 per pair is now regarded as a bargain-counter figure.

On Prince Edward Island, in the Gulf of St. Lawrence, black-fox breeding has been going on for ten years, and is now on a successful basis. One man has made a fortune in the business, and it is rumored that a stock company is considering the purchase of his ten-acre fox ranch at a fabulous figure. The enormous prices obtainable for live black foxes, male or female, make diamonds and rubies seem cheap and commonplace; and it is no wonder that enterprising men are tempted to enter that industry.

The price of a black fox is one of the wonders of a recklessly extravagant and whimsical age. All the fur-wearing world knows very well that fox fur is one of the poorest of furs to withstand the wear and tear of actual use. About two seasons' hard wear are enough to put the best fox skin on the wane, and three or four can be guaranteed to throw it into the discard. Even the finest black fox skin is nothing superlatively beautiful! A choice "cross" fox skin costing only $50 is *far more beautiful, as a color proposition;* but London joyously pays $2,500 or $3,000 for a single black-fox skin, to wear!

Of course, all such fads as this are as ephemeral as the butterflies of summer. The Russo-Japanese war quickly reduced the value of Alaskan blue foxes from $30 to $18; and away went the Alaskan fox farms! A similar twist of Fortune's fickle wheel may in any year send the black fox out of royal favor, and remove the bottom from the business of producing it. Let us hope, however, that the craze for that fur will continue; for we like to see our friends and neighbors make good profits.

PHEASANT REARING.—This subject is so well understood by game-breeders, and there is already so much good literature available regarding it, it is not necessary that I should take it up here.

CHAPTER XLI

TEACHING WILD LIFE PROTECTION TO THE YOUNG

Thousands of busy and burdened men and women are to-day striving hard, early and late, to promote measures that will preserve the valuable wild life of the world. They desire to leave to the boys and girls of to-morrow a good showing of the marvelous bird and animal forms that make the world beautiful and interesting. They are acting on the principle that the wild life of to-day is not ours, to destroy or to keep as we choose, but has been given to us *in trust*, partly for our benefit and partly for those who come after us and audit our accounts. They believe that we have no right to squander and destroy a wild-life heritage of priceless value which we have done nothing to create, and which is not ours to destroy.

DUTY OF PARENTS.—This being the case, it is very necessary that the young people of to-day should be taught, early and often, the virtue and the necessity of wild-life protection. There is no reason that the boy of to-day should not take up his share of the common burden, just as soon as he is old enough to wander alone through the woods. Let him be taught in precise terms that he must *not rob birds' nests*, and that he *must not shoot song-birds, woodpeckers and kingfishers* with a 22-calibre rifle, or any other gun. At this moment there lies upon my side table a vicious little 22-calibre rifle that was taken from two boys who were camping in the woods of Connecticut, and amusing themselves by shooting valuable insectivorous birds. Now those boys were not wholly to blame for what they were doing; but their fathers and mothers were *very much to blame!* They should have been taught at the parental knee that it is very wrong to kill any bird except a genuine game bird, and then only in the lawful open season. Those two fathers paid $10 each for having failed in their duty; and it served them right; for they were the real culprits.

Small-calibre rifles are becoming alarmingly common in the hands of boys. *Parents must do their duty in the training of their boys against bird-shooting!* It is a very serious matter. A million boys who roam the fields with small rifles without having been instructed in protection, can destroy an appalling number of valuable birds in the course of a year. Some parents are so slavishly devoted to their children that they wish them to do everything they please, and be checked in nothing. Such parents constitute one of the pests of society, and a drag upon the happiness of their own children! It is now the bounden duty of each parent to teach each one of his or her children that the time has come when the resources of nature, and especially wild life, must be conserved. To permit boys to grow up and acquire guns without this knowledge is very wrong.

THE DUTY OF TEACHERS AND SCHOOLS.—A great deal of "nature study" is being taught in the public schools of the United States. That the young people of our land should be taught to appreciate the works of nature, and especially animal life and plant life, is very desirable. Thus far, however, there is a screw loose in the system, and that is the shortage in definite, positive instruction regarding *individual duty* toward the wild creatures, great and small. Along with their nature studies all our school children should be taught, in the imperative mood:

1. That it is wrong to disturb breeding birds, or rob birds' nests;

2. That it is wrong to destroy any harmless living creature not properly classed as game, except it be to preserve it in a museum;

3. That it is no longer right for civilized man to look upon wild game as *necessary* food; because there is plenty of other food, and the remnant of game can not withstand slaughter in that basis;

4. That the time has come when it is the duty of every good citizen to take an active, aggressive part in *preventing* the destruction of wild life, and in *promoting* its preservation;

5. That every boy and girl over twelve years of age can do *something* in this cause, and finally,

6. That protection and encouragement will bring back the almost vanished birds.

We call upon all boards of education, all principals of schools and all teachers to educate our boys and girls, constantly and imperatively, along those lines. Teachers, do not say to your pupils,—"It is right and nice to protect birds," but say:—"It is your *Duty* to protect all harmless wild things, and *you must do it!*"

In a good cause, there is great virtue in "Must."

Really, we are losing each year an immense amount of available wild-life protection. The doctrine of imperative individual duty never yet has been taught in our schools as it should be taught. A few teachers have, indeed, covered this ground; but I am convinced that their proportion is mighty small.

TEXT BOOKS.—The writers of the nature study text books are very much to blame because nine-tenths of the time this subject has been ignored. The situation has not been taken seriously, save in a few cases, by a very few authors. I am glad to report that in 1912 there was published a fine text book by Professor James W. Peabody, of the Morris High School, New York, and Dr. Arthur E. Hunt, in which from beginning to end the duty to protect wild life is strongly insisted upon. It is entitled "Elementary Biology; Plants, Animals and Man."

Hereafter, no zoological or nature study text book should be given a place in any school in America unless the author of it has done his full share in setting forth the duty of the young citizen toward wild life. Were

I a member of a board of education I would seek to establish and enforce this requirement. To-day, any author who will presume to write a text book of nature study or zoology without knowing and doing his duty toward our vanishing fauna, is too ignorant of wild life and too careless of his duty toward it, to be accepted as a safe guide for the young. The time for criminal indifference has gone by. Hereafter, every one who is not for the preservation of wild life is against it· and it is time to separate the sheep from the goats.

From this time forth, the preservation of our fauna should be regarded as a subject on which every candidate for a teacher's certificate should undergo an examination before receiving authority to teach in a public school. The candidate should be required to know *why* the preservation of birds is necessary; why the slaughter of wild life is wrong and criminal; the extent to which wild birds and mammals return to us and thrive under protection; why wild game is no longer a legitimate food supply; why wild game should not be sold, and why the feathers of wild birds (other than game birds) never should be used as millinery ornaments.

As sensible Americans, and somewhat boastful of our intelligence, we should put the education of the young in wild-life protection on a rational business basis.

STATE EFFORTS.—In several of our states, systematic efforts to educate children in their duty toward wild life are already being made. To this end, an annual "Bird Day" has been established for state-wide observ ance. This splendid idea is now legally in force in the following states:

California, Connecticut, Delaware, Illinois, Louisiana, Minnesota, Ohio and Wisconsin.

Bird Day is also more or less regularly observed, though not legally provided for, in New York, Indiana, Colorado and Alabama, and locally in some cities of Pennsylvania. Usually the observance of the day is combined with that of Arbor Day, and the date is fixed by proclamation of the Governor.

Alabama and Wisconsin regularly issue elaborate and beautiful Arbor and Bird Day annuals; and Illinois, and possibly other states, have issued very good publications of this character.

THE PHILLIPS EDUCATIONAL CAMPAIGN FOR THE BIRDS.—Quite recently there has come under my notice an episode in the education of school children that has given the public profound satisfaction. I cite it here as an object lesson for pan-America.

In Carrick, Pennsylvania, just across the Monongahela River from the city of Pittsburgh, lives John M. Phillips, State Game Commissioner, nature-lover, sportsman and friend of man. He is a man who does things, and gets results. Goat Mountain Park (450 square miles), in British Columbia, to-day owes its existence to him, for without his initiative and labor it would not have been established. It was the first game preserve of British Columbia.

Three years ago, Mr. Phillips became deeply impressed by the idea

BIRD DAY AT CARRICK, PA.

Marching Behind the Governor

that one of the best ways in the world to protect the wild life, both of to-day and the future, would be in teaching school children to love it and protect it. His fertile brain and open check-book soon devised a method for his home city. His theory was that by giving the children *something to do*, not only in protecting but in actually *bringing back* the birds, much might be accomplished.

In studying the subject of bringing back the birds, he found that the Russian mulberry is one of the finest trees in the world as a purveyor of good fruit for many kinds of birds. The tree does not much resemble our native mulberry, but is equally beautiful and interesting. "The fruit is not a long berry, nor is it of a purple color, but it grows from buds on the limbs and twigs something after the manner of the pussy-willow. It is smaller, of light color and has a very distinct flavor. The most striking peculiarity about the fruit is that it keeps on ripening during two months or more, new berries appearing daily while others are ripening. This is why it is such good bird food. Nor is it half bad for folks, for the berries are good to look at and to eat, either with cream or without, and to make pies that will set any sane boy's mouth a-watering at sight." —(Erasmus Wilson).

Everyone knows the value of sweet cherries, both to birds and to children.

Mr. Phillips decided that he would give away several hundred bird boxes, and also several hundred sweet cherry and Russian mulberry trees. The first gift distribution was made in the early spring of 1909. Another followed in 1910, but the last one was the most notable.

On April 11, 1912, Carrick had a great and glorious Bird Day. Mr. Phillips was the author of it, and Governor Tener the finisher. On that day occurred the third annual gift distribution of raw materials designed to promote in the breasts of 2,000 children a love for birds and an active desire to protect and increase them. Mr. Phillips gave away 500 bird boxes, 500 sweet cherry trees and 200 mulberry trees. The sun shone brightly, 500 flags waved in Carrick, the Governor made one of the best speeches of his life, and Erasmus Wilson, faithful friend of the birds, wrote this good story of the occasion for the *Gazette-Times*, of Pittsburgh:

The Governor was there, and the children, the bird-boxes, and the young trees. And was there ever a brighter or more fitting day for a children and bird jubilee! The scene was so inspiring that Gov. Tener made one of the best speeches of his life.

The distribution of several hundred cherry and mulberry trees was the occasion, and the beautiful grounds of the Roosevelt school, Carrick, was the scene.

Mr. John M. Phillips, sane sportsman and enthusiastic friend of the birds, has been looking forward to this as the culmination of a scheme he has been working on for years, and he was more than pleased with the outcome. The intense delight it afforded him more than repaid him for all it has cost in all the years past.

But it was impossible to tell who were the more delighted,—he, or the Governor, or the children, or the visitors who were so fortunate as to be present. County Superintendent of Schools Samuel Hamilton was simply a mass of delight. And how could he be otherwise, surrounded as he was by 2,000 and more children fairly quivering with delight?

Children will care for and defend things that are their very own, fight for them and stand guard over them. Realizing this Mr. Phillips undertook to show them how they could have birds all their own. Being clever in devising schemes for achieving things most to be desired, he began giving out bird-boxes to those who would agree to put them up, and to watch and defend the birds when they came to make their homes with them. And he found that no more faithful sentinel ever stood on guard than the boy who had a bird-house all his own.

Here was the solution to the vexed problem. Provide boxes for those who would agree to put them up, care for the birds, and study their habits and needs. The children agreed at once, and the birds did not object, so Mr. Phillips had some hundreds, four or five, blue-bird and wren boxes constructed during the past winter. These were passed out some weeks ago to any boys or girls who would present an order signed by their parents, and countersigned by the principal of the school.

He knows enough about a boy to know that he does not prize the things that come without effort, nor will he become deeply interested in anything for which he is not held more or less responsible. Hence the advantage in having him write an order, have it indorsed by his parents, and vouched for by his school principal.

That he had struck the right scheme was proven by the avidity with which the girls and boys rushed for the boxes. The fact that a heavy rain was falling did not dampen their ardor for a moment, nor did the fact that they were tramping Mr. Phillips' beautiful lawn into a field of mud.

Mr. Phillips, seeing the necessity of providing food for the prospective hosts of birds, and wishing to place the responsibility on the boys and girls, offered to provide a cherry tree or mulberry tree for every box erected, provided they should be properly planted and diligently cared for.

DISTRIBUTING BIRD BOXES AND FRUIT TREES

This was practically the culmination of the most unique bird scheme ever attempted, and yesterday was the day set apart for the distribution of these hundreds of fruit trees, the products of which are to be divided share and share alike with the birds.

Nowhere else has such a scheme been attempted, and never before has there been just such a day of jubilee. The intense interest manifested by the children, and the earnest enthusiasm manifested, leaves no doubt about their carrying out their part of the contract.

Up to date (1912) Mr. Phillips has given away about 1,000 bird boxes, 1,500 cherry and Russian mulberry trees, and transformed the schools of Carrick into seething masses of children militantly enthusiastic in the protection of birds, and in providing them with homes and food. As a final coup, Mr. Phillips has induced the city of Pittsburgh to create the office of City Ornithologist, at a salary of $1200 per year. The duty of the new officer is to protect all birds in the city from all kinds of molestation, especially when nesting; to erect bird-houses, provide food for wild birds, on a large scale, and report annually upon the increase or decrease of feathered residents and visitors. Mr. Frederic S. Webster, long known as a naturalist and practical ornithologist, has been appointed to the position, and is now on active duty.

So far as we are aware, Pittsburgh is the first city to create the office of City Ornithologist. It is a happy thought; it will yield good results, and other cities will follow Pittsburgh's good example.

CHAPTER XLII

THE ETHICS OF SPORTSMANSHIP

I count it as rather strange that American and English sportsmen have hunted and shot for a century, and until 1908 formulated practically nothing to establish and define the ethics of shooting game. Here and there, a few unwritten principles have been evolved, and have become fixed by common consent; but the total number of these is very few. Perhaps this has been for the reason that every free and independent sportsman prefers to be a law unto himself. Is it not doubly strange, however, that even down to the present year the term " sportsmen " never has been defined by a sportsman!

Forty years ago, a sportsman might have been defined, according to the standards of that period, as a man who hunts wild game for pleasure. Those were the days wherein no one foresaw the wholesale annihilation of species, and there were no wilderness game preserves. In those days, gentlemen shot female hoofed game, trapped bears if they felt like it, killed ten times as much big game as they could use, and no one made any fuss whatever about the waste or extermination of wild life.

Those were the days of ox-teams and broad-axes. To-day, we are living in a totally different world,—a world of grinding, crunching, pulverizing progress, a world of annihilation of the works of Nature. And what is a sportsman to-day?

A SPORTSMAN is a man who loves Nature, and who in the enjoyment of the outdoor life and exploration takes a reasonable toll of Nature's wild animals, but not for commercial profit, and only so long as his hunting does not promote the extermination of species.

In view of the disappearance of wild life all over the habitable globe, and the steady extermination of species, the ethics of sportsmanship has become a matter of tremendous importance. If a man can shoot the last living Burchell zebra, or prong-horned antelope, and be a sportsman and a gentleman, then we may just as well drop down all bars, and say no more about the ethics of shooting game.

But the real gentlemen-sportsmen of the world are not insensible to the duties of the hour in regard to the taking or not taking of game. The time has come when canon laws should be laid down, of world-wide application, and so thoroughly accepted and promulgated that their binding force can not be ignored. Among other things, it is time for a list of species to be published which no man claiming to be either a gentleman or a sportsman can shoot for aught else than preservation in a public museum. Of course, this list would be composed of the species that are threatened with extermination. Of American animals it should include the prong-horned antelope, Mexican mountain sheep, all the mountain sheep and goats in the United States, the California grizzly bear, mule deer, West Indian seal and California elephant seal and walrus.

In Africa that list should include the eland, white rhinoceros, blessbok, bontebok, kudu, giraffes and southern elephants, sable antelope, rhinoceros south of the Zambesi, leucoryx antelope and whale-headed stork. In Asia it should include the great Indian rhinoceros and its allied species, the burrhel, the Nilgiri tahr and the gayal. The David deer of Manchuria already is extinct in a wild state.

In Australia the interdiction should include the thylacine or Tasmanian wolf, all the large kangaroos, the emu, lyre bird and the mallee-bird.

Think what it would mean to the species named above if all the sportsmen of the world would unite in their defense, both actively and passively! It would be to those species a modus vivendi worth while.

Prior to 1908, no effort (so far as we are aware) ever had been made to promote the establishment of a comprehensive and up-to-date code of ethics for sportsmen who shoot. A few clubs of men who are hunters of big game had expressed in their constitutions a few brief principles for the purpose of standardizing their own respective memberships, but that was all. I have not taken pains to make a general canvass of sportsmen's clubs to ascertain what rules have been laid down by any large number of organizations.

The Boone and Crockett Club, of New York and Washington, had in its constitution the following excellent article:

"Article X. The use of steel traps, the making of large bags, the killing of game while swimming in water, or helpless in deep snow, and the unnecessary killing of females or young of any species of ruminant, shall be deemed offenses. Any member who shall commit such offenses may be suspended, or expelled from the Club by unanimous vote of the Executive Committee."

In 1906, this Club condemned the use of automatic shotguns in hunting as unsportsmanlike.

The Lewis and Clark Club, of Pittsburgh, has in its constitution, as Section 3 of Article 3, the following comprehensive principle:

"The term 'legitimate sport' means not only the observance of local laws, but excludes all methods of taking game other than by fair stalking or still hunting."

At the end of the constitution of this club is this declaration, and admonition:

"*Purchase and sale of Trophies.*—As the purchase of heads and horns establishes a market value, and encourages Indians and others to "shoot for sale," often in violation of local laws and always to the detriment of the protection of game for legitimate sport, the Lewis and Clark Club condemns the purchase or the sale of the heads or horns of any game."

In 1906 the Lewis and Clark Club condemned the use of automatic shotguns as unsportsmanlike.

The Shikar Club, of London, a club which contains all the big-game hunters of the nobility and gentry of England,* and of which His Majesty King George is Honorary President, has declared the leading feature of its "Objects" in the following terms:

"To maintain the standard of sportsmanship. It is not squandered bullets and swollen bags which appeal to us. The test is rather in a love of forest, mountains and desert; in acquired knowledge of the habits of animals; in the strenuous pursuit of a wary and dangerous quarry; in the instinct for a well-devised approach to a fair shooting distance; and in the patient retrieve of a wounded animal."

In 1908 the Camp-Fire Club of America formally adopted, as its code of ethics, the "Sportsman's Platform" of fifteen articles that was prepared by the writer and placed before the sportsmen of America, Great Britain and her colonial dependencies in that year. In the book of the Club it regularly appears as follows:

CODE OF ETHICS

OF THE

CAMP-FIRE CLUB OF AMERICA

Proposed by Wm. T. Hornaday and adopted December 10, 1908

---

1. The wild animal life of to-day is not ours, to do with as we please. The original stock is given to us *in trust*, for the benefit both of the present and the future. We must render an accounting of this trust to those who come after us.

2. Judging from the rate at which the wild creatures of North America are now being destroyed, fifty years hence there will be no large game left in the United States nor in Canada, outside of rigidly protected game preserves. It is therefore the duty of every good citizen to promote the protection of forests and wild life and the creation of game preserves, while a supply of game remains. Every man who finds pleasure in hunting or fishing should be willing to spend both time and money in active work for the protection of forests, fish and game.

3. The sale of game is incompatible with the perpetual preservation of a proper stock of game; therefore it should be prohibited by laws and by public sentiment.

4. In the settled and civilized regions of North America there is no real *necessity* for the consumption of wild game as human food; nor is there any good excuse for the sale of game for food purposes. The maintenance of hired laborers on wild game should be prohibited everywhere, under severe penalties.

5. An Indian has no more right to kill wild game, or to subsist upon it all the year round, than any white man in the same locality. The Indian has no inherent or God-given ownership of the game of North America, any more than of its mineral resources; and he should be governed by the same game laws as white men.

6. No man can be a good citizen and also be a slaughterer of game or fishes beyond the narrow limits compatible with high-class sportsmanship.

*This organization contains in its list of members the most distinguished names in the modern annals of British sport and exploration. Its honorary membership, of eight persons, contains the names of three Americans: Theodore Roosevelt, Madison Grant and W. T. Hornaday; and of this fact at least one person is extremely proud!

7. A game-butcher or a market-hunter is an undesirable citizen, and should be treated as such.

8. The highest purpose which the killing of wild game and game fishes can hereafter be made to serve is in furnishing objects to overworked men for tramping and camping trips in the wilds; and the value of wild game as human food should no longer be regarded as an important factor in its pursuit.

9. If rightly conserved, wild game constitutes a valuable asset to any country which possesses it; and it is good statesmanship to protect it.

10. An ideal hunting trip consists of a good comrade, fine country, and a *very few* trophies per hunter.

11. In an ideal hunting trip, the death of the game is only an incident; and by no means is it really necessary to a successful outing.

12. The best hunter is the man who finds the most game, kills the least, and leaves behind him no wounded animals.

13. The killing of an animal means the end of its most interesting period. When the country is fine, pursuit is more interesting than possession.

14. The killing of a female hoofed animal, save for special preservation, is to be regarded as incompatible with the highest sportsmanship; and it should everywhere be prohibited by stringent laws.

15. A particularly fine photograph of a large wild animal in its haunts is entitled to more credit than the dead trophy of a similar animal. An animal that has been photographed never should be killed, unless previously wounded in the chase.

This platform has been adopted as a code of ethics by the following organizations, besides the Camp-Fire Club of America:

The Lewis and Clark Club, of Pittsburgh, John M. Phillips, President

The North American Fish and Game Protective Association (International).

Massachusetts Fish and Game Protective Association, Boston.

Camp-Fire Club of Michigan, Detroit.

Rod and Gun Club, Sheridan County, Wyoming.

The platform has been endorsed and published by The Society for the Preservation of the Wild Fauna of the British Empire (London), which is an endorsement of far-reaching importance.

Major J. Stevenson-Hamilton, C.M.Z.S., Warden of the Government Game Reserves of the Transvaal, South Africa, has adopted the platform and given it the most effective endorsement that it has received from any single individual. In his great work on game protection in Africa and wild-animal lore, entitled "Animal Life in Africa" (and "very highly commended" by the Committee on Literary Honors of the Camp-Fire Club), he publishes the entire platform, with a depth and cordiality of endorsement that is bound to warm the heart of every man who believes in the principles laid down in that document. He says, "It should be printed on the back of every license that is issued for hunting in Africa."

I am profoundly impressed by the fact that it is high time for sportsmen all over the world to take to heart the vital necessity of adopting high and clearly defined codes of ethics, to suit the needs of the present hour. The days of game abundance, and the careless treatment of wild life have gone by, never to return.

CHAPTER XLIII

THE DUTY OF AMERICAN ZOOLOGISTS AND EDUCATORS TO AMERICAN WILD LIFE

The publication of this chapter will hardly be regarded as a bid for fame, or even popularity, on the part of the author. However, the subject can not be ignored simply because it is disagreeable.

Throughout sixty years, to go no further back, the people of America have been witnessing the strange spectacle of American zoologists, as a mass, so intent upon the academic study of our continental fauna that they seem not to have cared a continental about the destruction of that fauna.

During that tragic period twelve species of North American birds have been totally exterminated, twenty-three are almost exterminated, and the mammals have fared very badly.

If "by their works ye shall know them," then no man can say that the men referred to have been conspicuous on the firing line in defense of assaulted wild life. In their hearts, we know that in an academic way the naturalists of America do care about wild-life slaughter, and the extermination of species; and we also know that perhaps fifty American zoologists have at times taken an active and serious interest in protection work.

I am speaking now of the general body of museum directors and curators; professors and teachers of zoology in our institutions of learning —a legion in themselves; teachers of nature study in our secondary schools; investigators and specialists in state and government service; the taxidermists and osteologists; and the array of literary people who, like all the foregoing, *make their bread and butter out of the exploitation of wild life.*

Taken as a whole, the people named above constitute a grand army of at least five thousand trained, educated, resourceful and influential persons. They all *depend upon wild life for their livelihood.* When they talk about living things, the public listens with respectful attention. Their knowledge of the value of wild life would be worth something to our cause; but thus far it never has been capitalized!

These people are hard workers; and when they mark out definite courses and attainable goals, they know how to get results. Yet what do we see?

For sixty long years, with the exception of the work of a corporal's guard of their number, this grand army has remained in camp, partly neglecting and partly refusing to move upon the works of the enemy. For sixty years, with the exception of the non-game-bird law, as a class and a mass they have left to the sportsmen of the country the dictating of laws for the protection of all the game birds, the mammals and the game fishes. When we stop to consider that the game birds alone embrace *154 very important species,* the appalling extent to which the zoologist has abdicated in favor of the sportsman becomes apparent.

It is a very great mistake, and a wrong besides, for the zoologists of the country to abandon the game birds, mammals and fishes of North America to the sportsmen, to do with as they please! Yet that is practically what has been done.

The time was, thirty or forty years ago, when wild life was so abundant that we did not need to worry about its preservation. That was the golden era of study and investigation. That era ended definitely in 1884, with the practical extermination of the wild American bison, partly through the shameful greed and partly through the neglect of the American people. We are now living *in the middle of the period of Extermination!* The questions for every American zoologist and every sportsman to answer now are: Shall the slaughter of species go on to a quick end of the period? Shall we give posterity a birdless, gameless, fishless continent, or not? Shall we have close seasons, all over the country, for five or ten years, or for five hundred years?

If we are courageous, we will brace up and answer these questions now, like men. If we are faint-hearted, and eager for peace at any price, then we will sidestep the ugly situation until the destroyers have settled it for us by the wholesale extermination of species.

If the zoologist cares to know, then I will tell him that to-day the wild life of the world *can* be saved by law, but *not by sentiment alone!* You cannot "educate" a poacher, a game-hog, a market-gunner, a milliner or a vain and foolish woman of fashion. All these must be curbed and controlled *by law.* Game refuges alone will not save the wild life! *All* species of birds, mammals and game fishes of North America must have more thorough and far-reaching protection than they now have.

Do not always take your cue from the sportsmen, especially regarding the enactment of long close seasons! If you need good advice, or help about drafting a bill, write to Dr. T. S. Palmer, Department of Agriculture, Washington, and you will receive prompt and valuable assistance. The Doctor is a wise man, and there is nothing about protective laws that is unknown to him. Go to *your* state senator and *your* assemblyman with the bills that you know should be enacted into law, and assure them that those measures are necessary for the wild life, and beneficial to 98 per cent of the people *who own the wild life.* You will be heard with respectful attention, in any law-making body that you choose to enter.

People who cannot give time and labor must supply you with money for your campaigns. *Ask*, and you will receive! I have proven this many times. With care and exactness account to your subscribers for the expenditure of all money placed in your hands, and you will receive continuous support.

In times of great stress, print circulars and leaflets by the ten-thousand, and get them into the hands of the People, calling for *their* help. Our 42,000 copies of the "Wild Life Call" (sixteen pages) were distributed by organizations all over the state of New York, and along with Mr. Andrew D. Meloy's letters to the members of the New York State League, aroused such a tidal wave of public sentiment against the sale of game that the Bayne bill was finally swept through the Legislature with only one dissenting vote! And yet, in the beginning not one man dared to hope that that very revolutionary measure could by any possibility be passed in its first year in New York State, even if it ever could be!

It was the aroused Public that did it!

This volume has been written (under great pressure) in order to put the whole situation before the people of America, including the zoologists, and to give them some definite information, state by state, regarding the needs of the hour. Look at the needs of your own state, in the "Roll Call of States," and you will find work for your hand to do. Clear your conscience by taking hold now, to do everything that you can to stop the carnage and preserve the remnant. Twenty-five or fifty years hence, if we have a birdless and gameless continent, let it not be said that the zoologists of America helped to bring it about by wicked apathy.

At this juncture, a brief survey of the attitude toward wild life of certain American institutions of national reputation will be decidedly pertinent. I shall mention only a few of the many that through their character and position owe specific duties to this cause. *Noblesse oblige!*

The Biological Survey of the U. S. Department of Agriculture is a splendid center of activity and initiative in the preservation of our wild life. The work of Dr. T. S. Palmer has already been spoken of, and thanks to his efforts and direction, the Survey has become the recognized special champion of preservation in America.

The U. S. Forestry Bureau is developing into a very valuable ally, and we confidently look forward to the time when its influence in preservation will be a hundred times more potent than it is to-day. *That will be when every national forest is made a game preserve, and every forest ranger is made a game warden.* Let us have both those developments, and quickly.

In 1896 the AMERICAN MUSEUM OF NATURAL HISTORY became a center of activity in bird protection, and the headquarters of the New York State Audubon Society. The president of the Museum (Professor Henry Fairfield Osborn) is also the president of that organization.

In several of the New York State movements for bird conservation, especially those bearing on the plumage law, the American Museum has been active, and at times conspicuous. No one (so I believe) ever appealed to the President of the Museum for help on the firing line without receiving help of some kind. Unfortunately, however, the preservation of wild life is not one of the declared objects of the American Museum corporation, or one on which its officers may spend money, as is so freely and even joyously done by the Zoological Society. The Museum's influence has been exerted chiefly through the active workers of the State Audubon Society, and it was as president of that body that Professor Osborn subscribed to the fund that was so largely instrumental in creating the New York law against the sale of game.

There is room for an important improvement in the declared objects of the American Museum. To the cause of protection it is a distinct loss that that great and powerful institution should be unable to spend any money in promoting the preservation of our fauna from annihilation. An amendment to its constitution is earnestly recommended.

The activities of the NEW YORK ZOOLOGICAL SOCIETY began in 1896, and they do not require comment here. They have been continuous, aggressive and far-reaching, and they have been supported by thousands of dollars from the Society's treasury. It is true that the funds available for protection work have not represented a great annual sum, such as the work demands, but the amount being expended from year to year is steadily increasing. In serious emergencies there is *always something available!* During the past two years, to relieve the Society of a portion of this particular burden, the director of the Park secured several large subscriptions from persons outside the Society, who previously had never entered into this work.

The MILWAUKEE PUBLIC MUSEUM has entered actively and effectively into the fight to preserve the birds of Wisconsin from annihilation by the saloon-loafer element that three years ago determined to repeal the best bird laws on the books, and throw the shooting privilege wide open. Mr. Henry L. Ward, Director of the Museum, went to the firing line, and remained there. Last year the saloon element thought that they had a large majority of the votes in the legislature pledged to vote their way. It looked like it; but when the decent people again rose and demanded justice for the birds, the members of the legislature stood by them in large majorities. The spring-shooting, bag-limit and hunting-license laws were *not* repealed.

THE UNIVERSITY OF KANSAS (Lawrence) scored heavily for the cause of wild-life protection when in 1908 it gave to the Governor of the state the services of a member of its faculty, Professor Lewis Lindsay Dyche, who was wanted to fill the position of State Fish and Game Commissioner. Professor Dyche proved to be a very live wire, and his activities have covered the State of Kansas to its farthest corners. We love him for the host of enemies he has made—among the poachers, game-butchers, pseudo-"sportsmen" and lawbreakers generally. The men who thought they had the "pull" of friendship for lawbreaking were first warned, and then as second offenders hauled up to the bar, one and all. The more the destroyers try to hound the Commissioner, the more popular is he with the great, solid mass of good citizens who believe in the saving of wild life.

THE MUSEUM OF COMPARATIVE ZOOLOGY has at last made a beginning in the field of protection. Last winter, while the great battle raged over the Wharton no-sale-of-game bill, several members of the Museum staff appeared at the hearings and otherwise worked for the success of the measure. It was most timely aid,—and very much needed. It is to be hoped that that auspicious beginning will be continued from year to year. The Museum should keep at least one good fighter constantly in the field.

THE BOSTON SOCIETY OF NATURAL HISTORY takes a very active part in promoting the preservation of the fauna of Massachusetts, and in resisting the attempts of the destroyers to repeal the excellent laws now in force. Its members put forth vigorous efforts in the great campaign of 1912.

THE BROOKLYN INSTITUTE OF ARTS AND SCIENCES is well represented in the field of protection by Director Franklin W. Hooper, now president of the American Bison Society, and an earnest promoter of the perpetuation of the bison. When the Wind Cave National Bison Herd is fully established, in South Dakota, as it practically *is already*, the chief credit for that coup will be due to the unflagging energy and persistence of Professor Hooper.

THE BUFFALO ACADEMY OF SCIENCES in 1911 entered actively and effectively, under the leadership of Dr. Lee H. Smith, into the campaign for the Bayne bill. Besides splendid service rendered in western New York, Dr. Smith appeared in Albany with a strong delegation in support of the bill.

THE UNIVERSITY OF CALIFORNIA was the first institution of learning to enter the field of wild-life protection for active, aggressive and permanent work. W. L. Taylor and Joseph Grinnell, of the University Museum, have taken up the fight to save the fauna of California from the dangers that now threaten it.

At this point our enumeration of the activities of American zoological institutions comes to an unfortunate end. There are many individuals to be named elsewhere, in the roll of honor, but that is another story. I am now going to set before the public the names of certain institutions largely devoted to zoology and permeated by zoologists, which thus far seem to have entirely ignored the needs of our fauna, and which so far we know have contributed neither men, money nor encouragement to the Army of the Defense.

PARTIAL LIST OF INSTITUTIONS OWING SERVICE TO WILD LIFE.

The United States National Museum contains a large and expensive corps of zoological curators and assistant curators, some of whom long ago should have taken upon themselves the task of reforming the laws of the District of Columbia, Virginia and Maryland, at their very doors! This museum should maintain at least one man in the field of protection, and the existence of the Biological Survey is no excuse for the Museum's inactivity.

The Field Museum of Chicago is a great institution, but it appears to be inactive in wild-life protection, and indifferent to the fate of our wild life. Its influence is greatly needed on the firing line, especially in Illinois, Wisconsin, Iowa and northern Minnesota. First of all the odious sale-of-game situation in Chicago should be cleaned up!

The Philadelphia Academy of Sciences has been represented on the A. O. U. Committee on Bird Protection by Mr. Witmer Stone. The time has come when this Academy should be represented on the firing line as a virile, wide-awake, self-sacrificing and aggressive force. It is perhaps the oldest zoological body in the United States! Its scientific standing is unquestioned. Its members *must* know of the carnage that is going on around them, for they are not ignorant men. The Pennsylvania State Game Commission to-day stands in urgent need of active, vigorous and persistent assistance from the Philadelphia Academy in the fierce campaign already in progress for additional protective laws. Will that help be given?

The Carnegie Institute of Washington (endowment $22,000,000) unquestionably owes a great duty toward wild life, no portion of which has yet been discharged. Academic research work is all very well, but it does not save faunas from annihilation. In the saving of the birds and mammals of North America a hundred million people are directly interested, and the cause is starving for money, men and publicity. Education is not the ONLY duty of educators!

The Carnegie Museum at Pittsburgh should be provided by Pittsburgh with sufficient funds that its Director can put a good man into the field of protection, and maintain his activities. The State of Pennsylvania, and the nation at large, needs such a worker at Pittsburgh; and this statement is not open to argument!

The California Academy of Sciences;
The Chicago Academy of Sciences;
The New York Academy of Sciences;
The National Academy of Sciences;
The Rochester Academy of Sciences;
The Philadelphia Zoological Society;
The National Zoological Park;

Appear to have done nothing noteworthy in promoting the preservation and increase of the wild life of America.

A Few of the Institutions of Learning Which Should Each Devote One Man to this Cause.

Columbia University, of New York, has a very large and strong corps of zoological professors in its Department of Biology. No living organism is too small or too worthless to be studied by high-grade men; but does any man of Columbia ever raise his voice, actively and determinedly, for the preservation of our fauna, or any other fauna? Columbia should give the services of one man wholly to this cause.

There are men whose zoological ideals soar so high that they can not see the slaughter of wild creatures that is so furiously proceeding on the surface of this blood-stained earth. We don't want to hear about the "behavior" of protozoans while our best song birds are being exterminated by negroes and poor whites.

Cornell University should now awaken to the new situation. All the zoological Neros should not fiddle while Rome burns. For the sake of consistency, Cornell should devote the services of at least one member of its large and able faculty to the cause of wild-life protection. Cornell was a pioneer in forestry teaching; and why should she not lead off now in the new field?

Yale University, in Professor James W. Toumey, Director of the School of Forestry, possesses a natural, ready-made protector of wild life. From forestry to wild life is an easy step. We hopefully look forward to the development of Professor Toumey into a militant protectionist, fighting for the helpless creatures that *must* be protected by man *or perish!* If Yale is willing to set a new pace for the world's great universities, she has the Man ready at hand.

The University of Chicago should become the center of a great new protectionist movement which should cover the whole Middle West area, from the plains to Pittsburgh. This is the inflexible, logical necessity of the hour. *Either protect zoology, or else for very shame give up teaching it!*

Every higher institution of learning in America now has a duty in this matter. Times have changed. Things are not as they were thirty years ago. To allow a great and valuable wild fauna to be destroyed and wasted is a crime, against both the present and the future. If we mean to be good citizens we cannot shirk the duty to conserve. We are trustees of the inheritance of future generations, and we have no right to squander that inheritance. If we fail of our plain duty, the scorn of future generations surely will be our portion.

CHAPTER XLIV

THE GREATEST NEEDS OF THE WILD-LIFE CAUSE AND THE DUTY OF THE HOUR

The fate of wild life in North America hangs to-day by three very slender threads, the names of which you will hardly guess unaided. They are Labor, Money and Publicity! The threads are slender because there is so little raw material in them.

We do not need money with which to "buy votes" or "influence," but money with which to pay workers; to publish things to arouse the American people; to sting sportsmen into action; to hire wardens; to prosecute game-hogs and buy refuges for wild life. If a sufficient amount of money for these purposes cannot be procured, then as sure as the earth continues to revolve, our wild life will pass away, forever.

This is no cause for surprise, or wonder. In this twentieth century money is essential to every great enterprise, whether it be for virtue or mischief. The enemies of wild life, and the people who support them, are very powerful. The man whose pocket or whose personal privilege is threatened by new legislation is prompted by business reasons to work against you, and spend money in protecting his interests.

Now, it happens that the men of ordinary means who have nothing personal at stake in the preservation of wild life save sentimental considerations, cannot afford to leave their business more than three or four days each year on protection affairs. Yet many times services are demanded for many days, or even weeks together, in order to accomplish results. Bad repeal bills must be fought until they are dead; and good protective bills must be supported until the breath of life is breathed into them by the executive signature.

With money in hand, good men aways can be found who will work in game protection for about one-half what they would demand in other pursuits. With the men *whom you really desire*, sentiment is always a controlling factor. It is my inflexible rule, however, in asking for services, that men who give valuable time and strength to the cause shall not be allowed to take their expense money from their own pockets. Soldiers on the firing line *cannot* provide the sinews of war that come from the paymaster's chest!

Campaigns of publicity are matters of tremendous necessity and importance; but their successful promotion requires hundreds, or possibly thousands of dollars, for each state that is covered.

I believe that the wealthy men and women of America are the most liberal givers for the benefit of humanity that can be found in all the

OUR VANISHING WILD LIFE

world. New York especially contains a great number of men who year in and year out work hard for money—in order to give it away! The depth and breadth of the philanthropic spirit in New York City is to me the most surprising of all the strange impulses that sway the inhabitants of that seething mass of mixed humanity. Every imaginable cause for the benefit of mankind,—save one,—has received, and still is receiving, millions of gift dollars.

Some enterprises for the transcendant education of the people are at this moment hopelessly wallowing in the excess of wealth that has been thrust upon them. Men are being hired at high salaries to help spend wealth in high, higher, highest education and research. It is now fashionable to bequeath millions to certain causes that do not need them in the least! In education there is a mad scramble to educate every young man to the topmost notch, often far above his probable station in life, and into tastes and wants far beyond his powers to maintain.

In all this, however, there would be no cause for regret if the wild life of our continent were not in such a grievous state. If we felt no conscience burden for those who come after us, we would not care where the millions go; but since things are as they are, it is heartbreaking to see the cause of wild-life protection actually starving, or at the best subsisting only on financial husks and crumbs, while less important causes literally flounder in surplus wealth.

This regret is intensified by the knowledge that *in no other cause for the conservation of the resources most valuable to mankind will a dollar go so far, or bring back such good results, as in the preservation of wild life!* The promotion of "the Bayne bill" and the enactment of the Bayne law is a fair example. That law is to-day on the statute books of the State of New York because fifty men and women promptly subscribed $5,000 to a fund formed with special reference to the expenses of the campaign for that measure; and the uplift of that victory will be felt for years to come, just as it already has been in Massachusetts.

At one time I was tempted to show the financial skeleton in the closet of wild-life protection, by inserting here a statement of the funds available to be expended by all the New York organizations during the campaign year of 1911-1912. But I cannot do it. The showing is too painful, too humiliating. From it our enemies would derive too much comfort.

Even in New York State, in view of the great interests at stake, the showing is pitiful. But what shall we say of Massachusetts, Pennsylvania, Connecticut, New Jersey, and a dozen other states where the situation is much worse? In the winter of 1912 a cry for help came to us from a neighboring state, where a terrific fight was being made by the forces of destruction against all reform measures, and in behalf of retrogression on spring shooting. The appeal said: "The situation in our legislature is the worst that it has been in years. Our enemies are very strong, well organized, and they fight us at every step. We have *no funds*, and we are expected to make bricks without straw! Is there not *something* that you can do to help us?"

There was!

Only one week previously, a good friend (who declines to be named) gave us *two thousand dollars*, of real money, for just such emergencies.

Within thirty-six hours an entirely new fighting force had been organized and equipped for service. Within one week, those reinforcements had made a profound impression on the defenses of the enemy, and in the end the great fight was won. Of our small campaign fund it took away over one thousand dollars; but the victory was worth it.

With money enough,—a reasonable sum,—the birds of North America, ánd some of the small-mammal species also, can be saved. The big game that is hunted and killed outside the game preserves, and outside of such places as New Brunswick and the Adirondacks, can *not* be saved—until *each species* is given perpetual protection. Colorado is saving a small remnant of her mountain sheep, but Montana and Wyoming are wasting theirs, because they allow killing, and the killers are ten times too numerous for the sheep. They imagine that by permitting only the killing of rams they are saving the species; but that is an absolute fallacy, and soon it will have a fatal ending.

With an endowment fund of $2,000,000 (only double the price of the two old Velasquez paintings purchased recently by a gentleman of New York!) a very good remnant of the wild life of North America could be saved

But who will give the fund, or even a quarter of it?

Thus far, the largest sums ever given in America for the cause of wild life protection, so far as I know personally, have been the following:

Albert Wilcox, to the National Association of Audubon Societies,	$322,000
Mary Dutcher Fund, to the National Association of Audubon Societies	12,000
Mrs. Russell Sage, for the purchase of Marsh Island	150,000
American Game Protective and Propagation Association, from the manufacturers of firearms and ammunition, annually	25,000
Charles Willis Ward and E. A. McIllhenny, purchase of game preserve presented to Louisiana	39,000
Mrs. Russell Sage, miscellaneous gifts to the National Audubon Society	20,000
The American Bison Society for the Montana National Herd	10,526
New York Zoological Society, total about	20,000
John E. Thayer, purchase of game preserve	5,000
Caroline Phelps Stokes Bird Fund, N. Y. Zoological Society	5,000
Boone and Crockett Fund for Preservation	5,000
A Friend in Rochester	2,500
Henry C. Frick	1,500
Samuel Thorne	1,250

Of all the above, the only endowment funds yielding an annual income are those of the National Association of Audubon Societies and the Caroline Phelps Stokes fund of $5,000 in the treasury of the Zoological Society.

A fund of $25,000 per year for five years has been guaranteed by the makers of shot-guns, rifles and ammunition, to the American Game Protective and Propagation Association. This is like a limited endowment.

In the civilized world there are citizens of many kinds; but all of them can be placed in two groups: (1) those with a sense of duty toward mankind, and who will do their duty as good citizens; and (2) those who from the cradle to the grave meanly and sordidly study their own selfish interests, who never do aught save in expectation of a quick return benefit, and who recognize no such thing as duty toward mankind at large.

Men and women of the first class are honored in life, mourned when dead, and gratefully remembered by posterity. They leave the world better than they found it, and their lives have been successful.

Men and women of the second class are merely so many pieces of animated furniture; and when they pass out the world cares no more than when old chairs are thrown upon the scrap-heap.

There are many men so selfish, so ignorant and mean of soul that even out of well-filled purses they would not give ten dollars to save the whole bird fauna of North America from annihilation. To all persons of that brand, it is useless to appeal. As soon as you find one, waste no time upon him. Get out of his neighborhood as quickly as you can, and look for help among real MEN.

The wild life of the world cannot be saved by a few persons, even though they work their hearts out in the effort. The cause needs two million more helpers; and they must be sought in Group No. 1. They are living, somewhere; but the great trouble is to find them, *before it is too late.*

There are times and causes in which the good citizen has no option but to render service. The most important of such causes are: the relief of suffering humanity, the conservation of the resources of nature, and the prevention of vandalism. If the American Nation had refused aid to stricken San Francisco, the callous hard-heartedness of it would have shocked the world. If the German army of 1871 had destroyed the art treasures and the libraries of Paris, it would have set the German nation back ten centuries, into the ranks of the lowest barbarians.

And yet, in America, and in the regions now being scourged by the feather trade, a wonderful FAUNA is being destroyed! It took *millions of years* to develop that marvelous array of wild life; and when gone *it never can be replaced!* Yet the Army of Destruction is sweeping it away as joyously as a hired laborer cuts down a field of corn.

That wild life *can* be saved! If done, it must be done by the men and women of Group No. 1. The means by which it can be saved are: *Money, labor* and *publicity. Every man* of ordinary means and intelligence can contribute either money or labor. The men on the firing line must not be expected to furnish their own food and ammunition. The Workers MUST be provided with the money that active campaign work imperatively demands! Those who cannot conveniently or successfully labor should give money to this cause; but at the same time, every good citizen should keep in touch with his lawmaking representatives, and in times of need ask for votes for whatever new laws are necessary.

With money enough to arouse the American people in certain ways, the wild life of North America (north of Mexico) can be saved. *Money* can secure labor and publicity, and the People will do the rest. For this campaign work I want, *and must have*, a permanent fund of $10,000 per annum,—cash always ready for every emergency in field work. I greatly need, *and must have, immediately*, an endowment Wild-Life Fund of at least $100,000, and eventually $250,000. I can no longer "pass the hat" each year. This is needed in addition to the several thousands of dollars annually being expended by the Zoological Society in this work. The Society is already doing its utmost in wild-life protection, just as it is in several other fields of activity.

Outside of New York many wealthy men will say, "Let New York do it!" That often is the way when national campaigning is to be done. In *national* wild-life protection work, New York is to-day bearing about nine-tenths of the burden. It is my belief that in 1912 outside of New York City less than $10,000 was raised and expended in wild-life protection save by state and national appropriations. We know that in the year mentioned New York expended $221,000 in this cause, all from private sources.

In a very short time I shall call for the $100,000 that I now must have as an endowment fund for nation-wide work, to be placed at $5\frac{1}{2}$ per cent interest for the $5,500 annual income that it will yield. How much of this will come from outside the State of New York? Some of it, I am sure, will come from Massachusetts and Pennsylvania; but will any of it come from Cleveland, Cincinnati, Chicago, St. Louis and San Francisco?

The Duty of the Hour

I have now said my say in behalf of wild life. Surely the path of duty toward the remnant of wild life is plain enough. Will those who read this book pass along my message that the hour for a revolution has struck? Will the millions of men commanded by General Apathy now arouse, before it is too late to act?

Will the true sportsmen rise up, and do their duty, bravely and unselfishly?

Will the people with wealth to give away do their duty toward wild life and humanity, fairly and generously?

Will the zoologists awake, leave their tables in their stone palaces of peace, and come out to the firing-line?

Will the lawmakers heed the handwriting on the wall, and make laws that represent the full discharge of their duty toward wild life and humanity?

Will the editors beat the alarm-gong, early and late, in season and out of season, until the people awake?

On the answers to these questions hang the fate of the wild creatures of the world,—their preservation or their extermination.

INDEX

Abundance of wild life, 1.
Accuracy, value of, in campaigning, 262.
Acklen, J. H., 252.
Actinomycosis, 82, 83.
Adams, Cyrus C., on the lion, 183.
Adirondack State Park, 347.
Adjutant, 123.
Africa, big game of, 181; game preserves in, 364, 367; rinderpest in, 83; "soon to be shot out," 206.
African big game disappearing, 187.
African game that needs exemption, 383.
Agriculture, Department of, 208, 212.
Aigrette, 120.
Akeley, C. E., 186.
Alabama, 42, 46, 59, 106; deer killed in, 172; laws of, 268.
Alabama Game Commissioner, 252.
Alaska, 46; brown bears of, 178; new laws needed in, 264; game of, 270; Sitka National Monument in, 344.
Alaska—Yukon region, 157.
Albatross, steamer, seals taken by, 40.
Albatrosses, Laysan, 138; 140.
Alberta, 45, 51, 158, 162, 165; at fault on antelope-shooting, 351; laws of parks of, 352.
Alden, M.P., Percy, 135.
Algonquin National Park, 351.
Aliens, game wardens killed by, 103; prohibited from owning firearms, 103; slaughter of song-birds by, 100.
Altai Mountains of western China, 190.
American Bison Society, 180.
American Game Protective and Propagation Association, 257, 395.
"American Natural History" on hawks and owls, 224, 338.
American, North, Fish and Game Protective Association, 385.
American private game preserves, 358.
Amsterdam, 120.
Animallai Hills to-day and in 1877, 188.
"Animal Life in Africa," on status of settlers, 365.
Animals, predatory, 73; caught by cats, 73; wild, may become nuisances, 234.

Antelope, prong-horned, 2; attempts to transplant, 163; in Alberta, 51; in Montana, 287; in Nevada, 288; in Texas, 51; in Wyoming, 51; lumpy jaw in, 83, 84; physical weakness of, 160; present status of, 159; preserve in Montana, 2; wrong to kill, 351.
Anthony bill for migratory birds, 267, 306.
Antelopes, African, for the South, 242.
Aphis devouring potato-tops, 213.
Apple crop, losses on, 210.
Aquarium, West Indian seals in, 39.
Areas inhabitated by big game, 157.
Argali, Siberian, 191.
Arizona, 42, 46; new laws needed in, 270; national monuments in, 344.
Arizona elk exterminated, 35.
Arkansas, 42, 106; new laws needed in, 270.
Army of Defense, 248, 257.
Army of Destruction, 54, 59.
Army worm, 221.
Arnold, Craig D., 43.
Ashe, T. J., 133.
Asia, future of big game of, 188.
Asiatic game that should be close-seasoned, 383.
Askins, Charles, article in *Recreation* by, 107.
Association in Pennsylvania fighting Game Commission, 245.
Association, Wool-Growers, fighting antelope preserve, 2, 348.
Astley, Hubert D., 94.
Atkinson, George, 86.
Atlanta Journal, 106.
Audubon Societies, National Association of, 28, 254, 256, 291, 395.
Auk, Great, 9, 10.
Austrians in Minnesota, 49.
Australia, animal pests in, 331, 332; game preserves in, 364.
Automatic and pump shot-guns, 61, 65, 144; campaign against, won in New Jersey, 289; denounced by organizations, 152; use of, prohibited by law, 152.
Automobile, use of, in hunting forbidden, 60.
Automobiles detrimental to wild life, 293.

399

BOOKS BY W. T. HORNADAY

CHARLES SCRIBNER'S SONS, 153-157 FIFTH AVENUE, NEW YORK

THE AMERICAN NATURAL HISTORY

Illustrated by 220 original drawings by Beard, Rungius and Sawyer, and 100 photographs by Sanborn, Keller and Underwood, and with numerous maps and diagrams. Treats of the most important mammals, birds, reptiles and fishes of North America. More than 400 pages, double column, $5\frac{1}{2}$ x 8 inches. $3.50, net.

CAMP-FIRES IN THE CANADIAN ROCKIES

Illustrated photographically by John M. Phillips. Adventures and observations in the home of the White Goat, Grizzly Bear and Mountain Sheep. Awarded gold medal by Camp-Fire Club of America. 8vo., pp. 353. Net, $3.00.

CAMP-FIRES ON DESERT AND LAVA

Illustrated by MacDougal, Phillips, and the author. Explorations and adventures in the wonderland of the Sonoran Desert; Tucson, Arizona to the Pinacate Mountains. 8vo., pp. 366. Net, $3.00.

TWO YEARS IN THE JUNGLE

The adventures and explorations of a hunter-naturalist in India, Ceylon, the Malay Peninsula and Borneo. (Eighth edition). Illustrated. 8vo., pp. 512. Net, $2.50.

TAXIDERMY AND ZOOLOGICAL COLLECTING

A complete handbook for the amateur taxidermist, collector, osteologist, sportsman and traveller. (Seventh edition). Illustrated. 8vo., pp. 364. Net, $2.50.

OUR VANISHING WILD LIFE: Its Extermination and Preservation

A book of warning and appeal, for use in defense of wild life. Illustrated. 8vo., pp. 428. Net, $1.50.

18745556R00241

Made in the USA
Middletown, DE
01 December 2018